KANT'S POLITICAL THEORY

KANT'S POLITICAL THEORY

INTERPRETATIONS AND APPLICATIONS

edited by Elisabeth Ellis

THE PENNSYLVANIA STATE UNIVERSITY PRESS
UNIVERSITY PARK, PENNSYLVANIA

Library of Congress Cataloging-in-Publication Data

Kant's political theory : interpretations and applications /
edited by Elisabeth Ellis.
p. cm.
Includes bibliographical references and index.
Summary: "A collection of essays examining Immanuel Kant's
lectures and minor writings as well as his political essays.
Offers a comprehensive introduction to Kant's political thought
from a position of engagement with modern political and
philosophical questions"—Provided by publisher.
ISBN 978-0-271-05377-6 (cloth : alk. paper)
ISBN 978-0-271-05378-3 (pbk. : alk. paper)
1. Kant, Immanuel, 1724–1804—Political and social views.
I. Ellis, Elisabeth.

JC181.K4K379 2012
320.01—dc23
2011051036

Copyright © 2012 The Pennsylvania State University
All rights reserved
Printed in the United States of America
Published by The Pennsylvania State University Press,
University Park, PA 16802-1003

The Pennsylvania State University Press is a member of
the Association of American University Presses.

It is the policy of The Pennsylvania State University
Press to use acid-free paper. Publications on uncoated
stock satisfy the minimum requirements of
American National Standard for Information Sciences—
Permanence of Paper for Printed Library Material,
ANSI Z39.48-1992.

CONTENTS

List of Abbreviations *vi*
Introduction / *Elisabeth Ellis* 1

1 Kant and the Social Contract Tradition / *Onora O'Neill* 25

2 Kant and the Circumstances of Justice / *Arthur Ripstein* 42

3 Is Kant's *Rechtslehre* a
"Comprehensive Liberalism"? / *Thomas W. Pogge* 74

4 Realizing External Freedom: The Kantian
Argument for a World State / *Louis-Philippe Hodgson* 101

5 The Progress of Absolutism in
Kant's Essay "What Is Enlightenment?" / *Robert S. Taylor* 135

6 Unsocial Sociability: Perpetual Antagonism
in Kant's Political Thought / *Michaele Ferguson* 150

7 Kant's Political Thought in the
Prussian Enlightenment / *Ian Hunter* 170

8 Kant on Education / *Mika LaVaque-Manty* 208

9 Kant, Freedom of the Press,
and Book Piracy / *John Christian Laursen* 225

Selected Bibliography 239
Index 253

ABBREVIATIONS

A note on citation of Kant's works:

Page references in parentheses are to the Prussian Academy (now the Berlin-Brandenburgische Akademie der Wissenschaften) edition of Kant's works (Berlin: de Gruyter, 1900–). These standard volume and page numbers are reproduced in most translations of Kant's writings, including *The Cambridge Edition of the Works of Immanuel Kant*, edited by Paul Guyer and Allen W. Wood (Cambridge: Cambridge University Press, 1992–), which, unless otherwise indicated, is the source of the translated quotations in this volume. The volume and page numbers of the Academy edition are preceded by an abbreviation or short title referring to the individual work in which the text appears.

A   *Anthropology* is the short title for *Anthropology from a Pragmatic Point of View* (1798). In *Anthropology, History, and Education*, edited by Günter Zöller and Robert B. Louden (Cambridge University Press, 2007).

CB   *Conjectural Beginning* is the short title for *Conjectural Beginning of Human History* (1786). In *Anthropology, History, and Education*, edited by Günter Zöller and Robert B. Louden (Cambridge University Press, 2007).

CF   *Conflict* is the short title for *The Conflict of the Faculties* (1798). In *Religion and Rational Theology*, edited and translated by Allen W. Wood and George di Giovanni (Cambridge University Press, 1996).

CJ   *Judgment* is the short title for *Critique of the Power of Judgment* (1790). In *Critique of the Power of Judgment*, edited by Paul Guyer, translated by Paul Guyer and Eric Matthews (Cambridge University Press, 2000).

CPR   *Critique of Pure Reason* (1781 [cited as A]/1787 [cited as B]). In *Critique of Pure Reason*, edited, translated, and with an introduction by Paul Guyer and Allen W. Wood (Cambridge University Press, 1998).

CPrR *Critique of Practical Reason* (1788). In *Practical Philosophy*, translated and edited by Mary J. Gregor, introduction by Allen W. Wood (Cambridge University Press, 1996).

GW *Groundwork* is the short title for *Groundwork of the Metaphysics of Morals* (1785). In *Practical Philosophy*, translated and edited by Mary J. Gregor, introduction by Allen W. Wood (Cambridge University Press, 1996).

MM *Metaphysics of Morals* (1797) contains two parts: *Doctrine of Right* is the short title for the first half of the *Metaphysics of Morals*; *Doctrine of Virtue* is the short title for the second half of the *Metaphysics of Morals*. In *Practical Philosophy*, translated and edited by Mary J. Gregor, introduction by Allen W. Wood (Cambridge University Press, 1996).

OT *Orient in Thinking* is the short title for "What Does It Mean to Orient Oneself in Thinking?" (1786). In *Religion and Rational Theology*, translated and edited by Allen W. Wood and George di Giovanni (Cambridge University Press, 1996).

P *Pädagogik* is the short title for Kant's *Lectures on Pedagogy* (1803). In *Anthropology, History, and Education*, edited by Günter Zöller and Robert B. Louden (Cambridge: Cambridge University Press, 2007).

PP *Perpetual Peace* is the short title for *Toward Perpetual Peace* (1795). In *Practical Philosophy*, translated and edited by Mary J. Gregor, introduction by Allen W. Wood (Cambridge University Press, 1996).

RE *Religion* is the short title for *Religion Within the Boundaries of Mere Reason* (1793). In *Religion and Rational Theology*, edited and translated by Allen W. Wood and George di Giovanni (Cambridge University Press, 1996).

TP *Theory and Practice* is the short title for "On the Common Saying: 'That May Be Correct in Theory, but It Is of No Use in Practice'" (1793). In *Practical Philosophy*, translated and edited by Mary J. Gregor, introduction by Allen W. Wood (Cambridge University Press, 1996).

UH *Universal History* is the short title for "Idea for a Universal History with a Cosmopolitan Aim" (1784). In *Anthropology, History, and Education*, edited by Günter Zöller and Robert B. Louden (Cambridge University Press, 2007).

VN *Vigilantius* is the short title for *Kant on the Metaphysics of Morals, Vigilantius's Lecture Notes* (1793–94). In *Lectures on Ethics*, edited by

Peter Heath and J. B. Schneewind, translated by Peter Heath (Cambridge University Press, 1997).

WE *Enlightenment* is the short title for "An Answer to the Question: What Is Enlightenment?" (1784). In *Practical Philosophy*, translated and edited by Mary J. Gregor, introduction by Allen W. Wood (Cambridge University Press, 1996).

INTRODUCTION

Elisabeth Ellis

The study of Kant's politics is undergoing what Patrick Riley has called "a remarkable renaissance."[1] Recent years have seen a flowering of interest in Kant's politics among social scientists, political theorists, philosophers, legal scholars, historians, and many others. Among political scientists, research on transnational organizations, the democratic peace hypothesis, just war theory, human rights, and other areas has led to renewed interest in Kant's thought.[2] In political theory, one of the most influential new schools of thought is the deeply Kantian deliberative democratic theory, whose precepts are not only being discussed in academic journals but are also being implemented in new political institutions.[3] Interestingly, critics of deliberative democratic theory's perhaps too idealized notion of reasonableness have also found support in Kant's work, though they have tended to focus on Kant's political, anthropological, and historical work rather than his ethical theory.[4] Political philosophers are turning to Kant for his concepts of provisionality, agency, cosmopolitan right, the public sphere, and of course for his systematic treatment of human freedom in general.[5]

Kant's critical account of freedom is at the root both of the extraordinary appeal of his political thought and of its formidable interpretive challenge. Asking as he does about the conditions of possibility for human freedom in the world, Kant is able to offer authoritative and vigorous criticism of given social and political institutions while refraining from the construction of what he calls "castles in the air" (that is, idealized, specific models meant to apply across space and time). Focusing on the real and manifestly imperfect institutions of his day, Kant asks whether each political practice "leaves open the possibility" for progress toward freedom. Kant is much more interested in the drivers of actually possible, necessarily incremental improvement in human conditions than he is in describing profound but unreachable political perfection. His sustained interest in the public sphere,

---

I would like to thank Brad Goodine, Zeke Anglim, and Megan Dyer for their research assistance on this project. The Institute for Advanced Studies in Princeton, New Jersey, the National Endowment for the Humanities, the Glasscock Center for Humanities Research at Texas A&M University, and the Ray A. Rothrock '77 Fellowship each supported this project, for which I am very grateful.

for example, attests to Kant's conviction that it is more important to assure the underlying mechanisms that might promote political progress over time than it is to make pronouncements about exactly what is wrong with our present circumstances.

Kant's historical circumstances as a university teacher subject to the censorship regime of late eighteenth-century Prussia made it difficult for him to offer blunt political critique in any case.[6] From his early essay on enlightenment through his later political essays, Kant tends to approach his targets obliquely, allowing his readers to draw analogies between, for example, his criticism of paternalism in church governance and an implied general critique of domination. If Kant's own reticence has made it hard to discover his powerful critical political thought, superficial interpretations of his moral theory have compounded that difficulty. The relationship between Kant's ethics and his politics is complex and interesting (and the subject of much discussion in this volume), but it is by no means as straightforward as scholars used to presume. The soaring precepts of the *Groundwork of the Metaphysics of Morals* govern all human beings, according to Kant. Yet these same principles cannot simply be applied to political life directly. As Kant argues in the introduction to the *Metaphysics of Morals*, a system of political right is necessarily empirical and therefore always incomplete (6:205). Kant cannot provide a set of answers that will be right for every historically embedded political circumstance. Instead, he consistently asks about the conditions that might enable human freedom.

This reading of Kant's political thinking has itself been made possible by recent advances in the interpretation of Kant's ethics. Scholars of Kant's moral philosophy have definitively revised old images of Kant's ethics as rigoristic and sterile. In a series of important books and essays, Christine Korsgaard has demonstrated that Kant's moral theory is no dry summation of abstract and formulaic duty, but in fact envisions a rich and embedded life of ethical value whose applications are quite relevant to present-day problems.[7] Like Korsgaard, Barbara Herman rejects the reading of Kant's ethics as a sterile system of deontological rules of duty. In her pathbreaking work, *The Practice of Moral Judgment* (1993), Herman argues that Kant's moral theory is better understood as advocating practical rationality. She demonstrates the relevance of such a view to the present day in that book and in later work, focusing especially on moral education.[8] Onora O'Neill's 1989 work, *Constructions of Reason,* resolves persistent difficulties in the interpretation of Kant's moral theory by taking Kant's critical task very seriously and reading the *Critiques* together. She reveals the moral and political substructures of Kant's *Critique of Pure Reason*, using the resulting coherent picture of Kant's ethics to argue for the values of trust and autonomy in spheres of present-day life from development economics to bioethics.[9]

Following the work of Herman, Korsgaard, and O'Neill, philosophers are finding in Kant's moral work a vigorous theory relevant to such diverse contemporary issues as reconciliation, international humanitarian intervention, environmental ethics, and political violence. Scholars from many disciplines have a renewed interest in Kant thanks to the recent publication of politically relevant new material in the Berlin Academy edition of Kant's works.[10] Finally, recent years have seen important contributions not only to the interpretation of Kant's political work, but also to the body of Kantian political philosophy generally. This collection seeks both to introduce Kant's political thought to a new generation of readers and to demonstrate the fruitfulness and vibrancy of a broadly Kantian approach to political philosophy.

Why Kant? Why Now?

Kant's most profound and influential works are the three critiques (of pure reason, practical reason, and the power of judgment) and the *Groundwork of the Metaphysics of Morals*; not one of these works is explicitly political.[11] Moreover, his name almost never appears on short lists of canonical political theorists in the Western tradition, which tend to include the likes of Plato, Aristotle, Machiavelli, Hobbes, Locke, Rousseau, Mill, and Marx, but not Kant. His explicitly political writings take the form mostly of occasional essays written for magazines like the *Berlinische Monatsschrift*. The more formal treatment of political topics that appears in the first half of Kant's *Metaphysics of Morals* (the *Rechtslehre*) is obscure in its exposition, a late product of Kant's scholarly life, and probably so neglected by Kant himself that he missed a series of critical printers' errors that resulted in key paragraphs appearing out of order.[12] Other late works of political relevance, including the second essay of *The Conflict of the Faculties* and parts of Kant's lectures on anthropology, have similarly troubled publication and reception histories.[13]

In 2005 I wrote that "it is no longer necessary to begin a work on Kant's political philosophy defensively."[14] Though I stand by the claim I made then (and that I make again here) that Kant offers the best available lens through which to view many of the present-day world's most crucial political questions, I see now that I was wrong about the necessity of defensiveness among scholars of Kant's political thought. Two of the authors represented here (Arthur Ripstein and Michaele Ferguson) even choose to introduce their essays with admissions about Kant's low status in the field and defensive reactions to that status: Kant is "not widely seen as an important political thinker on par with Aristotle, Locke, or Rousseau" (Ferguson), and he "lies outside the primary canon in the history of political philosophy" (Ripstein). Though in her opening pages Onora O'Neill claims that Kant is known "as a social contract theorist, and a good one," within a few paragraphs she admits that "if Kant is a social contract theorist he is a peculiar one." Mika LaVaque-Manty notes early in his essay that Kant's pedagogical work has generated so little interest that "there was no high-end scholarly English translation until 2007." Though the remaining essays (safely, I should say) presume that Kant's political philosophy is of an interest too obvious to belabor, we Kant scholars should ask ourselves why the Kantian outlook that illuminates the political world so brightly for us is so obscure to many of our fellow students of politics.

Ripstein and many others have suggested that Kant's "writings on the topic are frequently opaque, even by the standards of his other writings." Although this is certainly an accurate description, it would also be an accurate description of many of the competing providers of analytical lenses for the study of politics (Hegel, for example, surely fits this description). Moreover, as LaVaque-Manty points out in his contribution to this volume, "Kant's lecture-based books and essays often are [eminently readable], and the structure accessible even to nonexperts." So I do not think that sheer obscurity in his writing can be the main explanation for the relative obscurity of Kant's political thought.

If we attend to some of the most successful uses of Kant for understanding politics, such as those offered by John Rawls, or Jürgen Habermas, or even to the less sweeping but still important applications of Kantian ideas such as those of Michael Doyle, Onora O'Neill, or Amy Gutmann, one very basic fact stands out: in order to arrive at their Kantian perspectives on the political world, these thinkers had first to understand Kant's full critical system. By "full critical system" I mean the three *Critiques* and accompanying shorter works like the *Groundwork of the Metaphysics of Morals* at a minimum. (I am not saying that years of study of Kant's system are necessary to understand his political thought, and in fact I frequently assign isolated political essays to my undergraduate students, who understand them. Instead, I am interested in the level of understanding necessary to construct an original contemporary political theory in the Kantian tradition.)

To follow Locke's thinking about property or revolution, by contrast, it is by no means necessary to have a deep grasp of the metaphysics and epistemology of his *Essay Concerning Human Understanding*.[15] Of course, it would be preferable to have achieved such knowledge, but what matters here is that the political theory of Locke's *Treatises* and *Letter Concerning Toleration* does not fundamentally depend on the apparatus of the *Essay*. As the contributions to this volume demonstrate, Kant's political theory depends essentially on the critical method, on arguments that consider the conditions of possibility for those elements of political life in question. Again, as demonstrated in the volume, even the apparently straightforward political essays that Kant published in monthly magazines only really make sense in the context of the critical project.

This systematic element of his work is both Kant's great drawback as a political theorist (among other things, it makes for a ferocious learning curve for new students), but also his great strength. Kant's political thought, asking as it does about the conditions of possibility of things like freedom, can achieve a broad historical and geographical sweep without committing the usual imperialist indecencies.[16] Rather than taking a principle—sticking with the contrast to Locke, we might think of a natural right to property taken from seventeenth-century struggles for sovereignty—from some historically specific context and then applying it willy-nilly across space and time, Kantian political theory asks about the conditions of possibility for realizing freedom in context. Unlike contemporary heirs to Locke, who treat the historically specific natural right to property as an unassailable starting point from which to reason about politics at every time and place, a theorist with a Kantian perspective would ask whether the institution of property rights as it works in context promotes the possibility of freedom. In his *Metaphysics of Morals*, Kant defends a provisional right to property in just this way (see Arthur Ripstein's, Ian Hunter's, and Thomas Pogge's contributions to this volume).

Of course, Kant did not consistently maintain an attitude of critical detachment when confronted with empirical social facts of his day. Much as present-day Kant scholars would prefer him to have done so, Kant failed to transcend local views about women, non-Europeans, and laborers (see LaVaque-Manty, Hunter, Taylor, Pogge, and O'Neill, this volume). Robert

Taylor explains Kant's relegation of some people to the status of passive citizens as an effort to prevent people in situations of dependency from representing something other than their own autonomous interests. "From our own perspective, such restrictions on voting may seem highly reactionary," Taylor notes. However, as Inder Marwah and others have argued, Kant's views on women as necessarily immature cannot be written off as incidental to his political theory, especially since, as Taylor acknowledges, the resources for a more inclusive view are present in his own system.[17] In an interesting twist, Pogge argues that Kant's clear inegalitarianism with regard to women and members of the lower classes ("these views occur too frequently and are too sharply expressed to be discounted as slips of the pen") actually supports his (Pogge's) contention that Kant's political theory is freestanding, since it can accommodate even a view as inegalitarian as Kant's apparently is.

Why, then, even bother with Kant's political theory? The short answer is this: because Kant is *the* philosopher of freedom, and the possibility of freedom is *the* political question par excellence. The question of freedom touches both political thought and the very possibility of knowledge of politics. Arthur Ripstein writes in this volume that it is not too strong to call freedom *the* problem, demonstrating the point with the example of slavery: "if the other problems a slave has—low welfare, limited options, and so on—were addressed by a benevolent master, the *relationship* of slavery would perhaps be less bad, but it would not thereby be any less wrong." As the essays in this volume demonstrate, all three *Critiques* make substantial contributions to the political philosophy of freedom. Moreover, and despite their somewhat disjointed and haphazard presentation, Kant's specifically political works together comprise a body of ideas that not only occupies a rightful place in the canon but also offers a number of original theories directly relevant to present-day politics.

These ideas will be treated in some detail below and in the volume's essays. For now, to give the reader an idea of the importance of Kant's contributions to political theory, I shall select a few elements of the work for brief mention. First on the list would have to be the Kantian basis of present-day international, national, and subnational human rights regimes. As O'Neill and others demonstrate in this volume, Kant defends human rights as the only possible basis for moral interaction among limited rational beings.

Next on this list of mention-worthy Kantian achievements in political thought would come Kant's ethics of peace and the accompanying political theory for an international pacific regime. Whether or not political scientists eventually conclude in favor of the "democratic peace hypothesis," the underlying ideals and pragmatic suggestions of Kant's system continue to exert enormous influence. Moreover, Kantian ideals provide perhaps our most powerful moral lens through which to view historical and contemporary actors. Kant gives us both optimistic and very dark moments when contemplating the human propensity for war, revealing simultaneously our potential for peaceful coexistence and our repeated failures to achieve it. When it comes international right, Kant observes, "we are still barbarians."[18]

Third on our short list of Kantian achievements in political theory might be the Kantian basis for several of today's most important theories of justice, including especially those of Habermas and Rawls. Rawls's move toward a "political, not metaphysical" theory that can accept the fact of pluralism owes more to Kant than Rawls himself acknowledges (see Pogge's essay in this volume). As I put the point in 2008, "What matters for politics is not the conclusiveness of any particular ethical system, even Kant's own, but the abstract ubiquity of moral argument in political life."[19] Habermas's adaptation of Kant's theory of the public sphere builds on this same, fundamental Kantian idea of the ubiquity of moral reasoning in politics; in addition to Habermas's work, there is an important and influential body of theory on discursive and deliberative modes of politics based on the Kantian idea of the public sphere.[20] Of course, not everyone agrees about the value of these achievements. Ian Hunter argues here, for example, that "the historical understanding of Kant's political thought has suffered from its modernizing adaptation to meet the needs of two highly successful twentieth-century normative philosophies, those of John Rawls and Jürgen Habermas." Michaele Ferguson similarly notes that Kant's adaptation to serve the needs of neo-Kantian contemporary theory has oversimplified Kant's nuanced philosophy. Arguing that antagonism is essential to Kant's system, Ferguson writes that Kant "is a moral philosopher who attends to the undesirability of the elimination of conflict and the importance of its perpetuation. . . . This is a Kant who can help us understand the neo-Kantian impulse to regulate antagonisms . . . [and] who can help us see how this impulse draws strength from its own failure to ever fully eliminate the antagonisms that bring it into being."

In addition to these primarily normative theories of political reason giving, we have the fundamentals for a number of more empirically oriented theories of discourse in Kant's dynamic account of public reason.[21] Kantian political theory includes important accounts of justice, revolution, pedagogy, autonomy, international relations, press freedom, regime change, citizenship, republicanism, property rights, punishment, cosmopolitanism, the rule of law, and many other critical political topics. Across Kant's different modes of inquiry—from the *Critiques* through the political treatises and essays to his university lectures, letters, and even the marginalia[22]—we find his consistent concern with the possibility of realizing human freedom.

Overview of Kant's Political Ideas

Kant's political works are concerned not with moral or internal freedom, but with external freedom. This topic is treated in an assortment of essays and books, the most important of which is the first part of the *Metaphysics of Morals* (the *Doctrine of Right*). Kant defines this kind of freedom as "independence from being constrained by another's choice" (6:237). To be subject to another's choice would be to be tyrannized over, to suffer despotism. Kant consistently opposes despotism, whether it is the despotism of paternalistic government, or the social despotism of an inherited nobility, or even the despotism of having one's will determined by material rather than ideal considerations (though this is more a moral and less a political concern). The goal is human emancipation—from the institutions of the old regime, from social and political domination generally, and even from traditional patterns of thinking. "*Sapere aude!*" Kant writes in *Enlightenment*. "Have the courage to make use of your *own* understanding!" (8:35).

For Kant there are many paths to human emancipation, most of them explored in the contributions to this volume. LaVaque-Manty, for example, ably demonstrates that for Kant the achievement of moral and political autonomy depends on and is analogous to the achievement of natural autonomy in the sense of using one's body to fulfill the ends one has set oneself. This will surprise some readers of Kant, for whom his exclusion of empirical conditions from the moral calculus of the *Groundwork* implies a rejection of the natural world *tout court*. However, LaVaque-Manty persuasively argues that physical autonomy is for Kant an irreplaceable step on the way to autonomy generally. This view explains many of Kant's otherwise inexplicable positions: his support for play and physical education for children, his opposition to rote memorization, his consistent attacks on leading strings and walkers for young children (these three are LaVaque-Manty's examples), and even the otherwise puzzling inclusion of a chapter on health regimens with detailed instructions on proper breathing in *The Conflict of the Faculties*.

Though he never wrote a critique of politics, Kant does apply his famous critical method to the question of political freedom. How, Kant asks, is freedom possible? What are the conditions of possibility for human freedom? As Ripstein demonstrates here, this question leads Kant to coercion under the rule of law almost as soon as he posits freedom as the only innate human right. Louis-Philippe Hodgson explains that the idea is "fundamental for Kant's entire political philosophy: . . . human beings have, in virtue of their rational nature, a *right to freedom,* that is, a right to 'independence from being constrained by another's choice . . . insofar as it can coexist with the freedom of every other in accordance with a universal law.' (*MM*, 6:237)." For everyone to enjoy freedom in the sense of independence from others' determination, we need to be able to prevent people from exercising unilateral force on one another (and any coercion authorized by less than a united will counts as unilateral, including for example one class coercing another). But if coercive force is required to stop people from interfering with one another's legitimate exercises of freedom, how can it be reconciled with freedom as independence from another's determination? I have already hinted that Kant's answer will be that legitimate coercion can only be exercised on behalf of a universal will. As Ripstein explains here, law, and not any one person or group, must determine the limits within which free citizens interact. The answer to Kant's critical question about the conditions under which political freedom is possible is this: only under the republican rule of law is human freedom possible.

What, then, counts as republican? The crucial test of republican legitimacy is whether the state's laws reflect the universal will of the people. As mentioned above, laws that reflect any partial will, whether the will of a societal group like the clergy or the aristocracy, or the will of a single despot, always subject individuals to determination by another, and are thus illegitimate. According to Kant the "mixed constitution" of Great Britain is illegitimate, because the royal house can decide whether or not to go to war, and thus real legislative power lies with the king and not with the people. This does not mean that Kant expects actual unanimity or even actual majorities to support laws before they can be viewed as legitimate. Instead, he argues that the test of legitimate legislation is whether a whole people could have reasonably supported it.

Like other Enlightenment republicans of his day, Kant supports the separation of powers. However, it is the problem of realizing freedom as independence from determination by another's choice that motivates Kant's insistence on the separation of powers rather than the usual concerns about power. As O'Neill notices in her contribution, Kant often adapts a familiar structure from mainstream republican thought while giving it an entirely new justification. Like Montesquieu and other advocates of the separation of powers, Kant argues for a three-branch style of government, including executive, legislative, and judicial authorities. Unlike them, however, Kant uses this structure only to insure that citizens are insulated from unilateral will. Kant is interested in making sure that the exercise of coercive power always represents the united will of the people and not the private will of some individual or group. The executive branch, according to Kant, must never treat the state as a private holding, but only perform the universal will of the people as best as this can be understood. Kant illustrates this norm in *Perpetual Peace* with the example of the absolutist but relatively progressive Prussian king Frederick II, who "at least *said* that he was only the highest servant of the state" (8:352). This Kantian version of the separation of powers also explains why he is so critical of ancient direct democracies, which might strike us as surprising from the author who inspired the democratic peace hypothesis.

Ripstein writes in this volume that for Kant, "the state of nature is devoid of justice. The solution is to leave the state of nature and enter a rightful condition in which we are subject to common standards." For Kant, then, if we are to enjoy freedom as independence of determination by another's choice, we must be subject to a state that enforces the universal rule of law. In this sense, Kant joins the social contract tradition by arguing that everyone is obliged to leave the state of nature and submit to common adjudication of disputes. However, here as elsewhere, Kant's innovative use of familiar terms can be misleading. Ripstein reminds us that Kant's reason to enter the civil condition is not like those of other social contract thinkers: the state and its coercion are not meant just to keep "corrupt, lazy, or selfish beings in line." Only under conditions of universal law is freedom possible. It is wrong, therefore, to refuse to enter into lawful relations with anyone with whom one might interact. Again, thinking with Ripstein: "Coercion is central to [Kant's] analysis because the possibility of interference with freedom arises simply from the existence of a plurality of free beings setting their own purposes, not the empirical likelihood of people using force."

Kant, then, does not argue for the entry into the civil condition on any of the usual grounds: for protection of prepolitical rights to one's body or the fruits of one's labor, for instance, or in the service of a rational interest in peaceful coexistence, to take another example. Rather, the idealized Kantian reasoner exits the state of nature for the rule of law, the only condition under which the exercise of human freedom is possible.

We all know there is no actual ideal reasoner. As O'Neill argues in her essay in this volume, for Kant the social contract is important as an idea [*Idee*], not as an historical reality or as a personal obligation. Kant calls the original contract a norm for all actually existing states; he means that real states can be judged according to how well they achieve the standards entailed by the idea of original contract. Kant glosses freedom as independence from determination by another's choice; that is to say, freedom means obeying laws of one's own making (however indirect that lawmaking may in fact be). Kant argues in *Theory and Practice* that the idea of original contract has "undoubted practical reality" just because it functions as a norm for states, in particular binding legislators to make only laws "in such a way that they *could* have arisen from the united will of a whole people" (8:297). O'Neill summarizes: "Kant's version of the social contract can count as an idea of reason because he derives it from his account of practical reason, rather than from any appeal to actual or hypothetical consent."

Once we realize that the original contract is not empirical or historical reality but rather an idea of reason, we can understand why Kant would insist that subjects must not investigate the origins of the state that rules them. Kant argues that investigation into the origins of actual states would certainly reveal illegitimate coercion, adding that such an inquiry would likely be futile, since "savages draw up no record of their submission to law" (*MM*, 6:339). Citizens must not seek critical leverage in the material and historical origins of their particular state, though they may compare their states with the principles derived from the idea of original contract as a norm. As Taylor describes in his essay in this volume, Kant views this kind of judgment and petition as citizens' main mode of political expression. Acting only in the public sphere, they may expose duplicity, artifice, and other failures of the regime to conform to republican principles of accountability. To do more than this, Taylor's Kant argues, would undermine the rule of law that makes their very freedom possible. The exercise of freedom of the pen, of participation in the public sphere unconstrained by social or political hindrances, should according to Kant be the driving force that moves regimes from despotism to freedom without risking revolutionary setbacks. As John Christian Laursen demonstrates in this volume, Kant could be quite strategic in his political arguments, aiming to transform the legal context in a progressive direction, but not always by the most obvious means. Discussing Kant's arguments against book piracy, for example, Laursen shows us Kant inculcating associations between authorship and natural right subtly, "in the most abstract, uncontroversial, and innocuous language, so that by the time the reader had finished reading he would find himself having to agree with Kant's outcome."

This has not, however, been the experience of readers of Kant's remarks on the right of revolution. Far from being drawn into unavoidable agreement, most readers find themselves remarking on the irony that the philosopher of freedom calls for obedience even to unjust authorities. One argument Kant makes against revolution is that for any revolutionary action to succeed, it would have to be kept secret, and would thus violate the norm of publicity. He also employs more empirical arguments, including the claim that quick transitions cannot effect the substantive social changes that are required to make progress toward genuine republicanism. As Taylor demonstrates here, Kant's preferred mode of regime change is gradual to the point of being invisible to its very agents: "By a series of policy innovations, each tactically sound, an absolute monarchy (or more likely a dynasty) thus engineers its own downfall and the creation of a republic. Moreover, this end is . . . accomplished without any violations of right, which would inevitably occur in a revolution."

As Taylor suggests, Kant's main argument against revolutionary activity is that it undermines the conditions of civil freedom itself. For Kant, the kind of gradual reform that is possible through public critique is both more likely to succeed and more legitimate (since it depends on potentially universal arguments, rather than unilateral force). In his late writings, Kant expresses sympathy for the goals of the French Revolution; in fact, he cites the daring of Prussian partisans of the French revolutionaries as indirect evidence of the empirical reality of moral reason itself. As Ferguson notes, Kant sometimes recognizes that revolutionary activity, viewed historically, can promote progress toward freedom. Moreover, as Ripstein argues here, Kant distinguishes among regimes, however despotical, that provide a civil condition (law), and what he calls barbarian regimes that do no such thing. Though Kant's remarks on the topic are all too brief, resistance to barbarism may not only be permitted, but may also be obligatory. However, Kant consistently advocates gradualism and the public sphere over revolutionary action in the streets or on the battlefield.

"Now morally practical reason pronounces in us its irresistible *veto: there is to be no war*" (*MM*, 6:354). Like individuals, states must exit the state of nature and enter into peaceful coexistence in the international sphere. Just as the idea of an original contract justifies the surrender of lawless freedom to a state that guarantees the rule of law, so the idea of perpetual peace ought to move states to enter into lawful relations with one another. The analogy is imperfect; we see in Hodgson's account that a Kantian should actually support a global federal system with the minimum necessary powers, though Kant himself resists this conclusion (*PP*, 8:355–56). Kant does not conflate all potential world states with the one he criticizes as despotic (universal monarchy). Incidentally, this common mistake (conflating universal monarchy with all potential world states) reminds us of the continuing value of detailed historical research into Kant's intellectual historical context. Without the understanding provided by Hunter, Laursen, Georg Cavallar, and others that discussion of the "universal monarchy" advocated by Dante, for example, was quite common, it is impossible to follow Kant's subtle distinction.

Returning to the analogy between exiting the state of nature on the domestic and international levels, however, we see that the logic is the same: the idea of perpetual peace, like the idea of original contract, functions as a norm to which everyone ought to conform. Kant does not expect states to make themselves vulnerable by behaving as if the peaceful norm were already reality. As Ferguson notes here, Kant does not expect war to disappear entirely. Instead, he argues that even in war, states ought to "always leave open the possibility of leaving the state of nature among states . . . and entering a rightful condition" (*MM*, 6:347).

Kant provides a series of arguments that have become associated with the democratic peace hypothesis. The general idea is that what we would call democratic accountability under the rule of law on the domestic front leads to peace internationally. First, he claims that under republican governance, the people's will would be reflected in policy decisions, and the people, he thinks, will not support costly aggressive wars. By contrast, the incentives facing despotic heads of state would tend to encourage them to "decide upon war, as upon a kind of pleasure party" (*PP*, 8:350). Second, he argues that republican governments' peaceful examples will serve as a kind of focal point for an expanding, and commercially profitable, pacific league.

Finally, Kant offers both an idealized picture of peaceful international relations and a set of principles that should promote its realization. As Ferguson points out in this volume, Kant does not expect cosmopolitan harmony to be achieved, and his references to such an outcome are invariably ironic, using terms like "illusory." However, "we must act as if it is something real, though perhaps it is not; we must work toward establishing perpetual peace and the kind of constitution that seems to us most conducive to it" (*MM*, 6:354).

But of course this peaceful condition is not real. How can actual human beings work to achieve progress toward such ideal, even unreachable, conditions? At the international level, Kant suggests a number of norms to which principled heads of state ought to adhere, including bans on such practices as debt-financed military adventure and the use of assassins as weapons of international intrigue. Any practice undermining the possibility of future peaceful relations among states must be eliminated. However, Kant does admit the possibility that some practices that conflict with right, such as the maintenance of standing armies, might under the right circumstances promote rather than prevent eventual peaceful international relations. In these cases, he argues, they are provisionally acceptable.

Kant also applies the idea of provisional right to domestic politics. Hodgson explains why "there are no conclusive rights in the state of nature. . . . Because the conditions that must obtain for rights to be legitimately adjudicated and enforced are jointly constitutive of the civil condition." However, as Ripstein notes in his contribution, a defective civil condition is still obligatory compared with no civil condition at all. Kant is well aware of the enormous gap between the near-feudal reality of much of contemporary politics and the republican ideal of political freedom. Therefore, he argues not that leaders must instantly revolutionize their world to reflect republican perfection, but instead that real-world leaders ought to consider whether their actions promote or retard the possibility of progress.

For example, as Hunter notes in this volume, "when Kant applies the test [of political legitimacy as the possible unified will of the people] . . . to show the illegitimacy of the laws arbitrarily privileging a noble social estate—he does so not by asking whether republican governments might actually pass such laws (clearly they have), but by asking whether such a law could be universalized in a community of rational beings." Even once he has determined that a policy—say, of granting privileges to members of an hereditary nobility—is illegitimate, however, Kant does not propose eliminating them outright. Instead, "the only way the state can then gradually correct this mistake it has made, of conferring hereditary privileges contrary to right, is by letting them lapse . . . it has a provisional right to let these titled positions of dignity continue" (*MM*, 6:329). Kant is much more interested in preventing actual despotism than in reproducing the ideal forms of republican governance; if public opinion values ancient formalities, Kant supports their continuation, so long as the real distribution of the power to decide becomes steadily more rightful.

"Two things fill the mind with ever new and increasing admiration and reverence, the more often and more steadily one reflects on them: *the starry heavens above me and the moral law within me* (5:162)," Kant writes in *Critique of Practical Reason*. The elements of human existence most relevant to political freedom are our physical location on what Kant called the *globus terraqueus* and the fact that we all apply moral norms to political reality. Not only are individuals obliged to enter into law-governed conditions with all potential interacting agents, but states also "are condemned by their power to find a way to share the surface of the earth; they cannot escape this plight, because there is a very real sense in which, to use Kant's words, they 'cannot help mutually affecting one another'" (Hodgson). Given our residence on a round earth connected by waterways, we are always at least potentially interacting with everyone else: "a violation of right on *one* place of the earth is felt in *all*" (*PP*, 8:360). Even if we do not always agree about the nature of such violations, we can all recognize wrongs by comparing reality with norms of rightful relations. In Kant's vision of politics, we are on the way to a civil condition under which human freedom is possible. Freedom from determination by another's choice is the innate right of individuals; freedom to decide to make progress toward enlightened self-rule is the "highest right of the people" (*MM*, 6:327).

Overview of This Volume's Contributions

We begin our volume of essays by asking basic questions about Kant's political theory. What, if anything, justifies the state? If political power is instrumental to some other good, what is that good and why should it serve to legitimate sovereignty? Philosopher Onora O'Neill opens this collection with a critical and rarely recognized claim about Kant's political thought: for Kant, the state solves a problem that arises from the basic structure of our existence as reason givers, applied to our specific condition as human beings. As Michaele Ferguson puts it later in the volume, politics is a necessary aspect of our human condition (as plural end setters) rather than an unfortunate makeshift necessitated by our flawed human nature. While the flaws in our human nature may be remediable, the human condition of plurality is not: "As Kant's imaginative example of rational extraterrestrials suggests, in order to rid ourselves of the human condition of plurality, we would have to become entirely different beings." Even without our character faults, we would still exist as inhabitants of space on a closed, round planet, necessarily interacting and each setting ends ourselves. Addressing the same set of questions, Arthur Ripstein in this volume emphasizes that for Kant, politics is not remedial. "Justice is required because human beings are capable of setting and pursuing their own purposes. That capacity is not a limitation; it is our humanity itself."

So in contrast to other thinkers in the social contract tradition, for Kant the state and its coercive enforcement of law is necessitated by practical reason in a human context. Kant's idea of the social contract plays an important but subordinate part in his political philosophy. As O'Neill writes, for Kant, "the social contract is a special case of his universal principle of justice: it spells out what this principle requires in actual human conditions. The universal principle of justice is in turn a special case of the categorical imperative: it spells out the most basic maxims to which our lives must conform if the structures of the public domain are to meet the requirements of the categorical imperative. The categorical imperative is the supreme principle of practical reason, indeed an idea of reason, because its double modal requirement formalizes the recognition that we are not in the business of offering reasons to others unless we can take it that they can follow those reasons. Kant's version of the social contract can count as an idea of reason because he derives it from his account of practical reason, rather than from any appeal to actual or to hypothetical consent." Therefore, O'Neill argues, Kant grounds political justification in reason itself, rather than in explicit or tacit, actual, or hypothetical consent. O'Neill's theme of Kant's ambivalent relationship to the social contract tradition recurs throughout the volume, but especially in Ripstein's and Hodgson's contributions.

The concept of consent is a fraught one for scholars of Kant's political thought. On the one hand, the idea of a united will overcoming the problem of the injustice of should-be autonomous agents subordinated to unilateral will, that is, of individuals being objects of some other person's or people's choice, is the linchpin of Kant's system of right. On the other hand, however, as O'Neill neatly demonstrates in the first part of her essay, Kant cannot adopt any of the standard contractarian views of consent. Explicit consent could not be the basis for the kind of reliable mutual enforcement that guarantees the exercise of free choices within the bounds of everyone else's free choice, since if I had to agree to each law that binds me, I might well pick and choose, exposing my fellow citizens to arbitrary determinations of mine. Tacit consent also cannot be Kant's answer, for, as O'Neill remarks, "a conception of tacit consent sufficiently diluted to endorse all legitimate coercion would be so indeterminate that it would endorse everything—and justify nothing." A final possible consent option is hypothetical consent; this option holds wide appeal for contemporary scholars seeking to, as Hunter acerbically puts it in this volume, transform Kant's "esoteric" doctrine into something "exoteric" and useful in the modern day.[23] Kant certainly provides some textual evidence for this view, recommending for example that we must treat laws as authoritative if a people could possibly have willed them (but remember that crucial word, "possibly"). Unfortunately for hypothetical consent theory, O'Neill shows why it must be a nonstarter for Kant: either we base hypothetical consent on idealized conditions (deliberative rationality, say) that are impossible for empirical choosers to fulfill, or we begin with empirically existing features shared by the choosers, in which case we must presume what we are trying to justify. Abandoning these three consent theories, O'Neill returns to Kant's basic critical apparatus for the answer: we need to understand the conditions of possibility for universal consent. Kant's criterion is *"modal and not hypothetical."*

Arthur Ripstein explains Kant's contract theory and his rejection of the right of revolution by distinguishing sharply between Kant's views and those of his predecessors (by contrast with Ian Hunter's contribution). Most of these predecessors, including both natural lawyers and contractarians, view justice as remedial, and law as a makeshift solution to problems arising from human imperfection. Kant's view is fundamentally different, Ripstein argues: "neither justice nor law is remedial ... [they] are required for any finite and embodied free beings that interact with one another." To be sure, Kant is concerned with how human beings "come to terms with their imperfections." But these questions come into play for Kant only after the fundamentals of justice and law have been established, whereas for his predecessors they form the first step of the arguments for the necessity of government. Toward the end of the chapter, Ripstein draws on a range of distinctions among political regimes from Kant's *Anthropology* to explain Kant's oft-criticized rejection of the right to rebellion. People have misunderstood Kant if they claim that his support of the rule of law would include orderly but lawless regimes such as Nazi Germany. The Nazi regime was no republic, and no despotism, but only barbarism, a regime of force with neither freedom nor law, and thus merely a "defective form of a state of nature" for Kant.

Thomas Pogge argues that "we can gain a better understanding of Kant's *Rechtslehre* by confronting it with the distinction [between political and comprehensive conceptions of justice] Rawls developed two centuries later." With a subtle and powerful reading of Kant's most important political work, Pogge argues that we need not presume that Kant's political theory is dependent on his moral philosophy, even though Kant sometimes writes as if it were. Instead, we should analyze the text of the *Rechtslehre* to discover whether the account of political justice there can be interpreted as freestanding in the Rawlsian sense. Pogge argues that it can, and calls on "those who dismiss Kant's political philosophy as dependent on metaphysical or moral views that we cannot expect to be freely endorsed by the citizens of modern societies" to answer his case.

With Hodgson's chapter on the Kantian case for a world state, we move from the background of Kant's international legal thought to its application in perhaps the most ambitious possible way. As with the other contributors, Hodgson places Kant's effort to realize moral ideals at the center of his argument. Hodgson, however, departs from Kant's own well-known worries about the institution of a global government to argue that the best Kantian view supports a federally organized world state with enforcement powers. Such an institution, Hodgson argues, is made necessary by the same arguments that Kant uses to justify the exit from the state of nature in the case of individuals. Thoughtfully deploying Kant's distinction between conclusive and provisional right, Hodgson argues that only under an enforceable system of rights can states and the individuals within them enjoy genuine freedom. These rights could be enforced only by a federally organized international authority. Hodgson's conclusions regarding a proposed world state could apply to rest of the contributions in this volume: "Kant's doubts notwithstanding, there is thus good reason to believe that realizing the ideal set by external freedom is possible in this world."

For Robert Taylor, a close reading of Kant's famous essay, "An Answer to the Question: What Is Enlightenment?," allows us to understand how absolutist rule could fit comfortably within Kant's republican political philosophy. Reading the essay against the background of debates in the Prussian journals of the time and in the context of Kant's other political writings, Taylor demonstrates the critical importance of Kant's contrast between man and machine for his account of the fundamental political human "aptitude for active, republican citizenship." Along the way, Taylor demonstrates how Kant's philosophy of history leads him to expect that absolute rulers, including those not motivated by moral duty, will take the steps leading ultimately to their replacement by republican government.

In her chapter, Michaele Ferguson examines a central concept in Kant's teleological thought: unsocial sociability. Focusing in particular on Kant's accounts of friendship and cosmopolitanism, Ferguson argues that for Kant unsocial sociability drives human progress but produces unavoidable antagonism. "The seeds of mistrust, suspicion, and conflict are forever embedded in human affairs." Rejecting pessimism about the human condition, however, Ferguson identifies unsocial sociability as a "constitutive tension," both for Kant's philosophy and for would-be cosmopolitans. While both Ferguson and Ripstein agree that the human condition of a plurality of end setters drives the necessity of the entry into the civil condition, they disagree about what Ferguson calls Kant's phenomenology. For Ferguson, the source of all social conflict "from interpersonal strife all the way up to interstate war . . . [is] the result of the free choices of individuals acting in accord with their natural unsociability." Ferguson corrects the common impression that this view of the human condition is pessimistic: antagonism is a productive force in Kant's theory of history, moving humanity toward cosmopolitan life, if not toward some impossible perfect harmony.

The historian Ian Hunter uses the context of the journal wars of the Prussian eighteenth century to demolish anachronistic readings of Kant's political and religious thought. Hunter begins with the historical point that Kant's moral, political, and religious ideas existed in competition with rival strands of Enlightenment ideology; we ought to examine Kant's ideas as part of a "concrete struggle for dominance in the field of competing moral programs." In the first half of his chapter, Hunter argues persuasively for setting Kant's ideas in the context of Protestant rationalist metaphysics, identifying Kant's central metaphysical construct—his conception of man as a pure intelligence mortgaged to sensuous inclinations—with its roots in

"German university metaphysics." This done, Hunter proceeds in the second half of the chapter to overturn the dominant reading of Kant's engagements in religious controversies of his day. This dominant reading sees Kant as the representative of enlightened, rational religion against (minister for religious affairs) Johann Christoph Wöllner's anti-Enlightenment dogmatic conservatism. Hunter argues instead that the Prussian religious establishment attacked by Kant and defended by Wöllner was in fact more pluralist, secular, and tolerant than the "factional cultural politics of the Protestant metaphysical rationalists" like Kant. "However alien it might be to the political sensibilities of those now living in religiously pacified societies under politically secularized states, the occasional action taken against outbreaks of religious rationalism in Brandenburg-Prussia during the seventeenth and eighteenth centuries was neither anti-Enlightenment nor indicative of the state's attempt to block the progress of reason and freedom."

The intersection of moral ideals and social reality continues to concern us in Mika LaVaque-Manty's contribution to the volume. Reading Kant's pedagogical writings, and reporting on Kant's personal involvement in progressive educational movements of the time, LaVaque-Manty demonstrates in the context of education Kant's concern with the possible realization of critical moral philosophy. In the first place, Kant thought of education and politics as essentially connected: "Two human inventions can be considered the most difficult, namely, the art of government and the art of education" (P, 9:446). They are both means of realizing human autonomy, and both fraught with similar conundra of paternalism and enlightenment. What LaVaque-Manty says about Kant's views on education applies just as well to progressive politics: "too much fostering, and independence won't come about . . . too little, and people will remain metaphorical children all their lives." For Kant as for his fellow reformer Johann Bernhard Basedow, education serves the state by producing good citizens. Note also, as Ian Hunter mentions in his essay, that for Kant the Prussian state is an *Erziehungsstaat* or "pedagogical or tutelary state."

More generally, Kant associated the field of education with the possibility of progress for humanity: musing on the contemporary barbarism that is the international system, Kant proceeded to complain that "we" have not yet come up with a unified religion, nor a system of education.[24] The results of LaVaque-Manty's investigation into Kant's pedagogical theory and practice support his important reading of Kant's concept of autonomy. Kant's "emphasis on free play on children's own terms . . . and an opposition to rote memorization and physical punishment" constitute a pragmatic application of an ideal of autonomy that is "far more dynamic than it sometimes seems." LaVaque-Manty shows us that Kant's pedagogical work, like his theory of citizenship, promotes an ideal of autonomy through context-sensitive instantiations intended to bring imperfect, unequal circumstances closer to the egalitarian goal.

John Christian Laursen's contribution also examines Kant's views in their historical context. He begins with the following puzzle. It is well known that Kant called for intellectual freedom and freedom of the press in his famous essay of 1784, "What Is Enlightenment?," and that in many of his later works he promotes a politics of publicity. Why, then, is there no clearly established right to freedom of the press in his great *Metaphysics of Morals* of 1797? Laursen examines Kant's engagement in the eighteenth-century controversy over book piracy, including especially his response to Martin Ehlers, in order to illuminate the important question of Kant's commitment to press freedom. Interpreting Kant's writings on contemporary political controversies as "a sort of Trojan horse, designed to plant ideas inside the city walls, which can later break out and tear down those walls," the chapter begins with the context of the book piracy debate and ends up providing a new and persuasive explanation for the curious absence of a right of press freedom in the *Rechtslehre*.

Conclusion

The contributors to this volume represent a variety of disciplines (political science, history, philosophy, international relations), and they present even more different perspectives on Kant's political theory. Their conclusions often overturn accepted wisdom about Kant's work: LaVaque-Manty compares Kant's pedagogy favorably with the educational innovations of both Locke and Rousseau, for example, and Ripstein shows us that some regimes (barbaric ones) may rightly be opposed. There are certainly strong disagreements among the contributors, including for example between Pogge and Hunter on the value of Rawls's adaptation of Kant's ideas, or between Taylor and Pogge on the consequences of Kant's sexism. However, across these differences, certain continuities remain. One area of agreement is that the status of Kant's relation to mainstream social contract theory is an important and difficult topic. Another is the continuing interest of

Kant's political philosophy. Even Hunter defends the Kant that he views as an authentic representative of Protestant rationalism against modern misreadings.

Most important, the contributors to this volume share a conviction that Kant offers a crucial touchstone for thinking about the conditions of human freedom today. In imitation of Kant's own orientation, the contributors in their writings maintain an openness to new ideas and evidence; an ecumenical view with regard to sources of interest; a nonparochialism of discipline, region, and topic; and a consistent fallibilism with regard to their own and others' work; in short, this group represents a genuinely Kantian attitude toward the investigation of the world. Kant is the great inquirer, the great antidogmatist who took uncertainty and limited human knowledge as a starting point and still dared to conjecture. We hope to have honored these commitments with our interpretations and applications of Kant's political theory.

NOTES

1. Patrick Riley, "Review Essay of O'Neill and Flikschuh," *Political Theory* 31, no. 2 (April 2003): 315.

2. For a good overview, see Vesna Danilovic and Joe Clare, "The Kantian Liberal Peace (Revisited)," *American Journal of Political Science* 51, no. 2 (April 2007): 397–414.

3. See, for example, the experiments described in John Gastil and Peter Levine, eds., *The Deliberative Democracy Handbook: Strategies for Effective Civil Management in the Twenty-first Century* (San Francisco: John Wiley and Sons, 2005).

4. Elisabeth Ellis, *Provisional Politics: Kantian Arguments in Policy Context* (New Haven: Yale University Press, 2008). See also Christian F. Rostbøll, "Preferences and Paternalism: On Freedom and Deliberative Democracy," *Political Theory* 33, no. 3 (2005): 370–96; and Ferguson, chapter 6 of this volume.

5. See, for example, some recent works by contributors to this volume, including: Ellis, *Provisional Politics*; Mika LaVaque-Manty, *Arguments and Fists: Political Agency and Justification in Liberal Theory* (London: Routledge, 2002); Onora O'Neill, *Autonomy and Trust in Bioethics* (Cambridge: Cambridge University Press, 2002); and Arthur Ripstein, *Force and Freedom: Kant's Legal and Political Philosophy* (Cambridge: Harvard University Press, 2009).

6. See, for example, the essays in this volume by John Christian Laursen and Robert S. Taylor on this topic.

7. Christine Korsgaard, *Creating the Kingdom of Ends* (Cambridge: Cambridge University Press, 1996); *The Sources of Normativity* (Cambridge: Cambridge University Press, 1996); and *The Constitution of Agency: Essays on Practical Reason and Moral Psychology* (Oxford: Oxford University Press, 2008).

8. Barbara Herman, *The Practice of Moral Judgment* (Cambridge: Harvard University Press, 1993); and *Moral Literacy* (Cambridge: Harvard University Press, 2007).

9. Onora O'Neill, *Constructions of Reason: Explorations of Kant's Practical Philosophy* (Cam-

bridge: Cambridge University Press, 1989); *Bounds of Justice* (Cambridge: Cambridge University Press, 2000); and *Autonomy and Trust in Bioethics* (Cambridge: Cambridge University Press, 2002).

10. Immanuel Kant, *Anthropology, History, and Education*, ed. Günter Zöller and Robert B. Louden (Cambridge: Cambridge University Press, 2007).

11. Although, as contributor Onora O'Neill has demonstrated, Kant's critical opus takes the (inherently political) question of freedom as its central task, and the (also inherently political) structure of a tribunal as its mode of investigation. See O'Neill, *Constructions of Reason*.

12. See Gregor's discussion of printer error and the subsequent scholarship on it in her translator's note, *Immanuel Kant: Practical Philosophy*, trans. and ed. Mary Gregor, intro Allen W. Wood (Cambridge: Cambridge University Press, 1996). See also my discussion of the importance of these matters in a review of *Toward Perpetual Peace and Other Writings on Politics, Peace, and History*, ed. Pauline Kleingeld (New Haven: Yale University Press, 2006) that appears in *Ethics* 117, no. 4 (2007): 766–67. But see Hunter's note 24, this volume, 204.

13. On *Conflict*, see my remarks in Elisabeth Ellis, *Kant's Politics: Provisional Theory for an Uncertain World* (New Haven: Yale University Press, 2005), 160–61. See also John Zammito, "A Text of Two Titles: Kant's 'A Renewed Attempt to Answer the Question: "Is the Human Race Continually Improving?"'" *Studies in History and Philosophy of Science* 39 (2008): 535–45, who argues that if Kant is attempting in this late work to improve on his earlier philosophy of history, than it must be considered a failure. On *Anthropology from a Practical Point of View*, see Robert Louden's introduction to the collection of Kant's writings on *Anthropology, History, and Education*, ed. Günther Zöller and Robert B. Louden (Cambridge: Cambridge University Press, 2007), 1–17; and Todd Hedrick, "Race, Difference, and Anthropology in Kant's Cosmopolitanism," *Journal of the History of Philosophy* 46, no. 2 (2008), 245–68.

14. Ellis, *Kant's Politics*, 2.

15. John Locke, *An Essay Concerning Human Understanding*, ed. P. H. Nidditch, based on the 4th ed. (New York: Oxford University Press, 1975 [1700]).

16. I tried to demonstrate this point with a series of applications of Kantian political thinking to diverse case studies in *Provisional Politics*.

17. Inder S. Marwah, "What Nature Makes of Her: Kant's Gendered Metaphysics," paper presented at the Western Political Science Association meeting, 2010.

18. "Wir sind in Ansehung des Völkerrechts noch Barbaren. Wir haben noch kein System der Vereinigung der Religionen, Vornehmlich noch kein Erziehungssystem. Neue Epoche" (Refl. 1453), *Reflections on Anthropology*, 15:634. Reprinted in *Materialen zu Kants Rechtsphilosophie*, ed. Zwi Batscha (Frankfurt am Main: Suhrkamp, 1976), 39.

19. Ellis, *Provisional Politics*, 3.

20. The locus classicus is Habermas's little essay on Kant in Jürgen Habermas, *Structural Transformation of the Public Sphere: An Inquiry into a Category of Bourgeois Society* (Cambridge: MIT Press, 1989 [1962]), 102–17; see also *Habermas and the Public Sphere*, ed. Craig Calhoun (Cambridge: MIT Press, 1992).

21. Though their work is very different, and neither presents himself as a Kantian, both Reinhart Koselleck and Michel Foucault offer theories of the development of discourses in society that are indebted to Kant's work on the topic. See Koselleck, *The Practice of Conceptual History: Timing History, Spacing Concepts* (Stanford: Stanford University Press, 2002), especially chapters 13 and 15; and *The Foucault Reader*, ed. Paul Rabinow (New York: Pantheon, 1984).

22. Kant's marginalia and other notes are an important source for political theorists and other students of Kantian philosophy. See Zwi Batscha, *Materialen*; Richard Velkley, *Freedom and the End of Reason: On the Moral Foundation of Kant's Critical Philosophy* (Chicago: University of Chicago Press, 1989); John Zammito, *The Genesis of Kant's Critique of Judgment* (Chicago:

University of Chicago Press, 1992); and Kant, *Notes and Fragments*, ed. Paul Guyer (Cambridge: Cambridge University Press, 2005).

23. I confess that I, too, describe Kant's consent theory in hypothetical terms in *Kant's Politics*, though I am now convinced that O'Neill's modal model is the right one.

24. See note 18.

KANT AND THE SOCIAL CONTRACT TRADITION
Onora O'Neill

The fundamental idea of the social contract tradition is that consent or agreement can justify basic social and political institutions: just societies are based on the consent of the governed, unjust societies are not. As is well known, the tradition has had many forms, notably in political philosophies of the early modern period and in the luxuriant variety of contemporary contractualisms. As is equally well known, a discouraging list of standard difficulties stands in the way of the thought that consent can justify fundamental political and social arrangements.

One long-standing dispute is about the sort of consent needed for justification: should it be the *actual* consent of those involved, or the *hypothetical* consent that would be given by beings with a distinctive (e.g., reasoned, informed, disinterested) view of the matter? If actual consent is needed, should it be explicit or is tacit consent enough? Neither view of actual consent seems satisfactory for purposes of justification: we consent explicitly to too little, but (as it seems) tacitly to far too much. If, on the other hand, consent is only hypothetical, then it is quite obscure why it justifies. Why should the consent of hypothetical idealized rational agents, or of

---

This essay originally appeared in François Duchesneau, Guy Lafrance, and Claude Piché, eds., *Kant actuel: Hommage à Pierre Laberge* (Montreal: Bellarmin 2000), 185–200. Reprinted with permission from Copibec. Alas, this paper was written too late for me to discuss it with Pierre Laberge. Earlier versions were given as the Paton Lecture at the University of St. Andrews in 1998 and at the University of Santa Clara in 1999; I am indebted to many helpful commentators, and in particular to Ken Westphal and Katrin Flickschuh.

hypothetical beings in an ideal speech situation, or of persons in an artfully tailored hypothetical original position, justify the principles by which we are to live, who have never been any of these supposedly ideal beings, and probably cannot and do not aspire to become any of them? Moreover, even if hypothetical consent could justify, how should we choose among the many versions of hypothetical consent that have been proposed? And if there is a choice to be made, does not this very fact suggest that considerations other than consent are basic to justification?

On the surface it seems that Kant too must encounter these difficulties. He is generally taken to be a social contract theorist, and a good one. In the most distinguished formulation of twentieth-century contractualism, John Rawls writes: "My aim is to present a conception of justice which generalizes and carries to a higher level of abstraction the familiar theory of the Social Contract as found, say, in Locke, Rousseau and Kant."[1] Many knowledgeable writers on Kant's political philosophy speak confidently of him as a social contract theorist.[2] Patrick Riley has even titled an article "On Kant as the Most Adequate of the Social Contract Theorists."[3]

In his great political writings of the 1790s—*Theory and Practice, Perpetual Peace,* and *The Doctrine of Right,* which forms the first part of *The Metaphysic of Morals*—Kant provides a fair amount of evidence for the view that he is a social contract theorist. Numerous passages in *Theory and Practice,* and some in the other political writings, discuss and apparently endorse a conception of the social contract. Yet Kant's basic justification of political institutions appeals to a quite different universal principle of justice (right). This principle is stated at the beginning of section 2 of *Theory and Practice*; a particularly clear formulation is given early in the *Doctrine of Right*: "Any action is *right* if it can coexist with everyone's freedom in accordance with a universal law, or if on its maxim the freedom of choice of each can coexist with everyone's freedom in accordance with a universal law" (*MM,* 6:230; see also *TP,* 8:289).

This universal principle of justice makes no obvious reference to consent, and Kant does not identify it as the principle of a social contract. Moreover, many of his central writings on justice, and specifically on the justification of state power, barely refer to the notion of a social contract.

It is not then wholly surprising that some recent writers have argued that Kant does not fall within the social contract tradition at all. For example, Reinhardt Brandt stresses both premodern elements in Kant's political philosophy and the importance of the so-called *lex permissiva* rather than of consent in justifying coercive state power.⁴ Leslie Mulholland argues systematically in *Kant's System of Rights*⁵ that Kant's account of justice belongs not in the social contract but in the early modern natural law tradition.⁶

Clearly, if Kant is a social contract theorist he is a peculiar one. Here I shall look at some of the peculiarities, and suggest that they may enable Kant to avoid some standard difficulties both of social contract theory and of contemporary contractualism. If I am right about the distinctiveness of Kant's relationship to the social contract tradition, it may not be feasible to construct a seriously Kantian form of contractualism.

1. Justification by Actual and Hypothetical Consent

Before turning to Kant, I shall consider some of the underlying claims of consent theories, including classical social contract theories and contemporary contractualist positions. Their basic thought is that consent can justify basic principles for social and political structures, hence indirectly justify those structures and even the coercion they inflict. This thought may seem intuitively plausible. When we have consented to something, we have no basis for objecting; we are not wronged when it happens; we have authorized what is done: *volenti non fit iniuria*.

On second thought, matters are far more complex. A start can be made by looking at the role of actual consent in justification. There are some cases where actual consent is not sufficient to justify and others where it is not necessary. Its importance is nevertheless not hard to discern.

Consider first how ordinary it is for us to think that actual consent is not sufficient to justify because it has been given to an action or policy of an unacceptable type. Suppose that A agrees that B may practice surgery on him, or agrees to sell B one of his body organs (a kidney, say), or agrees to let B push him from a dangerous height in return for payment, or to let B bully him, or to be B's slave. In these and countless similar cases we are likely to think that, all legalities apart, consent does not provide sufficient justification. We may be tempted to "save" the claim that actual consent is necessary for justification by arguing that in such cases there was something defective about the consent. We may argue, for example, that the danger or plain stupidity of consenting to dangerous treatment or the profound violation of one's rights is evidence that such action cannot have been *genuinely* consented to by competent adults, that here consent is defective, just as in other cases it is defective because the consenting parties were not adequately rational, informed, free from duress, and the like. However, this is a desperate line of argument: there is all too much evidence that people sometimes genuinely consent to action that may seem deeply unacceptable, even to action that profoundly injures, oppresses, or degrades them.[7] Across the board insistence that any consent to such action must be flawed merely suggests an underlying refusal to consider the possibility that justification requires more than actual consent.

On the other hand there are plausible cases where actual consent does *not* seem necessary to justification. When laws are enforced, when parents control their children, when public authorities take emergency action, we have compliance rather than consent: yet the action taken may be wholly legitimate. No form of the social contract tradition even claims to show that *all* justifiable action receives actual consent. If we had to consent to every particular act of state for it to be legitimate, the central purpose of the social contract tradition—the justification of government—would be undermined.[8] Clearly, actual consent is not always needed: it is no more necessary than it is sufficient for justification or just action.

Justification that appeals to consent in ethics and politics might, I suggest, more plausibly be thought of as having *two* stages, which are (generally) individually necessary and only jointly sufficient. First a certain *type* of action (relationship, institution, policy) must be shown acceptable; second, the parties involved in or affected by a particular instance of such an action (relationship, institution, policy) must (generally) consent to it. The only cases in which this second element of actual consent is not required are where the particular action (relationship, policy, institution) is of a type that has been shown exempt from such a requirement—for example, because it is an instance of legitimate coercion.

Daily life is full of examples of two-stage justifications. The myriad activities and transactions of domestic, commercial, and professional life can be justified by showing that they are consensual, *provided that* such activities and transactions are of acceptable types, but not otherwise. Political life incorporates processes for allowing for actual consent and dissent: democratic consent given in elections, more rarely in referenda, most rarely in constitutional conventions,[9] can justify governments, policies, and states, *provided that* they are of acceptable types.

Actual consent is not then unimportant either in political or in other forms of justification; but it presupposes other arguments to show that the *types* of action (relationship, institution, policy) to which consent is given are acceptable. Moreover, even when actual consent is given to an action (relationship, institution, policy) that is of an acceptable sort, its justifying power reaches only a certain distance. Actual consent is a propositional attitude, so is given to a particular act or policy or institution *as described by the agent*. Since propositional attitudes are referentially opaque, actual consent will not automatically transfer from its initial object to the logical or causal implications of that initial object. This is why actual consent theories, although well designed to take note of consent given by those affected to action (relationships, policies, institutions) *as they perceived these*, is not well designed to show whether those affected also consent to related, even closely and necessarily related matters. Actual consent bears on aspects of the particular action (relationship, institution, policy) that an agent may (take herself to) encounter, and can complete a justification when these are of an acceptable type; it does so in a clear but necessarily narrow way. It cannot justify aspects of action (relationship, institution, policy) of acceptable types to which agents do not attend.

These considerations may suggest that any social contract theorist, and any contractualist, should rely as much as possible on appeals to hypothetical consent. Hypothetical consent theories are well designed to justify types of action (relationship, institution, policy); they do not demand demonstrations that anybody actually consents, so avoid the tiresome chore of demonstrating that consent has actually been given, and under which descriptions it has been given.

Although they are clearly designed to reach far, hypothetical consent theories do so at high cost. For two linked reasons a switch of focus to hypothetical consent fails to provide reasons for thinking that consent can justify. First, if hypothetical consent theories invoke conceptions of rationality (reasonableness, disinterestedness, etc.), their applicability to the human case will be in question unless they deploy empirically plausible conceptions of each notion. But many versions of hypothetical consent theory have invoked empirically false, highly idealized conceptions of rationality (reasonableness, disinterestedness, etc.). Second, if hypothetical consent theories do without idealizing assumptions, and use only empirically accurate assumptions true of all choosers, they may not get very far. To repair the deficit of premises, hypothetical consent theories usually add more specific, empirical premises that refer to features and characteristics that are distinctively true of certain choosers, such as references to their citizenship or membership in certain states or communities. However, in doing this hypothetical consent theories forfeit the possibility of justifying the very features or characteristics they presuppose.[10]

Hypothetical consent theories face an uncomfortable choice between idealized ("metaphysical") justifications and restricted ("political") justifications.[11] A metaphysical justification fails insofar as it relies on idealized claims that are false of many, even all, choosers; a political justification fails insofar as it relies on conceptions it aims to justify. For example, John Rawls's version of a political justification in *Political Liberalism* uses conceptions such as those of *peoples* and *citizens* in its basic justificatory arguments, so also presupposes *boundaries,* and thereby also presupposes some *exercise of state powers.*[12] Appeals to hypothetical consent that assume and build on political notions such as these cannot justify fundamental political arrangements.

Analogous dilemmas arise for contractualisms that appeal either to hypothetical preference orderings that meet idealized conceptions of coherence (connectedness, transitivity) or to the empirically established preference orderings true of specific choosers. If idealized accounts of preferences cannot be established, hypothetical consent theories may well slide toward actual consent theories, and in so doing presuppose not just the structure of preferences orderings but also the content of preferences—but as they do so problems about the capacities of preferences to justify, and in particular about appeals to adaptive and addictive preferences, will become pressing.

However, the profound limitations of hypothetical consent theories do not show that theories of justice are impossible. There is no particular reason for thinking that all reasoning that aims to show which *types* of action (relationship, institution, policy) are acceptable (so setting the context for justifying their particular instances by reference to actual consent) needs to build on a conception of hypothetical consent. The claim that actual consent is a second step, needed to complete a justificatory process (in all but a restricted set of cases, where coercion is shown to be legitimate), rather than a complete justification by itself, could be linked with a variety of conceptions of justification and of justice. However, if the basic moves of a theory of justice do not appeal to consent, we may no longer be considering any recognizable version of the social contract tradition. With these thoughts, back to Kant.

2. Kant's Social Contract: Hypothetical Consent?

Kant states his views on the social contract most clearly in part 2 of *Theory and Practice*. The section begins with the assertion that the social contract is completely distinctive and is the "unconditional and first duty in any external relation of people in general, who cannot help mutually affecting one another" (*TP*, 8:289). He then drops all discussion of the social contract for several pages in order to set out the universal principle of justice and to explain why it entails the three components of republican justice, namely, freedom, dependence on law, and equality under law (*TP*, 8:290).

Only toward the end of the section does Kant resume discussion of the idea of the social contract. When he does so, he makes a negative and a positive claim: the social contract should not be thought of as an historical event; it should be thought of as an idea [*Idee*] of reason offering practical guidance.

Kant expresses the negative point as follows:

> But it is by no means necessary that this contract (called *contractus originarius* or *pactum sociale*), as a coalition of every particular and private will within a people into a common and public will (for the sake of a merely rightful legislation), be presupposed as a *fact* (as a fact it is indeed not possible)—as if it would first have to be proved from history that a people, into whose rights and obligations we have entered as descendants, once actually carried out such an act, and that it must have left some sure record or instrument of it, orally or in writing, if one is to hold oneself bound to an already existing civil constitution. (*TP*, 8:297)[13]

Here Kant is on uncontroversial ground. His position amounts to selective rejection of the claim that actual (past) consent (by others) can justify state coercive powers.[14]

Kant's second, positive claim can be, and often has been, read as showing his adherence to some version of hypothetical consent theory. For he asserts that the idea of the social contract is an idea of reason. In *Theory and Practice* the point is summarized as follows: "the idea [*Idee*] of the social contract would remain . . . not however as a fact . . . but only as a rational principle for appraising any public rightful constitution" (*TP*, 8:302).[15]

However, I believe it would be a misreading to take this passage as showing that Kant belongs with the majority of contemporary, contractualist exponents of the social contract tradition in thinking that hypothetical consent of some sort is the source of political justification. Consider the most explicit passage on the social contract in *Theory and Practice*; consider in particular its modalities, which Kant repeatedly italicizes:

> [The social contract] is instead *only an idea* of reason [eine bloße Idee der Vernunft], which, however, has its undoubted practical reality, namely to bind every legislator to give his laws in such a way that they *could* have arisen from the united will of a whole people and to regard each subject, insofar as he wants to be a citizen, as if he has joined in voting for such a will. For this is the touchstone of any public law's conformity with right. In other words, if a public law is so constituted that a whole people *could not possibly* give its consent to it (as, e.g., that a certain class of *subjects* should have the hereditary privilege of *ruling rank*), it is unjust; but if it is *only possible* that a people could agree to it, it is a duty to consider the law just, even if the people is at present in such a situation or frame of mind that, if consulted about it, it would probably refuse its consent. (*TP*, 8:297)[16]

Kant does not say here that the hypothetical consent of (idealized) rational beings constitutes the touchstone for justifying constitutions and laws, and thereby fixes the terms of the social contract. He also explicitly rejects the thought that actual consent can do so. He suggests that it is *possible* agreement that is decisive. He appeals to *possible* universal consent, not to hypothetical consent. The criterion is apparently *modal and not hypothetical*.

At first consideration there are unappealing aspects to a modal conception of justification. One problem of any modal view is that it looks too weak either to identify determinate constitutional requirements or to justify them. Surely all sorts of constitutions and legislation, including much that seems palpably unjust, *could* be universally consented to. A second problem is that it is far from obvious why an appeal to possible consent should count as an idea of reason.

3. Kant's Social Contract: Republican Institutions

However, on Kant's view the criterion of possible consent has crucial substantive implications, and can itself be justified. I shall turn to the implications first. Kant argues that the criterion of possible consent can vindicate a republican constitution that guarantees freedom within the law: constitutions that lack this structure *cannot*, he claims, be universally consented to; constitutions with this structure *can* be universally consented to.

A succinct formulation of the components of a republican constitution is given in *Perpetual Peace*: "A constitution established, first on principles of the *freedom* of the members of a society . . . second on principles of the *dependence* of all upon a single common legislation . . . third on the law of their *equality* . . . the sole constitution that issues from the idea of the original contract, on which all rightful legislation of a people must be based—is a *republican* constitution" (*PP*, 8:349–50; cf. *MM*, 6:340; *TP*, 8:290).

Kant's arguments from the idea of the social contract to the three basic components of a legitimate republican constitution are no doubt overly compressed. Yet I do not think it is hard to discern how his thoughts run. If the idea of a social contract is that of a constitution that *could* secure universal consent, then any constitution that exemplifies it must require the *freedom of individuals*, without which the possibility of genuine consent or dissent is undermined, at least for some, and universal consent becomes impossible. Second, it requires their *common dependence on or subordination to law*: if anyone were above or outside the law, freedom could be systematically or gratuitously undercut, and once again the possibility of genuine consent or dissent is undermined, at least for some, and universal consent becomes impossible.[17] Third, it must endorse the *legal equality* of citizens, since the subordination of some individuals to others (rather than to the law) would once again undercut freedom, and with it the possibility of genuine consent or dissent, at least for some, and universal consent becomes impossible. In saying that these principles must be exemplified in any constitution that can be derived from the idea of the original contract, Kant does not insist on constitutional uniformity, but be does claim that all just constitutions must meet these three quite demanding "republican" conditions.[18]

There has, of course, been much criticism of Kant's limited conception of a republican constitution, and in particular of his lack of concern with democracy, his exclusion from full citizenship of those whom the world he knew made socially dependent (women, day laborers), and his tough views on the duty of obedience even to unjust rulers.[19] I shall leave these interesting issues largely aside[20] and comment on the fundamental reasoning that lies behind Kant's idea of the social contract, and so behind the three elements of any republican constitution.

4. Kant's Social Contract: The Universal Principle of Justice

Kant's peculiar conception of the social contract undoubtedly also has appealing features. These lie not just in the particular constitutional demands for which he argues, but also in his distinctive conception of the reasoning that lies behind his accounts of justice and of justification. These features of Kant's argument may enable him to avoid some of the difficulties of social contract theory and of contemporary contractualism discussed in section 1.

To see this it is necessary to trace the steps by which Kant reaches the view that his, and only his, conception of the social contract is *"only an idea of reason"* (*TP*, 8:297). The notion of an "idea of reason" is a technical term that Kant explicates as early as the beginning of the Transcendental Dialectic of the *Critique of Pure Reason*, where he writes: "A concept is either an **empirical** or a **pure concept**, and the pure concept, insofar as it has its origin solely in the understanding . . . is called *notio*. A concept made up of notions, which goes beyond the possibility of experience, is an **idea [Idee]** or a concept of reason" (A320/B377).[21]

Already in this section of the *Critique of Pure Reason* Kant offers his version of the social contract as an example of an idea of reason: "A constitution providing for the **greatest human freedom** according to laws that permit **the freedom of each to exist together with that of others** . . . is at least a necessary idea, which one must make the ground not merely of the primary plan of a state's constitution but of all the laws too" (A316/B373).[22]

What lies behind the idea that this constitutional principle, unlike others, is an idea of reason?

Put schematically, Kant's justification of the social contract as an idea of reason relies on three linked claims. Proceeding from the most to the least abstract, these claims are:

A. *The categorical imperative is the supreme principle of practical reason, so an idea of reason.*
B. *The universal principle of justice states a version of the categorical imperative, restricted to the public domain.*
C. *The republican conception of the social contract is a special case of the universal principle of justice, adjusted to certain historical conditions.*

These three stages of justification may be traced as follows:

A1. From the Supreme Principle of Practical Reason to the Categorical Imperative

Despite the fact that critique of reason is evidently Kant's central task, the way in which be proceeds is often overlooked or slurred, and the frequently asserted status of the categorical imperative as a principle of reason—the supreme principle of practical reason—is left quite obscure. I think this obscurity is remediable. Kant presents extensive and coherent accounts of his views on the vindication of reason in a number of works, and in particular in the *Doctrine of Method* of the *Critique of Pure Reason*.[23] A bald summary is all that I can offer here. I think that it would run along these lines.

Kant holds that we should take seriously the thought that we may lack any adequate account of reason, in that we may be unable to vindicate any generally authoritative ways of disciplining and organizing either thinking or doing. What we provisionally take to be the powers of human reason may, as Kant suggests vividly in the prefaces of the *Critique of Pure Reason*, betray us and leave us in darkness and confusion. Moreover, we cannot expect to find any transcendent vindication of reason, such as rationalists have sought. In the *Doctrine of Method* of the *Critique of Pure Reason*, Kant argues that if *any* ways of proceeding, any theoretical or practical principles, are to have a general or unrestricted authority for organizing our thinking and doing, they must be principles that all for whom they are relevant can follow: principles could hardly have authority for those unable to follow them. The fundamental requirement of reason is modal: any reasoned way of thinking or acting must be one that is (viewed as) possible for its intended audience to follow.

This line of thought can be seen as vindicating at least a very abstract and minimal, doubly modal principle for anything to count as theoretical and practical reasoning. Anything that is to count as theoretical reasoning *must* at least be based on principles that are *followable in thought* by those whom it is to reach: intelligibility for its intended audience is an indispensable condition for any theoretical reasoning. Anything that is to count as practical reasoning *must* at least be based on principles that are *followable in choosing or willing*, that is *adoptable* by those whom the reasoning is to reach. Universalizability, alias the categorical imperative, is a doubly modal requirement, which insists that principles of action *must* be ones that *can* be adopted by all for whom they are to provide reasons.[24]

B1. From the Categorical Imperative to the Universal Principle of Justice

The categorical imperative is broader in scope than the universal principle of justice. Its most familiar version, and the one that makes its doubly modal character most explicit, is the formula of universal law: *act only on that maxim through which you can at the same time will that it be a universal law* (GW, 4:421). It covers maxims for all sorts of action, inward and outward, personal and public. By contrast the universal principle of justice is restricted in two ways. First, it is concerned only with maxims for *outward* action, that is, with the aspects of action that could be enforced (hence not, for example, with maxims for virtue or with moral worth). Second, it is concerned only with maxims for *structuring* individuals' external freedom, that is, with maxims for shaping the public domain, hence not with maxims for other outward aspects of individual conduct, such as the outward aspects of duties to self or personal relations. The universal principle of justice formulates a restricted version of the categorical imperative for structuring the domain of *"the external use of freedom"*—that is to say the domain of justice: it requires the rejection of any basic maxims for structuring the domain of the external use of freedom that *could not* be consented to or adopted by all.

Accordingly the universal principle of justice states a restricted version of the categorical imperative. This is wholly explicit in the formulation from the *Rechtslehre* quoted in section 1: "Any action is *right* if it can coexist with everyone's freedom in accordance with a universal law, or if on its maxim the freedom of choice of each can coexist with everyone's freedom in accordance with a universal law" (*MM*, 6:230).

Here there is no appeal to actual or to hypothetical consent: there is only a doubly modal criterion of justice, *requiring* action on principles that *can* be adopted by all.

C1. Universal Principle of Justice to Social Contract

The universal principle of justice remains very abstract; it might be satisfied in many different ways. It does not even claim that state structures and coercion are needed to secure a world in which people do not infringe one another's freedom. Indeed, since state coercion obstructs external freedom it may seem incompatible with the universal principle of justice.

Kant argues that, contrary to initial assumptions, *in our world* only coercive structures can secure the universal principle of justice. We are neither reliably altruistic nor sufficiently scattered across the surface of the earth to avoid interaction: without a system of enforced laws we will inevitably injure one another's external freedom. In our world justice requires coercion: we need a power that will "hinder hindrances to freedom" and cannot achieve any more complete realization of freedom for all.[25] The universal principle of justice conjoined with coercive enforcement is the basis for Kant's version of the social contract. Kant's social contract is a less abstract idea than his universal principle of justice, in that it takes account of specific historical circumstances of human life in which unsociable beings "cannot help mutually affecting one another" (*TP*, 8:289), so demands a constitution that deploys state power to enforce a law to which all are subordinate and that guarantees legal equality. *Theory and Practice* contains Kant's most significant discussion of the idea of the social contract, because these specific historical conditions are borne in mind throughout the essay. By contrast, in the *Doctrine of Right* Kant's initial focus is broader, and the specific historical conditions that make coercion essential are addressed in a second move, after consideration of the more abstract universal principle of justice.[26]

There is good reason to distinguish the two principles. The universal principle of justice, as stated in the *Doctrine of Right* and elsewhere, might or might not require coercive powers. For example, if certain rational beings were never inclined to do one another injustice, or if human beings lived the isolated lives of Rousseau's earliest state of nature and could not interact or do one another injustice, they would not need coercive structures. But Kant thinks that this is not the human condition: we are evidently not perfect altruists; unsociability runs through our sociability.[27] And we unavoidably interact since we are now numerous yet still inhabit the closed space of the earth's surface. In the conditions in which we now live, the universal principle of justice can only be realized by way of the more specific idea of a social contract, which makes explicit that for us only constitutional structures of a republican type are objects of possible universal consent.

5. Is Kant a Social Contract Theorist?

The strands of argument can now, I think, be pulled together. Kant's conception of the social contract is a special case of his universal principle of justice: it spells out what this principle requires in actual human conditions. The universal principle of justice is in turn a special case of the categorical imperative: it spells out the most basic maxims to which our lives must conform if the structures of the public domain are to meet the requirements of the categorical imperative. The categorical imperative is the supreme principle of practical reason, indeed an idea of reason, because its double modal requirement formalizes the recognition that we are not in the business of offering reasons to others unless we can take it that they can follow those reasons. Kant's version of the social contract can count as an idea of reason because he derives it from his account of practical reason, rather than from any appeal to actual or to hypothetical consent.

Can the fact that Kant labels a derivative, but still very general, principle of reason, "the social contract" make him into a social contract theorist? Labels perhaps do not matter much, and it is probably not useful to make essentialist claims about what makes a theorist a social contract theorist. But I think that Kant has in fact moved away from the basic insights of other versions of the social contract tradition to a different type of justification, to which neither actual nor hypothetical consent is fundamental. His basic thought is that when we think that others cannot adopt, a fortiori cannot consent to, some principle, we cannot offer them reasons for doing so.

This distinctive if minimalist approach to justice and to justification has the advantage that it avoids some of the central difficulties of justification of the social contract tradition. Kant's thought is not that coercion is justified because its exercise, or the institutions that exercise it, or the principles behind these institutions, have been, are, or would be consented to, but because certain types of republican coercive institutions *could* be consented to by those who live under them, whereas their rejection *could not* be consented to by all. Nonrepublican institutions are nonstarters for universal consent. The rejection, destruction, and replacement of nonrepublican institutions is the foundation of justice, the basis for identifying acceptable types of action (policies, institutions), and for establishing the proper contexts for actual consent by those who will be actually affected by particular acts (policies, institutions).

Constitutions that cannot be objects of possible universal consent are all of them unjust on Kant's view. Societies that do not secure the rule of law (anarchic or despotic societies) undermine or jeopardize external freedom for some or for all, so do not secure even the possibility of universal consent; societies that leave some persons above or outside the law (monarchies, dictatorships, states within states) undermine or jeopardize external freedom for some or for all, so do not secure even the possibility of universal consent; societies that do not secure equality of status under law (feudalism, caste societies) undermine or jeopardize external freedom for some or for all, so do not secure even the possibility of universal consent.[28] We may think that Kant's position would be improved by adding that further forms of social subordination that he accepted, but that also obstruct the possibility of consent, are unjust, and so that the rejection of patriarchy and the institution of full democracy are also required components of a just constitution.

If Kant is "the most adequate of the social contract theorists" this may ironically be because he abandons the idea that the social contract is some sort of agreement or contract, actual or hypothetical, and thinks of it simply as formulating the necessary conditions for the possibility of universal consent to a political order for unsociable yet interacting rational beings.

NOTES

1. John Rawls, *A Theory of Justice* (Cambridge: Harvard University Press, 1971), 11.
2. For example, Susan Meld Shell, *The Rights of Reason: A Study of Kant's Philosophy and Politics* (Toronto: Toronto University Press, 1980), 152: "Kant's theory of justice is, substantially, a theory of contract"; and Howard Williams, *Kant's Political Philosophy* (Oxford: Blackwell, 1983), 94.
3. Patrick Riley "On Kant as the Most Adequate of the Social Contract Theorists," *Political Theory* 1, no. 4 (1973): 450–71. *MM*, 6:230; see also *TP*, 8:289.
4. Reinhardt Brandt, "Das Erlaubnisgesetz," in *Rechtsphilosophie der Aufklärung*, ed. Reinhardt Brandt (Berlin: de Gruyter, 1982), 233–85; see also Heinrich Böckerstette, *Aporien der Freiheit und ihre Aufklärung durch Kant* (Stuttgart: Frommann-Holzboog, 1982), esp. 235ff.
5. Leslie A. Mulholland, *Kant's System of Rights* (New York: Columbia University Press, 1990). See also Katrin Flickschuh, who argues that Kant is neither a social contract nor a natural law theorist, in "Freedom and Constraint in Kant's Metaphysical Elements of Justice," *History of Political Thought* 20 (1999): 250–71.

6. On Kant and the natural law tradition, see Ripstein, Hunter, and Laursen, this volume.

7. Phenomena such as adaptive and addictive preferences are deeply unsettling for attempts to base justification on actual consent. Some people adapt their preferences to the world and then go along with, accept, endorse, consent to being injured, exploited, and oppressed; others are dominated by preferences they cannot adapt. See John Elster, *Sour Grapes* (Cambridge: Cambridge University Press, 1983), and *Alchemies of the Mind: Rationality and the Emotions* (Cambridge: Cambridge University Press, 1999); John Elster and O.-J. Skog, eds., *Getting Hooked* (Cambridge: Cambridge University Press, 1999); and Onora O'Neill, "Justice, Capabilities, and Vulnerabilities," in *Women, Culture, and Development*, ed. Martha Nussbaum and Jonathan Glover (New York: Oxford University Press, 1995), 140–52.

8. This thought might be resisted by arguing that there is tacit consent whenever there is legitimate coercion. However, a conception of tacit consent sufficiently diluted to endorse all legitimate coercion would be so indeterminate that it would endorse everything—and justify nothing.

9. These simple examples do not show that actual consent is a simple matter. On standard views, any actual consent that justifies must be *informed consent*. This small phrase covers a multitude of conditions: possession and use of adequate capacities to understand, to reason, and to exercise choice, the absence of duress, ignorance, and the like. Consent is a defeasible notion that an indefinite number of conditions can render void, so without justifying power.

10. A third option would be to invoke only weaker assumptions that are empirically true of all persons. Although I cannot argue the matter explicitly here, I believe Kant's position is among those that take this option.

11. The terms "metaphysical" and "political" are distinguished in Rawls's later work, first appearing in "Justice as Fairness: Political not Metaphysical," *Philosophy and Public Affairs* 14, no. 3 (1985): 223–51; and is included in revised form in *Collected Papers: John Rawls*, ed. Samuel Freeman (Cambridge: Harvard University Press, 1999), 388–414.

12. Onora O'Neill, "Political Liberalism and Public Reason: A Critical Notice of John Rawls, *Political Liberalism*," *Philosophical Review* 106 (1997): 411–28.

13. Kant repeats this criticism of actual consent approaches quite often: "these writers have assumed that the idea of an original contract (a basic postulate of reason) is something which must have taken place *in reality*, even where there is no document to show that any contract was actually submitted to the commonwealth" (*TP*, 8:302); translation by H. B. Nisbet, in Hans S. Reiss, ed., *Kant's Political Writings* (Cambridge: Cambridge University Press, 1970), 83. See also *MM*, 6:318–19, 6:339–40; and *WE*, 8:39.

14. It is selective because in this passage he challenges only the view that the social contract was an historical event, and does not address the thought that actual consent to basic institutions might be currently but tacitly expressed.

15. The term *Idee* ("Idea," capitalized in many translations) is a technical one for Kant; see section 5 of this chapter, "Is Kant a Social Contract Theorist?". In *Theory and Practice* Kant writes, "die Idee von einem ursprünglichen Vertrag, die immer in der Vernunft zum Grunde liegt" (*TP*, 8:302); "It [the social contract] is instead *only an idea* of reason, which, however, has its undoubted practical reality, namely to bind every legislator to give his laws in such a way that . . ." (*TP*, 8:297).

16. See also the following passage that articulates the modal character of the universal principle of justice: "For, provided it is not self-contradictory that an entire people should agree to such a law, however bitter they might find it, the law is in conformity with right" (*TP*, 8:299). The German is even sharper: "Denn wenn es sich nur nicht widerspricht, daß ein ganzes Volk zu einem solchen Gesetze zusammenstimme, es mag ihm auch so sauer ankommen, wie es wolle: so ist es dem Rechte gemäß."

17. Kant means quite specifically dependence *on law*. He sometimes speaks of dependence and at other times of independence in this context. However, he has closely similar ideas in mind. *Common dependence on law* is one of the guarantees of adequate independence, an independence that Kant in fact extends only to some (active citizens). In *PP* he states that the social

contract mandates common *dependence* or *subordination to law*. In *MM* he makes the same point by referring to *independence*: "civil *independence* . . . allows him to owe his existence and sustenance not to the arbitrary will of any one else among the people, but purely to his own rights and powers as a member of the commonwealth," but once again distinguishes the case of the active and passive citizen (*MM*, 6: 314); trans. Nisbet, in Reiss, *Kant's Political Writings*, 139–40.

18. For a different view, see Hunter, chapter 7 of this volume.

19. Kant makes well-known and severe comments on the duty to obey and the wrongness of all rebellion even against a harsh ruler (*TP*, 8:299–305), yet insists that his position is entirely different from Hobbes's (*TP*, 8:303–5, 84–85). Hobbes had claimed that the sovereign has no obligations to the people, so can do no injustice to a citizen. Kant insists: "Whatever a people cannot impose upon itself cannot be imposed upon it by the legislator either" (*TP*, 8:304); trans. Nisbet, in Reiss, *Kant's Political Writings*, 85. He characterizes Hobbes's position as "quite terrifying [*erschrecklich*]" (*TP*, 8:304, 84). However, although Kant insists that the people have inalienable rights, these rights do not include a right to rebel against rulers who violate their rights, "a coercive right against the one who has done him injustice." In many (arguably not in all) of his discussions of obedience Kant argues that the only legitimate action of citizens in the face of injustice is to make representations: "the *freedom of the pen* is the only safeguard of the rights of the people" (*TP*, 8:304, 85; cf. *WE*, 8:37–39).

20. But see the discussions of Kant's views on women and on social classes in Pogge and LaVaque-Manty, this volume, chapters 3 and 8.

21. "Der Begriff . . . sofern er lediglich im Verstande seinen Ursprung hat . . . heißt *Notio*. Ein Begriff aus Notionen, der die Möglichkeit der Erfahrung übersteigt, ist die Idee oder der Vernunftbegriff" (*CPR*, A320/B377).

22. It might be argued that this is a statement of the universal principle of right rather than of the idea of the social contract. I have taken it as stating the latter, although it does not distinguish the three elements of a republican constitution, because it does refer explicitly to a constitution.

23. For textual analysis of Kant's vindication of practical reason, see Onora O'Neill, *Constructions of Reason: Explorations of Kant's Practical Philosophy* (Cambridge: Cambridge University Press, 1989), part 1; and Onora O'Neill, "Vindicating Reason," in *The Cambridge Companion to Kant*, ed. Paul Guyer (Cambridge: Cambridge University Press, 1992), 280–308.

24. This should not be understood as a claim that all must be able to *act*, or *act successfully*, on any principle for which reasons can be given, either on a given occasion or at all times; the success of any action (policy, institution) always depends on many contingent circumstances.

25. "If a certain use of freedom is itself a hindrance to freedom in accordance with universal laws (i.e., wrong), coercion that is opposed to this (as a *hindering of a hindrance to freedom*) is consistent with freedom in accordance with universal laws, that is, it is right. Hence there is connected with right by the principle of contradiction an authorization to coerce someone who infringes upon it" (*MM*, 6:231).

26. See *MM*, 6:230ff.

27. See Kant's 1784 essay, *Idea for a Universal History with a Cosmopolitan Purpose*, in Reiss, *Kant's Political Writings*, 41–53.

28. See also Ripstein, chapter 2 of this volume.

KANT AND THE CIRCUMSTANCES OF JUSTICE

Arthur Ripstein

Kant lies outside the primary canon in the history of political philosophy, in part because his writings on the topic are frequently opaque, even by the standards of his other writings.¹ That opacity often leads readers to take him to hold positions that are not importantly distinct from those of others in the natural law or social contract traditions. So he is sometimes compared, or assimilated, to Aquinas, Grotius, or even the elusive Pufendorf. More frequently, his work is lumped together with that of Rousseau, or taken to occupy some sort of middle ground surrounded by the trio of Hobbes, Locke, and Hegel.

Yet Kant's political writings, particularly in the *Doctrine of Right,* resist assimilation to either the natural law or social contract traditions. For both of those traditions are rooted in a pair of ideas that Kant rejects.² The first of these, common to both traditions, is the idea that law is a compromise that we must accept because of our corrupt, willful, troubling, or fallen condition. For natural lawyers, positive law is needed to coerce people into

---

I am grateful to Lisa Austin, Abraham Drassinower, Evan Fox-Decent, Robert Gibbs, Louis-Philippe Hodgson, Tom Hurka, Dennis Klimchuk, Sophia Moreau, Christopher Morris, Horacio Spector, Gopal Sreenivasan, Sergio Tenenbaum, Catherine Valcke, Helga Varden, Ernest Weinrib, Jacob Weinrib, and Karen Weisman for comments on an earlier draft of this paper, and to the members of the Law and Philosophy discussion group at the University of Toronto for joining me in reading the *Doctrine of Right* at glacial speed over the last several years. An earlier version of this paper was presented at a conference sponsored by the University of Pennsylvania Law School in May 2003 and at the Toronto Workshop in Moral and Political Philosophy in September 2003.

doing what justice requires.³ The second idea, which takes elements of the social contract tradition a step further, contends that *justice* itself is a response to unfortunate circumstances, or unfortunate human nature.⁴ That idea finds favor in the Christian tradition, with its idea of the centrality of the fall from grace to human life and history, but also in secular thinkers, such as Hume or Rawls, each of whom limits the application of justice to what they call "the circumstances of justice." In circumstances of moderate scarcity and limited benevolence, human purposes are likely to conflict to the peril of all. Were objects of desire more plentiful, or people more generous, we could dispense with justice. In our less happy circumstances, however, we need it in order to get along.

Both of these traditions thus accept a distinction between justice and the other virtues, supposing justice to be of value only in specific circumstances, however pervasive those circumstances might be. The idea that justice is a remedial virtue is widespread in contemporary legal and political thought. Michael Sandel compares the virtue of justice to that of courage, a virtue that, he suggests, is less a human perfection than an important expedient in the unfortunate circumstances of a war zone.⁵ Grant Gilmore, in *The Ages of American Law,* remarks: "The better the society, the less law there will be. In Heaven, there will be no law, and the lion will lie down with the lamb. . . . The worse the society, the more law there will be. In Hell, there will be nothing but law, and due process will be meticulously observed."⁶ For this tradition, the cold, institutional world of law and justice contrasts with the kinder, gentler, more personal world of virtue. Virtue consists in the human task of self-perfection, that is, in realizing what is best in our natures. No artifice is required, but, through virtue and agreeable circumstances, we can enable ourselves to dispense with law and justice.

Kant believes that neither justice nor law has circumstances in the sense in which they are usually supposed to. Canonical early modern political philosophers present a spectrum of possible positions on these issues. Hobbes, for example, appears to believe that both justice and law only apply in a limited range of circumstances, but also that those circumstances differ. As a result, he makes his argument in two steps, first explaining why the rules of justice are required as the solution to a problem about human interaction in circumstances of scarcity and potential conflict, before going on to explain the further reason why those rules themselves require an enforcer if anyone is to have the benefit of them. Locke, by contrast, believes that the demands of justice can be known by human reason, and, although those demands make reference to empirical circumstances, such as the possibility of spoilage, nonetheless, justice places demands on us even in conditions of abundance and goodwill. Locke contends, however, that men in a state of nature are nonetheless in what we might call "the circumstances of law," because, as he puts it, they are subject to certain "inconveniences" chief among which is the lack of an impartial arbiter to adjudicate disputes. Although disputes presumably *arise* in part because of scarcity and limited benevolence—otherwise, each person might happily yield to others—the source of conflict that Locke focuses on is primarily epistemic. Factual disputes arise even among people motivated by justice, and they require impartial adjudication by magistrates. Hume takes the opposite approach, arguing that justice itself is an "artificial virtue" that only emerges and makes demands in circumstances of moderate scarcity and limited benevolence. Were scarcity too severe, or completely overcome, justice would make no claim. Were people completely benevolent, justice would be unnecessary; if they were so selfish that they could never moderate their conduct in light of the claims of others, it would be impossible. Hume argues that the artificial nature of justice leaves the question of *law* open. Perhaps rational beings could moderate their claims, provided they live in small enough groups and interacted in sufficiently regular ways. So for Hobbes, then, both justice and law are remedial; for Locke, only law is, and for Hume, justice is.

Kant stands in contrast to each of these positions in his insistence that neither justice nor law is remedial. He argues that both justice and law are required for any finite and embodied free beings that interact with one another. Finitude and embodiment do not enter his account as the basis of appetite or need, but only as expressions of the idea that such beings are in space and time, so that their purposes and pursuits *could* be incompatible.[7] That possibility of incompatibility is modified further by the contingent fact that we are embodied rational beings that are able to use things other than our own bodies for setting and pursuing our purposes, and the still further contingent fact that the earth on which we live is a finite sphere rather than an unbounded plane. Yet none of these generic features of our condition matter in relation to what Kant describes as the *matter* of choice, that is, the particular ends that human beings tend to, or even need to pursue. Justice is required because human beings are capable of setting and pursuing their own purposes. That capacity is not a limitation; it is our humanity itself.

Although some of Kant's earlier formulations of his political philosophy appeal to the idea of man's unsocial sociability and malevolence, the *Doctrine of Right* does not treat appetite, pride, or quarrelsomeness as the sources of conflict.[8] Law is required "[n]o matter how well-disposed and law-abiding men might be" (*MM*, 6:312). Free beings require justice if they are to act rightly toward one another. More strikingly, they require legal institutions if they are to do so.

Although human imperfection plays no part in Kant's theory of justice, it is a central issue in the other part of the *Metaphysics of Morals*, the *Doctrine of Virtue*. Kant's discussion is concerned with the ways in which rational beings must come to terms with their imperfections. As a result, it contains discussion of, among other things, the ways in which we should think about embodiment, health, sexuality, and such matters as the proper disposal of one's hair.

Kant's rejection of the circumstances of justice does not rest on a naïve denial of human selfishness or corruption. The philosopher who is famous for saying that "nothing straight will ever be made from the warped wood of humanity," that "nature does not seem to have been concerned with seeing to it that the human being should live agreeably" (*UH*, 8:20), also says that a person need not "wait until he has learned from a bitter experience" of humanity's quarrelsome nature (*MM*, 6:307), but in so doing he concedes that the experience of the motives and means adopted by others is indeed bitter. Moreover, some of the examples through which he develops his account incorporate his negative assessment of human sociability.[9] Nonetheless, his position is not that the rule of law, in fact, makes life more bearable and manageable, but rather that its claim to underwrite the use of force does not depend on those effects, however welcome they may be. In this, his attitude toward the obvious but contingent benefits of civil life is parallel to his attitude toward the obvious though no less contingent benefits of truthfulness. Welcome though they are, those benefits do nothing to redeem the claim that every legal system makes to be entitled to force citizens to do certain things. That claim must be understood in terms of the metaphysics of morals, not their anthropology, even as it is explained through anthropological examples.

The Metaphysical Conditions of Justice 1: The Universal Principle of Right and "The Innate Right of Humanity"

Kant's starting point is what he calls the "universal principle of right," according to which "[a]ny action is *right* if it can coexist with everyone's freedom in accordance with a universal law, or if on its maxim the freedom of choice of each can coexist with everyone's freedom in accordance with a universal law" (*MM*, 6:230). The universal principle of right incorporates the familiar vocabulary of the categorical imperative, but does not simply restate it or even apply it. Instead, Kant explains, it enters as a "postulate that is incapable of further proof" (6:231)[10] because it extends the basic moral ideas underlying the categorical imperative to the case in which rational beings occupy space. Such an extension requires a postulate because the categorical imperative governs only logical relations between maxims.[11] As such, it does not presuppose anything about the occupation of space. Once the postulate is introduced, however, the actions of separate rational beings can come into conflict, and the universal principle of right regulates this external use of freedom so as to guarantee its consistency.[12]

The universal principle of right, in turn, governs both the rights that persons have prior to any affirmative acts they might perform, and in relation to affirmative acts they have performed. Each person has an "innate right of humanity" in their own person, the right to "independence from being constrained by another's choice," insofar as it can coexist with the freedom of others (*MM*, 6:237). This right is innate because it does not require an affirmative act to establish it. Kant offers different formulations of it, each of which elaborates an aspect of the idea that one person must not be subject to the choice of another, which Kant glosses in terms of one person being a mere means for another. This familiar Kantian theme is explained in terms of the classic distinction, from Roman law, between persons and things. A person is a being capable of setting its own purposes. A thing is something that can be used in the pursuit of whatever purposes the person who has it might have. The classic example of a person being treated as a mere thing is the slave, for a slave is entirely at the disposal of his or her master. The slave's problem is that he is subject to the master's choice: the master gets to decide what to do with the slave and what the slave will do. The slave does not set his own ends, but is merely a means for ends set by someone else.[13] To call it *the* problem is not too strong: if the other problems a slave has—low welfare, limited options, and so on—were addressed by a benevolent master, the *relationship* of slavery would perhaps be less bad, but it would not thereby be any less wrong.

If right is independence, then wrong is a matter of the dependence of one person on the choice of another. There are two basic ways in which such dependence can occur: you can be made to serve someone else's purposes, without your consent, or you can be deprived of the ability to choose by being deprived of your powers. If I enslave you or trick you into serving me, I wrong you in the first sense. If I break your arm I wrong you in the second sense.

This idea of independence is explicitly contrastive and interpersonal. A person could avoid wronging others by "shunning all society" (*MM*, 6:236); if there were only one person in the world, no issues of independence or rightful obligation would arise (6:261). This interpersonal idea of independence contrasts with the idea of freedom as independence from empirical determination that some interpreters find in Kant's *Groundwork*.[14] It also contrasts with prominent contemporary views that regard natural and social obstacles as impediments to freedom.[15] These differences are fundamental to Kant's argument.

Kant articulates the same idea of independence as the right to be beyond reproach, that is, the right to have your reputation depend only on what you say and do, and the right to freedom, which he explains as the right to do to others anything that does not violate their rights. These are all aspects of the same idea of independence, and each of them is important to one or more aspects of the social contract. He brings them together under the idea of equality, since none has, simply by birth, either the right to command others or the duty to obey them.

The innate right of humanity serves as a constraint on how people can be treated, but also on how they can allow themselves to be treated by others, and so on the public institutions that they can authorize via contract. Kant formulates this aspect of innate right as an internal duty in terms of Ulpian's precept *honeste vive* (6:236), which he interprets as the demand of rightful honor: do not allow yourself to become a mere means for others.[16] As Thomas Pogge points out in chapter 3 of this volume, the independence on which Kant focuses is not the thing that everybody most obviously wants. Kant begins with this idea, rather than with appetite, the capacity for a conception of the good, or need, because any violation of independence subjects one person to the choice of another, and so treats the former as a mere thing.

Putting the familiar Kantian distinction between means and ends in this way turns it into a measure of types of interaction that free beings can authorize, and so an account of the legitimate uses of coercion. In order to choose something, rather than merely wish for it, I must take myself to have means available to me to pursue it (*MM*, 6:213).[17] Your independence sets limits on the ways in which you and your deeds can be among the things available to me in the pursuit of my ends. In private interaction, rightful honor demands that nobody be able to use your powers without your consent. In the contract argument for public right, it sets limits on the kind of state powers you can authorize.

This emphasis on coercion is easy to misunderstand if Kant's argument is assimilated to those of social contract thinkers for whom coercion is understood in terms of threats needed to keep corrupt, lazy, or selfish beings in line.[18] Coercion is central to his analysis because the possibility of interference with freedom arises simply from the existence of a plurality of free beings setting their own purposes, not the empirical likelihood of people using force or the need to use force to constrain them. Well-meaning and conscientious people can interfere with one another's freedom, even in a world of plenty, simply because they have separate purposes. No assumption about limited benevolence or scarcity is required.

The Metaphysical Conditions of Justice II: Equal Freedom and Coercion

The innate right of humanity can only be honored in a rightful condition, but the connection between them is not direct. The basic principles of justice governing human interaction are not themselves the subject of a contract. Instead, they are explicated and developed in terms of the more basic idea of reciprocal limits on external freedom.

The basic idea is that equal freedom requires that one person not interfere with the person of another, that I not injure you or draw you into my purposes without your consent. The same interferences are also wrongful in relation to your possession or use of what Kant refers to as "external" things, that is, that exist apart from your body. Kant introduces this idea again by means of a postulate, because the principles governing acquired rights constitute an extension of innate right, since innate right presupposes only purposive beings who occupy space, not the existence of things a person could use in setting and pursuing purposes. Such objects can be mine or yours generally in a way that your own person cannot. The owner of a piece of property has rights with respect to a thing, the holder of a contractual entitlement has rights to another person's action, and the beneficiary of a status relation has rights in relation to another person. At the same time, some other person might equally have had the same rights to the thing, action, or person in question. Who has particular acquired rights depends on who has performed the requisite affirmative acts.

Once possible objects of choice are introduced, the postulate extends the idea of right to include them. The core idea is that it must be possible to have such objects as your own. The only alternative is a limit on freedom that is imposed for the sake of something other than freedom. Those who suppose that natural objects have a type of intrinsic value that creates a legitimate basis for coercion that has nothing to do with limits on freedom may bridle at this thought. But that is just to say that they must reject the idea that reciprocal limits on freedom could provide a complete account of the legitimate use of force. Starting with this idea, Kant concludes that it must be possible to have external objects of choice as one's own, since the alternative would be usable things that could not be used, or that could only be used with the consent of everyone else. The first of these possibilities would be an arbitrary limit on freedom; the second would subject a person to the arbitrary choice of others (*MM*, 6:246). The argument does not aim to show that arbitrary limits on freedom are somehow unprincipled, or at odds with some fundamental value (not even the value of freedom), but rather that nobody could ever have standing to limit the freedom of another on grounds of something other than freedom, since to do so would be to coerce the other on grounds related to some particular purpose, which the person being coerced does not share (6:246).[19]

Having external things available to you enables you to choose purposes that you could not choose without them, and if I deprive you of those things, or use them without your consent, I thereby interfere with your freedom. So it must be possible to acquire those things, and have them as your own, independently of the choice of others, provided that you can have and acquire them in a way that is compatible with the independence of others.

Kant divides the external things to which private parties can have rights through an analysis of the Roman legal categories of acquisition, *facto* (deed), *pacto* (contract), and *lege* (status). Property rights enable people to acquire things through their deeds, contract enables people to acquire rights to the powers of other persons through agreement, and status governs relationships between persons, such as parents and children, in which one party cannot consent to the terms or particulars of the relationship. In each case, a distinctive form of wrongdoing is possible: if I damage your property, or use it without your consent, I deprive you of powers with which you were entitled to choose. If I renege on my agreement to do something for you, I deprive you of the use of a power I had given you. And if I use my children for my own benefit, I treat them as mere things. In each case, the wrong is coercive because in each case it interferes with another person's freedom. Justice regulates the interactions of free beings, and is necessary if they are to interact in a way that is consistent with the freedom of all.

This is not the place to examine in detail Kant's reasons for supposing that these types of interaction are exhaustive, or his reasons for articulating them in terms of the categories of substance, causality, and community.[20] Instead, my present focus is on the way in which Kant deploys those ideas of private right in introducing his argument for the need for public right. It is, however, worth noting that the analysis proceeds without reference to ideas of harm or benefit. As we will see below, the conferral of a benefit by another person does not create an obligation to pay for it. Conversely, the withdrawal of a mere benefit does not amount to a wrong, no matter how costly it is to the person from whom it is withdrawn, because, outside of relations of contract or status, you do not need to tailor your pursuits to the interests or needs of others. By framing the structure of justice without reference to harm or benefit, Kant distances himself from the idea that it is remedial. Instead, it governs a structure of interaction that is required by the existence of a plurality of free beings who occupy space. The material circumstances and empirical vulnerabilities and weaknesses of humans probably make up what Kant would call the "matter" of many actual trespasses, injuries, and breaches of contract. Categories of right protect against *forms* of wrongdoing. Free beings can be wronged by trespasses or injuries because they interfere with the ability to set and pursue purposes, even if the purposes of free beings are not mandated by the inadequate provisions of nature. With different vulnerabilities, or even none at all, the same structures would be required.[21]

Kant's discussion of private right articulates the structure of rightful interaction between private persons, and so sets the stage for the contract argument for public right. Each aspect of private right also provides the apparatus for part of that argument. The discussion of property frames the problem of unilateral acquisition. Rightful relations are always relational: your right to property, for example, is that right that all others forbear from using or interfering with your possession and use of your things without your consent. As such, relations of property must implicate everyone, because nobody can be bound by an act to which they are not a party. The problem is that any act of acquiring unowned property is unilateral: you acquire an apple by grabbing it with your hand in a way that does not appear to implicate anyone else. If you suppose, as Locke sometimes seems to have, that property is a relation between a person and a thing, this need not be a problem, because you can claim that the apple that you acquire becomes part of you and is subject to the very same constraints that govern the ways in which other people may treat you (*MM*, 6:260). That route is not open for Kant. An adequate account of property must explain how a person can be wronged through the unauthorized use of his property even when no wrong is committed directly against his person. That can only be explained if property is a relation between persons with respect to things, which in turn requires an explanation of how everyone can be bound by some other person's unilateral act.

Kant's discussion of contract illustrates the structure of the solution to this problem in the form of a united will. In order for you and me to make an agreement, we must do so together. No pair of respective powers each of us has individually could do the job. Contract shows how two people can be party to a single act. It still lacks the generality needed to explain how *everyone* can be party to a transaction, let alone a transaction in which not everyone participates explicitly. Relations of status reveal how someone can be bound by an act without being a party to it explicitly, and how such a relationship can be mandated by law.[22]

Kant's exposition in terms of the acquisition of property must not be mistaken for the subject matter of the argument: Kant's concern is with the enforceability of rightful relations in general, even though he articulates the first part of his analysis in discussing property, and is not always forthcoming in reminding his readers that a point he has already made has further application (*MM*, 6:256). Acquired rights are pivotal to his account because the innate right of humanity sets limits that apply independently of anyone's deeds; provided that one person does not physically displace another from where the second happens to be, nobody does wrong. Acquired rights govern interacting persons, who do more than occupy space.[23] Freedom requires that people be able to acquire property and enter into relations of contract and status, but only public law can secure any relationships more complex than the disjunctive occupation of different regions of space.

From Private Right to Public Law: The Metaphysical Circumstances of Law

Reciprocal limits can only be binding if they are, in fact, reciprocal. Kant denies that there is an enforceable obligation to do what I would do in an ideal condition, not because there is no moral obligation to do so,[24] but because outside of the civil condition, nobody is entitled to enforce claims of right, since anyone appointing him- or herself to do so would be violating the requirement of reciprocity. Since there are no reciprocally enforceable obligations, there are no obligations of right (*MM*, 6:256). Thus, "human beings do *one another* no wrong at all when they feud among themselves [in a state of nature].... But in general they do wrong in the highest degree," because they remain in a condition in which each is subject to the choice of others (6:307–8).

Kant elaborates this point in explaining the principle of what he calls "original" acquisition of property, which, he says, can only be "provisional," that is, awaiting a civil condition to become conclusive.[25] Absent a civil condition, there can be no enforceable rights with respect to external things, because right requires everyone to limit their freedom in the same ways. Those limits must apply at both the primary level of conduct and the remedial level of enforcement. The standards of private right require reciprocal limits on conduct; if they are to be standards of right, they must also require reciprocal limits on enforcement. Unless there is a way of creating reciprocal limits on enforcement, people have the rights that they do to things that they have—and thus to the forbearance of others in relation to those rights—only provisionally, because they cannot be integrated into a full set of reciprocal limits on freedom.

The full details of Kant's account of property need not concern us here.[26] We can focus instead on the way in which legitimate appropriation of an unowned thing presupposes the idea of a general will (*MM*, 6:261).[27] Unlike most contemporary accounts of property that focus on acquisition, Kant first examines the nature of a property right, how such a thing could be possible and consistent with the freedom of all, before turning to questions of acquisition. The core of his answer to this first question is that a property right is a right to exclusive possession and use of the thing, such that others wrong the owner if they use the thing without his or her authorization.

The first part of Kant's account of property explains how my owning something can set limits on your freedom. If I own something, it is subject to my choice, and so I am entitled to exclude you from it. Moreover, my right to have the thing subject to my choice continues even when I am not in physical possession of it. Kant notes that you interfere with my innate right if you peel my fingers off of an apple I am holding in my hand (*MM*, 6:250), even though you commit no wrong against my person if you manage to extract the pulp from it without displacing my hand. If I own the apple, however, you can interfere with my ownership without interfering with me.

The freedom to exclude others from whatever you already have is consistent with the freedom of all under universal law. So too is the freedom to alienate whatever it is that you happen to have: if you and I each have something that the other wants, there does not seem to be anything particularly puzzling about the possibility of our making a trade, since we have agreed to alter our respective rights. In the case of both ownership and exchange, the rights in question are ones that everyone could have with respect to whatever they happen to have as their own, without anyone being subject to the choice of anyone else.

The second, derivative part of Kant's account concerns acquisition. Kant needs a theory of acquisition to explain the transition from unowned things that are available for all to use to exclusive possession, such that one person's unilateral act of acquisition can alter the normative situation in a way that is consistent with the freedom of all. Each time someone acquires something previously unowned, they limit the freedom of others. As a matter of each person's innate right of humanity in their own person, each is allowed to be "wherever nature or chance has placed them." Kant frames the issue in terms that sound familiar: he speaks of "(original or instituted) possession in common" (*MM*, 6:261). He presents this medieval and Lockean image of the world prior to private appropriation in terms of innate right—to say that the world is held in common prior to appropriation is just to say that nobody does wrong merely by occupying space.[28] Ownership changes that. If I own a piece of land, you wrong me if you occupy my space without my permission. The problem is not that I decrease your welfare by appropriating it, but that I have the power to obligate you to refrain from using something that you were at liberty to use.

Kant explains the significance of a unilateral act by embedding it in a broader context. The postulate of practical reason explains that it must be possible to have things, from which it follows that it must be possible to acquire them.²⁹ But acquisition is a unilateral act, so Kant must provide a further account of how one person's unilateral act can make a difference to the rights of others who are not parties to it.

Acquisition is only consistent with the freedom of all if it can be understood in terms of "a will that is united *a priori*" (*MM*, 6:263). The point is not that I actually need to get everyone's permission before acquiring something, but rather that a unilateral act can only bind others if the transition in status from unowned to owned is licensed through a process that everyone has authorized. The particular acquisition inherits its rightfulness from the possibility of such a general law, and until the general law is laid down in a civil condition, any acquisition is merely provisional, in the sense that the owner's claim to have it as her own can only be understood through implicit reference to such a law.

Kant writes that "something external can be *originally* acquired only in conformity with the idea of a civil condition, that is, with a view to it and to its being brought about, but prior to its realization" (*MM*, 6:264). That does not mean that I can simply invoke the *idea* of a civil condition as grounds for excluding you. Until we have entered such a condition, any reference that I make to it is as unilateral as my act itself. Any further reference to a further civil condition would have exactly the same problem, creating a regress of unilateral deeds and claims.³⁰ The authorization to acquire an unowned thing is incomplete outside of the civil condition through which we authorize acquisition together.

There is a second problem of unilateral action created by the introduction of property, which also arises for both contract and status. That is the problem of disputes about rights. Some disputes can arise about innate rights: if I injure you by startling you without physically touching you, we might disagree about how this engages our respective rights to occupy space.

Acquired rights introduce a further source of potential disputes. The boundaries in space and time of an object I have acquired may be unclear (although some objects that can be acquired rightfully, such as animals or islands, may have perfectly determinate boundaries), but more important, it may be unclear whether some other person had acquired the same thing in the distant past. Again, you and I may disagree about the terms of an agreement we entered into, or about what exactly is required by my obligation to act on your behalf. These problems all arise because there are acts of acquisition through which one person acquires a right in relation to others.

How much land did I claim as I walked over it? What exactly did you authorize me to do when you said "okay"?

These questions generate disputes because they concern changes in the rights of persons. It is a familiar and inescapable feature of the law of contract, on Kant's or any other understanding of it, that two people cannot make a contract to change the rights of a third. This familiar and plausible idea runs up against the peculiar structure of initial acquisition, in which it appears one person *is able* to change the rights of all others. Just as the possession of external objects needs to be made consistent with the will of all, so too does each particular act of acquisition. Otherwise it is simply a unilateral imposition, a version of the rule of the stronger, and so the subjection of others to one person's choice.

If disagreement about rights arise in a state of nature, each party makes what, from the point of view of the other, can appear to be nothing other than a unilateral assertion. When you and I disagree about our rights, it may be prudent for one or the other of us to give in, but as a matter of our respective rightful honor, each of us is also entitled to stand our ground. Each of us has a right to be beyond reproach, and so each of us is entitled to repudiate what we regard as any unjust claims against us—and any unilateral claim will be a reproach in just this sense. You may give in to me because I seem to be stronger or better connected than you, but your rightful honor demands that you not allow yourself to be treated in this way. Even though our respective rights form the subject matter of this dispute, given just the two of us, there seems to be no resolution that is consistent with the universality that structures those rights. We make competing claims, each of us purporting to speak for right, that is, for the common standard that applies to us both, but in so doing each of us is merely expressing our own private standard. A private standard, however, is just a unilateral will. That is just to say, the state of nature is devoid of justice (*MM*, 6:312). The solution is to leave the state of nature and enter a rightful condition in which we are subject to common standards.

Kant articulates the role of a court in rendering private rights conclusive in a discussion that includes three examples of what he calls "ideal acquisition," followed by another four examples of what he calls "right that is subjectively dependent on the choice of a court" (*MM*, 6:291–305). The examples look like a miscellany of eighteenth-century legal doctrines—acquisition by prolonged possession, wills, the right to a good reputation after a person's death, contracts to make gifts or loans, recovery of stolen objects, and the compulsion of witnesses to take oaths. Underneath this apparent chaos, however, is a dual structure: the first three cases concern rights that are required by equal freedom, but impossible to demarcate in a state of nature. The next four are cases in which a court seems compelled to reach a conclusion contrary to natural right.

A single theme emerges from all seven examples: closure. Acquisitions and transfers must fit into a single closed system. Such a system is only possible if a state has powers that no private party could have.

Kant's first example concerns acquiring land by long-term possession, a feature of all modern legal systems. After enough time has passed, previous owners of a piece of land lose their title. Although this is often defended on some version of utilitarian grounds, Kant argues that it is actually a formal precondition of secure ownership of land. If the passage of time were not sufficient to vest ownership, a piece of land could never be subject to its owner's choice, because some person claiming prior title could dislodge him. This requirement of natural right can only be secured in a civil condition, because the general requirement of title closure does not specify either the precise act required to acquire land or the amount of time that must pass. Those conditions must be stipulated by a competent authority. Again, Kant's fourth example concerns a contract to make a gift. Such a contract could not be binding in a state of nature, because nobody could ever have standing to assert that the person who promised to make a gift meant to be bound by his promise if he subsequently asserts otherwise. A court is authorized to treat such contracts as binding unless the promisor expressly stipulates to the contrary, because he is in a position to make such a stipulation. Were the promisor required to expressly undertake responsibility, the same issue would arise with respect to the express undertaking: did the promisor mean to be bound by *it*? To avoid such a regress of undertakings, Kant says the court must presume the initial promisor meant to be bound unless an express declaration to the contrary is made.[31] In this, as in the other examples of subjective right,[32] the court has powers that no private person could have.

The first three of Kant's examples show that there are powers that citizens have as a matter of natural right that they could not enjoy outside of the state; the next four examples show that there are rights that a court can have that no private citizen could have. Both sets of cases show that in order for acquired rights to form a complete and consistent set, there must be a public authority competent to individuate acts of acquisition and transfer.

In acquisition from an unowned condition, institutions must be competent to declare an acquired object previously unowned, and they must be able to do so without investigating back to time immemorial. In acquisition from others through contract, institutions must be competent to declare a contract binding without investigating what the parties actually consciously contemplated at the time of formation. The power of the state to do these things is the precondition of rights that are closed, that is, rights that are not subject to dispute because they are merely unilateral expressions.

Kant explains the transition to a rightful condition through the "postulate of public right." This time, a postulate is required because the concept of rightful possession of external things is silent on the possibility of disputes about rights. Once again, Kant uses the vocabulary of Roman law, referring to the third of Ulpian's precepts, "*suum cuique tribue*," which he loosely renders: "*Enter* a condition in which what belongs to each can be secured to him against everyone else" (*MM*, 6:237).[33] Kant notes that a literal translation, "give each his own," appears to make no sense, because each already has whatever is his own (6:237). It makes sense, however, as the mark of the distinction between provisional and conclusive rights: by making rights conclusive, we give each person (conclusively) what is already his (provisionally).[34]

Pactum. In his discussion of contract, Kant elaborates the manner in which agreement is something that people must do together. To complete the simplest of transactions, the present transfer of a piece of property from one person to another, the two parties must do more than abandon and acquire the object in sequence. The transfer of physical possession of the apple requires only a sequence of empirical steps. First I am holding it, and then you are. The transfer of rightful possession requires more. If I want to give you an apple, I cannot do so by abandoning it in your presence. To do so would be to renounce *all* of my rights to it, including my right to give it to you rather than have it go to some other person who happens along just as I let go of it. To transfer the right to a thing, the two parties must act together, with a "united will" (*MM*, 6:272). The example of a present transfer illustrates a point that any account of the power to enter into contracts must explain: *whatever* powers are exercised in making contracts, they must be powers that the contracting parties have in relation to each other: I must have the power to transfer *to you*, and you must have the power to accept *from me*. No power that one of us has independently of the other could complete the transaction.

Uniting two choices in the requisite sense is not an empirical achievement. Even if we had a clear sense of what it would be for two separate minds to be empirically in perfect unison, that would not count as something they did together, but merely as a coincidence of their separate choices, and so no different than the case of one person abandoning and the other acquiring the object. My wish to give you something and your wish to receive it aren't enough. We need an affirmative act that unites us, but it cannot just be my act, or even the pairing of my act with yours. If the two parties were to fall into this sort of coincidental harmony, it would be irrelevant to any question of a transfer of rights.[35] Instead, the united will is an idea that we must presuppose to understand how a transaction can change the rights of the parties. Kant notes that people making agreements are aware of this need for unity, and awkwardly try to symbolize it by shaking hands (*MM*, 6:272). The handshake itself is not binding; only the united choice is. If people are to be able to unite their choices by doing things like shaking hands, there must be a public way for them to do so. But the resulting agreement is not an imperfect copy of a united choice, because it is neither a copy nor imperfect—it really does bind the parties.[36]

A bilateral contract isn't a perfect model of the agreement that creates a rightful condition, because, as Kant says, "For a unilateral will (and a bilateral but still *particular* will is also unilateral)" (*MM*, 6:263). Two people cannot enter into an agreement to change the rights of a third person; more generally, your consent to my appropriation of unowned property cannot entitle me to exclude anyone else. Moreover, a bilateral will is not sufficient to underwrite its own enforcement in cases of dispute.

The deficiencies of a binary contract to make up a general will reveal the need for a *more general* united will. Right requires reciprocal limits in accordance with a universal law. Universality needs to apply to conduct, to transactions, and to enforcement and remedies in cases of wrongdoing. The acquisition of property through unilateral acts is permissible, but only under a general will; the resolution of disputes can only be reconciled with the idea of reciprocal limits under the idea of a universal law. Without universal law, everyone would be subject to the particular choice of anyone else they encountered. Each would pursue his or her particular purposes, and "no matter how good and law abiding" they might be, each could have no measure of what is right except what seems right and good to him (*MM*, 6:312). In such a state of nature, rightful honor cannot require one person to moderate his or her conduct simply for the sake of another, since to do so would be to allow himself to be treated as a mere means toward some other person's particular purposes.

Philosophers who talk about the circumstances of justice represent them as conditions in which people are likely to be jealous of what is their own. Kant sees that rightful honor confers an *entitlement* to be jealous of what is your own. Where Hobbes, Locke, and Hume have drawn attention to the tendency of people to be unwilling to benefit others because of observed features of human behavior, Kant focuses on the entitlement to be unwilling to benefit others as a consequence of the entitlement to be the one who decides what purposes you will pursue. His claim is not that people should be selfish—the *Doctrine of Virtue* demands that *you* make the happiness of others *your* end[37]—but rather that no *other* private person could ever be entitled to set your ends for you. Thus nobody has standing to assume, much less demand, that you act for anyone's purposes but your own.

Those who make war on each other in a state of nature "do each other no wrong," because there are no obligations of right for them to violate, but they "do wrong in the highest degree" by willingly remaining in a "condition that is not rightful," because to refuse to secure your rights is inconsistent with rightful honor (*MM*, 6:308). You can only do so through public legal institutions.

So we must consent to the existence of public procedures—lawmaking, law applying and enforcement—needed to make rights reciprocal. Those procedures, in turn, require public institutions to give effect to them. Only institutions can create offices, and only officials acting in official capacities under law can render decisions that represent the united will of all, rather than their own particular wills. Unless law has this institutional form, it cannot do justice, even if its matter is morally appealing.

The significance of institutions rests on the distinctive nature of public offices. Officials have powers that private citizens lack: the elected official can pass laws, the police officer can arrest you, the judge can pass judgment on you. They are also constrained in distinctive ways: they can only act within their offices, which are in turn specified by law. Legislative officials are constrained by the constitution; the judiciary and the executive are constrained both by the constitution and by positive law as it has been laid down. Acts *ultra vires* are without legal effect. These familiar powers and restrictions reflect the ways in which properly constituted powers are able to act on behalf of everyone, making their actions exercises of the citizens as a collective body rather than as their own private acts.

As a result, any refusal to consent to public institutions of justice can only be a private reservation of a prerogative to make, apply, or enforce laws from my own private standpoint. That is nothing more that a demand that I be free to subject others to my choice, to set my terms of interaction with them unilaterally, and so is a demand to which others cannot consent consistent with their innate right of humanity. The only thing to which everyone can consent is entering a rightful condition by setting up public legal institutions.

I am now in a position to make good on my earlier claim that neither law nor justice is remedial for Kant. Justice is not remedial because its demands are an expression of human freedom, not a reflection of the unfortunate features of the human condition. At the same time, justice is not possible without law. The Lockean contention that, so long as I do not interfere with the rights of other persons I do not really need the state,[38] cannot even be coherently stated. There is no such thing as respecting the entitlements of others outside of a civil condition, because both entitlements and respect for them must be systematic and reciprocal, and they can only be reciprocal under public laws. You can only respect another person's rights if those rights are part of a consistent system of rights, as prescribed by a law that both applies to all and can be thought of as legislated by all. Neither the systematicity of right nor omnilateral lawgiving, judgments, and enforcement can be achieved without public institutions.

Justice can only be an individual virtue if it is a public one. Absent a civil condition, I can understand that the moral law requires me to return your deposit, and I return it. I might even convince you of my reliability by giving you a hostage.[39] Even if I can do all these things, I cannot respect your rights, nor you mine, because to respect rights at all we must do so systematically. Absent such systematic limits, conflict is not inevitable, but mutual vulnerability to wrong is. Only by uniting our wills can our independence be rendered consistent.

Three Private Law Models of Political Power

To say that we must unite our wills to create institutions if we are to have justice is not yet to explain how it is possible to do so in a way consistent with the innate right of humanity. Kant invokes the Roman law maxim *volenti non fit iniuria* (MM, 6:314)—the idea that one cannot be wronged through one's own act—in explaining why the state does no wrong in enforcing the law against citizens.[40] At other points he speaks of the "creation" and even the "acquisition" (6:259) of a rightful condition. This may seem to simply deepen the puzzle: what work could these ideas of private interaction be doing? Just as the idea of holding something in my hand provides a model of the acquisition of property, and a present transfer provides a model of acquisition by contract, so the idea of a social contract provides a model through which the idea of a rightful condition can be understood. Just as the model of holding something in my hand must not be taken to lead to the conclusion that I can only acquire what I can hold, so too the model of agreement must not be mistaken for its incidental features. Like all such models, it is potentially misleading.

The idea of the consent of the governed has taken three general forms in the social contract tradition, each of which reflects one of the standard forms of acquired obligations. The first of these is the idea of a contract, understood as a voluntary undertaking of a commitment, in consideration of something to be gained. Hobbes and Locke both emphasize aspects of this first idea. The second is the idea of cooperative fairness: those who benefit from their participation in a joint venture must bear their share of the costs of sustaining it. Locke's idea of tacit consent can be read as a version of this. The third is the idea of authorization, whereby one person accepts responsibility for deeds done by another person. Hobbes represents the relation between the state and its citizens this way.

It should be clear from Kant's account of both the nature of private rights and the inadequacies of a state of nature, understood as a pure system of private right, that none of these can, in and of themselves, serve as a model for a rightful condition. For the fundamental problem outside of a rightful condition is that rights are provisional and thus not enforceable. The acquisition of a right that is not enforceable could not generate enforceable rights. This difficulty is clear for each of the familiar models: if contracts, cooperative arrangements, and authorizations are not enforceable outside a rightful condition, then none of them can be used to generate a rightful condition.

Each of the private law models has other difficulties as well. Consent serves to make rightful what would otherwise be wrongful: what would have been a battery becomes a welcome caress; what would have been theft become a gift.[41] Political justification has to be different because entering states exercise powers such as making laws, resolving disputes, and enforcing those resolutions that nobody is entitled to enforce in a Kantian state of nature. Nor is consent relevant in other familiar ways: entering into a state is not an otherwise wrongful act of theft, battery, or defamation that is made rightful through the consent of its victims.[42] Images like this pervade contractarian writing precisely because both are images of law as a remedy, a bitter pill that it nonetheless makes sense to swallow. For Kant, these images go wrong by assuming a background of rightful interaction against which the otherwise wrongful deed might be consented to. Outside of a rightful condition, we don't have enforceable rightful claims without law, so ordinary consent lacks its condition of application.[43]

A different difficulty confronts what H. L. A. Hart and Rawls have called "the principle of fair play," according to which people have a moral obligation to contribute to a cooperative venture from which they benefit.[44] Insofar as the principle of fair play is characterized as a principle of private right, it is too narrow to be of any use even if it were enforceable. Critics have pointed out that not every effect of the cooperative activities of others gives rise to an obligation on the part of those who benefit.[45] Once the principle is narrowed appropriately, it only applies to cases in which the benefits in question are freely accepted. So understood, it has no obvious application to the case of the state, in which participation is mandatory. The person who judges that he would do better without the state is still subject to legal obligation and liable to coercion. There is little hope of assimilating this to the willing acceptance of benefits that might have been declined.

Both consent and cooperative fairness fail for another reason as well: they presuppose not only enforceable obligations but also some form collective agent entitled to enter into binding relationships. Yet the question of how the state can have the power to enter into binding arrangements is subordinate to the question that we were trying to answer, namely, that of how there can be a state at all. So we cannot presuppose the state as a party to it in explaining the contract.

Another Way of Looking at the Social Contract

In light of all of the things that appear to distance Kant from the rest of the social contract tradition, it may seem puzzling that he remains attracted to its central metaphor, that of a voluntary agreement. An alternative to both of these models must explain the distinctive normative relation between the individual and the state, and also how it can obtain in a way that is consistent with the *volenti* principle, despite the lack of a datable act of consent. The private relation that comes closest to this task is the idea of authorization: if I authorize you to handle my finances, then I am responsible for whatever you decide to do, and (provided you act within your mandate) I cannot be wronged by your acts, even if you mismanage those finances, no matter how badly I am harmed as a result.[46]

The idea of you acting for me is in one respect a promising model for the relation between the individual and the state, but, in another sense, it repeats the difficulties of the other two models. I can only authorize you to do what I am entitled to do, and, since I am not entitled to enforce my rights, I cannot authorize somebody else to enforce them. There is also no datable act of authorization through which I transfer this power (which I did not have to begin with.) Nonetheless, the idea of authorization does capture one important structural feature of the relationship between a state and its citizens: the state acts on behalf of its citizens; its acts are their acts. It also captures the idea that the relationship between the state and its citizens is not one of actual agreement, but instead is an arrangement that must be understood as required by law.[47]

How can authorization proceed without running afoul of the difficulties with other models of agreement? Kant defines public right as "a system of laws for a people, that is, a multitude of human beings" (*MM*, 6:311). "Multitude," in turn, is a technical term for Kant; in both his *Lectures on Logic* and in the *Critique of Pure Reason,* Kant articulates three different forms of quantity: unity, plurality, and totality. As always with Kant's triads, the third member represents the second member considered as the first; in this case a totality is a plurality considered as a unity. Public right represents the plurality of persons whose activities are regulated by private right as a unity, and it is as a unity that they consent.

Focusing on an already united people may appear to just push matters back a step. As Rousseau asked of Grotius, don't we first need an account of how a people becomes a people before we ask about anything in particular that it does?[48] Kant's solution to this problem is that the lack of conclusive rights is not just your problem or my problem, considered separately; it is also *our* problem, considered together. Inasmuch as rights in a state of nature are merely provisional, we do *each other* no wrong by remaining in a state of nature, because neither of us has conclusive rights to external things with respect to which we can be wronged. We do each other wrong "in the highest degree," however, because we act in a way inconsistent with the possibility of rightful relations between us, and "take away any validity from the concept of right as such" (*MM*, 6:308). If there are no wrongs against you or me, considered separately, then we don't have an individual problem (at least not one about our rights). The wrong in the highest degree, however, is *our* problem. Our joint problem requires a joint solution: the state. Any legitimate act of dispute resolution or enforcement must be understood as the act of a united will of those who are subject to it. Further, any *claim* to legitimate enforcement must also be understood as a claim to represent a people.

Any authorization cannot be explicit, but must instead be *lege*, that is, deemed as a matter of law. Models of deemed authorizations are familiar enough: parents are deemed to be acting on behalf of their children; the doctor who performs life-saving surgery is deemed to be acting on behalf of the unconscious patient; and, in many legal systems, rescuers of property are deemed to be acting on behalf of its owners, and so entitled to recompense for their services.[49] In these private examples, the relationship must be deemed because the power that one person has in relation to another must be analyzed so as to render it consistent with innate right.

Private examples of relationships *lege* make those particular relationships possible. Public law must be deemed in order to make rightful relations possible at all.

The idea that the relationship between the individual and the state is deemed rather than deed explains the two senses of the word "must" in the claim that citizens must authorize the state. First, it is deemed by law, not as a matter of fact, in the same way in which the relation between a parent and child is mandated by law, and so consistent with the freedom of both parent and child, even if neither of them consciously chose to take it on as such. So too the state must be taken to be acting on behalf of its citizens, because otherwise the private actions of citizens are inconsistent with their respective freedom.

Second, any person who wishes to remain in a state of nature may be forced by others to enter into a rightful condition, because neither choices nor deeds in a state of nature give rise to any rights. A fortiori, they give rise to no right to resist the attempts by others to bring you into a rightful condition.[50] A person in a state of nature is "permitted to constrain everyone else with whom he comes into conflict about whether an external object is his or another's to enter along with him into a civil constitution" (*MM*, 6:256). Force can be used, because those who would resist it can only be demanding that they set their terms of interaction unilaterally. In the same way, when a civil condition exists, everyone in it can be taken to have authorized the state to act for them, because the only alternative would be to "renounce all conceptions of right" (6:312) by remaining in a condition in which others could treat you as a mere thing, and neither you nor anyone else would have any entitlement to stop them. So to refuse to authorize a civil condition is, paradoxically, to make yourself wholly subject to the choice of others. You cannot be taken to have done so, any more than you can be taken to have voluntarily become a slave. To authorize a civil condition, by contrast, is to protect your independence.

At the same time, as we each authorize the state, authorizing it is something we do together: to enforce my own rights would be to act unilaterally; the reason the state can, with my authorization, do that thing is that an omnilateral will makes its so doing no longer unilateral. We announce, interpret, and enforce laws through our institutions and their officials. The need for those laws, and their announcement and enforcement, is not rooted in agreement (or disagreement) but in the nature of human freedom. If they are to be anything but unilateral impositions, they must be expressions of an omnilateral will, so all must authorize the institutions that make such a will possible. Institutions enable each person to take shared responsibility for the nonunilateral use of force; the taking of responsibility is what makes that force nonunilateral.

The postulate of public right thus establishes the need to enter a rightful condition, and, further, establishes that the entry to a defective rightful condition is nonetheless rightful. The idea for the latter claim is that a choice provides a further criteria through which a rightful condition can be evaluated, which Kant calls "the idea of the original contract." As the ideal case of a rightful condition, it serves as the moral standard against which particular rightful conditions can be evaluated. In *Enlightenment* Kant characterizes possible agreement as the "touchstone" of all legitimate lawgiving. This contractarian idea does not say that laws are binding because people have agreed to them. The laws are binding because of the postulate of public right; they are fully adequate to the underlying demands of all if they are parts of a system of equal freedom.[51]

Absolutism and the Circumstances of Justice?

I want to close by briefly considering the implications of this argument for Kant's widely noted opposition to claims that citizens have a right to revolution. Philosophers who think of law as remedial can go either way on the question of revolution. Hobbes notoriously thought that life outside the state was so terrible that citizens could never have reason to believe that overthrowing the state would improve their lot. Locke, who shared Hobbes's view of the state as remedial, also thought that sometimes, at least, the cure could be worse than the disease it was supposed to remedy, and so justify revolution. Neither of these lines of thought is available to Kant. Any similarity between his conclusions and Hobbes's must be coincidental. Instead, his attitude toward revolution reflects his rejection of the idea that law and justice are remedial.

Kant's discussion of revolution occurs in his "General Remark" concerning "effects with regard to rights that follow from the nature of the civil union." Like the sections that follow it—discussions of entailed estates, religious orders, hereditary nobility, and crime—Kant's discussion of revolution articulates the supremacy of the rule of law against other normative claims that seek to contest it.

The first consequence Kant draws is that it is pointless to inquire into the historical origin of the state's authority or search for a datable act of authorization. This is a straightforward implication of Kant's rejection of the idea that setting up the state is just another private transaction. History can never establish that a condition is rightful, because there could be no datable event of agreement that would count as the creation of a rightful condition. Any search for one is guaranteed to disappoint. Kant also writes that to search for one with a practical aim is inconsistent with right (*MM*, 6:318). If the legitimacy of the state depends on its past, the rights of those now living depend upon the deeds of past generations. The fact that a state was founded on violence cannot deprive you of your right to freedom, because no act to which you were not party could deprive you of the entitlement to join others in a rightful condition.[52]

Kant uses the irrelevance of history to make the further claim that the people have "a duty to put up with even what is held to be an unbearable abuse of supreme authority" (*MM*, 6:320).[53] Three claims need to be distinguished here. The first and second are claims that Kant makes, and are relevant to the point he is making; the third is often attributed to him, but he does not make it explicitly and it bears no connection to the rest of his discussion.

The first is the claim that bad laws are possible in a rightful condition. This claim *is* a development of the more general point about the irrelevance of history to the existence of a rightful condition. The existence of a rightful condition can no more be conditional on the prudence of its current rulers than it can on the justice of its founders. The second is the claim that no private party or faction can take it upon itself to exercise coercive authority. This also follows from the more general claim about the contract making rightful interaction possible, and is immediately relevant to the discussion of the irrelevance of history. The social contract is an idea of reason through which we can understand coercion as legitimated by the creation of institutions. Nobody could claim authorization to take up arms in the absence of such institutions, or to appoint themselves as a sort of counterinstitution.

These claims have gotten less attention than a third claim, which Kant does not make: every organized exercise of power is a civil condition. It does not follow from the claim that the legitimate use of force requires procedures of making, applying, and enforcing rules that any regularized and effective use of force is legitimate. The warlord who pillages in an orderly fashion does not thereby make himself a legitimate ruler.[54] If neither the state of nature nor the contract that enables us to escape it is to be understood historically, there may be cases of "lawless freedom" (*MM*, 6:307) in which it is legitimate to use force to create a rightful condition. Whether some particular situation fits this description cannot be determined a priori, nor can it be determined by the existence of partial apparatus of government.

In the final section of *Anthropology from a Pragmatic Point of View* Kant distinguishes between four combinations of force with freedom and law.

1. Law and freedom without force, which is anarchy (this is a state of nature understood as an idea of reason).
2. Law and force without freedom, which is despotism.
3. Force without freedom and law, which is barbarism.
4. Force with freedom and law, which is a republic (this is a civil condition understood as an idea of reason). (*A*, 7:330–31)

Despotism is a defective form of a republic, and Kant's remarks about resistance presumably are meant to apply to it. Barbarism, by contrast, is not a form of a republic at all, not even a defective one. Instead, it is a defective form of a state of nature, because it is simply a unilateral use of force. A state of nature can be represented as an idea of reason[55] insofar as it is thought of as a situation of perfect conformity with private right in the absence of public right. Persons have an obligation to leave a state of nature, even a peaceful one; to remain in it is to do wrong in the highest degree, because in the absence of a united will each person's independence is entirely subject to the goodwill (that is, the choice) of his or her neighbors.

Barbarism, as a defective form of a state of nature, also has no united will. All force is unilateral, so no issue arises of whether it may be resisted with right. Those who resist barbarism with the aim of entering a rightful condition do right; those who uphold barbarism "do wrong in the highest degree" (*MM*, 6:307). Despotism, which may lead to various forms of unfairness, could be a possible form of the general will.[56] Barbarism is not a possible form of the general will, and so is simply arbitrary force. Thus no argument for preserving a united will has any application. Only an argument for creating one does.

Kant's conception of barbarism is important for understanding his opposition to revolution. The examples that are supposed to embarrass him—most notably Nazi Germany—are conditions of barbarism in Kant's sense. In such a condition there is no united will, only the use of force and prerogative by a powerful group of people who make no pretence of representing all.[57]

Conclusion

In rejecting the idea that political society is ultimately remedial, Kant is able to provide an account of why it is distinctive, and how the state can be *entitled* to use force even if people are so well-disposed and law abiding that it is never actually used. The account he provides has profound implications for the world of bitter experience in which we find ourselves. It too is a world in which we can only be independent together.

NOTES

1. Mary Gregor remarks that "Kant has never been accused of underestimating his readers, but he seldom treats them so harshly." Mary Gregor, "Kant's Theory of Property," *Review of Metaphysics* 41 (1988): 787.
2. For a different view, see Hunter, chapter 7 of this volume.

3. Grotius's claim that "maintenance of the social order ... is the source of law" is representative. For a historical survey of Kant's natural law antecedents, see Jerome Schneewind, "Kant and Natural Law Ethics," *Ethics* 104 (October 1993): 53–74.

4. Rousseau is admittedly hard to classify on this spectrum; on prominent readings, such as that offered by David Gauthier, he regards law and justice as remedial solutions to the problems of life outside oneself described in the *Second Discourse*. David Gauthier, *Rousseau: The Sentiment of Existence* (Cambridge: Cambridge University Press, 2006). On Kant's own reading, in "Conjectural Beginning of Human History," the *Social Contract* and *Second Discourse* are not connected in this way.

5. Michael Sandel, *Liberalism and the Limits of Justice* (Cambridge: Cambridge University Press, 1982), 35.

6. Grant Gilmore, *The Ages of American Law* (New Haven: Yale University Press, 1977), 110–11.

7. This incompatibility is in addition to the incompatibility of a maxim with its own universalization that is at the heart of Kant's treatment of moral obligation in the *Groundwork of the Metaphysics of Morals*. As Kant notes in the *Critique of Pure Reason*, objects in space differ externally, while concepts differ only internally (A25/B40). The distinction between internal and external relations, in turn, corresponds to the contrast between two different forms of generality: the relations between a concept and its instances, and the relation between a whole and its parts.

8. For Kant on unsocial sociability, see Ferguson, chapter 6 of this volume.

9. Allen Wood emphasizes these aspects of the Kantian enterprise in *Kant's Ethical Thought* (Cambridge: Cambridge University Press, 1999)

10. Kant's discussion of God, freedom, and immortality as postulates in the *Critique of Practical Reason* is well known, as are the postulates of empirical thought in the *Critique of Pure Reason*. I explained the relation between these and the postulates in the *Doctrine of Right* in "A Postulate Incapable of Further Proof," the appendix to *Force and Freedom: Kant's Legal and Political Philosophy* (Cambridge: Harvard University Press, 2009).

11. The various formulations of the categorical imperative focus on contradictions within the will of a single agent, or in the conception of a maxim, rather than in any incompatibility between separate persons.

12. The idea that spatial relations introduce forms of incompatibility that are distinct from logical relations is a central theme in the *Critique of Pure Reason*, both in the Transcendental Aesthetic and in the "Amphiboly of Concepts of Reflection" appendix to the chapter on noumena and phenomena. I examine these relations in more detail in "A Postulate Incapable of Further Proof."

13. Kant famously distinguishes between will (*Wille*) understood as pure practical reason, and choice (*Willkur*) understood as the capacity to decide what purposes to pursue. (*MM*, 6:214.) The classic discussion is still Lewis White Beck, "Kant's Two Conceptions of Will," *Annales de Philosophie Politique* 4 (1962): 119–37.

14. I postpone to another occasion the question of whether this reading of the *Groundwork* is correct, noting only that it is familiar.

15. For example, in *A Theory of Justice* Rawls speaks of freedom in terms of independence from natural contingencies and natural fortune. See John Rawls, *A Theory of Justice* (Cambridge: Harvard University Press, 1971), 73.

16. Ulpian, *Rules*, Book 1, recorded in Justinian's *Digest*, Book One, 1.10. A more literal translation would be the infinitive "to live honorably." Kant uses the Latin phrase *Lex iusti* (what is right), as well as the phrases "the law of outer freedom" and "the axiom of outer freedom," to mark this idea elsewhere in the *Doctrine Of Right*.

17. Writing in a very different tradition, Elizabeth Anscombe makes the same point: "The wanting that interests us, however, is neither wishing nor hoping nor the feeling of desire, and cannot be said to exist in a man who does nothing toward getting what he wants." Elizabeth Anscombe, *Intention* (Cambridge: Harvard University Press, 2000), 67–68.

18. Paul Guyer takes Kant to be concerned with coercion in this sense. See Paul Guyer, "Kant's Deductions of the Principles of Right," in *Kant's Metaphysics of Morals: Interpretive Essays*, ed. Mark Timmons (Oxford: Oxford University Press, 2002), 23–64.

19. Kant makes this argument by means of an explicit analogy with the "Refutation of Idealism" in the preliminary materials for the *Doctrine of Right*, *Vorarbeiten zum Privatrecht* (preliminary unpublished material on private right, 23:309).

20. I argue for their completeness in "Authority and Coercion," *Philosophy and Public Affairs* 32, no. 1 (2004): 2–35.

21. I explain this in more detail in "Beyond the Harm Principle," *Philosophy and Public Affairs* 34, no. 3 (2006): 216–46.

22. This modeling is layered over the modeling already contained in private right. The concepts of property, contract, and status are each introduced with an example of a bodily deed: property is introduced with the example of taking something in my hand; contract with that of me giving you a thing; and status with two people taking possession of each other sexually, followed by a secondary example of childbirth. In each case, the bodily example can only be understood by abstracting away from its bodily features: I can have a property right in a thing even when I am not holding it; I can have a contractual right to your deed even though you have not performed it; and two persons can rightfully enjoy each other only if they are in more general, indeed complete, possession of each other. Parents have duties to their children because they were brought into the world without their consent. Kant's point with these models is not that I can only own things that I can hold, or that the only genuine form of contract is barter, or that only heterosexual intercourse can be rightful, or that adoptive parents don't owe the same obligations to their children as biological parents do. Instead, the examples serve as models because practical concepts can only be understood through models: right is "a rational concept for which no corresponding intuition can be given" (*MM*, 6:252). The incompatibility of two bodies occupying different regions of space provides the model for innate right; the same spatial model analyzes property by treating the ownership of land (space) as the basic case from which others are derivative (6:261–62). Kant makes a more general point about models for practical concepts in *Critique of the Power of Judgment*, section 59 (5:351).

23. In the "right of nations," only war raises questions of right. States occupy their territory in a way that is formally equivalent to each person's occupation of his or her own body. Unlike natural persons, however, territory is immovable, so only war can interfere with the right of states as against each other. Neither peaceful trade nor migration between states raises any issues of right.

24. In a dispute in the state of nature, it may be that only one party's act is consistent with the categorical imperative. Kant's point is that this is not sufficient to generate a title to coerce. Defensive force in a state of nature does not satisfy the requirement of reciprocal limits on choice any more than initial aggression does. Physical exclusion of others from the space I occupy is consistent with innate right. Standard cases of self-defense require more because they concern the entitlement to use force against an aggressor before he or she actually invades my space.

25. The argument is introduced in the discussion of property, but the conclusion about the need for institutions is also supposed to apply to contract and status (*MM*, 6:255).

26. But see Laursen, chapter 9 of this volume, for Kant's theory of property with regard to book publishing.

27. Kant first describes the same three-stage sequence for external things in general (6:259), so it applies to contract and status as well as the property example in which he develops it in detail.

28. This point is explicit in the *Vorarbeiten* at 311; it is also implicit in Kant's characterization of original possession in common as "disjunctive." In both the *Jasche Logic* and the Metaphysical Deduction in the *Critique of Pure Reason*, Kant explicates disjunction in terms of mutual exclusion. The earth's surface is possessed disjunctively if different persons occupy different parts of it.

29. Kant uses the vocabulary of "permissive law" to make this point. A permissive law is an extension of the idea of right, through which an act that is merely permissible can create a correlative obligation on the part of others (MM, 6:223), in this case an obligation to respect what belongs to another, even though the other person's ownership of something is not entailed by the concept of right as such, but requires the postulate of practical reason. Kant's other example is marriage, though which a conjugal act that is merely permissible obligates the parties (6:276–80). In "Kant on Property: The Problem of Permissive Law," *Journal of the History of Ideas* 62, no. 2 (2001) 301–12, Brian Tierney contends that this idea mires Kant in paradoxes that cannot be resolved, but can only explained in terms of their history. Tierney's paradoxes are a result of saddling Kant with the view that a permissive law serves to make an otherwise wrongful act acceptable. For a more favorable assessment of Kant and his predecessors, see Joachim Hruschka, *Das deontologische Secheck bei Gottfried Achenwall in Jahre 1767* (Gottingen: Vandenhoeck & Ruprecht, 1986), and "The Permissive Law of Practical Reason in Kant's 'Metaphysics of Morals,'" *Law and Philosophy* 23, no. 1 (2004): 45–72. Hruschka rightly locates the idea of permission as implicit within the broader structure of rightful relations: a law is required for a merely permissible act to be imputable to a person, because imputation must be in accordance with a rule.

30. Kant's argument is formally parallel to the Transcendental Deduction of the Categories in the *Critique of Pure Reason*. Each begins with apprehension, proceeds through giving a sign/reproduction, and concludes with inclusion in a whole—in the *Critique*, a public world of enduring objects in space, and in the *Doctrine of Right* a rightful condition under public laws. The parallels are not accidental, because in each case the philosophical issue turns on the application of a rational concept to a (potentially) absent object. I am only entitled to apply the categories of the understanding to objects of possible experience, that is, those objects that I can represent as existing apart from me by representing them in space. I am only entitled to claim property as my own if my claim to it constrains the conduct of others even when the object is apart from me in space.

31. Kant's analysis pervades the modern law of negligent misrepresentation. See, for example, *Glanzer v. Shepard*, 135 N.E. 275 (N.Y. Ct. App. 1921); and *Hedley Byrne & Co. Ltd. v. Heller* [1964] A.C. 465 (House of Lords). Lord Reid's speech in *Hedley Byrne* is especially instructive: the ground of the obligation to make good on a representation lies in the failure of the representor to qualify his representation by explicitly refusing to take responsibility.

32. The other examples include the bearing of risk in a contract to lend a thing; the recovery of a lost object, in which the thief can transfer title through sale in a public market; and requirement of oaths. In each case, the apparent requirement of natural right would lead to a regress; a public procedure must thus reverse it.

33. He refers to this idea as *Lex iustitae* throughout the *Doctrine of Right*, sometimes rendering it as, "What is laid down as right." The three precepts are brought together as "what is right, what is rightful, and what is laid down as right" in explaining the nature of public law (6:306). He also describes this as the "postulate of public right." A postulate is required because *actual* interaction with others is not contained in the concept of what is rightful, though in the case of humans it is guaranteed by the spherical shape of the globe (6:311).

34. Kant describes this as "subsumption." Like subsumption in the *Critique of Pure Reason*, it serves to create a systematic relation between things that are by their nature heterogeneous, namely, particular deeds and normative concepts. In the *Vorarbeiten*, Kant explicitly talks about the need for "schemata" to do so (23:228).

35. This point is an application of the more general criticism that Kant makes of Leibniz, when he notes that the idea of preestablished harmony cannot explain the concept of necessity. See *Critique of Pure Reason* (B339/A283).

36. There are several places where Kant treats ideas of reason in what appears to be a more platonic way. In the *Critique of Pure Reason* he makes an explicit comparison with Plato's forms; in the *Lectures on the Philosophical Doctrine of Religion* he says that ideas must outstrip any actual exemplification of them so as to leave room for the concept of perfection (28:995).

In the appendix to the *Doctrine of Right* he appears to take a similar line, arguing in response to a reviewer that "no object given in experience can be adequate" to a perfectly rightful constitution; and continues, a few lines below, to describe the empirical constitution as "afflicted with great defects and gross faults" (*MM*, 6:372). That his words here do not support a platonic reading becomes clear if they are applied, as he plainly means them to, to deeds more generally. He introduces the point by saying that actual deeds are mere appearances, which we must understand in terms of ideas of reason to which they are not adequate (6:371). Acquisition of property and transfer by contract really do take place; it is not that we somehow need to treat the slipshod attempts people make to achieve each process *as if* they were successful, because they approximate some ideal that is radically independent of them. The acquisition of an unowned thing isn't an imperfect approximation of some other process; when we shake hands we really do have a deal. The claim is that only by presupposing the ideas of acquisition and agreement can we understand how they can have normative consequences. In the same way, we need to presuppose the idea of a rightful condition created by a general will to understand how coercion can be authorized. On ideas of reason, see also O'Neill, chapter 1 of this volume.

37. The requirement that you make the happiness of others your end is an internal duty, which gets its moral worth from the fact that you choose it as your end. As Kant explains in the *Groundwork*, mere conformity to duties of virtue is without moral worth (4:397).

38. For a prominent recent version of this objection, see John Simmons, "Justification and Legitimacy," in John Simmons, *Justification and Legitimacy* (Cambridge: Cambridge University Press, 2001).

39. In his "dogmatic division" of rights that can be acquired by contract, Kant includes the Roman legal categories of *pignus* (pledge), *fideiusssio* (guarantor), and *praesatito obsidis* (hostage) (*MM*, 6:286). Each of these provides a way in which people can make themselves vulnerable to others and so create a basis for cooperation, without anything like a centralized system of enforcement or a generalized system of assurances.

40. On the maxim *volenti non fit iniuria*, see also O'Neill, chapter 1 of this volume.

41. Although on Kant's view there are some things that cannot be consented to rightfully, such as slavery, mutilation, and murder.

42. Kant makes this point in explaining the inability of a religious order to bind its future members in perpetuity: any such binding would be incompatible with the innate right of humanity, because it would be giving up one's ability to determine purposes for oneself (*MM*, 6:328). A consensual organization cannot acquire any powers that its members lack. The powers of the state are even broader than those of a private party (or religious order) and so cannot be the subject of ordinary consent.

43. Kant thus escapes Hegel's charge against the idea that the state is founded on contract. See Hegel, *Elements of the Philosophy of Right*, trans. H. B. Nisbet, ed. Allen W. Wood (Cambridge: Cambridge University Press, 1991) paragraphs 40, 75.

44. H. L. A. Hart, "Are There Any Natural Rights?" *Philosophical Review* 64, no. 2 (1955): 175–91; and Rawls, *A Theory of Justice*. The same general idea may underlie Locke's doctrine of "tacit consent," according to which living in a state and accepting its benefits amounts to consent. In a similar way, Locke's theory of property generates the right to exclude from the right to prevent others from benefiting from my efforts. That is why he insists that the person who gives chase to a hare is wronged by the intruder who captures it: Locke seeks to ground the right to property in the injustice of appropriating the fruits of another person's labors (*Second Treatise*, section 30). Kant is one of the few writers on property who does not discuss the capture of hares or foxes, but says that the person who expends effort on land that is not already his "has lost his pains and toil" (*MM*, 6:269). The classic discussion of acquisition of wild animals is in Justinian's *Digest*, Book 41; the classic common law discussion, which considers the writings of Pufendorf, Grotius, and Barbeyrac, can be found in *Pierson v. Post*, 3 Cai. R. 175 (N.Y. 1805). All of the classic discussions reject the Lockean view.

45. Robert Nozick, *Anarchy, State, and Utopia* (New York: Basic Books, 1974), 90–94. A. John Simmons, "The Principle of Fair Play," *Philosophy and Public Affairs* 8, no. 4 (1979):

307–37, argues that there are some cases in which the principle applies, but that all of them require free participation in a cooperative practice.

46. A version of this idea can be found in Hobbes, although it has not been the primary focus of recent Hobbes scholarship. For discussion, see David Copp, "Hobbes on Artificial Persons and Collective Actions," *Philosophical Review* 89, no. 4 (1980): 579–606.

47. On authorization, see also Hodgson, chapter 4 of this volume.

48. Jean-Jacques Rousseau, *The Social Contract*, book 1, chapter 5.

49. In civilian systems based on Roman law, this relation is *gestio negotii*. The common law of the English-speaking world repudiates this category and treats noncontractual improvers of property as volunteers acting on their own behalf. This disdain for volunteers does not extend to finders of property who take care of it.

50. The structure of the argument is parallel to more familiar passages in Kant: the "ought implies can" passage in the *Critique of Pure Reason*, in which my obligation proves that I am free, and the passage in the *Groundwork* in which Kant says that the "noumenal 'would' becomes the phenomenal 'ought.'" In the *Doctrine of Right*, the noumenal "would" becomes the phenomenal "must," that is, the authorization to use force. In private right, you can be compelled to pay your debts (*MM*, 6:230) or to pay compensation if you wrong someone (6:271). Your creditor's right to payment is noumenal, and so is not defeated by your failure to pay; the person whom you injure has a right to be uninjured, a right that Kant treats as continuing to exist in spite of the payment makes it as though the right in question was intact. In each case, the payment makes it as though the right in question was intact. In public right the noumenal "would"—the authorization of a civil condition—becomes the phenomenal "must"—others can force you into a civil condition.

51. For detailed discussion, see O'Neill, "Kant and the Social Contract Tradition," chapter 1 of this volume.

52. Kant makes the same point in discussing the legal doctrine of uscupation ("adverse possession" in the common law), according to which a trespasser can acquire title to land merely by occupying another person's land for a sufficient period of time. It must be possible for a wrongdoer to pass good title, otherwise nobody could have conclusive ownership in land acquired from another, because there could be no way to establish that no wrong had been involved in the past (*MM*, 6:292).

53. This passage appears to be a paraphrase of his comment in *Theory and Practice*: "[I]f a people now subject to a certain actual legislation were to judge that in all probability this is detrimental to its happiness, what is to be done about it? . . . The answer can only be that, on the part of the people, there is nothing to be done about it but to obey." Kant then clarifies this point by arguing that happiness cannot be the basis for valid laws (8:298), a point he reiterates at 8:302.

54. See Pogge, chapter 3 of this volume, note 47.

55. In the Vigilantius notes recording Kant's lectures on the metaphysics of morals from 1793, Kant is reported as describing *status naturalis* as a mere idea of reason (*VN*, 27:589).

56. Kant makes this point in the middle of the first paragraph of section 52, when he notes that the people could want autocracy (6:340).

57. The classic study of Nazi barbarism is still Ernst Fraenkel, *The Dual State: A Contribution to the Theory of Dictatorship* (New York: Oxford University Press, 1941). Fraenkel focuses on the prerogative nature of Nazi rule, that is, the deployment of force without freedom or law.

IS KANT'S *RECHTSLEHRE* A "COMPREHENSIVE LIBERALISM"?

Thomas W. Pogge

I. Introduction

Beginning in 1985, John Rawls repeatedly emphasized that modern, pluralistic societies should be structured in accordance with a *political* conception of justice.[1] In doing so, he has insisted that his own liberalism should be understood as political, in contrast to the *comprehensive* liberalisms of Kant and John Stuart Mill.[2] While this refinement in Rawls's position has been discussed by many scholars, his characterization of Kant's liberalism as comprehensive has not been critically explored in the literature. My interest in beginning such an exploration here is entirely focused on Kant. My guiding thought is that we can gain a better understanding of Kant's *Rechtslehre* by confronting it with the distinction Rawls developed two centuries later.[3]

By calling a conception of social justice comprehensive, Rawls means that it relies on "conceptions of what is of value in human life, as well as ideals of personal virtue and character, that are to inform much of our nonpolitical conduct" (*PL*, 175; cf. 13). He contends that "Kant's doctrine is a

---

This essay appeared originally as "Is Kant's *Rechtslehre* Comprehensive?" in *The Southern Journal of Philosophy* 36, no. 1, Spindel Supplement: Kant's *Metaphysics of Morals* (1998): 161–87. Reprinted with the kind permission of *The Southern Journal of Philosophy*. For revising this essay, I learned a lot from the lively discussions the paper evoked in Memphis and Lawrence. Many thanks also to Rüdiger Bittner, Ernesto Garcia, Samuel Kerstein, and Fang-Li Zhang for their detailed and very helpful critical comments and suggestions.

comprehensive moral view in which the ideal of autonomy has a regulative role for all of life" (*PL*, 99),⁴ and also, more cautiously, that "the basic conceptions of person and society in Kant's view have, let us assume, a foundation in his transcendental idealism" (*PL*, 100).

Evoking Isaiah Berlin, Rawls mentions as one main drawback of comprehensive conceptions of social justice that they are likely to be socially divisive, for example in their approach to public education: "The liberalisms of Kant and Mill may lead to requirements designed to foster the values of autonomy and individuality as ideals to govern much if not all of life" (*PL*, 199). But such requirements lead to a fatal dilemma, given what Rawls calls the "fact of oppression," namely, "that a continuing shared understanding on one comprehensive religious, philosophical, or moral doctrine can be maintained only by the oppressive use of state power" (*PL*, 37). The comprehensive liberalisms of Kant and Mill can maintain their social preeminence only by violating their own strictures against the use of state oppression (*PL*, 37, note 39).

Rawls does not define political conceptions of social justice simply as ones that are noncomprehensive or *freestanding*. Rather, he adds two further elements to his definition, namely, that political conceptions of social justice apply to, and only to, the basic structure of a closed and self-contained society (*PL*, 11–12) and that they are "expressed in terms of certain fundamental ideas seen as implicit in the public political culture of a democratic society" (*PL*, 13).⁵ To avoid the problems Rawls points to, Kant's liberalism need only be freestanding, not political; and so I ignore these two further elements. Simply put, our question is then whether Kant's *Rechtslehre* is freestanding—or beholden to and hence biased toward other parts of his philosophical corpus, such as his teachings about good will and autonomy or his transcendental idealism.

Let us begin with some straightforward points. It can hardly be disputed that Kant did develop and endorse the doctrine of transcendental idealism and an ideal of autonomy. But this cannot decide our question. For the fact that the author of a conception of social justice has also held and expressed broader religious, moral, or philosophical views—and surely Rawls himself has held, and presumably expressed, such views as well—does not show that the conception of social justice he sets forth depends upon these broader views in any way.

Nor can our question be settled by pointing to Kant's claim that his *Rechtslehre* fits into the broader worldview of his critical philosophy or by noting that Kant presents his entire philosophy as a system unified by certain key terms, propositions, and methods. For it does not follow from the fact that a conception of social justice fits into one comprehensive worldview that this is the *only* comprehensive worldview into which it fits or that it cannot *also* "be presented without saying, or knowing, or hazarding a conjecture about, what such doctrines it may belong to, or be supported by" (PL, 12–13). We can see this clearly by considering that Rawls presents his own political conception of social justice as "a module, an essential constituent part, that fits into and can be supported by various reasonable comprehensive doctrines" (PL, 12), and even claims, in developing his model case of an overlapping consensus, that his own *justice as fairness* fits into *Kant's* comprehensive worldview (PL, 145, 169).

What must be shown, then, to disqualify Kant's liberalism as comprehensive is not that it is entailed by his broader philosophical system, but, conversely, that Kant's broader philosophical system is presupposed by his liberalism. This liberalism is comprehensive if it cannot be presented as anything but an integral part of Kant's philosophical worldview.

I will here make the case for the hypothesis that the liberalism set forth in Kant's DR is *not* comprehensive, does *not* presuppose either Kant's moral philosophy or his transcendental idealism. I do not pretend that this case is fully conclusive. But it is a case that should be answered by those who dismiss Kant's political philosophy as dependent on metaphysical or moral views that we cannot expect to be freely endorsed by the citizens of modern societies.[6]

Before devoting the rest of this essay to supporting my hypothesis, let me concede that Kant, even if innocent of the charge of comprehensive liberalism, is guilty of the expositional flaw that Rawls come to criticize[7] in his own earlier work: Kant sometimes (falsely) suggests that his liberalism is dependent on his philosophical worldview and is hence comprehensive.[8] That he does so is not surprising. Kant is deeply committed to his moral philosophy and to his transcendental idealism; and these teachings would be more significantly vindicated by his liberalism if this liberalism were dependent upon rather than merely supported by them.[9]

II. Kant's Definition of *Recht* (§§A–B)

The liberalism Kant develops in the DR is constructed from a sparse arsenal of basic elements. Some of these are definitions. Thus Kant declares that, in contrast to a *thing*, a *"person* is a subject whose actions are capable of imputation" (*MM*, 6:223, 24–25). He continues: "*Moral* personality is therefore nothing other than the freedom of a rational being under moral laws ... from which it follows that a person is subject only to laws that it (either alone or at least jointly with others) gives to itself" (6:223, 25–31). With much help from Rüdiger Bittner and Joachim Hruschka, but following neither of them, I read this as follows. By italicizing "moral," Kant flags that this word narrows the meaning of "personality." The most plausible specification, which would also vindicate the word "therefore," is this: having *moral* personality means being a subject whose *inner* actions are capable of imputation, a subject with (transcendental) freedom of the will. This is the narrow, strong concept of person at work in Kant's moral writings.[10] Persons in the wider, weaker sense are then subjects whose *external* actions can be imputed to them as expressive of their will, choice, or intentions. Kant makes clear that—while the *DV* has to do with both inner and external actions and freedom and thus must work with the stronger concept of *moral* personality—the *DR* has to do with only the *external* actions and only the *external* freedom of persons and therefore requires only the weaker concept of person *simpliciter* or (what one might call) juridical personality (*MM*, 6:214, 13–30).[11]

Suppose there are persons—not just one, but a plurality. And suppose they move in the same space in such a way that the actions of one may obstruct those of another. Let us say that a person's external freedom is constrained exactly insofar as others are obstructing actions that she could otherwise perform if she so chose, and that her external freedom is insecure insofar as others *can* obstruct her otherwise possible actions. A person's external freedom is *secure,* then, insofar as others' actions that would obstruct her own are themselves obstructed. The security of a person's external freedom thus requires that the external freedom of others (to obstruct her external freedom) be constrained. Therefore, a plurality of persons can have security of their external freedom only if and insofar as the external freedom of each is constrained so as to be consistent with the constrained external freedom of all others.

Kant defines the word "Recht" as "the whole of the conditions under which the choice of one can coexist [*zusammen vereinigt werden kann*] with the choice of the other according to a universal law of freedom" (*DR*, 6:230, 24–6).[12] The word "choice" here is Mary Gregor's rendition of "*Willkür.*" And this translation seems all right if we attach two clarifications. First, "choice" must be understood not in the sense of decision (as in "she came to regret her choice"), but in the sense of domain of control (as in "this is her choice; for her to decide, up to her"). Second, we must understand someone's choice not locally, as what is up to her on some occasion, but globally, as what is up to her over a lifetime. I read Kant's expression "external freedom" as synonymous with choice in this sense. As a final clarification one might add that although Kant speaks of only two persons here, his definition is meant to cover an indefinite plurality. He defines the term "Recht" then as the whole of the conditions under which the external freedom of any person can coexist with that of all others according to a universal law of freedom.

Domains of external freedom can coexist when there is no action any person might perform within her domain that would render impossible another's action within his. To ensure such mutual consistency of choice, a universal law will need to include a large variety of restrictions and should thus be thought of as a *body* of law—a familiar meaning of the word "law," exemplified in such locutions as "Grundgesetz" or "common law." To ensure mutual consistency, such a law must apply to all persons, must specify precisely for each what she may, must, and must not do. But it need not treat all equally by making ultimately the same demands on each. I propose then to read the word "universal" ("allgemein") here in the weak sense of "applying to all," not in the stronger sense that also entails equality of persons under the law.[13] To be sure, Kant's liberalism does require equality under the law. But this requirement is not a matter of what *Recht* is by definition, but a matter of what Kant claims *Recht* ought to be. *Recht* may be instantiated in many different ways, only some of which involve equality under the law.

We have yet to explain what Kant means by "the whole [Inbegriff] of the conditions." I take this expression to have a twofold significance. First, by referring to conditions in the plural, Kant suggests that *Recht* is more than merely this single condition: that there be a universal law restricting everyone's external freedom so as to ensure mutual consistency. Such a universal law is insufficient for *Recht* because—as the familiar case of human beings illustrates convincingly—persons may not pay attention to it. A universal law makes it possible for persons' choices to coexist only if it is *effective*; and the conditions that render it effective must then be included among "the whole of the conditions" of Kant's definition. These effectiveness conditions may include institutional mechanisms through which the universal law is authoritatively formulated and announced, authoritatively interpreted and applied, and also enforced.[14] A particular instantiation of *Recht* may then—and among human beings *will*—have two components: a body of law that delimits each person's domain of external freedom, and institutional mechanisms that make this law effective.

Second, in associating *Recht* with a *complete* set of conditions, Kant is also suggesting the exclusion of any redundant restrictions. The set of conditions must not only be *in*clusive so that conditions it contains are jointly sufficient, but must also be *ex*clusive so that no restriction is dispensable for the maintenance of mutually secure domains of external freedom. *Recht* excludes any restrictions that make no contribution to such mutual security and thus involves (in modern jargon) a Pareto-efficient distribution of external freedom.[15] Kant displays this limitation rather clearly in the paragraph preceding his canonical definition of *Recht,* saying that "the concept *Recht* . . . has to do only with the external and indeed practical relation of one person to another insofar as their actions, as [imputable] deeds, can mutually influence one another" (*DR,* 6:230, 7–11) and is not concerned with persons' inner states, such as their wishes, needs, or ends (6:230, 11–19). It may well be desirable that persons' actions should harmonize with their own and others' wishes, needs, and ends. But this, for Kant, is a concern of ethics—not of *Recht,* which deals with, and only with, the preconditions for mutually secure domains of external freedom. *Recht* solves the problem of possible conflicts among actions and leaves aside all other possible conflicts that may arise among actions, wishes, needs, and ends.[16]

My explication of Kant's canonical definition makes "Recht" essentially equivalent to "Rechtszustand," which should be translated as "juridical state" or "juridical condition."[17] As Kant defines it here, *Recht* is not a system of rules such that, if all persons correctly observed them, no person's action would ever obstruct another's. Rather, *Recht* is a property of a world of persons capable of obstructing one another's actions—or capable of constraining one another's external freedom. It is instantiated in such a world if and only if this world is so structured that the external freedom of persons is, in accordance with a universal law, constrained in such a way that each person's constrained external freedom is secure. *Recht* is instantiated when persons coexist under an effective legal order that delimits and sustains mutually secure domains of external freedom. This explication of "Recht" strongly confirms my above conjecture that the word "universal" must be read in the weak sense. A complete and effective legal order, even without equality under the law, instantiates *Recht* or a juridical condition.

All that is required for such a condition is that there be an effective body of public standing laws that constrains each person's freedom in predictable ways and thereby predictably delimits and secures each person's constrained external freedom.[18]

If this is what *Recht* is, what then is *Rechtslehre*? This is not a trivial question, because there is a significant ambiguity in the German ending "-lehre." In one sense, this ending indicates an intellectual discipline or field of study. This use occurs, for instance, in the word "Arzneimittellehre," which is the study of medical remedies, or pharmacology. Taken in this sense, *Rechtslehre*—or *the Rechtslehre*, with the definite article—would be the intellectual discipline that reflects upon the establishment and maintenance of *Recht*, that is, of mutually secure domains of external freedom among persons. This field of study might be thought of as consisting of two branches: empirical *Rechtslehre*, which reflects upon our historical experience with actual attempts to establish and maintain *Recht*—and philosophical *Rechtslehre*, which reflects more abstractly on whether and how *Recht* can be and should be established and maintained. Kant, of course, would be operating within the latter branch of the philosophical *Rechtslehre*.

In its other sense, the ending "-lehre" indicates a particular theory, doctrine, or approach within some field of study. This use occurs, for instance, in the expression "Mendelsche Vererbungslehre," which is a biological theory yielding specific predictions about the transmission of traits from plants and animals to their offspring.[19] Taken in this sense, *a Rechtslehre* (now with an *indefinite* article) would be a particular theory about *Recht*; and a philosophical—or, as Kant likes to say, metaphysical (*DR*, 6:284, 9)—*Rechtslehre* would then be a particular theory about whether and how *Recht* can be and should be established and maintained. From here on I will use the word in this latter sense, as a substitute for "Kant's liberalism" (and as distinct from *DR*, the text).

Kant acknowledges and at once downplays the ambiguity, stressing that there can be only one true doctrine within each field of study (*MM*, 6:207, 11–29), hence only one philosophical doctrine of *Recht*, so that the study of *Recht* should ideally coincide with the study and refinement of the one true doctrine of *Recht*. Highlighting the distinction is worthwhile nonetheless in that it provides a helpful perspective on Kant's enterprise. We can expect the *DR* to contain two main components. The first component consists of Kant's definition of *Recht* and his analysis thereof, which generates whatever propositions follow from this definition analytically. The second component consists of whatever substantive elements Kant adduces to show the possibility and desirability of *Recht* and of certain instantiations thereof. It is this second component that might most plausibly be suspected of presupposing other parts of his philosophical worldview.

III. Kant's Universal Principle of *Recht* (§C)

After explicating the notions of *Recht* and *Rechtslehre* in §§A–B, Kant goes on, without any transition, to enunciate what he calls the universal principle of *Recht*. He does not make clear what the canonical text of this principle is supposed to be, but two formulations seem pertinent. One has the look of a definition and is given in quotes as the first paragraph of the section; the other has the look of an imperative, is given in the fourth paragraph, and is specifically referred to as the universal law of *Recht*. The first formulation is:

(1)   Any action is *right* [*recht*] if it, or if pursuant to its maxim the freedom of choice of each, can coexist with everyone's freedom according to a universal law (*DR*, 6:230, 29–31).

That this sentence is meant to provide a sufficient *and necessary* condition for the rightness of actions is shown by the very next sentence, which infers that certain actions, because they "cannot coexist with freedom according to universal laws" (*DR*, 6:231, 1–2), commit a wrong (*Unrecht*).

The second formulation demands:

(2)   [S]o act externally that the free use of your choice can coexist with the freedom of everyone according to a universal law (*DR*, 6:231, 10–12).

Since Kant offers no argument for either formulation, and since at least the second formulation looks like a straightforward variant or application of the categorical imperative, one can easily be led to presume that Kant is here presupposing the moral philosophy he had developed in the *Groundwork* and *CPrR*. The end of §C, however, must count strongly against this presumption. Kant writes there that his principle in its second formulation "does not at all expect, far less demand, that I *myself ought to* restrict my freedom to those conditions just for the sake of this obligation; instead, reason says only that my freedom *is* in its idea restricted to those conditions and also may forcefully [*tätlich*] be so restricted by others" (*DR*, 6:231, 13–17; cf. 6:231, 3–9). What looks like an imperative addressed to me turns out then to be a permission addressed to my fellows, who may force me to act externally so that the free use of my choice can coexist with the freedom of everyone according to a universal law. And this permission exists of course quite generally, not just with regard to myself: persons may force any person to act externally so that the free use of his or her choice can coexist with the freedom of everyone according to a universal law.

One might think that the second formulation—even if it is really a permission rather than an imperative—is still a *moral* claim whose justification presumably depends on Kant's moral philosophy. There is, however, a far more convincing alternative interpretation, which seeks support for the permission in question not from other parts of Kant's corpus, but from the immediately preceding discussion of *Recht*, and thus understands it not as a moral, but as a *juridical* permission. We saw in the previous section that Kant defines *Recht* as a property of a world of persons capable of obstructing one another's actions. Now Kant is using this definition to define a property of external actions. The relation of these two properties to one another will turn out to be complex, and I will deal with it in a moment. But that there is this connection is strongly suggested by the fact that both the definition of *Recht* as well as the two formulations now before us are dominated by expressions of the form "can coexist . . . according to a universal law."[20] My conjecture then is that Kant thinks of actions as either fitting or not fitting with *Recht*, which, as we have seen, is a certain organization of a world of persons. Let us say then that depending on whether actions satisfy or fail to satisfy the "can coexist . . . according to a universal law" expression, they either accord or fail to accord with *Recht*. The two formulations of §C can now be put, simply, as follows:

(1a) Any action is right if it accords with *Recht*, and wrong otherwise.
(2a) So act externally that your actions accord with *Recht* (i.e., are right).

As we have seen, Kant reads the second formulation as tantamount to a permission:

(2b) Persons may force any person to act rightly, or: persons may obstruct wrong actions.

Now the idea of reading the "may" in the sense of a juridical permission is simply to read statements about what persons may do as equivalent to statements about what it is right, in the sense of (1a), for them to do. Making this substitution turns (2b) into

(2c) It is right to force a person to act rightly (i.e., it is never wrong to obstruct wrong actions).

On this reconstruction of the text, (1) then turns out to be a definition of "right" (and "wrong") as applied to actions; and (2) turns out to be a theorem about the rightness and wrongness of action-obstructing actions—the theorem proven in §D.[21]

We have yet to unpack the predicate "accords with *Recht*." As is to be expected, Kant gives the most elaborate and careful explication in the definition, that is, in (1). This explication involves a disjunction. This may suggest that Kant is here offering persons a choice between two different ways of acting rightly.[22] But I find it more plausible to read him as distinguishing two cases, implying that what it means for an action to accord with *Recht* varies depending on whether the action takes place in a context where *Recht* is instantiated or in one where it is not. So I propose the following rendition of (1):

(1b) When *Recht* is instantiated, an action is right if and only if it can coexist with everyone's freedom according to a universal law (which we must presume to be the universal law that figures in the existing instantiation of *Recht*). When *Recht* is not instantiated, an action is right if and only if pursuant to its maxim the freedom of choice of each can coexist with everyone's freedom according to a universal law.

The basic idea of this definition is then the following. When *Recht* is instantiated (case 1), an action is right if it conforms to the existing law, and wrong otherwise. Here, actions accord with *Recht* if and only if they comply with existing law. When *Recht* is not instantiated (case 2), an action is right if and only if its maxim is consistent with a possible universal law. Here, actions accord with *Recht* if and only if they anticipate a possible instantiation of *Recht*.

Case 2 is problematic in at least two respects. The first problem is that, if we read the word "universal" in the weak sense I have advocated above, then it would seem that, when *Recht* is not instantiated, any (or almost any) action can be juridically permissible—provided only that the agent's maxim anticipates some, however ludicrously inegalitarian, instantiation of *Recht*.[23] The second problem with case 2 is that Kant's focus on agent maxims is odd because he insists so strongly—even in this very section (*DR*, 6:231, 3–5)—on the irrelevance of inner states. He does not seem to want to allow for the possibility that whether some given action is juridically right or wrong depends on the maxim on which it is performed. If we take this insistence seriously,[24] then we seem compelled to say that, when *Recht* is not instantiated, an action is right if and only if it *could* be performed on a maxim pursuant to which the freedom of choice of each can coexist with everyone's freedom according to a universal law.

A common element in both these problems is that, when *Recht* is not instantiated, the threshold for juridically right conduct may turn out to be implausibly low. This difficulty can be alleviated by strengthening what it means for conduct to anticipate a possible instantiation of *Recht*—along the following lines. When *Recht* is not instantiated, then my conduct is right if and only if there is an instantiation of *Recht* that (a) is practicable and such that my conduct is consistent with (would be legal under) it, and (b) is realistically attainable and such that my conduct facilitates (or at least does not hamper) its realization. It must be possible, that is, to understand my conduct as proceeding from maxims that are mindful of the *exeundum e statu naturali*. There is good evidence that Kant did indeed hold this view and took the goal-directed element (b) to be contained in (1). In §42, he writes: "In a situation of unavoidable proximity, you ought, with all others, to leave the state of nature and make the transition into a juridical condition" (*DR*, 6:307, 9–11).[25] He immediately goes on to say that "the reason for this can be developed analytically out of the concept of Recht" (6:307, 12–13) and, in explicating this reason, he identifies a person's being obliged to leave the state of nature with others being permitted to coerce him to do so (6:307, 24; *Refl.* 19:503, 28–30 [Reflection 7730]). So Kant clearly considered it juridically impermissible not to cooperate with others toward the establishment of *Recht* (for only those whose conduct is juridically impermissible are targets for juridically permissible coercion).

Let us take stock. I have tried to show that Kant conceives the core of his *Rechtslehre* as independent from the rest of his philosophy. What this means can be made vivid by conceiving of his *Rechtslehre* as a game—though doing so is misleading insofar as games are normally limited, for instance to a chessboard or soccer field, while this game covers everything persons might do externally. Kant's *Rechtslehre* game is governed by rules, which are binary by exhaustively dividing all possible actions by persons into those that are right (*recht*) and those that are wrong (*unrecht*) or, equivalently, into juridically permissible and juridically impermissible moves. One important theorem about this game is that coercive moves are permissible (right) *if* and *only if* any moves they obstruct are impermissible (wrong).[26] Both conditionals follow from Kant's definition of *Recht*: It cannot be permissible to obstruct a permissible move, because under any instantiation of *Recht* all permissible choices are compatible ("can coexist"). And it cannot be impermissible to obstruct an impermissible move, because any such restriction would be redundant; *Recht* excludes any conditions that make no contribution to the maintenance of mutually secure domains of external freedom.[27] This is not a trivial theorem—no conception of ethics I know of, Kant's included, makes it permissible to oppose any and all wrong actions—and Kant appears to be rather pleased that so substantial a result can be derived from so slender a basis.

The basic idea behind the metaphor of the *Rechtslehre* game is straightforward. To play this game is to be disposed to prefer juridically permissible over juridically impermissible conduct. Given Kant's theorem, this preference will spread: The fact that we have it will give others, who know that we have it, a reason to develop the same preference, because they know that we are less likely impermissibly to obstruct their permissible conduct than permissibly to obstruct their impermissible conduct. As these players' dispositions strengthen, and as more persons are drawn into the game, mutually secure domains of (constrained) external freedom emerge.

Starting out from §C, I have in this section sketched the rudiments of a game by saying something about its norms and something about how it might tend to go. As indicated, this game is connected to Kant's definition of *Recht* in this way. If the conduct of all persons consisted exclusively of juridically permissible (right) moves, then *Recht*—mutually secure domains of external freedom—would be established and maintained. Still, describing such a game, some principled way of sorting all external actions into juridically permissible and juridically impermissible ones, would seem to be a pointless exercise. Seeking the point of this exercise finally gets us to the second, substantive component of Kant's *Rechtslehre*.[28]

While we can view the universal principle of *Recht* as its core, Kant's *Rechtslehre* goes beyond this core in two related directions. On the one hand, it aims to offer a justification of this principle—seeking to give persons a reason for pursuing the instantiation of *Recht* through playing the *Rechtslehre* game. To be sure, each of us may have reason to play along if we know that the others are; but why should we, all of us as a group, play this game? The mere fact that the norms of the game instruct us to do so by defining certain conduct options as permissible and the remainder as impermissible cannot provide an answer to this question. We still need a reason for paying any attention to these norms. On the other hand, Kant also aims to strengthen the norms by going beyond what can be derived from his universal principle of *Recht*. He aims to specify the *Rechtslehre* game in such a way that it manifests a preference not merely for the instantiation of *Recht* (for a juridical condition over a state of nature) but also for a particular way of instantiating *Recht* over all alternative instantiations. The second of these projects presupposes the first in that at least some of Kant's attempts to strengthen the norms are justified by appeal to the point of the *Rechtslehre* game. I will discuss these two projects in the final two sections.

IV. The Point of *Recht*

Kant holds that persons have reason to take an interest in the *Rechtslehre* game because of their prior interest in securing the external freedom of (at least some) persons against obstructing actions by others. When *Recht* is not instantiated, persons' attempted actions are likely to be obstructed in various and unpredictable ways, and they will often fail to complete the actions they want to perform on account of such obstructions and will frequently not even attempt to do what they want to do for fear of being so obstructed. When *Recht* is instantiated, the conduct options of persons are constrained by firm restrictions on their external freedom. These constraints are, however, regular and predictable and give each person a clearly delimited space of options that are secure from the obstructing actions of others. The external freedom of persons is enhanced far more by the security that some of their options gain by being protected through an effective legal order than it is reduced by the added obstacles that legal prohibition imposes on their remaining options. Therefore persons tend to benefit, on balance, from the existence of a juridical condition.[29] Since the *Rechtslehre* game tends toward the establishment and maintenance of a juridical condition, it makes sense for persons interested in securing their own and/or others' external freedom against obstructing actions to play this game.

The text leaves little doubt, I believe, that Kant saw the point of mutually secure domains of external freedom in the enhancement of external freedom it makes possible.[30] He seems to be at some pains, however, to present the superiority (in terms of external freedom) of a juridical condition as knowable a priori.[31] The argument I have loosely sketched in the preceding paragraph, by contrast, sounds rather empirical; and this is so because I am unable to conceive of a plausible a priori argument. We cannot know a priori, for example, how severely persons can obstruct one another's conduct, how insecure their options would be in the absence of an effective legal order, how constraining the rules imposed by such an order would be, and how securely it would protect the options it permits. We also cannot rule out a priori that capacities and vulnerabilities are distributed very unevenly among persons, so that the balance of pros and cons differs from person to person. Without taking such empirical complexities into account one cannot endorse Kant's conclusion that persons with an interest in external freedom have reason to play the *Rechtslehre* game.[32]

But reaching this conclusion involves still further difficulties. Playing the *Rechtslehre* game is supported insofar as persons have an interest in having a large and stable set of valued options that are secure from obstructing actions by other persons. But then it is hard to see why persons should not also have an interest in having their options expanded and protected against obstacles and threats of other kinds. So Kant must show either that persons do not have this further interest or that this further interest does not furnish a reason that might outweigh their reason—based on their interest in securing their external freedom against obstructing actions by other persons—in favor of playing the *Rechtslehre* game.[33] This difficulty can be generalized to other interests that might be attributed to persons—interests in happiness, knowledge, wisdom, salvation, moral perfection, and so on. With respect to any such purported interest, Kant needs to show either that persons do not have it, or that it should not count as providing a relevant reason, or that the reason it provides does not affect the balance of reasons so as to upset the claim that persons have reason, all things considered, to play the *Rechtslehre* game.[34]

Kant may not have a fully satisfactory response to these further difficulties, but I think his key idea for such a response would be that *Recht* must be based on, and only on, interests that we necessarily have as (interacting) agents. Only if it is so based can we show that the instantiation of *Recht*, and hence participation in the *Rechtslehre* game, is in the interest of each and every person. Only if it is so based can *Recht* stand above the potentially contested, divisive, and shifting interests that persons may contingently attribute to themselves and to others. But the only interest that persons, whom Kant defines by reference to a capacity to choose their conduct, can be said to have necessarily is the interest in the fullest exercise of this capacity and hence in the availability of a wide range of secure options from which to choose. As agents, we want our lives to be determined by our own choices rather than by the choices coercively imposed on us by others.[35]

On this reconstruction, Kant emerges as the freestanding liberal par excellence. Rather than presuppose much more than Rawls does—his moral philosophy and transcendental idealism—he in fact presupposes much less. He makes no appeal to fundamental ideas prevalent in the public culture of his society, nor does he insist that persons have certain moral powers and matching higher-order interests in their development and exercise, nor does he seek to identify all-purpose means needed for realizing the conceptions of the good that citizens of a society like his own are likely to have. Rather, he bases the establishment and maintenance of *Recht* exclusively on persons' fundamental a priori interest in external freedom.[36]

This freestanding argument for *Recht* can be embedded in diverse comprehensive views. It can be embedded, for instance, in a Kantian morality that holds each person to be duty-bound to afford tangible assurance to every other person: because I owe it to those around me to help secure their external freedom against obstructing actions by myself (and by others?), I morally ought to contribute to the establishment and maintenance of *Recht*. At another extreme, it can also be embedded in a Hobbesian prudential account: because my fundamental interest is to secure my external freedom against obstructing actions by others, I prudentially ought to contribute to the establishment and/or maintenance of *Recht*. Kant himself stresses the availability of this latter embedding in a famous passage from *Perpetual Peace*, where he discusses the best instantiation of *Recht*: "Now the *republican* constitution is the only one that is fully appropriate to the right of human beings. But it is also the most difficult one to establish and even more so to maintain, so that many claim that it could function only in a state of angels" (*PP*, 8:366, 1–4). He goes on to write that, on the contrary, even utterly selfish persons, intelligent devils, would have reason to establish and maintain such a constitution:

The problem of setting up a state . . . is solvable even for a people of devils (if only they have understanding). It is this: A set of rational beings who on the whole need for their preservation universal laws from which each is however secretly inclined to exempt himself is to be organized and their constitution arranged so that their private attitudes, though opposed [to one another], nevertheless check one another in such a way that these beings behave in public as if they had no such evil attitudes. (*PP*, 8:366, 15–23)

This passage shows clearly, I believe, that Kant wants his argument for *Recht,* and for a republican instantiation thereof, to be independent from his morality. This morality may well give its adherents moral reasons for supporting *Recht* and a republican constitution in particular. But it does not therefore have a special status with respect to *Recht,* because it is, as the quote shows, just as true that selfishness gives its immoral adherents selfish reasons for supporting *Recht* and a republican constitution in particular.

This conclusion seems to go against the very core of Kant's philosophy: If everyone's participation in the *Rechtslehre* game were prudentially motivated, no one would be playing this game from duty or for the sake of genuine moral principles, and there would then presumably be no value in human beings living on this earth, even if *Recht* prevails.[37] But this is no reason to lament the fact that *Recht,* and a republican constitution, can be achieved without moral motives. To the contrary! This fact makes it much easier to establish and maintain an enlightened juridical condition, which in turn greatly facilitates the development of our moral dispositions.[38]

The conclusion also seems to collide head-on with the basic structure of the *Metaphysics of Morals,* of which the *DR* is of course an integral part. In the introductory materials preceding the *DR* (which has its own introduction), and elsewhere as well, Kant stresses the unity of the entire work, claiming that he is providing a systematic account of both *Recht* and ethics—an account that develops both of them out of their common root in human freedom and the categorical imperative (see *MM,* 6:207, 6:214, 6:215, 16–23, 6:221–22, 6:225–26): "The supreme principle of the *Metaphysics of Morals* [i.e., of both the *DR* and the *DV*] is therefore: act on a maxim that can also be valid as a universal law" (*MM,* 6:226, 1–2).

My conclusion, however, is not in fact threatened by these passages. It is true Kant seeks to establish not merely the consistency of his *Rechtslehre* with the rest of his philosophy, but also its unique standing as the one and only *Rechtslehre* firmly grounded in morality. Thus he aims to show that those who accept his moral philosophy must also accept his *Rechtslehre*. But it does not follow from this that he also aims to show that anyone who accepts his *Rechtslehre* must also accept his moral philosophy. We should be careful to avoid this erroneous inference and should therefore take care to distinguish between the two directions of support—a distinction that tends to get lost when the issue is framed in terms simply of "dependence" or "independence."

Failure to make this distinction vitiates Wolfgang Kersting's critique of what he calls the independence thesis (*Unabhängigkeitsthese*) and attributes to Julius Ebbinghaus, Klaus Reich, and Georg Geismann.[39] Kersting correctly explicates this thesis as asserting "a complete independence of the *Rechtslehre* from both the doctrine of transcendental idealism and from the critical moral philosophy."[40] On the next page, however, he refers to the "independence between [sic] transcendental idealism and critical moral philosophy on the one hand and the *Rechtslehre* on the other," and immediately proceeds to demolish this thesis by pointing out that Kant argues for *Recht* by appeal to moral notions, then asking rhetorically: "What sense does it make to develop *Recht* as part of a metaphysics of morals, if the *Rechtslehre* does not care whether or not natural causality is humanity's fate?"[41] Doing this would indeed make no sense, if Kant were committed to the *mutual* independence of his *Rechtslehre* and morality. But the independence thesis does not assert this. And so we can easily answer Kersting's question: Developing Kant's *Rechtslehre* as part of a metaphysics of morals makes sense because Kant wants to show that it has a basis in morality, is the only doctrine of *Recht* that fits into his moral philosophy. By showing that M entails R, Kant establishes merely a one-sided dependence of M on R; he establishes that R's failure would entail the failure of M, that M cannot stand without R. And this does *not* imply, of course, that R is dependent upon (cannot stand without) M.[42]

Some minor textual obstacles remain even after this clarification. Thus Kersting correctly points out that Kant "employs elements of his theoretical philosophy" when he uses the terms *sensible* and *intelligible* to distinguish between physical and juridical possession.[43] But I dare say that, in a pinch, this distinction can be drawn without recourse to Kant's theoretical philosophy and has in fact been so drawn long before Kant ever put pen to paper. It does not follow from Kant's eagerness to present his *Rechtslehre* as an integral part of his overall philosophy that he did not *also* want it to be freestanding: presentable on its own. The two modes of presentation are compatible, and Kant thus does not have to choose between them.

V. The Fine-Tuning of *Recht*

When *Recht* is not instantiated, persons are juridically obliged to cooperate in its establishment. In light of the vast range of possible instantiations of *Recht*, such cooperation involves an immense coordination problem. Persons must coordinate on a single set of descriptions in terms of which legal rules are to refer to action tokens, and they must coordinate on a division of labor between rigid and generative rules[44] and ultimately on one particular complete set of such rigid and generative rules.[45] If the *Rechtslehre* game is to be effective in guiding persons toward the fulfillment of their presumed interest in external freedom, then it must involve not merely a preference for *Recht* as such, but also a preference ordering over the many possible instantiations of *Recht*. This is an important point for my interpretation. For it may well seem that the interest in external freedom is too indeterminate to justify clear-cut rankings of alternative instantiations of *Recht*. But this appearance is deceptive, as the justification may proceed indirectly: our interest in external freedom justifies the master preference for the instantiation of *Recht* over its noninstantiation, and the fulfillment of this master preference *requires* secondary preferences sufficient to solve the coordination problem.

The secondary preferences Kant proposes, which often seem rather arbitrary and ad hoc,[46] become far less implausible if we view them as resting on such a two-stage justification. Kant is then not engaged in sorting possible rules into those that are correct and those that are incorrect by the lights of reason. Rather, he evaluates rules as more or less suitable for solving a coordination problem that simply has to be solved. Since he feels compelled by the task of a *Rechtslehre* to offer a salient solution that can guide the establishment of *Recht*, he does not feel that he has the luxury to confine himself to rationally compelling solutions. If no rationally compelling solution can be found, then the most salient one will have to do, even if it looks to Kant just barely more salient than some competitor.

It is clear what the juridical status of these secondary preferences must be. When *Recht* is not instantiated, then these preferences are juridically relevant by determining who is cooperating in the establishment of an effective legal order and who is not. While it is juridically permissible to coerce the latter, it is juridically impermissible to coerce the former. When *Recht* is instantiated, then the secondary preferences are juridically irrelevant. It is juridically permissible for the sovereign to maintain an inferior instantiation, and juridically impermissible for citizens to obstruct the sovereign's efforts to do so. And this, of course, is the position Kant in fact defends.[47]

There is space to discuss, at least briefly, the most important secondary preference of Kant's *Rechtslehre*—its general and pervasive preference for equality among persons. This preference for equality may seem to furnish the most powerful challenge that those who read Kant in the spirit of Kersting and Rawls can level at those who—like Ebbinghaus and myself—view Kant as holding that his *Rechtslehre* can stand on its own, independently from his moral philosophy and transcendental idealism. It is surprising that it has not, to my knowledge, been posed.

This is how the challenge might go. In the instructions it gives to the holders of sovereign power when *Recht* is instantiated and to all persons when *Recht* is not instantiated, Kant's *Rechtslehre* favors equal domains of external freedom, ultimately to be secured under a republican constitution, which requires equal access to political participation and thus popular sovereignty on equal terms. It is not hard to sketch how this preference for equality can be supported on the basis of Kant's moral philosophy: it would be morally wrong for some to claim more external freedom and more access to political participation than can possibly be granted to all others as well.[48] Now, if the independence thesis were correct, then Kant would need to offer for his egalitarian preference another defense that appeals solely to the interest of persons in their own external freedom and not to any principle of universalizability. However, no such defense appears in the text. One can still insist, of course, that Kant really meant his *Rechtslehre* to be presentable on its own, but one can do so only at the cost of accusing Kant of introducing the egalitarian preference surreptitiously—either by equivocating on the word "universal"[49] or by illicitly appealing to morality while pretending not to do so. Because the independence thesis requires such a severe accusation, it should be abandoned in favor of the more charitable interpretation defended by Kersting and assumed by Rawls.

I am not sure whether I can adequately meet this challenge, but the following points may make a decent start. To begin with, let me note that I would not view it as a great disaster to have to accuse Kant of the smuggling operation effected by the equivocal use of the word "universal," because, as far as I can see, Kant is undeniably involved in precisely this smuggling operation in the important §2 (*DR*, 6:246–47). He gives there two formulations of a "juridical postulate of practical reason," apparently without noticing the difference between them. One formulation suggests that it would violate the universal principle of right (would constitute "a contradiction of external freedom with itself"—6:246, 24–25) if the use of a usable object were forbidden to all persons (6:246, 10–17; cf. 6:252, 13–15, 6:301, 9–10).[50] The other formulation asserts that each person is equally permitted, and on the same terms of original appropriation, to acquire unowned objects (6:247, 1–6). Obviously, the latter claim is stronger than the former by demanding not merely that each usable object must be accessible to some person(s), but that each such object must be accessible to *any* person on *equal* terms (that is, on the basis of temporal priority). Insofar as the smuggling accusation is true (at least in regard to this passage), it must count against Kant himself and, if anything, *for* my interpretation.

Still, it would be much nicer if the enterprise I read Kant as engaged in could be reconstructed as successful, or at least promising. And, indeed, I believe that a defense of the egalitarian preference in terms of salience is no less promising than many of Kant's rather weak arguments—especially in part 1, (*Privatrecht*) of the *DR*—for more specific solutions ("secondary preferences"). Kant actually presents an argument of this kind:

> "All actions relating to the right of other human beings whose maxim is incompatible with publicity are wrong (*unrecht*)."
>
> This principle should be considered not merely an *ethical* one (belonging to the *Tugendlehre*), but also a *juridical* one (concerning the *Recht* of human beings). For a maxim that I must not *declare openly* without thereby ruining my own intention, that must absolutely be *kept secret* if it is to succeed, and that I cannot *publicly acknowledge* without thereby inevitably provoking the resistance of all against my plans—such a maxim can derive this necessary and universal, hence a priori foreseeable, resistance of all against me only from the injustice with which it threatens everyone (*PP*, 8:381, 24–35).

I read this passage as further explicating our juridical obligation to cooperate in the establishment and maintenance of *Recht*. To be juridically permissible, the conduct of persons must anticipate a practicable and realistically attainable effective legal order. Conduct that, if fully public, would mobilize widespread resistance fails this test and thus is juridically impermissible. Conduct that anticipates an inegalitarian legal order is a special case: there would be widespread resistance to such conduct, if it were fully public, and the attempt to establish such an inegalitarian legal order, too, would be widely resisted and is thus unrealistic.

This argument works, however, only if persons are roughly equal in strength and competence. If they are not, then it is the attempt to establish equality under the law that is unrealistic, because this bargain offers a much more favorable cost-benefit ratio to the weak and to those who lack the competence to follow the rules reliably than to the strong and competent. A legal order that is to find broad support and is to maintain an enduring equilibrium among rationally self-interested persons (or intelligent devils) must achieve a more equal distribution of incentives toward participation, must accommodate persons in rough proportion to the cost and value of their participation. If it is to govern rational persons concerned to maximize the security and extent of their own external freedom, such an order must assign larger domains of external freedom to the strong and competent. These thoughts lead to the objection that, even if the publicity argument does, without appeal to a (moral) universalizability principle, support a secondary preference for equality, this preference is for the wrong, un-Kantian sort of equality.

But is it really? Consider how Kant relates the egalitarian preference to the legally inferior status of women, which he repeatedly endorses (e.g., *TP*, 8:292, 4, 8:295, 15; *DR*, 6:314, 29): "Thus, if the question is raised whether it conflicts with the equality of spouses that the law says about the man in relation to the woman: he shall be your master (he the commanding, she the obeying part), then [the answer is that] this cannot be viewed as conflicting with the natural equality of a human couple so long as this mastership is based only on the man's natural superiority in the capacity to further the common interest of the household" (*DR*, 6:279, 16–25).

It would seem then that the egalitarian preference Kant himself (here at least) endorses is rather like the one that can be supported by the morality-free argument I have sketched—and, sadly, rather unlike the one we would expect to flow from Kant's morality. There is some reason then to keep faith in my interpretation of Kant as holding that the *Rechtslehre*, its secondary preferences included, can successfully be presented on its own.

Here it may be said once again that my reading is uncharitable by saddling Kant with a political doctrine that is morally odious by our current standards as well as by Kant's own, properly understood. My response is that, while there may be more charitable *mis*interpretations, mine is actually the most charitable interpretation available to us. Kant clearly did hold inegalitarian views with respect to women and members of the lower classes—these views occur too frequently and are too sharply expressed to be discounted as slips of the pen. On my reading, these views can be explained and, to some extent, excused by reference to his goal of developing a *freestanding* liberalism—a goal that he may well have thought morally important for much the same reasons Rawls deems it so. I find this reading the most charitable even though it leads me to conclude that Kant's attempt fails in the end to specify a liberalism that both Kantian moralists and intelligent devils can endorse.

NOTES

1. John Rawls, "Justice as Fairness: Political not Metaphysical," *Philosophy and Public Affairs* 14, no. 3 (1985): 223–52.

2. When insisting on this point, Rawls was criticizing also the way he had described his conception of justice as described in *A Theory of Justice*, remarking that in this earlier work "no distinction is drawn between moral and political philosophy" and "nothing is made of the contrast between comprehensive philosophical and moral doctrines and conceptions limited to the domain of the political.... Although the distinction between a political conception of justice and a comprehensive philosophical doctrine is not discussed in *Theory*, once the question is raised, it is clear, I think, that the text regards justice as fairness and utilitarianism as comprehensive, or partially comprehensive, doctrines." John Rawls, *Political Liberalism* (New York: Columbia University Press, 1993), xv–xvi (hereafter cited parenthetically in the text as *PL*).

3. I will cite only the introductory materials (6:203–28) of Kant's *Metaphysik der Sitten*, or *Metaphysics of Morals*, as MM; materials from the first part, *Metaphysische Anfangsgründe der Rechtslehre*, or *Doctrine of Right* (6:229–372), as *DR*; and materials from the second part, *Metaphysische Anfangsgründe der Tugendlehre*, or *Doctrine of Virtue* (6:373–493), as *DV*. In quoting or citing these materials, I also append line numbers when appropriate. All translations of Kant's works are my own. I use the word "*Rechtslehre*" to signify Kant's liberalism as developed throughout his later political writings.

4. Cf. *PL*, 78, where Rawls holds that Kant's comprehensive liberalism expresses the "ethical value of autonomy."

5. His distinction between *comprehensive* and *political* conceptions of social justice is, then, not exhaustive, though the two labels are, of course, mutually exclusive.

6. For a different view, see Hunter, chapter 7 of this volume.

7. See Rawls's self-criticism cited in note 2.

8. Let me cite one sample passage suggesting that juridical possession presupposes (inner) freedom of the will and the categorical imperative: "No one should be surprised that the theoretical principles of external mine and thine trail off into the intelligible and represent no expanded knowledge: for the concept of freedom on which they rest is incapable of a deduction of its possibility and can only be inferred from the practical law of reason (the categorical imperative) as a fact of reason" (*DR*, 6:252, 24–30; cf. 6:245, 16–21). I should add that my own previous understanding of Kant's political philosophy was hardly clear on this point either. See Thomas W. Pogge, "Kant's Theory of Justice," *Kant-Studien* 79 (1988): 407–33.

9. Mark the sense of triumph Kant expresses when he finds himself compelled to conclude that his moral philosophy presupposes his transcendental idealism: "Practical reason itself, without any collusion with the speculative, provides reality to a supersensible object of the category of causality, viz., to freedom . . . ; i.e., it confirms through a fact what there could only be *thought*. This strange but incontrovertible assertion of the speculative Critique, that *the thinking subject is only an appearance to itself in inner intuition*, now finds its full confirmation in the critique of practical reason" (*CPrR*, 5:6, 7–16).

10. See, for example, *GW*, 4:428, 21–29, with 4:446–48; *CPrR*, 5:87, 3–4, and 5:162, 17–20; *RE*, 6:27–28; and *DV*, 6:434–35. Cf. also *CPrR*, 5:97, 6–7 on imputation pursuant to the moral law (categorical imperative).

11. On this reading, Kant may still be committed to the claim—synthetic and made outside the *Doctrine of Right*—that all persons have moral personality.

12. In an earlier parallel passage, Kant defines *Recht* as "the restriction of the freedom of each to the condition of its coexistence [*Zusammenstimmung*] with the freedom of everyone insofar as this freedom is possible according to a universal law" (*TP*, 8:289–90).

13. But does this not go against how Kant uses the same expression in the first formula of the categorical imperative: "Act only on that maxim through which you can at the same time will that it become a universal law" (*GW*, 4:421, 7–8)? It is true, of course, that the categorical imperative involves the idea of equality under the law. But this idea is not implicit in the concept of a universal law; rather, it arises through how the categorical imperative constructs universal laws from one agent's contemplated maxim(s): The very permission one is inclined to give to oneself is made universal, that is, extended to all. See Thomas W. Pogge, "The Categorical Imperative," in *Grundlegung zur Metaphysik der Sitten: Ein kooperativer Kommentar*, ed. O. Höffe (Frankfurt: Vittorio Klostermann, 1989), 172–93; reprinted in *Critical Essays on Kant's Groundwork of the Metaphysics of Morals*, ed. P. Guyer (Lanham, Md.: Rowman and Littlefield, 1998).

14. Kant suggests that these effectiveness conditions are not affected by empirical information about human beings: "However good-natured and law-abiding one may imagine human beings, it nevertheless lies a priori in the rational idea of such a (non-juridical) state that, before a public law-governed condition has been established, individual human beings, peoples, and states can never be secure from violence against one another resulting from each one's own right to do *what seems right and good to it* independently of another's opinion" (*DR*, 6:312, 6–12). I am not so sure that he can exclude a priori the possibility that some species of persons might spontaneously converge upon a single system of rules and then follow these rules correctly without any further incentives. Still, the main point, which I do not contest, is the converse: one cannot exclude a priori the possibility that persons will fail spontaneously to converge upon a single system of rules and then to follow these rules correctly without any further incentives. Kant's "whole of conditions" thus cannot be reduced to the merely notional existence of a universal body of law that, if correctly followed by all, would ensure mutual consistency.

15. This sentence states merely that such redundant restrictions are not part of *Recht*; and this does not entail that they are inconsistent with *Recht* or "unrecht"—though Kant, as we shall see, has a tendency to slide from one claim to the other.

16. It is worth correcting here three interrelated mistakes Kant tends to make in this context. The first is that he tends to associate the just explicated consequence of his definition of *Recht*, A, with the claim, B, that inner states *cannot* be made the object of external legislation. (He opens the *Doctrine of Right* proper by writing that it will have to do with "the laws for which an external legislation is possible"—6:229, 5–6; see also *MM*, 6:220, 12–13.) Claim B goes beyond the definition of *Recht* and is actually false. For it is surely not impossible to promulgate laws that require or forbid certain inner states, for example, setting oneself a certain end (intention). And it is also not impossible to apply such laws accurately and effectively—indeed, most existing legal systems rely on findings of intent (*mens rea*) in defining crimes (e.g., murder) and in dispensing punishments. What Kant should say about such external laws is not

that they are impossible, but that they make no contribution to the maintenance of secure domains of external freedom and are thus not among the conditions under which each person's freedom can coexist with that of all others according to a universal law of freedom. Such laws—among which is of course the categorical imperative, which governs the agent's inner choice of maxims—fall outside *Recht* as Kant defines it. What is necessary for *Recht* is only persons' outward conformity to law, the legality of their conduct—and not inner conformity or morality.

The second mistake is that Kant conflates the definitional point about the *content* of legal restrictions necessary for *Recht* with a similar point about the *criteria* involved in such restrictions. The former point, A, is that the laws necessary for any particular instantiation of *Recht* will not constrain persons' inner states. This point is true. The latter point, C, is that such a body of law will constrain persons' external conduct by reference only to outer criteria. This claim is false, as can easily be seen through an example. Conflicts over the use of external objects can be avoided by a body of law that ensures that each object has at most one owner. But such conflicts can also be avoided by a body of law that incorporates familiar exceptions—exceptions that, for example, allow me to use your boat and forbid you to prevent me from using your boat, if we have certain inner states (e.g., we both believe that someone else is drowning and that I need the boat to rescue her and intend to do so). These laws, which restrict your use of your boat in exceptional circumstances and my use of your boat otherwise, make just as necessary a contribution to one instantiation of *Recht* as the more straightforward law, which restricts only my use of your boat, makes to another. A body of law that makes *criterial* use of inner states does not thereby overstep the mandate of *Recht*, which is to maintain mutually secure domains of external freedom.

At times, Kant conflates the two points I have last distinguished, A and C, with yet a fourth point, D, according to which legal restrictions (and institutional mechanisms), in order to fall within the mandate of *Recht*, must be selected solely by reference to the purpose of maintaining mutually secure domains of external freedom. (We must not prefer one property regime over another on the grounds that the latter would engender hunger among the poor—unless such hunger would make them rebellious and thereby render persons' domains of external freedom less secure.) This claim D is distinct from the others and, like B and C, does not follow from the definition of *Recht*.

17. As Kant suggests through the Latin *"status iuridicus"* (*TP*, 8:292, 33; *PP*, 8:383, 13). He can appropriately use the adjectives *"rechtlich"* and *"gesetzlich"* in German, so long as these are understood as "instantiating *Recht*" and "governed by laws," respectively. Translations as "rightful," "lawful," or "legal" are mistaken because a juridical state may well be unjust (in reference to natural law), and, as constitutive of legality, cannot itself be legal, or lawful, in reference to positive law. (Cf. how *rechtlich* contrasts with *rechtmäßig* at *PP*, 8:373n, 30–31.)

18. If this explication of Kant's definition is correct, then the word *"Recht"* as used in this definition is not equivalent to either "law" or "(social) justice." When law is incomplete or ineffective, there is law without *Recht*. And when law is complete and effective, there may be *Recht* without justice, for example, *Recht* that imposes very different constraints on different persons. This is not to deny, of course, that Kant also uses the word *Recht* in its common meaning, as denoting a society's body of law, as well as of course in its even more common meaning of "(a) right (to)."

19. Gregor Johann Mendel (1822–1884) was an Austrian botanist.

20. The formulations of the condition differ, but they do not differ much. I will return to this point.

21. It is this theorem that, in the introduction to the *Doctrine of Virtue*, Kant refers to as the "supreme principle of the *Rechtslehre*" and as an "analytic proposition" (6:396, 2, 10–11).

22. Sam Kerstein has pointed out that the "or" could also be read as explicative. He adds that, though it is quite hard to see how the two phrases it connects could be equivalent, they are too obscure for this possibility to be ruled out. I concede all three points, but still find the interpretation I provide in the text more convincing than its two alternatives.

23. This problem may seem to be a reason for holding that at least here the word "universal" should be read in the strong sense, so that the mutually consistent domains of external freedom envisaged in (1b) are required to be *equal* domains. I reject this reading for two reasons. First, the word "universal" occurs in (1) only once, in reference to both cases 1 and 2. For case 1, however, Kant needs the word "universal" to have its weak sense because he holds it to be juridically impermissible to disobey *any* existing instantiation of *Recht*—whether it provides equality under the law or not (see note 47 below). Second, I want to avoid, if at all possible, the conclusion that the equal juridical standing of all persons is smuggled in, that Kant begs rather than answers the question why an action that anticipates an *in*egalitarian instantiation of *Recht* should count as juridically wrong (as not according with *Recht*). I will have much more to say on this issue below.

24. We need not take it seriously, if we allow ourselves to correct Kant's "second mistake," detailed in note 16 above.

25. See also *DR*, 6:343, 23–25, 6:350, 6–8; and *PP*, 8:349n, 16–24.

26. This needs to be put more carefully. The fact that a move is impermissible (does not accord with *Recht*) entails that it is permissible to obstruct it—but not necessarily that anyone may do so. For it is possible that, if several persons try to obstruct an impermissible move, these would-be obstructors will obstruct one another. A legal order may therefore have to restrict the permission to use coercion by further rules or to certain officials.

Also, the fact that a move is permissible does not entail that it is impermissible to preempt it, thus rendering it impermissible. It may be permissible for any person to occupy some as yet unoccupied piece of land or space with the consequence that moves into it by others become impermissible and obstruction of such moves permissible.

27. Kant offers a very compressed derivation of this theorem in §D (*DR*, 6:231). One might comment that it is indeed relatively straightforward to get from Kant's concept of *Recht* to the permission to use coercion against impermissible conduct if such coercion is a matter of preventing a transgression at the border (blocking someone's path into another's domain) or a matter of terminating a transgression (ejecting someone from another's domain). The connection is harder to make when it is a matter of punishing someone who is well within her or his own domain for a transgression that is now wholly in the past. One might try to argue here that such punishment is permissible because it is a necessary by-product of a permissible prior (unsuccessful) attempt at deterrence.

28. These two components are introduced at the end of section II above.

29. This reasoning could be strengthened significantly by detailing how the establishment of *Recht* will also engender many new conduct options—involving new social practices or new technologies, for example—that would never emerge without an effective legal order.

30. "Freedom (independence from the coercive choice of another), insofar as it can coexist with the freedom of everyone else according to a universal law of freedom, is this sole original right to which every human being is entitled by virtue of his humanity" (*DR*, 6:237, 29–32). "The concept of an external *Recht* derives entirely from the concept of *freedom* in the external relations of human beings to one another and has nothing whatever to do with the end that all human beings have by nature (the goal of happiness)" (*TP*, 8:289, 29–33). Note that asserting the avoidance of interpersonal conflicts as the rationale would not explain Kant's exclusion from *Recht* of what I have called redundant restrictions.

31. See once more, for example, the quote from *DR*, 6:312, 6–12, cited in note 14.

32. For a different view, see Ripstein, chapter 2 of this volume.

33. In particular, Kant must exclude the preferability of a legal order that, though it constrains the external freedom of persons more than is necessary to establish mutually secure domains, enhances their external freedom on the whole by facilitating (e.g., through technology) the removal of natural obstacles and threats or the creation of additional options. This difficulty does not come into view for Kant because he does not clarify his notion of external freedom and, in particular, does not discuss what obstacles and threats are to count as reducing a person's external freedom. Without explicit defense he thus reasons as if the interest in

securing one's external freedom against obstructing actions by other persons were exhaustive of the interest in external freedom. Having highlighted this problem, I will use the latter, briefer label from now on.

34. We can learn from this paragraph that Kant's position on the point of government and an effective legal order is quite close to that defended by Isaiah Berlin and differs dramatically from what Berlin attributes to Kant: the view that law and government should be concerned to enhance citizens' positive freedom or moral autonomy. Contrast Isaiah Berlin, "Two Concepts of Liberty," in Isaiah Berlin, *Four Essays on Liberty* (Oxford: Oxford University Press, 1969), 118–72, and the Rawls passages cited in note 4 (*PL*, 99), with, for example: "But woe to the legislator willing through coercion to bring about a constitution directed to ethical ends! For he would thereby not merely attain the opposite of the ethical [ends], but would also undermine and render insecure his political [ends]" (*RE*, 6:96, 1–4).

35. This is not, of course, meant to be a satisfactory argument, only the sketch of an argument that Kant might reasonably have thought to be available. It is not clear, in particular, how the argument can derive the interest from the capacity and how it can confer special significance upon obstructions *by other persons*.

36. Here it might be said that Kant's argument is after all comprehensive by declaring irrelevant all the other interests that persons actually have or that might be attributed to them. In one sense this charge is trivially true. But it is also self-defeating by dissolving the distinction between political and comprehensive conceptions of social justice: *any* argument seeking to justify social institutions by reference to the interests of persons affected by them—and how else are social institutions to be justified?—will attach relative weights to indefinitely many possible interests. The charge becomes more substantial if it accuses Kant of *idealizing* where he should have been *abstracting*. For this distinction, see Onora O'Neill, *Constructions of Reason: Explorations of Kant's Practical Philosophy* (Cambridge: Cambridge University Press, 1989), chapter 11, and *Towards Justice and Virtue: A Constructive Account of Practical Reasoning* (Cambridge: Cambridge University Press, 1996), chapter 2. Instead of assuming that all other interests have zero weight, Kant ought to have made no assumptions about their relative weights at all. But it is unclear how an argument that leaves open whether persons' interest in salvation, say, is infinitely greater or infinitely smaller than their interest in external freedom (or somewhere in between) can support any substantive conclusions at all. And yet, as the next paragraph of text brings out, Kant does accommodate O'Neill to some extent by showing that his argument covers at least a certain range of interest attributions: Thanks to a shared strong interest in their own external freedom, moral and selfish persons can, despite discrepancies among their other interests, converge upon the same set of social arrangements. This suggests how Kant might have tried to meet the accusation that, by focusing on persons' interest in external freedom, he is embracing an ideal of the "unencumbered self"—an accusation advanced in Michael Sandel, *Liberalism and the Limits of Justice* (Cambridge: Cambridge University Press, 1982). Kant could have argued that the interests of deeply social persons, just as those of rugged individualists, involve a basic interest in external freedom. Still, it remains possible to imagine persons for whom this interest is completely dominated by other (e.g., religious) interests.

37. I am here alluding of course to Kant's famous saying: "If justice perishes, then it no longer has any value that human beings are living on the earth" (*DR*, 6:332, 1–3).

38. Absent this fact, humankind might well have been caught in a catch-22 situation: needing the security of a juridical state in order to develop effective moral motives and needing effective moral motives to make the transition into a juridical state.

39. Wolfgang Kersting, *Wohlgeordnete Freiheit* (Berlin: Walter de Gruyter, 1984), 37–42. The foremost champion of the "independence thesis" is Ebbinghaus, who has (rather polemically) argued for it in a number of essays, which are collected in Julius Ebbinghaus, *Gesammelte Schriften*, vol. 2, *Philosophie der Freiheit* (Bonn: Bouvier, 1988). Kersting also cites Klaus Reich, *Kant and Rousseau* (Tübingen: Mohr-Siebeck, 1936), 17; and Georg Geismann: *Ethik und Herrschaftsordnung* (Tübingen: Mohr-Siebeck, 1974), 56 (55–88 are pertinent).

40. Kersting, *Wohlgeordnete Freiheit*, 37.

41. Ibid., 38.

42. Kersting commits this conflation several times in different guises. One interesting further example comes in a long footnote (*Wohlgeordnete Freiheit*, 41, note 63), which presents an apparently devastating refutation of Ebbinghaus. Kersting first quotes Ebbinghaus's acknowledgement that "*Recht*, as the a priori law of the determination of external freedom, is required by the categorical imperative as the law of pure practical reason" (Ebbinghaus, *Philosophie der Freiheit*, 242; Kersting quotes this essay from another source). Kersting then quotes further that the "attempt to conceive of *Recht* in its objective perfection as dependent on the legislation of inner freedom and hence of ethics is from Kant's point of view a wholly absurd conclusion ... that has been drawn from an erroneous interpretation of the dependence of both legislations on the categorical imperative as the highest moral principle comprising both *Recht* and ethics" (243). Since Kersting conflates the claim that the categorical imperative requires *Recht* with the claim that *Recht* is dependent on the categorical imperative, he infers from these quotes that Ebbinghaus is forced to attribute to Kant the absurd view that the categorical imperative, too, is independent from Kant's teachings on freedom and autonomy. But there is a much more plausible way of reading Ebbinghaus: In the first passage, Ebbinghaus says that the categorical imperative requires *Recht*. In the second passage, Ebbinghaus *denies* that *Recht* is dependent on the categorical imperative. Ebbinghaus is not saying there, as Kersting has it, that the dependence of both legislations on the categorical imperative exists but has been misinterpreted. Rather, Ebbinghaus is rejecting as erroneous the interpretation that takes both legislations (rather than ethical legislation alone) to be dependent on the categorical imperative. Kersting cannot see this reading of Ebbinghaus because he cannot see that Ebbinghaus, by saying that the categorical imperative requires (entails) *Recht*, has by no means conceded the dependence of *Recht* on the categorical imperative.

43. Kersting, *Wohlgeordnete Freiheit*, 38, note 57; cf. note 8 above.

44. By generative rules I mean rules enabling voluntary rule changes. Examples are rules governing unilateral appropriation, contracting, and political decision making. Kant briefly mentions the distinction at *DR*, 6:237, 18–23.

45. A set of rules is complete if and only if it uniquely sorts all possible actions into those that are legal and those that are not. I take for granted that the rules must also satisfy the universal principle of *Recht*—for example, must count as legal any action that it is illegal to obstruct.

46. His preferred rules for the unilateral appropriation of land are a good example: "as if the soil were saying: if you cannot protect me, then you cannot command me either" (*DR*, 6:265, 4–5). States therefore own oceanic fishing grounds and continental shelves as far as their land-based cannons reach (6:265, 5–10).

47. For example, when he insists again and again that it is wrong for subjects to disobey the sovereign or its authorized representatives (*DR*, 6:320–23, 6:371–72; *TP*, 8:299–305; *PP*, 8:382; *Refl* 7989, 19:574–5, and 594 [Reflections 7989 and 8051]). It is worth stressing that Kant does not declare it wrong to disobey a tyrant who rules by whim, who does not specify and maintain mutually secure domains of external freedom (*Rechtssicherheit*). But Kant does not clarify *how* law-governed an exercise of power must be for it to count as establishing a juridical condition. And he does not explain why the distinction between whimsical and law-governed oppression should have such great significance for persons interested in their external freedom. On this point, see Ripstein, chapter 2 of this volume.

48. Filling in such a sketch is much harder, as numerous attempts in the secondary literature attest. But let me here just stipulate, for the sake of the argument, that Kant has a promising argument of this sort.

49. This sort of "smuggling operation" was briefly discussed in note 23.

50. Such a universal prohibition would be a paradigm case of a redundant restriction, one that makes no contribution to the maintenance of mutually secure domains of external freedom.

REALIZING EXTERNAL FREEDOM:
THE KANTIAN ARGUMENT FOR A WORLD STATE

Louis-Philippe Hodgson

The central thesis of Kant's political philosophy is that rational agents living side by side undermine one another's freedom so long as they remain in a state of nature. The claim is primarily intended as an account of the legitimacy of existing states: it entails that a state is justified in imposing the rule of law on individuals sharing a territory, because doing so amounts to preventing them from undermining one another's freedom. But, as Kant noticed, the point also has implications for international relations. A state puts an end to the state of nature among those living on a given territory, but if a plurality of states do so on different territories, then *they* remain in a state of nature with respect to one another. In such a situation, Kant's thesis seems to entail that imposing the rule of law upon *states,* so as to prevent them from undermining one another's freedom, would be justified. In short, the ideal of universal freedom seems to demand nothing less than the establishment of a world state.

My aim in what follows is to argue that this radical conclusion does indeed follow from the principles of Kant's political philosophy. More precisely, I

Earlier versions of this paper were presented in the Harvard University Workshop on Moral and Political Philosophy, in the University of Toronto Workshop in Ethical and Political Philosophy, and in the Queen's University Political Philosophy Reading Group. Shorter versions were presented at the Annual Congress of the Canadian Philosophical Association at the University of Western Ontario, and at the Tenth International Kant Congress in São Paulo. The final version of this paper was submitted in 2008. I am grateful to the audiences on all these occasions for their questions and comments. I also wish to thank Christine Korsgaard, T. M. Scanlon, and Arthur Ripstein for invaluable advice and suggestions.

want to present a detailed Kantian argument for the thesis that states have a *duty of right* to form a world state—which means, as Kant uses the phrase, that they could justifiably be forced to do so.[1] Although I believe that there is much to be said for the Kantian principles I invoke along the way, I do not attempt to defend them here. In that sense, I am putting forward a conditional claim: I argue that *if* we accept Kant's starting point, then we find ourselves committed to the ideal of a world state. The claim remains important, however, both because it fleshes out an important consequence of Kant's political philosophy, and because the consequence is one about which Kant himself had serious misgivings. That said, I should stress that it is not my goal here to elucidate Kant's cryptic remarks on world government. I state briefly at two points (in sections 2 and 6) why his main qualms about a world state seem to me ill founded; otherwise, my focus is on the positive Kantian argument that can be constructed in defense of a world state rather than on Kant's own elusive treatment of the issue.[2]

One might question the point of arguing that states have a duty of right to form a world state, given that any attempt to establish a world state through force would lead to chaos and destruction. But the claim's importance lies elsewhere. For one thing, it means that we should strive to establish a world state, at least if we follow Kant in thinking that there is a moral requirement to do what right requires (*MM*, 6:394). What is more, it means that an established world state would be justified in imposing coercive laws on *all* states—rogue states as well as willing members. In other words, although using force to establish a world state from scratch would be unwise, the fact that doing so is in principle justifiable shows that the legitimacy of a world state would not depend on the actual agreement of states—just as the legitimacy of existing states does not depend on the actual agreement of their citizens.

I proceed as follows. I begin in section 1 with an account of Kant's argument for the state in the case of individuals living side by side. I then explain in section 2 how the problem faced by individuals living side by side also arises for states existing side by side. The point is fleshed out in sections 3 and 4, which together form the core of the argument for a world state. I first argue in section 3 that legitimate states have a right to freedom similar to that of individuals. The very suggestion that collective entities such as states can have rights may seem problematic; I show that the idea is metaphysically respectable by explaining how a state's right to freedom simply follows from that of its citizens. I go on to argue in section 4 that states existing side by side have a duty of right to form a world state. I show that the international state of nature is incompatible with the freedom of states, so that forcing states to leave that condition—as a world state would by imposing the rule of law upon them—is consistent with their right to freedom. I conclude my discussion in sections 5 and 6 by showing that the argument I present requires a world state that is federal in structure, and that this model escapes the main objections traditionally leveled at the idea of a world state.

I. Living Side by Side: The Case of Individuals

Let me begin by explaining briefly how I understand Kant's argument for the state in the case of individuals living side by side. Doing so will provide guidance for the rest of our discussion, since the same general considerations apply in the case of states existing side by side; it will also show how the establishment of a multiplicity of states gives rise to a problem that only a world state can solve. The argument for individuals starts with an idea that is fundamental for Kant's entire political philosophy: that human beings have, in virtue of their rational nature, a *right to freedom,* that is, a right to "independence from being constrained by another's choice ... insofar as it can coexist with the freedom of every other in accordance with a universal law" (*MM,* 6:237). That right, it should be noted, concerns exclusively what Kant calls *external freedom.* By contrast with internal freedom, whose demands provide the foundation for Kant's moral philosophy,[3] external freedom does not concern the quality of an agent's will, but only her freedom of action—that is, her ability to set and pursue ends for herself without being subject to others' choices.[4]

Two further points should be stressed about the right to freedom. The first is that Kant does not understand freedom of action merely in terms of noninterference (as Hobbes does, for instance).[5] Rather, he explicitly adopts a Rousseauian conception that requires "*independence* from being constrained by another's choice" (*MM,* 6:237; emphasis added).[6] The nuance is crucial, since it acknowledges that one person can undermine another's freedom without actually interfering with her choices. To take an obvious example, suppose that I order you at gunpoint to do something that you had already resolved to do. On a Hobbesian view, we have to say that I do not undermine your freedom, since I do not interfere with your choice. Yet that cannot be right: my ordering you at gunpoint is sufficient to make you unfree regardless of the content of my orders, since you are in any case subject to my choices. Kant's view acknowledges as much.

The second point I want to stress is the limitation built into the right to freedom. As we saw, an agent's right to independence from constraint extends "insofar as it can coexist with the freedom of every other in accordance with a universal law" (*MM*, 6:237). Positively, this means that a rational agent has the right to do anything that does not interfere with another's right to freedom. But it also means that an agent's right to freedom only extends to choices that are consistent with the right to freedom of all. The point is important because it shows how the use of force can be compatible with the right to freedom. If a certain action of mine—say, tying you down—would be incompatible with your freedom, then it follows that the use of force to prevent me from doing so would be, in Kant's words, a "*hindering of a hindrance to freedom*" (*MM*, 6:231). That particular use of force against me would accordingly be consistent with universal freedom, and hence justified. Note that, on Kant's view, this is the *only* way to make the use of force fully compatible with the right to freedom. Any argument to justify the state's coercive power must therefore proceed along such lines: it must show that existing side by side in the state of nature is a hindrance to freedom, and that coercively imposing the rule of law amounts to hindering that hindrance to freedom. Let us now try to see how these claims might be established.

Why is existing side by side in a state of nature *in itself* a hindrance to freedom? In a nutshell, because individuals can only exist side by side consistently with their freedom if they have certain rights against one another, and these rights are not to be had in a state of nature. More precisely, the idea is that free coexistence requires the possibility of having rights to external objects, such as property and contract rights;[7] but such rights can only be *provisional* in the state of nature, since no one has the authority to adjudicate and enforce them.[8] Rights to external objects must therefore remain ineffective in a state of nature, and that makes individuals dependent on one another's choices. There are thus two main claims to establish here: first, that the absence of determinate and enforceable external rights—what Kant calls *conclusive* external rights—is an unjustified restriction of freedom; and second, that external rights can only be conclusive in a civil condition.

The considerations supporting the first point are straightforward. Take first the case of property. Suppose I want to use a certain object as part of a project—say, a hammer to build a house. If I can have no determinate and enforceable right to the hammer, then others cannot rightfully be excluded from using the hammer; as a consequence, whether I can pursue my end or not depends on their choices, since they are entitled to grab the hammer as soon as I let go of it.[9] Clearly, in such a case I lack the kind of control over the hammer that is required for pursuing my project; and the same problem will arise for any other object or project. In short, under such a system, I cannot make external objects into means for my ends *even when I would wrong no one by doing so*.[10] Such a restriction on my ability to set and pursue ends for myself is unjustifiable.

Analogous considerations apply to the case of contract rights. If I can have no determinate and enforceable contract rights, then I cannot involve others in my projects without becoming dependent on their choices, since in the end the choice whether to do their share or not is entirely up to them. My partners may turn out to be respectful and cooperative, of course; but I remain entirely dependent on their being so. The absence of conclusive contract rights thus means that I cannot have the actions of another person available as a means in my projects *even if he agrees to the arrangement*. This particular means must remain beyond my control, even though I would wrong no one by availing myself of it. Once again, this constitutes an unjustifiable restriction on my freedom.

I should emphasize that the worry here is not that, absent conclusive rights, the *range* of projects open to me would be restricted. It is true that under such circumstances I could only pursue projects involving objects I can physically hold onto and requiring no help from others; but that is not the point of the argument. The point is that, absent conclusive external rights, I cannot have means that *should* be available to me—things that are no one else's property and actions that others are willing to make available to me. Since no rational agent would be wronged by my making such objects into means for my ends, there is no justification for my not being able to do so: my ability to set and pursue ends for myself is restricted in a way that is not required by the freedom of others. That is why the absence of conclusive property and contract rights violates my right to freedom.

Why can there be no conclusive rights in the state of nature? Because the conditions that must obtain for rights to be legitimately adjudicated and enforced are jointly constitutive of the civil condition: there is no conceptual space between adjudicating and enforcing rights on the one hand, and leaving the state of nature on the other. The argument for this point starts from a simple fact about rights enforcement: an action can count as the enforcement of a right only if it is consistent with the right to freedom of all, *including the person against whom the right is being enforced*.[11] If that condition fails to obtain, then the action is a wrong against someone, and therefore cannot be the enforcement of a right. The point is important because it means that whether external rights can be enforced in a state of nature depends on there being an agent who can enforce such rights in a way that wrongs no one. Kant's view—by contrast to Locke's, notably—is that there can be no such agent outside a civil condition.[12] I take his reasoning to be the following. When an agent enforces rights, it must act on its judgment of what right requires. But that can be compatible with everyone's freedom only if the agent has standing to impose its judgments about right upon others—that is, if the agent's judgments are *authoritative*. If that is not the case—if the agent's judgments are simply those of a private individual—then there is no reason for others to accept them rather than resist with force. And since there are only private individuals in a state of nature, it follows that, strictly speaking, there can be no enforcement of rights.[13]

An example will help. Suppose that you claim a piece of land as yours in the state of nature. Can you use force to protect that right against me? Kant's claim is that, so long as you remain a private individual, you cannot do so in a fully justified manner. For although you may judge that you have the right to use force against me to protect your property, I am entitled to disagree with you, and you have no authority over me with respect to such matters. That is the case, I should stress, even if you were on the land before I was, and even if you had already built a house on it and started growing crops. These facts may support your contention; they may even make it the case that anyone with the authority to adjudicate and enforce our rights against one another would recognize your claim; but they do not by themselves give you the authority to use force against me.[14]

How then can any agent ever be justified in adjudicating and enforcing rights? The demands set by the right to freedom in this respect are clarified by an important corollary that Kant adjoins to it: the right to equality, which requires "independence from being bound by others to more than one can in turn bind them" (*MM*, 6:237). The connection with the right to freedom should not be hard to see: if I can be bound by another in a unilateral manner, then I am subject to her choices; by contrast, if we can only bind each other according to reciprocal terms, then neither of us is subject to the other's choices, since each can be bound only by terms she also imposes on the other. The implication is that the imposition of a law can be compatible with freedom so long as it is not a law that one agent imposes upon another, but rather a law that the two agents jointly impose on each other. In this way, the right to freedom sets a requirement of *reciprocity* on the adjudication and enforcement of rights. Concretely, I take this to entail that two conditions must obtain for rights to be made conclusive: first, equal rights must be granted to all whose freedom is codependent; and second, the enforcement of rights must be uniform.[15] The first condition is the most straightforward: if you have rights that I lack (because the color of our skin differs, say), then the reciprocity requirement is plainly violated. Yet the second condition is no less important: if your rights are better protected than mine (because your gang is more powerful than mine, say), then we are no more on reciprocal terms than if our rights were unequal to begin with. To have the authority to adjudicate and enforce rights on a territory, an agent must not only lay down equal rights for all, it must also wield sufficient power to enforce those rights effectively, even in the face of widespread opposition.

It is now clear why you lack the authority to enforce rights in a state of nature. To have that kind of authority, you would have to set out to protect the rights of all whose external freedom is codependent—and hence, of all who dwell on the territory; and you would need the power to do so credibly. In other words, *to have the authority to enforce rights, you would have to make yourself into a state*—a minimal state, admittedly, but a state nonetheless. There is no conceptual space between having conclusive rights and being in a civil condition, because setting up an authority that can make rights conclusive is just the same thing as setting up a state.

Note that the requirement of reciprocity does not add anything new to the right to freedom we started with: it is already contained in that right, as Kant signals by calling the right to equality a corollary. Reciprocity is not an ideal that is added on to the requirement of independence we started with; rather, independence is *realized* for finite rational agents living side by side precisely by putting in place conditions of reciprocity. In other words, what the state must do to make its citizens suitably independent from one another is to establish conditions of reciprocity. Concretely, this means that it must put in place an effective legal system designed to protect the rights of all and to punish or exact compensation when rights are violated. In short, it must impose the rule of law on its territory.

It is thus the law's protection that grants individuals living together the independence required by their right to freedom. Of course, the rule of law does not guarantee that no rights will ever be violated; no human institution could do that, and in any case the right to freedom does not demand that much. What the right to freedom demands is the possibility of justifiably excluding others from the use of certain objects, and of justifiably forcing them to abide by their contracts. By realizing conditions of reciprocity, a well-functioning legal system allows both, and thus removes the hindrance to freedom constituted by the absence of conclusive rights.

II. The International Order (and Lack Thereof)

We have seen that individual rational agents living side by side can justifiably be forced to leave the state of nature because freedom requires conclusive rights and conclusive rights are only possible in a civil condition. In short, a state must be established on every inhabited territory. Now, were all individuals to enter into a *single* civil condition, the demands of external freedom would be fully satisfied, since no two rational agents would remain in a state of nature with respect to one another. No questions of international justice would arise, since there would be no international realm in which they could arise. But matters are different if several groups of individuals form separate civil conditions on their respective territories, as has been the case in our world: questions then arise concerning the relations of these groups to one another.[16] To be exact, the existence of multiple civil conditions gives rise to two types of problems: problems concerning the relations of states to one another (what Kant calls the *right of nations*), and problems concerning the relations of citizens of one state either to the citizens of another state or to that state taken as a whole (what Kant calls *cosmopolitan right*).[17] Kant has important points to make about both, but my focus here will be on the former issue, which provides the starting point for the argument I want to present.

I argue in what follows that states existing side by side run into the same problem as individuals: they claim rights against each other that can only be provisional in a state of nature. This may seem odd, given what I said in the previous section about the authority of states and their role in making rights conclusive. But recall how the argument goes: a state has the authority to make rights conclusive only to the extent that it realizes conditions of reciprocity; accordingly, its authority only extends to the territory that it effectively rules. Thus, although a state makes rights conclusive for all agents dwelling on its territory, it cannot make rights conclusive with respect to agents dwelling outside that territory, be they other states or individuals.

In light of that remark, it should be clear why I am not convinced by Kant's claim that, because states "already have a rightful constitution internally," they "have outgrown the constraint of others to bring them under a more extended law-governed constitution in accordance with their concepts of right" (PP, 8:355). A legitimate state has "outgrown the constraint of others" with respect to its *internal* actions—anyone trying to take over its internal powers undermines an existing rightful condition and therefore does wrong. But since a state has no authority with respect to other states, its external actions are no different in status from those of a private individual.[18] It is therefore unclear why a legitimate state could not be forced to submit to an international rule of law, so long as the rule of law only applies to its external actions; those actions stand in need of regulation in the exact same way that the actions of private individuals in a state of nature do.[19]

Perhaps Kant thinks that a state's being internally rightful is sufficient to guarantee that its external actions will be rightful. Perhaps he thinks that, insofar as a state is internally rightful, its external actions will be grounded exclusively in public purposes, and hence that they will be restricted to what is required to protect the rights of citizens. This would rule out aggressive wars fought for private purposes (territory, wealth, glory, and so on), which may suffice to make the international order rightful.[20] I see two problems with this suggestion. One is that it is unclear why one state's public purposes could not clash with another's. Feeding the population is a public purpose, but it is quite conceivable for two states to wage a war over water availability. The second problem cuts deeper, and will be at the heart of the argument I present in section 4. To put it very broadly for now, the idea is that a state should not have to depend for its safety on whether another state's inner constitution remains rightful. For even if it were true that a fully legitimate state will never wage an aggressive war, that would not prevent any *actual* state from doing so: it would simply prevent it from remaining legitimate while doing so. That hardly provides its neighbors with the independence to which they are entitled.

The idea I just invoked—that states are entitled not to depend on one another's choices—is central to the argument I want to present. More specifically, the argument's starting point will be the claim that states have a right to freedom—or at least a right that is relevantly analogous to individuals' right to freedom. That claim is likely to be controversial, and may appear to rest on a worrisome personification of the state. I try to address the concern in the next section by showing how a state's right to freedom is directly dependent on its citizens' right to freedom—not a separate, freestanding right. In this way, although the argument I go on to present in section 4 is concerned directly with the rights of states, individuals remain its essential starting point. States occupy a prominent place only because respecting individuals' right to freedom requires respecting the rights of the collective agents they constitute—including, crucially, the state.

III. Why States Have a Right to Freedom

I argue here for a conditional claim: that if individuals have a right to freedom, then states must have a similar right that extends to whatever actions are necessary to secure their citizens' rights. In this way, the state's right to freedom derives from individuals' right to freedom properly understood. I take this to be an instance of a general phenomenon, according to which a legitimate collective agent acquires from its members the right to set and pursue its ends freely. Since the case of states raises special difficulties, I consider first a collective agent of a comparatively straightforward kind to lend support to my general contention. I explain afterward how the result applies to the state.

Suppose that a firm's workers decide to unionize: they agree on procedures by which union leaders are elected, rules that determine what these leaders can legitimately do, and so on. I want to argue that, as a result of this, the union they form has the right to set and pursue its ends freely. I start with the idea that the act by which a group becomes a collective agent is fundamentally one of *authorization*: each member authorizes certain individuals—call them the *leaders*—to do certain things on her behalf, and in virtue of that fact a collective agent is constituted. Assume for instance that the workers authorize the union leaders to negotiate work conditions for them, following the terms specified by the union charter. The leaders thereby gain the authority to represent the members within a specified domain: so long as they act within the limits set by the charter, they act for the entire group.

To see how the workers can grant rights to the union, it is helpful to think of authorization in terms of enabling another agent to exercise a certain right for oneself.[21] To take a simple example, if I authorize you to take out money for me, using my bank card and access code, then I allow you to exercise the right to withdraw money from my bank account for me. Something similar takes place in the case of the union: when the union is formed, each worker grants the union leaders the authority to exercise a certain right for her, namely, the right to negotiate freely with the employer.[22] The leaders thereby acquire a right to negotiate freely that exceeds their individual right to do so, since not only their own rights, but also the rights of all workers are at stake when they negotiate in their official capacity. If the union leaders are prevented from negotiating freely—if intimidation tactics are used against them, say—then it is not only their individual rights that are violated, but also the rights of all union members, since the exercise of all these rights is interfered with.

One might object that what is at stake in such cases is really only an individual right of each worker, namely, the right to organize. Things are not so simple. The workers' right to organize is at stake when an employer insists on negotiating with workers on an individual basis. But an employer who uses intimidation tactics against union leaders does not violate his workers' right to organize, since that right has already been exercised in the formation of the union. Indeed, the exercise of the right to organize is *presupposed* by the employer's threats: they could not have their intended effect if the workers had not formed a union. What is at stake in such cases is the workers' right to negotiate freely—a right that the union now exercises collectively on their behalf.

The way I have been attributing rights to the union may seem metaphorical at best. Let me clarify what I take the exact content of the idea to be. To say that the union has a right to negotiate freely is to say that, once the authorization has taken place, the corresponding rights of the workers can only be exercised or violated through the collective agent formed by the union. The union leaders have acquired the exclusive authority to exercise certain rights of the workers, so that those rights have become inseparable from the union; only by leaving the union altogether can a worker regain the authority to exercise them. The workers' rights have thus been collectivized in the sense that they can no longer be exercised or violated individually—they stand or fall together, as a single right. This is not to grant any primacy to collectives as such; on the contrary, whatever rights the union has must ultimately come from its members. The emphasis placed on the role of the union simply underlines that to understand how the workers' rights operate, we need to acknowledge that these rights can only be exercised jointly—

that is, we need to acknowledge that the workers have structured their rights so as to form a collective agent together.

Before moving on to the case of states, I want to stress an important qualification, namely, that the workers allow the union to exercise their rights *only as specified by the union charter*. This significantly circumscribes the union's rights: the union leaders act legitimately, and thus exercise the workers' rights, only when they act in accordance with the charter. Thus, a union would normally not exercise its members' rights if it reached an agreement with the employer about where workers should spend their holidays or about how they should vote, since both matters exceed the bounds of its authority. This points to an important fact about collective agents: the extent of their right to freedom is determined by the terms of association that bring them into existence, because those terms determine what they can legitimately do—that is, which actions of the leaders can count as actions of the collective agent. Obviously, any realistic terms of association will give the leaders some discretion as to how exactly to pursue the general ends of the association—all the more so when the ends are complex. But there are limits to that discretion: beyond a certain point an action becomes illegitimate, and is therefore no longer protected by the collective agent's right to freedom. To put the point succinctly, one might say that a collective agent's right to freedom is restricted to performing the function specified by its constitution. In that respect, the right to freedom of collective agents is less robust than that of individuals.

I have argued so far that collective agents are constituted by their authority to exercise certain rights for a group of individuals within limits dictated by their constitution, as a result of which they have a restricted right to freedom. I believe that one can account for the case of states along similar lines. Now, as I suggested above, states are not standard collective agents: they pose certain specific difficulties. Most noticeably perhaps, there is in general no datable moment at which citizens have actually authorized their state to do certain things for them, and thus nothing analogous to the act by which a union is formed. Furthermore, even if citizens wanted to authorize their state to enforce rights, it is unclear how they could do so. On a Kantian view, as we saw in section 1, no private party can have the authority to adjudicate and enforce rights that a legitimate state has. How the state could acquire that authority through an act of authorization is thus far from transparent.

I begin with the second problem, which points to a crucial difference between states and voluntary associations. A union exercises rights that its members have independently of its existence and that could be exercised individually. Exercising the rights jointly may increase the likelihood that each worker will get what she wants, and thus present a pragmatic advantage, but it does not change the nature of the rights as such. By contrast, the state's authority to enforce external rights is not one that could be exercised individually: as we saw in section 1, there can only be such authority if it is exercised jointly for all who live on a given territory—that is, for all whose freedom is codependent. The difference is significant; yet it would be a mistake to conclude that the idea of authorization has no purchase in the case of the state. Saying that the authority to enforce rights can only be exercised jointly does not amount to saying that individuals in a state of nature are entirely devoid of such authority—were that the case, it would be unclear *what* exactly the state would be exercising jointly. Individuals in a state of nature do have the authority to enforce rights; Kant's point is that the authority can only be *provisional,* because exercising it amounts to leaving the state of nature. That is precisely what the argument of section 1 shows: a group of individuals sharing a territory can only exercise their authority to enforce rights by jointly enabling a unified agent to do so on their behalf, and thus by putting in place a state. My point here is that, in doing so, they take part in a special kind of authorization—one that can only be valid if it is carried out jointly by all who live on a territory. In this way, the state's authority to enforce rights does ultimately come from its citizens; hence the justification of its authority is fundamentally contractual in nature.[23]

All this may seem to make the first problem I mentioned above more pressing still. For what good is it that citizens *could* authorize their state to enforce rights if it is generally not the case that they have actually done so? The answer is that, insofar as a state is legitimate, its citizens can be *presumed* for legal purposes to authorize its every action; whether they actually consent or not is irrelevant. The point is a straightforward consequence of the argument of section 1. As we saw there, the right to freedom of a group of individuals sharing a territory can only be respected if they have a state to secure their rights against one another. If that is correct, then rejecting the state's authority would amount to throwing away one's freedom—something that a person can never legally be deemed to do. In other words, individuals are rightfully presumed to authorize their state for the same reason that they cannot sell themselves into slavery: because from the point of view of right they cannot validly will their own unfreedom.

The dissimilarities between the case of states and that of voluntary associations are thus not as profound as they initially seem. But the question remains whether the peculiar relation of authorization that obtains between a legitimate state and its citizens suffices to grant the state a right to freedom comparable to that of other collective agents. I believe that it does. The point is most obvious if we consider the state's relation to its own citizens. With respect to them, the state clearly has a right to perform its function freely: any citizen who interferes with the state's administration of justice commits a wrong, since she acts to undermine the conditions under which she can coexist freely with her fellow citizens. But the state must also have the right to perform its function freely with respect to external agents, and in particular with respect to other states, if it is to realize its citizens' right to freedom. The idea is the following. The right to freedom is concerned with an agent's independence from being constrained by the choices of others. As we saw in section 1, that is why individuals living side by side have a duty of right to enter the state. But an individual can only be truly independent from the choices of others if the agent that secures her independence is itself independent. In other words, to be genuine, independence must go *all the way up*. A state can thus only perform its function if it is entitled to the same kind of independence as are its citizens. The right to freedom of individuals percolates up, so to speak: it requires that the state have a right to perform its function freely, because otherwise individuals cannot be truly independent from the choices of others, and hence *their* right to freedom is violated.[24]

Let me emphasize that what holds for collective agents in general also holds for the state: its right to freedom only extends to legitimate actions. The right to freedom would not protect a genocidal policy, to take an obvious example, or any other policy that is inconsistent with the state's function and thus undermines the very source of its claim to noninterference. I say more about what this point entails for the powers of an eventual world state in section 5.[25] For now, I simply want to emphasize that the restriction to legitimate actions does not entail that a state's right to freedom only protects the actions it carries out within the territory it controls. Obviously, securing the rights of individuals on a given territory chiefly requires the adoption of internal measures—putting in place a reasonably fair and efficient legal system, training a disciplined police force, and so on. But it can also require taking external measures. A state may have to take military action against an external threat; and as was suggested above, it may have to take measures (military or otherwise) to secure external resources needed to maintain its population. If the aims are genuine, then these are legitimate state actions, since they are required for the performance of the state's function. They are therefore protected by the state's right to freedom. Such actions will not always be rightful; indeed, they will often violate the right to freedom of other states. But the point is that, unless they do so, interfering with them will not be justified.

The conclusion so far is that states have a right to freedom that extends to all their legitimate actions, whether internal or external. In other words, a state has the right to perform any legitimate action that does not interfere with another agent's right to freedom. Despite the restriction to legitimate actions, this is a very extensive right. At the same time, like an individual's right to freedom, the right only holds insofar as it is consistent with the freedom of all agents. That makes it substantially different from the right of sovereignty, understood as the "absolute liberty" that Hobbes and others have ascribed to states to do whatever they judge "most conducing to their benefit."[26] The right to freedom also stands in contrast to another right that is commonly discussed in the literature: the right to self-determination. Here the crucial difference is that it only makes sense to assign a right to freedom to a group if it is already constituted as a collective agent, whereas discussions of the right to self-determination tend to concern precisely the question whether a particular group has a right to *become* a collective agent—a state, typically—given that its members share a certain ethnicity, language, culture, or a particular history.[27] There is also a deeper way in which the right to freedom differs from both the right to self-determination and the right of sovereignty, namely, in its focus on independence from the wills of others. That idea does not appear in the two other notions, and builds into the right to freedom an ideal with implications that are nothing short of radical—as the argument of the next section shows.

IV. Rights in the International State of Nature

We now come to the heart of the argument to establish that states can justifiably be forced to form a world state. Given the justification of coercion I outlined in section 1, and given that states have a right to freedom, the way to proceed is clear: we need to show that being in a state of nature is an unjustifiable restriction of states' freedom, and that establishing a world state is necessary to take away that restriction. If such is the case, then the use of force to establish a world state would be, to use the expression again, a *hindering of a hindrance* to freedom; it would therefore be consistent with—indeed, required by—states' right to freedom. I proceed in two steps. First, I present the considerations that show that the rights that states claim against one another must remain provisional so long as there is no world state. These considerations were partly anticipated in section 2, but I now provide a fuller presentation and consider some important objections that are specific to the case of states. Second, I explain why the provisional status of rights poses a problem for states, despite the fact that differences between states and individuals appear to make the international state of nature more tolerable than a domestic one would be.

I begin with the provisional character of rights in the international state of nature. There are two main categories of right to consider here, which parallel those discussed in section 1: the right to territorial integrity, which is analogous to property rights;[28] and treaty rights, which are analogous to contract rights. My focus will be on the first category because its importance is most readily apparent. States must have a right to territorial integrity if they are to be able to make the rights of those who dwell on their territory conclusive, because rights can only be conclusive if there is an agent with the exclusive authority to adjudicate and enforce them. And of course exclusive authority is only possible if the state has a right to its territory that holds against all external agents—otherwise, external agents do no wrong by intervening on its territory, and the state's decisions lack the required effectiveness. The point should be obvious: a state's judgment that a given person is the rightful owner of a certain house can only make the right conclusive if other states are not allowed to step in and take control of the house. The right to territorial integrity is thus clearly necessary for the state to perform its function.[29]

Why must a state's right to its territory remain provisional in the absence of a world state? As I suggested in section 2, the problem arises because a state's authority is restricted to the territory it actually controls. Outside that territory, the state cannot realize conditions of reciprocity, and therefore its use of force cannot be fully consistent with everyone's right to freedom. This gives rise to a fundamental asymmetry in the state's standing. Within its territory, and with respect to all who live there, a state can legitimately adjudicate and enforce rights. It has the authority to determine who the rightful owner of a certain house is, say, and to enforce its decision against anyone who dwells on the territory. It thus makes the rights of all agents living on the territory—individuals, but also associations, corporations, and so on—conclusive with respect to all others who live there. With respect to outsiders, however, the state can claim no special authority: it is, to use the traditional expression, a mere *power*.[30] Two states fighting for a piece of land are in this respect no different from two individuals fighting in the state of nature—and their rights with respect to one another are no less provisional.[31]

The argument here parallels that of section 1. Once again, the key idea is that an agent lacks the standing to impose its judgments about matters of right on others unless it realizes conditions of reciprocity with respect to them. Applied to the international case, this means that, to have the standing to enforce rights on the international stage, a state would have to fulfill conditions of reciprocity with respect to all states whose freedom is codependent. That is, it would need to take on the task of securing the rights of all states against one another, which would entail granting equal rights to all states, and having the power to enforce them reliably when needed. In short, *to make rights conclusive at the international level, a state would have to make itself into a world state*. There is, once again, no conceptual space between having conclusive rights and being in a civil condition—which in this case requires a state regulating relations among states, and thus a world state.[32]

This account may seem to fly in the face of deep-seated intuitions we share about what can justify the use of force on the international stage. Don't we all accept that a state can enforce its territorial rights against outsiders in virtue of its right of first occupancy, or at least in virtue of the right to noninterference of a people forming a society on a given territory? Such intuitions partly result from a failure to distinguish between two questions: how good a claim of right is, and whether it can make the use of force consistent with the right to freedom. Claims of first occupancy and demands of noninterference are in many ways good claims—it may even be that any legitimate system of rights would have to recognize them; but it does not follow that a state acts rightfully when it takes it upon itself to enforce them against others, since an agent does not acquire the right to use force against another agent simply by being correct in its judgment. The right to freedom sets extremely high demands on what can count as a justified use of force, be it against states or against individuals. It demands that any use of force respect the requirement of reciprocity; and since neither the right of first occupancy nor the right of noninterference can guarantee that this requirement is met, they cannot by themselves justify the use of force.

There is a further factor that accounts for our intuitions about the right of states to use force on the international stage: the fact that the international order is bound to remain a state of nature for the foreseeable future, and that no single state has the power to change that state of affairs. This undoubtedly makes a difference to what states can justifiably do. Although the use of force in the state of nature cannot realize conditions of reciprocity, it may be provisionally justified if the agent with whom one has a conflict does not want to enter a civil condition—that is, if the ideal of reciprocity set by the right to freedom is out of reach.[33] Understandably, our judgments about what states may do are influenced by the fact that we find ourselves in such a situation. But our views about when states may justifiably use force in the current world order must be kept separate from our discussion of the ideal toward which they should strive. When states take it upon themselves to use force on the international stage, the justification they can aspire to is only partial, since it necessarily falls short of the ideal of a fully rightful use of force—one that is compatible with the right to freedom of all rational beings. Only a world state can realize that ideal, since only a world state realizes the conditions of reciprocity that it requires. Accordingly, only a world state can make the rights of states conclusive.[34]

We now need to ask why the provisional character of rights in the international order is incompatible with states' freedom. The task raises difficulties we did not encounter in the case of individuals. One can see how arguments analogous to those I presented for individuals would go: if a state cannot rightfully exclude other states from its territory, then it cannot perform its function freely; and if it cannot make enforceable treaties with other states when required, then its ability to perform its function is unjustifiably restricted. The difficulty is that states have ways to avoid external interference that require nothing as extravagant as a world state, and that seem sufficiently effective to allow them to perform their function in a way that leaves their citizens with no grounds for complaint. To mention the most obvious possibilities: a state can avoid contact with the outside world, it can agree with its neighbors on terms of peaceful coexistence, or it can build up strength to deter others from meddling in its affairs. The question is, why is anything more needed?

The short answer is that the issue is not whether a state can be sufficiently *reliable* in carrying out its function, but rather whether it can have the *independence* demanded by the right to freedom. As we saw in section 3, the state can only realize its citizens' right to freedom if it itself enjoys the right kind of independence, something that none of the strategies on offer can provide. Yet although that claim is correct as far as it goes, one may still think that, for all relevant purposes, an individual's right to freedom will be secure so long as her state has sufficient control of its territory—which will be the case provided that the international system is stable enough, or that the state has enough power to deter outside interference. To dispel that thought, we need to inquire into the shortcomings of the three strategies I just mentioned.

Consider first the strategy of isolation. It is plain that the nature of states, and in particular the extent to which they can be self-sufficient, makes this a real possibility for them in a way it is not for individuals. And the strategy does seem promising if one imagines it to be universally adopted: if no borders were disputed on land or sea, and if all states restricted themselves to internal actions—if they did not seek to trade with one another, to acquire new land, and so on—then the absence of conclusive rights at the international level would never be *felt* either by states or by their citizens. But the situation would still be problematic, and not just because the assumption of lasting harmony among states is implausible. The problem is that so long as states have the *capacity* to interact with each other, the fact that they reliably choose not to do so cannot afford them the independence to which they are entitled. On the contrary, each is left to depend on the goodwill of others for the sustenance of this fragile equilibrium. Such a situation plainly violates the right to freedom of states; and it is no less objectionable from the point of view of citizens, since their rights are left to depend directly on the choices of foreign states (which are, with respect to them, mere powers).

The strategy of isolation could perhaps work if it were taken to the extreme. If a state could *literally* place itself out of the reach of all others, then it would no longer be dependent on their choices, since none of their actions could affect it. But there is no such option in our world: so long as a state is within the reach of others' cannons, its ability to secure rights on its territory depends on whether or not others choose to recognize its territorial claims. States are in that sense condemned by their power to find a way to share the surface of the earth; they cannot escape this plight because there is a very real sense in which, to use Kant's words, they "cannot help mutually affecting one another" (TP, 8:289).[35]

The strategy of agreement runs into the same problem: it fails to grant states the right kind of independence from one another.[36] This may seem in tension with the claim that the ideal of independence is realized by conditions of reciprocity, since obligations of agreement are usually thought to be reciprocal. But we have to distinguish two questions here: whether the *moral* obligations created by an agreement are reciprocal, and whether the agreement can be *enforced* in a way that realizes conditions of reciprocity. An agreement among states may not require a world state to be reciprocal in the first sense, assuming that background conditions are such as to make fair agreements possible; but this kind of reciprocity is not sufficient to secure freedom. For even if two states agree to respect one another's territory, nothing stops one of them from breaking the agreement when it no longer finds that it serves its interests. Indeed, even if we assume that states recognize a moral obligation to respect the agreement, that does not suffice to make them independent from one another's choices, since states, like all rational agents, can very well choose to overlook their moral obligations.[37]

The inadequacy of the strategy of agreement is also directly apparent from the standpoint of citizens. Individual citizens can object to a situation in which their state relies exclusively on agreement to prevent other states from meddling in its business, because that makes their rights contingent on the choices of other states. As agents with a right to freedom, they are entitled to more than mere agreement can provide. The problem can be overcome, of course: all it takes is an agent with the authority to enforce agreements. But as we saw above, an agent can only have this kind of authority if it realizes conditions of reciprocity—which in this case requires the agent to make itself into a world state. In that sense, the strategy of agreement does not provide an alternative to putting in place a world state: it presupposes the need to do so.

Because it promises a kind of security that the two previous strategies could not provide, the strategy of building strength poses the most serious challenge to the Kantian approach. By becoming sufficiently powerful, a state both creates a deterrent against outside interference and increases its chances of prevailing in case of dispute. This gives it a form of assurance that it will retain control of its territory, and thus some kind of independence from other states. Obviously, this is not the kind of independence required by the right to freedom, since the conditions for reciprocity are not realized. A quick response to the challenge would thus be that, however strong it might be, a state ultimately lacks the authority to use force against other states; in that sense, it is *entirely* dependent on their choices. But this way of digging in one's heels is unlikely to prove persuasive against a strategy that is so central to the contemporary view of international relations.

The strategy of building strength is best understood, not as challenging the Kantian approach on its own terms, but rather as proposing an alternative picture of the way in which states can secure the rights of their citizens. Let me therefore try to articulate more concretely what I take the picture's shortcomings to be.

The most obvious drawback of the strategy is that it cannot provide a universal solution to the problem faced by states. Its success depends precisely on one state's being stronger than the others; thus, although it may afford a few privileged states a sense of independence, it cannot in general make states independent from one another.[38] Now, that is certainly an important problem from an impartial point of view, as it is from the point of view of weak states; but it does not address the case of powerful states. We thus face the following challenge: can we show that there is a problem with the strategy of building strength from the point of view of a state that has achieved a dominant status? To put it more starkly, why would the absence of a world state be a problem for a state that has, by building up strength, made it virtually impossible for anyone else's will to prevail against its own—a state that enjoys as high a level of protection against the outside world as it could hope to have under a world state?

Objections of this kind are familiar enough: one tries to show that an argument grounded in mutual vulnerability fails to deliver its intended conclusion by bringing in some kind of superagent who escapes the constraints of vulnerability altogether. The device has been used against Hobbes's argument for the authority of the state, and against Kant's argument for the duty of beneficence.[39] This is not quite how we should understand the objection here, however, since the Kantian argument for the state is based, not on an assumption of mutual vulnerability, but on the demands set by the right to freedom. The point of the objection is that a superpower would not have to depend on the choices of other states, because they would be too weak to oppose it in any way. It would thus be able to perform its function in a way that left its citizens no grounds for complaint. Note that the possibility here is not merely academic. There are no superindividuals among us, so the idea that they might not be subject to a duty of mutual aid is only remotely worrying; what matters is that *we* are subject to such a duty. By contrast, states evidently can achieve a level of dominance that makes them practically invulnerable for the indefinite future. An argument for a world state that failed to address this possibility would lack bite where it matters most.

Back then to our question: why would the independence provided by a world state be preferable to the *status quo* even from the point of view of a superpower that is as secure as it could ever hope to be? The answer, in short, is that in the absence of a world state, the superpower's independence is entirely contingent on its dominance of others. It has no claim to noninterference that goes beyond the brute fact that, at this particular point in history, no other state can seriously challenge it. The problem with this situation is not that the superpower's dominance is bound to end at some point, since it might be stable enough to alleviate worries for the indefinite future. The problem is that the superpower allows itself to be in a condition in which might makes right, and in which others do no wrong by trying to undermine its power in whatever ways they can. In fact, their doing so is *warranted* by the superpower's status: from their point of view, the superpower is a lawless power, and hence fundamentally a threat.[40] The kind of de facto independence that comes with being a superpower is in that sense self-undermining; dominance turns out to be a problem, not a solution.

The comparison with the situation in which a world state is in place is telling. A world state cannot prevent all violations of rights from taking place; it may not even offer the superpower as high a level of actual protection as it otherwise enjoys. Yet by realizing conditions of reciprocity, the world state grants the superpower an independence that is not contingent on strength alone, but rather grounded in rights that are secured by legitimate institutions of adjudication and enforcement, and that no one may justifiably overlook. That comes at a cost: the superpower has to give up its position of dominance to acquire these rights, since the world state must be the sole dominant power in order to enforce the rights of states effectively. But the superpower thereby gains a procedure for rightful conflict resolution, as well as the protection of international law, and it ceases to be a legitimate target for other states. One need not subscribe to Kant's exact conception of the right to freedom to find this kind of independence more valuable than what exuberant power by itself could afford.

V. A Federal State of States

Let us take stock of the argument. In section 3, we saw that states have a right to freedom, and hence that their freedom can only be restricted for the sake of freedom itself. In section 4, we saw that the current international order is incompatible with states' right to freedom, because states can only have conclusive rights, and thus the independence required for freedom, under an authority that effectively secures the rights of all states against one another—in short, under a world state. Now, the world state required by this argument is undoubtedly minimal. It would have the authority to enforce territorial rights; and although I did not press the matter in the previous section, it would also have the authority to enforce treaties among states concerning matters such as trade. What further rights a world state would be justified in enforcing is a question that the present discussion leaves open. There likely are such further rights—I have argued that territorial and treaty rights are necessary for the realization of states' right to freedom, not that they are sufficient. Pursuing that question would take us too far afield, as it would require a much fuller account of the ideal of independence contained in the right to freedom than I have given here.[41] In any case, my goal here is not to give a complete characterization of the world state that the ideal of freedom requires, but only to establish that the ideal does require at least a minimal world state.

In general, it should be clear that the argument I have presented has little to say about matters of institutional design. It requires that a world state fulfill the requirement of reciprocity, and thus that it effectively secure the rights of all states against one another. This means that a world state would need a well-functioning legal system, backed by an effective international police force. Other than that, the reasoning is compatible with numerous institutional arrangements. I do want to stress one institutional implication of the argument I have presented, however, partly because it departs from the received view, and partly because it makes the prospect of establishing a world state less utopian than it otherwise would be: the federal nature of the world state that the Kantian position requires.

Why does the argument of sections 3 and 4 require a federal world state rather than a centralized one? Because anything more than a federal world state would be incompatible with states' right to freedom. Recall that, because of that right, states can be constrained by a world state *only to the extent that freedom itself requires it*. In other words, the only powers that a world state could justifiably exert against legitimate states are those necessary to secure the rights of states against one another. A world state would thus have the authority to regulate matters concerning relations among states—territorial disputes, trade relations, immigration, and so on.[42] But its authority would stop there: it would in general have no right to intervene in the internal affairs of legitimate states, since each state's activity of enforcing rights within its territory is consistent with the freedom of other states. Accordingly, the world state would have no authority to adjudicate a dispute between two neighbors over the appropriate location of a fence, or over the ownership of a particular object: such matters are for their domestic state to decide. Only if the territory on which the neighbors lived was contested, or if they happened to live on either side of a border, would the case fall under the world state's jurisdiction; otherwise, the matter would be purely internal and would fall under the exclusive jurisdiction of the domestic state.

To press the point further, recall the asymmetry I described in the previous section: with respect to its citizens, a state is the authority that adjudicates and enforces rights; with respect to other states, however, it is a mere power. The federal structure of the world state springs from this dichotomy. The state's lack of authority with respect to its peers is what justifies the world state in regulating international relations; the world state is justified in doing so, because it thereby solves the problem states face in having to share a planet. But the authority the domestic state has with respect to its citizens means that whatever problem *they* face in having to share a territory is already solved. For all the citizens of a state, in all their dealings with one another, *rights are already conclusive*. If we are citizens of the same state, then there is no sense in which our rights with respect to one another are provisional—as if we could not *really* know which one of us is the rightful owner of your car until a world state was in place. Our domestic state already provides the answers to such questions. And of course the domestic state can only make rights conclusive in this way, and thus perform its function, if external agents—including the world state—refrain from interfering. By stepping in, the world state would violate the domestic state's right to perform its function, and thereby undermine the right to freedom of those living on its territory. Such an action would be unjustified. This is not to deny that a domestic state could choose to transfer some (or all) of its powers to the world state; how and to what extent it could do so would depend on its constitutional structure. The point is simply that the world state's authority to impose its rule through force would stop at the border of a legitimate domestic state.

One might have thought that the Kantian conception of state authority would support a more circumscribed view of states' right to nonintervention. As we saw in section 3, a state's right to freedom, like that of other collective agents, only extends to its legitimate actions. This seems to imply that the right only holds so long as the state's actions are consistent with its citizens' right to freedom; actions that are not so consistent undermine the state's legitimacy, and thus its right to nonintervention. Should we then conclude that a world state would be justified in preventing a state from taking measures that violate the right to freedom of its citizens—much in the same way that the domestic state is justified in preventing a corporation from taking measures that violate the rights of its members?

The matter is not so simple. Recall that the state's function is to make the rights of individuals living on a given territory conclusive. As I have already emphasized, this is only possible if the state has the exclusive authority to adjudicate and enforce rights on the territory. The claim is in part trivial: if rights are to be made determinate, then clearly there has to be a single agent securing rights on the territory. But it goes further than that: it entails that rights can only be made conclusive by the state if its decisions about matters of right are taken to be *final*. No external standard can determine what right demands in particular cases, since that would render the state's authority essentially contestable, leaving citizens with no principled way of deciding matters of right, and thus in a state of nature with respect to one another. If it is to fulfill its function, the state must get to determine exactly what the rights of its citizens are in particular cases. There can be no external standard by which to assess whether its decisions are legitimate: the decisions of the highest court of the land must count as establishing what is right.[43] To put the point starkly, there has to be a sense in which the state can do no wrong.[44]

But that cannot be the whole story. States sometimes do things—conducting genocide, say—that undeniably justify outside intervention. We can make room for this possibility by noting that, although there is no external standard of legitimacy that applies to individual state actions, there are standards that apply to the state *as a whole*. This should be obvious from the argument of section 3: since the state acquires its right to freedom from its essential role in making the rights of individuals conclusive, its right to freedom only holds insofar as it succeeds in achieving that aim. If a state utterly fails to secure the rights of its citizens—because it lacks the power to do so (as in the case of failed states), or because it lacks the will (as in the case of oppressive states)—then it loses its legitimacy, and by the same token its right to noninterference. In such cases, a world state would be justified in intervening to establish a proper state.[45] But so long as a state remains legitimate—so long as it can credibly claim to realize the right to freedom of its citizens—it retains its right to freedom, and the world state has no authority to meddle in its internal affairs.[46]

Given that it leaves all legitimate states standing, one might think that the federal world state I advocate does not really go beyond the sort of free association of states that is usually seen as the main alternative to a centralized world state.[47] Yet a significant distance separates the two ideas. Recall the two minimal conditions that a world state has to fulfill: it must aim to secure the rights of all states, and it must have the force necessary to enforce those rights effectively. A free association of states as traditionally conceived fails to satisfy either condition.[48] The point is obvious with respect to the second condition, since an independent military force would be in tension with the voluntary character of a free association. Such an association can require its members to commit troops for a prolonged period of time; but by hypothesis members ultimately remain free to withdraw their contribution—if nothing else, by leaving the association altogether. A world state could not allow itself to be dependent on the decisions of other institutions in this way, since it could grant states no independence from one another if its enforcement of rights was contingent on a sufficient number of states' being willing to provide troops when needed. A world state, federal or otherwise, must have its own standing army.

A free association also fails to satisfy the first condition. The aim of a free association of states is primarily to protect its members against attacks by outsiders, and possibly to adjudicate disputes among members. That is a far cry from the commitment a world state must take on, which is to protect the rights of *all* states—rogue states as well as law-abiding ones. To emphasize: the world state has the authority to punish any rogue state that breaks international law; but conversely, if a rogue state is itself attacked, the world state is required to step in and defend it, as it would any other state. The requirement of reciprocity demands as much.[49] By contrast, although a free association may at times decide to help an outsider—for humanitarian or strategic reasons, say—its standing commitment is to its members only. Hence from the point of view of outsiders, a free association has the exact same status as a single state: it is a mere power—a greater power than a single state, no doubt, but a mere power nonetheless. Its status is in that sense closest to that of the superpower we considered above; and it falls short of the kind of federal world state I have defended here for the same reasons.[50]

VI. Concluding Remarks

By way of conclusion, I want to explain briefly how the federal model I have advocated here helps to address two objections to the idea of a world state that are commonly made. The first is Kant's influential worry that a world state would be bound either to be a "soulless despotism" (*PP*, 8:367) or to sink into anarchy. That concern arises naturally if one imagines a world state forcibly taking over all the powers exercised by national states in order to govern single-handedly the whole planet. Thus construed, a world state would accumulate power on a frightening scale, and would have to rule with an iron fist, being constantly on the verge of imploding under the pressure of various secessionist groups.[51] Such worries are harder to motivate with respect to the federal model. Given the restrictions on what it could legitimately do, a federal world state would not accumulate power on the same scale as a centralized one. It would be a dominant military force but lack extensive instruments of local control, since its use of force would be primarily aimed at regulating relations among states. In addition, a federal world state would have no need to counteract fragmenting forces through repressive measures, since it would already grant national states autonomy with respect to all internal matters. Worries about despotism are thus largely put to rest by the adoption of a federal model.

The second objection concerns the difficulty of establishing a world state from our present starting point. The worry is that any attempt to do so would result in endless fighting and chaos, so that however desirable the ideal of a federal world state might be, it must remain out of reach for us. Accordingly, no state would be justified in using force to establish a world state, since none could credibly claim to be effectively establishing a world state through its use of force. The point is well taken. Given our starting point, a world state can only be put in place if all the most powerful states voluntarily agree to do so. The argument I have presented here shows that this is something they *should* do, since their freedom depends on it; whether they will do so is another matter. As Kant lamented over two centuries ago, states tend to place their pride precisely in "not being subject to any external lawful coercion at all" (*PP*, 8:354), a stance that is hardly compatible with the establishment of a world state. The federal model cannot solve that problem by itself, but it does alleviate the worry by minimizing the demands placed upon states: whereas establishing a centralized world state would require states to acquiesce to their own dissolution, establishing a federal world state demands only that they give up the liberty to settle their disputes by force. That makes the prospect of states' willingly joining a world state considerably more realistic than it otherwise would be.

I should emphasize in closing that these grounds for cautious optimism are reinforced by our general conclusion, which entails that it is not necessary for all states to join the world state voluntarily. As we have seen, a well-functioning world state could legitimately enforce the rights of all states against one another regardless of whether they recognized its authority, since by realizing a rightful condition it would create a duty of right for states to submit to its rule. All it takes to establish a world state is for a coalition of powerful states to vest enough power in an international governing body to enable it to secure effectively the rights of all states against one another. Kant's doubts notwithstanding, there is good reason to believe that realizing the ideal set by external freedom is possible in this world.

NOTES

1. On Kant's view, the statement "A has a duty of right to do X" just *means* that A can justifiably be forced to do X; there is nothing more to the idea (see *MM*, 6:232). I observe that usage in what follows.

2. For an excellent discussion of Kant's position, as well as a useful survey of the vast literature on the topic, see Pauline Kleingeld, "Approaching Perpetual Peace: Kant's Defence of a League of States and His Ideal of a World Federation," *European Journal of Philosophy* 12, no. 3 (2004): 304–25. I discuss briefly below what I take to be Kleingeld's main suggestion (see note 19). The received interpretation of Kant's position is that he rejects the ideal of a world state. See for instance John Rawls, *The Law of Peoples* (Cambridge: Harvard University Press, 1999), 36. But the textual evidence is ambiguous. Kant does say at times that his theory only requires a noncoercive league of states rather than a federal world state (see *PP*, 8:355–56). Yet he also explicitly says that the ideal set by his theory is "a universal *association of states* (analogous to that by which a people become a state)" (*MM*, 6:350). The problem then seems to be that the ideal cannot be realized for pragmatic reasons—either because having one unified entity govern the entire world is impracticable (see *MM*, 6:350; and *PP*, 8:367), or because such an entity cannot be put in place against the will of existing states (*PP*, 8:357). Kant seems on the whole more favorable to the establishment of a world state in his earlier writings (see, for instance, *UH*, 8:24–25).

3. On this point, see notably *CPrR*, 5:28–29.

4. Since Kant's political philosophy is exclusively concerned with the demands of external freedom, it is always in that sense that I use the word "freedom" in what follows. Kant is not as transparent as he might be about the relationship between his political philosophy and his moral views. It seems clear that the political philosophy is in some sense derivable from the moral philosophy (for interesting suggestions on this point, see Onora O'Neill, "Kant and the Social Contract Tradition," and Arthur Ripstein, "Kant and the Circumstances of Justice," chapters 1 and 2 of this volume, respectively); at the same time, I am inclined to think, along with Thomas Pogge, that the political philosophy can stand on its own (see "Is Kant's *Rechtslehre* a 'Comprehensive Liberalism'?" in chapter 3 of this volume).

5. See Hobbes, *Leviathan*, ed. Edwin Curley (Indianapolis: Hackett, 1994), chapter 14, par. 2, and chapter 21, par. 2.

6. Rousseau notably endorses this view of freedom in the eighth of his *Lettres écrites de la montagne*, where he writes: "Freedom consists less in doing one's will than in not being subject to the will of others." Jean-Jacques Rousseau, *Oeuvres complètes*, vol. 3, ed. Bernard Gagnebin and Marcel Raymond (Paris: Gallimard, 1964), 841; my translation.

7. Such external rights stand in contrast to a person's right to her own body. Note that Kant identifies a third category of external rights among individuals: "rights to persons akin to rights to things" (*MM*, 6:276). These include the rights of parents over their children, along with (more controversially) the rights of spouses over one another and (more controversially still) the rights of the head of a household over servants (see *MM*, 8:276–84). I leave the whole category aside here, since it has no obvious analogue in the international realm. For an illuminating discussion of the three categories of right that Kant considers, along with an argument that they are exhaustive, see Arthur Ripstein, "Authority and Coercion," *Philosophy and Public Affairs* 32, no. 1 (2004): 2–35, at 15–22.

8. On the notion of provisional rights, see *MM*, 6:256–57.

9. So long as I hold onto the hammer, they would be violating my right to my body by wrestling it from me.

10. On this point, see Kant's explanation of the Postulate of Practical Reason with Regard to Rights at *MM*, 6:246. Note that the argument is not that my freedom is violated if I cannot have a hammer at my disposal for my project: on a Kantian conception, one's freedom is not dependent on the availability of any *particular* means. The problem arises because I cannot make *any* object into a means to my ends, even if it is available for my use as far as others are concerned.

11. The last clause simply acknowledges that by committing a wrong an agent does not lose her right to freedom: the agent only makes it the case that certain actions become consistent with her right to freedom that previously were not. Thus, if you attempt to break the law, it is consistent with your right to freedom to restrain you or to punish you appropriately if you succeed. But that does not mean that you *lose* your right altogether—if you did, then any form whatsoever of restraint or punishment would be justified, which is not the case.

12. For Locke's position, see his *Second Treatise*, in John Locke, *Two Treatises of Government*, ed. Peter Laslett (Cambridge: Cambridge University Press, 1988), §§7–9. On Locke's view, every individual in the state of nature is entitled to use force, so long as she does so for the protection of a genuine right. In other words, private individuals have the standing to judge when their rights have been violated, and to use force according to that judgment. As I explain in the text, Kant's conception of the right to freedom rules out that possibility.

13. I say "strictly speaking" because I do not mean to rule out that some actions may count as a legitimate enforcement of rights in a state of nature when putting in place a civil condition is not possible (as is arguably the case in the current international order). But such actions would still fall short of the ideal set by freedom.

14. I am not denying that I have a *moral* obligation to stay off your land. But even if that is the case, it does not follow that you may *force* me to stay off. (I have a moral obligation not to lie to you, but that does not give you the right to hit me if you know I am about to do so.) Nor am I denying that you have a right to fight me, given that we are in a state of nature, and that it is beyond your power to establish a civil condition; but then I also have a right to fight you, for precisely the same reason (see *MM*, 6:307–8).

15. Kant suggests something along these lines when he says that rights can only be made conclusive by "a will putting everyone under obligation," by which he means "a collective general (common) and powerful will" (*MM*, 6:256). I should stress that I do not claim that the two conditions I identify in the text are sufficient for an agent to have the authority to enforce rights—only that they are necessary.

16. What Kant's principles require thus depends on our starting point. If there were no states, then the principles would require a single state to impose the rule of law on all rational

agents. But if we start with numerous legitimate states in place, then the problem we face in making the international realm rightful is to determine how these states must relate to one another. In that case, I argue below, Kantian principles require a federal world state, since the internally rightful orders established by existing states must be respected.

17. On the right of nations, see *MM*, 6:343–51 and *PP*, 8:354–55; on cosmopolitan right, see *MM*, 3:352–53 and *PP*, 8:357–60.

18. Kant seems to have acknowledged as much in his lectures: Vigilantius reports him as saying that "just as private persons stand to one another, so entire peoples stand to each other" (*VN*, 27:590). The thought echoes Rousseau's claim that "the will of the state, although general with respect to its members, is no longer so with respect to the other states and their members, but becomes for them a particular and individual will." Jean-Jacques Rousseau, *Discourse on Political Economy*, in *The Social Contract and Other Later Political Writings*, ed. and trans. Victor Gourevitch (Cambridge: Cambridge University Press, 1997), 7 (*Oeuvres complètes* III, 245).

19. Here I find myself in disagreement with the position defended by Pauline Kleingeld in a pair of recent papers: "Approaching Perpetual Peace" and "Kant's Theory of Peace," in *The Cambridge Companion to Kant and Modern Philosophy*, ed. Paul Guyer (Cambridge: Cambridge University Press, 2006), esp. 483–88. On Kleingeld's view, Kant advocates the establishment of a noncoercive league of states, but only as a necessary first step to the establishment of a world state. The latter remains the ideal of reason, but it can only rightfully be established with the consent of existing states, since "forcing an unwilling state into a federation would violate the autonomy of the individuals composing the state, collectively as co-legislating citizens" ("Kant's Theory of Peace," 485). I see two problems with this suggestion. First, the autonomy of individuals composing a state only seems to be unacceptably curtailed if the world state interferes in their state's *internal* affairs; not so if the world state's actions are restricted to protecting the rights of other states—as they have to be on my view (on which more in section 5). Second, Kleingeld's argument threatens to overshoot: it seems to imply that the *domestic* state can only be put in place with the consent of individuals, since otherwise their autonomy would be violated. That is flatly at odds with Kant's claim that individuals have a duty of right to leave the state of nature (see *MM*, 6:307).

20. This interpretation was suggested to me by Arthur Ripstein.

21. On this general idea, see Hobbes, *Leviathan*, chapter 16.

22. There may seem to be an important difference between the two cases, namely, that the authorization that creates the union involves several individuals *pooling* their rights to make them into a single collective right. But that fact is easily accounted for. What happens in standard acts of association is that different individuals allow the leaders to exercise the *exact same right* on their behalf. In our case, each worker allows the union leaders to exercise on her behalf the right to negotiate freely with the employer, according to the specific terms of the union charter. That amounts to pooling the rights together, because once the authorization has been given, the rights can only be exercised or violated *together*, as a single right, through the person of the union leader.

23. For different views on (and more detailed discussions of) Kant's relation to the social contract tradition, see O'Neill, "Kant and the Social Contract Tradition," and Ripstein, "Kant and the Circumstances of Justice," chapters 1 and 2 of this volume, respectively.

24. The point can be put slightly differently. We saw in section 1 that the state must realize conditions of reciprocity in order to make rights conclusive on its territory. One of these conditions demands that the state be able to enforce rights in a uniform manner on its territory. Since that is obviously not possible if it cannot exclude other states from its territory, it follows that the right to freedom can only be realized if states have conclusive rights against one another. The idea finds echo in Kant's suggestion that original acquisition of external object "will always remain only provisional unless [the original contract] extends to the entire human race" (*MM*, 6:266). As I suggest in section 4, I take the point to be that the acquisition remains

provisional *with respect to agents external to the state's territory*; it is not provisional with respect to those dwelling on that territory.

25. One point I make in section 5 is that the restriction of the right to freedom to legitimate actions is less constraining for the state than it is for ordinary collective agents because the state can only make rights conclusive if it is the ultimate judge of matters pertaining to those rights on its territory. Thus, although the state is constrained by its proper function, it inevitably has a greater latitude to act as it sees fit in performing that function than do ordinary collective agents.

26. Hobbes, *Leviathan*, chapter 11, par. 8. Here, the notion of a benefit is taken to go beyond the legitimate purposes of the state, and to include things like increasing the state's wealth or territory. On the view I am defending, such purposes do not count as benefits to the state (unless they are somehow necessary for the state to perform its function). They are merely benefits to the state's *ruler*, considered as a private person—a distinction that makes no difference on Hobbes's view, and all the difference on Kant's.

27. What I say does not as such rule out that there could be such a right; only it would have to be a right of individuals—unless of course it can be shown that rights are properly ascribed to ethnic or linguistic groups. For discussions of the right to self-determination, see notably Avishai Margalit and Joseph Raz, "National Self-Determination," *The Journal of Philosophy* 87, no. 9 (1990): 439–61; and Will Kymlicka, *Multicultural Citizenship* (Oxford: Clarendon Press, 1995).

28. Arthur Ripstein has suggested to me that a state's right to its territory is more like a person's right to her body than like a right to an external object. That seems correct in one way, since the state is constituted as an agent by its control of its territory, much in the way that a person is constituted as an agent by her control of her own body. In another way, however, the arbitrariness of the limits of a state's territory makes it more like property than like a person's body. In any case, I do not think the argument I present here is affected by this point: either way, a state's use of force to defend its territory fails to live up to the demands of external freedom, since the state fails to realize conditions of reciprocity with respect to external agents, and hence lacks the authority to impose its judgment about matters of right on them.

29. The importance of treaty rights is more complex, since they are not directly necessary for the state to perform its function in the way that territorial rights are. I believe that treaty rights are required for similar reasons as contract rights are—because otherwise a state's ability to pursue its legitimate purposes would be unjustifiably restricted, since it could not make the actions of another state into its means even if the other state agreed to the arrangement. But that question can be left to one side for present purposes.

30. See *MM*, 6:311. Cf. Rousseau, *Du contrat social*, book 1, chapter 6, in *Oeuvres complètes* III, 362.

31. See again the passage from Kant's *Lectures on Ethics* quoted in note 18 above.

32. Although I said at the beginning that I would not attempt to provide a detailed interpretation of Kant's position on world government, I do want to point out a passage from the *Doctrine of Right* in which he endorses the general point I make in the text. It goes as follows: "Since a state of nature among nations, like a state of nature among individual human beings, is a condition that one ought to leave in order to enter a lawful condition, before this happens any rights of nations . . . are merely *provisional*. Only in a universal *association of states* (analogous to that by which a people becomes a state) can rights come to hold *conclusively* and a true *condition of peace* come about" (*MM*, 6:350). Kant then goes on to point out what seems an essentially pragmatic problem: "But if such a state made up of nations were to extend too far over vast regions, governing it and so too protecting each of its members would finally have to become impossible, while several such corporations would again bring on a state of war" (ibid.). I say a few words in section 6 about the general worry that a world state would be ungovernable. For now, I simply want to emphasize that Kant acknowledges that his theory requires a world state in principle; his claim that a free association of states should be put in

place (at 6:345, for instance) seems to result from his belief that the ideal of a world state is unattainable.

33. Kant seems to acknowledge this at *MM*, 6:257 and 267.

34. To clarify, I am not denying that states can justifiably defend themselves against aggressors; what I deny is that, in doing so, they are enforcing their rights in the strong sense. Here I find myself in disagreement with a view defended by Michael Walzer in *Just and Unjust Wars* (New York: Basic Books, 1977). Walzer claims that states that are attacked, along with other states that want to help them, "are entitled not only to repel the attack but also to punish it. All resistance is also law enforcement" (59). On the view I defend, the conditions for genuine law enforcement are far more demanding than this suggests. Using force to back up reasonable claims is not in itself law enforcement. Thus, although the community of states may be justified in taking action against an aggressive state, it does not thereby *punish* it, for it has no authority to do so; all it does is to defend itself or one of its members. Walzer inadvertently supports the point when he claims that the decision of one state to help another that is being attacked is "best understood by analogy to the decision of a private citizen who rushes to help a man or woman attacked on the street" (62): private citizens have no authority to enforce the law or punish aggressors; all they can do is defend one another.

35. Recall how Kant celebrates the fact that, because of the earth's spherical shape, human beings "cannot disperse infinitely but must finally put up with being near one another" (*PP*, 8:358; cf. *MM*, 6:262).

36. For a defense of the strategy of agreement, see J. G. Fichte, *Foundations of Natural Right*, ed. Frederick Neuhouser, trans. Michael Baur (Cambridge: Cambridge University Press, 2000). On Fichte's view, the central problem is that property rights are not "thoroughly secure for the purpose of external right" (118) unless they are recognized by all humankind. His solution is to have each state recognize the property of all states with which it shares a border. This secures the claims of all states, he contends, because "even if the distant states have not recognized the property of the state within which *I* live (and thus indirectly my property), they have nevertheless recognized the property of the states that immediately border them. These states and their citizens cannot enter my state's territory without passing through and making free proprietary use of the territories that lie between my state and theirs, and this they are not permitted to do, in consequence of their recognition of the bordering state's territory" (ibid.). As I explain in the text, I think there are deeper problems with the strategy of agreement than Fichte recognizes. Even if all countries recognized the property of all other countries, it would still not suffice to make rights conclusive. Note that Fichte's approach finds echo in the widely held view that the law of treaties is the main source of international law. What I say in the text entails that, although the law of treaties may serve important pragmatic purposes in the development of a system of international law, it cannot on its own ground such a system—a proper world state is needed for that.

37. The problem is thus not that states tend to view international relations as a modus vivendi (as Thomas Pogge suggests in *Realizing Rawls* (Ithaca: Cornell University Press, 1989), 223–24). The problem is that even if they take themselves to be morally obligated to abide by their agreements, they may still *choose* to overlook their obligations.

38. The idea of a balance of power may seem the obvious universalist extension of the strategy of building strength, but it ultimately boils down to a strategy of agreement, since states must agree to do what is necessary to preserve the balance of power. As such, the idea is open to the objections I presented above. It was traditionally thought that a balance of power would be self-enforcing, of course, but that claim can hardly withstand scrutiny, or any awareness of the history of Europe. Kant mocks the idea outright in *Theory and Practice*, where he writes that "an enduring universal peace by means of the so-called *balance of power in Europe* is a mere fantasy, like Swift's house that the builder had constructed in such perfect accord with all the laws of equilibrium that it collapsed as soon as a sparrow alighted upon it" (*TP*, 8:312).

39. Hobbes's argument famously rests on the assumption that the weakest can always kill the strongest "either by secret machination, or by confederacy with others that are in the same

danger with himself" (*Leviathan*, chapter 13, par. 1). As for Kant's argument, it relies on the assumption that anyone may need help at some point (see *GW*, 4:423).

40. Kant puts the point forcefully (and somewhat surprisingly) when he writes that "the *condition* of the *superior power*, before any deed on its part" is "a wrong to the lesser power," so that "in the state of nature an attack by the lesser power is indeed legitimate" (*MM*, 6:346; cf., however, *PP*, 8:384).

41. The requirement of independence would most likely demand that the world state recognize a right to assistance for states whose population is in dire need. Otherwise, a state could be left to depend entirely on the goodwill of others for its survival. For a detailed argument that a right to assistance can be justified within a Kantian framework, see Ernest J. Weinrib, "Poverty and Property in Kant's System of Rights," *Notre Dame Law Review* 78, no. 3 (2003): 795–828.

42. Certain matters of public health would also belong on the list. For instance, a state's failure to respond adequately to the outbreak of a contagious disease constitutes a threat against which citizens of other states have the right to be shielded.

43. On this point, see *MM*, 6:316.

44. Here I am indebted to Christine Korsgaard's treatment of these ideas in "Taking the Law into Our Own Hands: Kant on the Right to Revolution," in *Reclaiming the History of Ethics: Essays for John Rawls*, ed. Andrews Reath, Barbara Herman, and Christine M. Korsgaard (Cambridge: Cambridge University Press, 1997), esp. 309–10. What I go on to say, however, is at variance with her conclusions.

45. In fact, any state would be justified in so intervening; the world state, however, is *required* to do so. To make rights conclusive on the international stage, the world state must secure the rights of all agents appearing on the international stage; that is what the reciprocity requirement demands. In the ideal situation I assumed in section 4, all agents on the international stage are states. But if a state collapses, then its citizens appear as lawless agents on the international stage; the world state must then make their rights conclusive along with everybody else's if it is to succeed in making rights conclusive at all.

46. This sets the threshold for the right to noninterference relatively low. Charles Beitz places it much higher when he argues that states only have a right to autonomy if they conform to liberal standards of justice (see *Political Theory and International Relations* (Princeton: Princeton University Press, 1979), 80–81). He evidently means the requirement to be fairly stringent, since he writes that intervening in a state's internal affairs is at least prima facie justified "when the state's institutions are unjust according to appropriate principles of justice and the interference would promote the development of a just domestic constitution within the state" (81–82). The criterion I put forth in the text coincides with Beitz's in cases where the injustice of a state's institutions is so egregious as to compromise its legitimacy—when fundamental human rights are violated, for instance. But a legitimate state can be unjust, at least up to a point. In such a case, given that the state in question still has a claim to realizing—albeit imperfectly—the right to freedom of its citizens, it is owed more respect than Beitz acknowledges.

47. See for instance *PP*, 8:354–57; *MM*, 6:350–51; and Rawls, *Law of Peoples*, 36.

48. This is not to deny that a free association of states could reform itself to fulfill the two conditions; but then it would simply make itself into a world state.

49. This goes back to the point I made in note 14, following which an agent that commits a wrong does not thereby lose its right to freedom. A rogue state may be punished, perhaps in some cases by the imposition of a regime change, but it cannot justifiably be left without the protection of international law—no more than a citizen could justifiably be left without the protection of the law for having committed a wrong.

50. I should note that, although free associations of states such as NATO clearly lack the commitment of a world state, the United Nations Organization has very much the right sort of commitment. But it falls short of the kind of world state I advocate here in its utter dependence on the choices of its members for any military action.

51. Rawls expresses the worry plainly when he writes: "I follow Kant's lead in *Perpetual Peace* (1795) in thinking that a world government—by which I mean a unified political regime with the legal powers normally exercised by central governments—would either be a global despotism or else would rule over a fragile empire torn by frequent civil strife as various regions and peoples tried to gain their political freedom and autonomy" (*Law of Peoples*, 36). Note how Rawls explicitly considers a centralized world state in this passage, as does Kant in the famous "soulless despotism" passage, where he is specifically concerned with what he calls "universal monarchy" (*PP*, 8:367).

THE PROGRESS OF ABSOLUTISM IN KANT'S ESSAY "WHAT IS ENLIGHTENMENT?"

Robert S. Taylor

Introduction: The Essay's Immediate Intellectual Context

In December 1784, Immanuel Kant published his essay "An Answer to the Question: What Is Enlightenment?" in the *Berlinische Monatsschrift* (*BMS*). The question that Kant was answering had been posed the previous December in the *BMS* by Johann Friedrich Zöllner, who was writing to defend the role of clergy in marriage ceremonies against a proposal to make them purely civil, as with other contracts.[1] After arguing that attacks on the role of religion in social life would only hasten an ongoing decline in morals and that writers should not, "in the name of enlightenment, confuse the hearts and minds of men," Zöllner asks in a note: "What is enlightenment? This question, which is almost as important as the question, what is truth? should really be answered before one begins enlightening! And yet I have not found an answer to it anywhere."[2]

Zöllner's question and his concerns about the possible negative effects of enlightenment arose in the context of an ongoing discussion within Berlin's *Mittwochsgesellschaft* (Wednesday Society), a secret society that was tied to the *BMS* and whose members included Zöllner, J. K. W. Möhsen, Moses Mendelssohn, and other notables of the German Enlightenment.[3] In the

---

Portions of this chapter were published in different form as "Democratic Transitions and the Progress of Absolutism in Kant's Political Thought" in the *Journal of Politics* 68, no. 3 (2006): 556–70. Cambridge University Press Copyright © 2006, Southern Political Science Association, reprinted here with permission.

same month that Zöllner's essay appeared, Möhsen had presented a paper to the society that asked a series of questions, the first of which was, what is enlightenment?; he went on to ask whether enlightenment was "useful or harmful, not only for the public, but also for the state and the government."[4] Möhsen's presentation sparked months of debate within the society, prompting Mendelssohn to address the issue in a contribution to the *BMS* in September 1784, three months before Kant's essay appeared.[5] Mendelssohn defines enlightenment as the cultivation of our theoretical reason through scientific inquiry; moreover, he entertains the idea that friends of enlightenment may have an obligation to withhold certain truths lest "prevailing religious and moral tenets" be destroyed, and worries that "the misuse of enlightenment weakens the moral sentiment and leads to hard-heartedness, egoism, irreligion, and anarchy."[6]

Kant's essay, which is easily the most famous of the many responses to Zöllner's original question, takes a radically different approach, as we shall see. Instead of emphasizing theoretical reason, Kant shifts the focus to practical reason, both pure and empirical. Rather than agonizing over the possible dangers of enlightenment, Kant argues that free and informed public discussion in a protective political environment is the only way to teach people to think for themselves and to prepare them for intellectual and political self-government.[7] In the remainder of the chapter, I will offer a detailed exegesis of Kant's essay, emphasizing its use of botanical and mechanical metaphors and showing how it anticipates his later works and their defenses of representative government and a progressive philosophy of history.

An Exegesis of "What Is Enlightenment?"

Kant begins his essay by defining the term "enlightenment" (*Aufklärung*) as "the human being's emergence from his self-incurred minority," where "minority" (*Unmündigkeit*) is defined as an "inability to make use of one's own understanding without direction from another" (*WE*, 8:35). Though our own "laziness" and "cowardice" are the primary reasons for our minority, those who guide us (priests, doctors, officers, tax officials) have an interest in maintaining and reinforcing it. How, then, are we to surmount such obstacles and achieve enlightenment? Kant discusses three possible paths to enlightenment, although two of them turn out to be false ones. The first path requires each individual to overcome immaturity through his own effort, but Kant argues that the "precepts and formulas" (*Satzungen und Formeln*) that weigh us down are too heavy to be removed by individual initiative alone—except for a talented few who succeed "by their own cultivation of their spirit, in extricating themselves from minority." The second path is through violent revolution against our guardians, but Kant believes that such a short cut to enlightenment will never produce "a true reform in one's way of thinking; instead new prejudices will serve just as well as old ones to harness the great unthinking masses" (*WE*, 8:36).[8]

After warning against these two false paths to enlightenment, Kant points to a third path. Unlike the first path, which counsels individualism, it recognizes that it "is more possible . . . that a public should enlighten itself" collectively; unlike the second path, which promises a quick fix, it realizes that "a public can achieve enlightenment only slowly." To identify this path, Kant says, we must determine "what sort of restriction hinders enlightenment, and what sort does not hinder it but instead promotes it." Contrary to the customary liberal prescription, Kant suggests that the "*public use* of one's reason" must be perfectly free, while the "*private use* of one's reason" may reasonably be subject to control—indeed, *must* be subject to control in order for the public use of reason to flourish and for enlightenment to be achieved, as we shall see (*WE*, 8:36–37).

But what does Kant mean by these terms? The private use of reason is that use of reason that we make in our capacity as members of social hierarchies; it is empirical practical reason (specifically, precepts of skill) for the achievement of ends given to us by our superiors (*GW*, 4:415).[9] Thus, soldiers cannot "engage openly in subtle reasoning about [the] appropriateness or utility" of the orders they receive, but must simply obey them; citizens must not argue with the tax collector over their tax bills, but must quietly discharge their obligations; and priests cannot attack church doctrine in the midst of communion, but must carry out their duties as required by their offices (*WE*, 8:37–38). Such obedience is required to maintain social order and to achieve important public ends, so our superiors in these hierarchies are justified in punishing us when we refuse to exercise our martial, ecclesiastical, or other skills for communal purposes.

The public use of reason, on the other hand, is that use of reason that we make in our capacity as members of learned society; the highest form of such reason is pure reason, whether theoretical or practical, which examines the foundations of science and mathematics, politics and religion. Kant says that each person may consider himself a "member of a whole commonwealth, even of the society of citizens of the world" who "in his capacity [as] a scholar . . . by his writings addresses a public in the proper sense of the word" (*WE*, 8:37). As literate individuals, we can step outside our roles as members of social organizations and participate in learned society, where we are free to discuss and to criticize. Thus, for example, while a soldier is not allowed to "engage openly in subtle reasoning" about his orders, he may offer his thoughts to the public regarding military matters on his own time, in print.

Kant repeatedly emphasizes that what is needed for the public use of reason to flourish and for enlightenment to be achieved is, first and foremost, *intellectual freedom*. The very existence of public reason depends on free and open inquiry, as Kant argues in the *Critique of Pure Reason*. "Reason must subject itself to critique in all its undertakings, and cannot restrict the freedom of critique through any prohibition without damaging itself and drawing upon itself a disadvantageous suspicion. . . . The very existence of reason depends upon this freedom, which has no dictatorial authority, but whose claim is never anything more than the agreement of free citizens, each of whom must be able to express his reservations, indeed even his *veto*, without holding back" (A738–39/B766–67). As this passage suggests, freedom of thought requires freedom of the press, without which the former would be endangered;[10] as Kant asks elsewhere, "how much and how correctly would we *think* if we did not think as it were in community with others to whom we *communicate* our thoughts, and who communicate theirs to us!" (*OT*, 8:144) Earlier in the enlightenment essay, however, Kant said that the "guidance of another" in intellectual matters was a sign of minority. How is the kind of guidance we receive by thinking "in community with others" different from the kind that our guardians provide for us?

The key to answering this question lies at the beginning of the sentence just quoted. First, consider how the two kinds of guidance affect *how much* we think. Our guardians have no desire to see us think for ourselves, as this would (ultimately) threaten their power over us. If it were up to them, we would hardly think at all—except for that instrumental reasoning necessary for us to discharge our duties within social hierarchies. Our interlocutors in learned society, on the other hand, are pressing us constantly to reason, question, and criticize. Their ideas, especially when different from our own, are an encouragement to thought, and their criticisms of our own ideas are a similarly fruitful provocation.

Now consider how the two kinds of guidance affect *how correctly* we think. To the extent that our guardians encourage us to think at all, they desire that we think in terms of "precepts and formulas" whose accuracy cannot be guaranteed in the absence of vigorous and open debate and whose function is to preserve social order rather than hone our reasoning skills. Our interlocutors in learned society, however, have no patience for dogmatic assertions and challenge us to defend our claims. By questioning our comfortable assumptions and noting our missteps, they compel us to develop our intellectual capacities, which atrophy under guardianship, and become more self-critical. In short, by challenging us to think more and think more correctly, by engaging us in a critical public culture, our fellow participants in cosmopolitan society can help us to overcome intellectual dependency (which makes us little more than the "domesticated animals" of our guardians) and thereby to achieve enlightenment *(WE,* 8:35).

The second necessity is *education.* In both "What Is Enlightenment?" and "Idea for a Universal History," Kant treats education as something that a public creates for itself, "if only it is left its freedom" (*WE,* 8:36).[11] As he puts it in the latter essay, while "the world's present rulers have no money to spare for public educational institutions or indeed for anything which concerns the world's best interests (for everything has already been calculated out in advance for the next war), they will nonetheless find that it is to their own advantage . . . not to hinder their citizens' private efforts in this direction, however weak and slow they may be" (*UH,* 8:28).[12] However, in *The Conflict of the Faculties,* published fifteen years later, Kant suggests a much more positive educational role for political rulers. He says there that "the education of young people in intellectual and moral culture" cannot hope to succeed "unless it is designed on the considered plan and intention of the highest authority in the state, then set in motion and constantly maintained in uniform operation thereafter." Kant admits, however, that such administration can be expected from political rulers "only . . . through their negative wisdom in furthering their own ends," a theme to which I will return below (*CF,* 7:92–93).[13]

Intellectual freedom and education are necessary but not sufficient for enlightenment; in addition, Kant argues, *civil unfreedom* is required, a finding he admits is "paradoxical." By the term "civil unfreedom," he appears to mean the restrictions on the private use of reason previously discussed, along with the political means to enforce them—specifically, a "well-disciplined and numerous army ready to guarantee public peace" as well as an enlightened absolute monarch to govern (*WE*, 8:41). Kant is not clear about why civil freedom would set up "insurmountable barriers" to intellectual freedom and therefore enlightenment, but his reasons are not difficult to discern. The intellectual freedom that Kant endorses is a wide-ranging one, embracing art, science, religion, and even legislation, but the critical public culture that this freedom makes possible is by its very nature subversive, leading its participants to question and criticize the "precepts and formulas" that buttress the authority of doctors, priests, and officers of the law. Without an enlightened absolute monarch at the head of a "well-disciplined and numerous army," such criticism might threaten the very public order that facilitates the long and laborious exploration of ideas needed for enlightenment; it might even provoke a popular uprising that would harness an insufficiently enlightened public with "new prejudices" as pernicious as the old ones they replaced (8:36).

A republic, by contrast, would be incapable of providing this kind of external discipline. Its natural responsiveness to the preferences and passions of a semi-enlightened citizenry would lead it to censor ideas that its citizens found threatening or offensive and to respond inadequately to outbreaks of lawlessness. This is why Kant argues that an enlightened absolute monarch "can say what a free state may not dare to say: *Argue as much as you will and about what you will; only obey!*" (*WE*, 8:41). Just as our interlocutors in learned society provide a guidance that differs in kind from that offered by our guardians, so the enlightened monarch imposes a constraint that differs in kind from that imposed by unenlightened rulers, who offer nothing but "personal despotism and . . . avaricious or tyrannical oppression" (8:36).

As I have just indicated, however, a tension exists between argument and obedience, a tension that motivates Kant to endorse enlightened absolutism but that promises to greaten with time. As a people grow increasingly enlightened, their hostility to established authority and its ideological supports will grow as well: the "precepts and formulas" formerly offered by their guardians will seem increasingly hollow and inadequate, and they will begin to question the legitimacy of rule that is not subject to the same mature public reason that governs the world of ideas. Kant indeed recognizes this dialectical tension and hints at a resolution in the last sentences of his essay: "A greater degree of civil freedom seems advantageous to a people's freedom of *spirit* and nevertheless puts up insurmountable barriers to it; a lesser degree of the former, on the other hand, provides a space for the latter to expand to its full capacity. Thus when nature has unwrapped, from under this hard shell [*harten Hülle*], the seed [*Keim*] for which she cares most tenderly, namely the propensity and calling to *think* freely, the latter gradually works back upon the mentality of the people (which thereby gradually becomes capable of *freedom* in acting) and eventually even upon the principles of *government,* which finds it profitable to itself to treat the human being, *who is now more than a machine,* in keeping with his dignity" (*WE,* 8:41–42).

This rich, somewhat obscure passage needs to be carefully unwrapped itself; I believe it holds the key to Kant's theory of enlightened absolutism. Attend first to the botanical imagery. Kant describes civil unfreedom (i.e., enlightened but militarily powerful absolute monarchy limiting the private use of reason) as a "hard shell" that safeguards our "propensity and calling to *think* freely," which he describes as a "seed" in need of development. This shell, hard but capacious, "provides a space" for the seed to grow and mature; this space is intellectual freedom, and the maturation of the seed is the steady process of enlightenment that culminates in our intellectual majority. A germinating seed soon presses against its shell, however, and the pressure gradually builds; this pressure is symbolic of the tension between argument and obedience that I discussed above. This tension is resolved when the seed is "unwrapped" by "nature": the shell, weakened by time and weather, is slowly penetrated and disintegrated by the germinating seed, which no longer needs its protection. The metaphor is most complex—and subversive—at precisely this point. If the shell is indeed civil unfreedom, then its penetration and disintegration suggests that an enlightened people attain not merely freedom in thinking but also "freedom in acting," i.e., it assumes responsibility for its own governance. Intellectual self-government, which is facilitated by a critical public culture flourishing under the protection of an enlightened absolute monarch, becomes a prelude to and preparation for *political* self-government. Nature (which is itself used as a metaphor for providence [*Vorsehung*] in Kant's other writings, notably *Perpetual Peace,* 8:360–63) makes this transition possible, but the details are difficult to infer from the metaphor itself: a shell may passively submit to disintegration by a germinating seed, but why would an absolute monarch allow himself to be displaced by his enlightened subjects, who are now able to govern themselves? In fact, why would he ever allow, much less encourage, his own subjects to grow into such a threat to begin with? Kant suggests in the above passage that a government may find the adoption of political principles more consistent with human dignity "profitable to itself"; in other words, self-interest may motivate an absolute monarch's early support for enlightenment and his eventual acquiescence in representative institutions, a possibility to which I will return below.

Additional support for my reading of this botanical imagery is provided by Kant himself in a strikingly similar passage in *Religion Within the Boundaries of Mere Reason* (1793), in which he uses gestation imagery to describe "the continuous development of the pure religion of reason [*reinen Vernuftreligion*] out of its present still indispensable shell [*Hülle*]" of historical faith: "The integuments [*Hüllen*] within which the embryo is first formed into a human being must be laid aside if the latter is to see the light of day. The leading-string of holy tradition, with its appendages, its statutes and observances, which in its time did good service, become bit by bit dispensable, yea, finally, when a human being enters upon his adolescence, turn into a fetter" (*RE*, 6:121, 135).[14] Historical faiths, which divide men from one another with their different holy texts and statutes, can only lay claim to being true faiths by serving as a "vehicle" for the pure religion of reason, which is a moral religion, i.e., a religion of "good life-conduct," not of ritual observance (6:123, 170–71). This moral religion will gradually displace the ecclesiastical elements of the historical faiths, including not merely "statutes and observances" but even religious hierarchy itself: "the degrading distinction between *laity* and *clergy* ceases, and equality springs from true freedom, yet without anarchy, for each obeys the law (*not* the statutory one) which he has prescribed for himself" (6:122). This vision of colegislation of the moral law by a priesthood of all believers has subversive implications for religion *and* politics.

Let us return to the last sentences of the enlightenment essay excerpted above. Attend now to the mechanistic imagery at the close of the passage. Hans Reiss suggests that this is an allusion to Julien Offray de la Mettrie's materialistic doctrine in *L'homme machine*.[15] However, it may also be a reference to another use of mechanistic imagery in the essay, which is in the midst of Kant's discussion of the *private* use of reason. He says there that a social hierarchy serving public ends (e.g., military, church, or civil service) is like a "mechanism" and that when an individual serves in one he acts as "part of the machine" (*WE*, 8:37). Therefore, to say that man is "*now more than a machine*" is to say that enlightened man is capable of service in institutions other than such hierarchies and is capable of reason beyond the limited, functional private reason proper to such hierarchies, which is exemplified by "precepts and formulas, those mechanical instruments of a rational use, or rather misuse, of his natural endowments" (8:36). In other words, man's capacity for the *public* use of reason identifies him as a potential participant not only in the cosmopolitan society of men of letters but also in the critical political culture of a self-governing people.

Similar mechanical imagery makes an appearance in Kant's other texts as well, especially the political ones, and once again reinforces the proposed interpretation. For example, Kant says that to employ someone as a soldier and to make use of his skills "to kill . . . seems to involve a use of human beings as mere machines and tools in the hands of another (a state)"; they become part of a larger mechanism, the military, which serves public purposes but demands of its participants qua soldiers that they simply exercise their limited, functional private reason to fulfill their duties (*PP*, 8:345). In *Theory and Practice*, Kant emphasizes that "there must be *obedience* under the mechanism of the state constitution to coercive laws" in order for public order to be maintained, an obedience requiring nothing more than a rudimentary instrumental reason (e.g., paying one's taxes, respecting others' lives and property, etc.) (*TP*, 8:305; cf. *CPrR*, 5:38). Going on to echo the theme of his enlightenment essay, however, Kant argues that citizens must be "convinced by reason that this coercion is in conformity with right," something they can only do with liberty of thought and press, which allows them to exercise their reason publicly and thereby develop their capacity for self-government. To deny this capacity, as Kant accuses the Machiavellian "political moralist" of doing in *Perpetual Peace*, is tantamount to "throwing human beings into one class with other living machines" (*PP*, 8:378; cf. *MM*, 6:355). To affirm the capacity, on the other hand, is to recognize man's aptitude for an active, republican citizenship, which is the ultimate way in which enlightenment "eventually even [works back] upon the principles of *government*" (*WE*, 8:41–2).

Conclusion: Republicanism and the Cunning of History

In "What Is Enlightenment?" Kant suggests that an enlightened absolute monarch (such as Frederick the Great, who ruled Kant's Prussia from 1740 to 1786) can and should lead his subjects to intellectual and political self-government. What form of political self-government does Kant have in mind, however, and why would any absolute monarch take such steps to empower his subjects and thereby jeopardize his own authority? Kant offers answers to these two questions in his later political and historical writings. As for the form of political self-government, Kant endorses *republicanism*, which for him means a separation of powers between a unitary executive and a representative-democratic legislature whose members are chosen by a limited electorate of "active" citizens. The separation-of-powers component of Kantian republicanism is described in *Perpetual Peace*, where Kant contrasts republicanism ("separation of the executive power . . . from the legislative power") with despotism ("the high-handed management of the state by laws the regent has himself given") (*PP*, 8:352).[16]

Kant lays out his views regarding the legislative branch most clearly in the first half of the *Metaphysics of Morals*, the *Doctrine of Right* (*Rechtslehre*). He argues there that "sovereignty" (*Souveränität*) resides in the "person of the legislator," and in addition that "legislative authority can belong only to the united will of the people" (*MM*, 6:313). The "active" citizens of a republic are described as those with an "equal right to vote within this constitution" as well as "the right to manage the state itself . . . [to] organize it or to cooperate for introducing certain laws" (6:314–15). But Kant was not an advocate of direct democracy: he goes on say that citizens are "represented by [their] deputies (in parliament)" and "[act] through their delegates (deputies)," i.e., their political agency is expressed by voting for and otherwise trying to influence their legislative representatives (6:319, 341). The legislature can grant or withhold war-making powers from the executive; citizens "must therefore give their free assent, through their representatives, not only to waging war in general but also to each particular declaration of war" (6:345–46). It also has power of the purse, for "the people taxes itself, since the only way of proceeding in accordance with principles of right in this matter is for taxes to be levied by those deputized by the people" (6:325). Finally, and most radically (given his political context), Kant gives the legislature the right to "take the ruler's [executive's] authority away from him, depose him, or reform his administration. But it cannot *punish* him (and the saying common in England, that the king, i.e., the supreme executive authority, can do no wrong, means no more than this)" (6:317). Given his experience with the Prussian censors, such an assertion may strike the reader as quite bold, bordering on reckless, but Kant does rule out punishment of the monarch (no doubt with Louis XVI in mind), and he later stresses that citizens can only "legally *resist* the executive authority and its representatives (the minister) by means of its representatives (in parliament)" (6:322).[17] Kant's motto, as always, is "Reform not revolution."

Kant believes that the vote should be limited to "active" (rather than "passive") citizens. He defines an active citizen as one who is "independent," i.e., capable of "acting from his own choice" and therefore not dependent "upon the will of others" (*MM*, 6:314–15). By this definition he apparently intends to exclude from the franchise whoever is personally dependent upon others for his "preservation in existence (his being fed and protected)," whether through employment or familial dependency (e.g., wives and children) (*TP*, 8:295–96). Although he does not discuss his reasons for restricting the franchise in this way, he seems to believe that passive citizens would be unduly influenced by those upon whom they were dependent; allowing them to vote would therefore undermine the integrity of republican governance by effectively giving multiple votes to employers, husbands, and fathers—though a secret ballot could surely diminish this kind of influence. From our own perspective, such restrictions on voting may seem highly reactionary. In fairness to Kant, though, we should also note that he says that the "natural laws of freedom and . . . equality" require that "anyone can work his way up from this passive condition to an active one," i.e., anyone who can escape personal dependency (by becoming an independent artisan, yeoman farmer, etc.) is entitled to the franchise (*MM*, 6:315; cf. *TP*, 8:292).

If republicanism so described is the enlightened absolute monarch's goal, then what is his motive? First, he has a *moral duty* to facilitate this transition to intellectual and political self-government, as Kant says clearly in the *Rechtslehre*:

> The spirit of the original contract (*anima pacti originarii*) involves an obligation on the part of the constituting authority to make the kind of government suited to the idea of the original contract. Accordingly, even if this cannot be done all at once, it is under obligation to change the kind of government gradually and continually so that it harmonizes in its effect with the only constitution that accords with right, that of a pure republic. . . . Any true republic is and can only be a system representing the people, in order to protect its rights in its name, by all the citizens united and acting through their delegates (deputies). (*MM*, 6:340–41)

Moreover, the monarch is authorized to guide this transition by a *lex permissiva*: he may defer the institution of a government fully consistent with right "until the people gradually becomes susceptible to the influence of the mere idea of the authority of law . . . and thus is found fit to legislate for itself"; such a delay must be allowed "lest implementing [self-rule] prematurely counteract its very purpose," as I discussed earlier (*PP*, 8:347–48, 372–73; cf. *WE*, 8:41–42).[18]

He may be morally authorized and even obligated to effect this transition, but given that it will demote him to a limited, constitutional executive, do we have any reason to believe that he will actually carry it out? As we saw above, Kant suggested in the enlightenment essay that *self-interest* might lead a monarch to reform. He maintains in "Idea for a Universal History" that "the mutual relationships between states are already so sophisticated that none of them can neglect its internal culture without losing power and influence in relation to the others" (*UH*, 8:27). In other words, geopolitical concerns will cause state leaders to engage in internal reform as a means of strengthening their societies for various forms of international competition. Among the reforms Kant mentions here are freedom of religion and freedom of thought more broadly, as well as the tolerance of (if not support for) citizens' efforts to educate themselves:

> Restrictions placed upon personal activities are increasingly relaxed, and general freedom of religion is granted. And thus, although folly and caprice creep in at times, *enlightenment* gradually arises. It is a great benefit which the human race must reap even from its rulers' self-seeking schemes of expansion, if only they realize what is to their own advantage. But this enlightenment . . . must gradually spread upwards towards the thrones and even influence their principles of government. While . . . the world's present rulers have no money to spare for public educational institutions . . . they will nonetheless find that is to their own advantage at least not to hinder their citizens' private efforts in this direction. (*UH*, 8:28; cf. *WE*, 8:41–42)

Unfortunately, Kant does not say why these reforms would be to the advantage of "self-seeking" rulers, but his reasons are not difficult to infer. To begin, religious toleration may promote social peace, thereby freeing up state resources (especially military ones) for other uses; moreover, it may secure the loyalty of oppressed but economically powerful religious minorities.[19] More generally, freedom of thought and the education to make it effective, by fostering a critical public culture and an enlightened citizenry, enlists the talents of the people in the reform process. As noted above, Kant believed that freedom of the press should be broad, including matters scientific, religious, and legislative (*WE*, 8:41). The critical public culture that results will therefore be a rich source of new ideas for improving the efficiency of public institutions—a desirable state of affairs for an ambitious, expansionist ruler.

But these initial rounds of reform can take a society only partway toward republican governance: economic and intellectual freedom can help create a prosperous and enlightened populace that is prepared for political self-rule, but political reforms are needed to realize such self-rule, and these are hard to square with the self-interest of an absolute monarch. One can imagine reasons, however, why an absolute monarch might set up representative institutions, albeit initially weak, advisory ones. For example, he might create them to learn the views of his subjects and to provide a venue for the peaceful expression of grievances. Kant even suggests a reason why actual powers might be ceded to them: the need for money. The very geopolitical competition that forces rulers to implement the initial rounds of internal reforms may compel them to make political reforms as a way to extract additional resources from the people without sparking serious opposition; the British parliament and other countries' representative assemblies gained much of their power as a consequence of monarchical penury. Kant himself offers Louis XVI and his convocation of the Estates General in 1789 as an example: "A powerful ruler in our time therefore made a very serious error in judgment when, to extricate himself from the embarrassment of large state debts, he left it to the people to take this burden on itself and distribute it as it saw fit; for then the legislative authority naturally came into the people's hands, not only with regard to the taxation of subjects but also with regard to the government, namely to prevent it from incurring new debts by extravagance or war. The consequence was that the monarch's sovereignty wholly disappeared (it was not merely suspended) and passed to the people, to whose legislative will the belongings of every subject became subjected" (*MM*, 6:341).

Thus, it can be in the short-run self-interest of a monarch to empower the citizenry legislatively. Myopia is apparently key here, for as Kant notes, "a republic, once established, no longer has to let the reins of government out of its hands and give them over again to those who previously held them and could again nullify all new institutions by their absolute choice" (*MM*, 6:341). The return of sovereignty to its original owner (the people) reduces the monarch to a mere executive, an "organ of the sovereign," who can now be rightfully deposed or otherwise constrained by a popular legislature, as noted above (6:319).

By a series of policy innovations, each tactically sound, an absolute monarchy (or more likely a dynasty) thus engineers its own downfall and the creation of a republic. Moreover, this end is (or at least can be) accomplished without any violations of right, which would inevitably occur in a revolution (*TP*, 8:298–304; *MM*, 6:318–23). Whatever one thinks of the likelihood of such a sequence of events unfolding, Kant's theoretical accomplishment here is impressive and largely unnoticed: he has shown how republicanism might emerge from absolute monarchy in a manner wholly consistent with both justice and the short-run interests of the regent himself—the immaculate conception of a republic, in brief, unsullied by revolutionary violence or monarchical resistance. In this way Kant completes his narrative of the progress of absolutism from despotism and dependence to popular self-government, both political and intellectual, and of the systematic political self-emasculation of enlightening rulers prompted by moral duty or (more likely) by the cunning of history.

NOTES

1. Zöllner, "Ist es rathsam, das Ehebündiß nicht ferner durch die Religion zu sanciren?" *Berlinische Monatsschrift* 2 (1783): 508–17; reprinted in *Was ist Aufklärung?: Beiträge aus der Berlinischen Monatsschrift*, ed. Norbert Hinske (Darmstadt: Wissenschaftliches Buchgesellschaft, 1977), 107–16. The proposal was made in a previous *BMS* article written under the pseudonym E. v. K. ("Vorschlag, die Geistlichen nicht mehr bei Vollziehung der Ehen zu bemühen," *Berlinische Monatsschrift* 2 (1783): 265–76; reprinted in Hinske, 95–106), which was commonly used by Johann Erich Biester, one of the founders of the *BMS*—on this point, see Hinske, xxxvii. Elisabeth Ellis provides an excellent discussion of the Biester/Zöllner exchange and its context in *Kant's Politics: Provisional Theory for an Uncertain World* (New Haven: Yale University Press, 2005), 28–30. (The entire *BMS* is now online: http://www.ub.uni-bielefeld.de/diglib/aufkl/berlmon.)

2. Zöllner, "Ist es rathsam," 516; Hinske, *Was ist Aufklärung?*, 115.

3. Günter Birtsch, "The Berlin Wednesday Society," in *What Is Enlightenment?: Eighteenth-Century Answers and Twentieth-Century Questions*, ed. James Schmidt (Berkeley and Los Angeles: University of California Press, 1996), 235–52.

4. J. K. W. Möhsen, "What Is to Be Done Toward the Enlightenment of the Citizenry?" in Schmidt, *What Is Enlightenment?*, 49, 51.

5. Kant writes in a note to his essay that he had unfortunately not received the issue of *BMS* that contained Mendelssohn's essay before completing his own (*WE*, 8:42). Moses Men-

delssohn, "Ueber die Frage: Was heißt aufklären?" *Berlinische Monatsschrift* 4 (1784): 193–200; "On the Question: What Is Enlightenment?" in Schmidt, *What Is Enlightenment?*, 53–57.

6. Mendelssohn, "Ueber die Frage," 198–99, in Schmidt, *What Is Enlightenment?*, 55–56.

7. On Prussian politics of the period, see Hunter, chapter 7 of this volume.

8. Kant's hostility to political revolution is a consistent feature of his practical philosophy. See, for example, *TP*, 8:297–305; *MM*, 6:318–23; and *RE*, 6:122. For Kant's views on citizen obedience under despotism and barbarism, see Ripstein, chapter two of this volume.

9. Cf. Ciaran Cronin, "Kant's Politics of Enlightenment," *Journal of the History of Philosophy* 41, no. 1 (2003): 56–57; and James Schmidt, "The Question of Enlightenment: Kant, Mendelssohn, and the *Mittwochsgesellschaft*," *Journal of the History of Ideas* 50, no. 2 (1989): 288, who see private reason as reason that is valid for the realm of contractual relations.

10. On freedom of the press, see Laursen, chapter 9 of this volume.

11. On education, see LaVaque-Manty, chapter 8 of this volume.

12. Kant may have in mind here Frederick the Great's ill-funded 1763 attempt to create a universal primary education system in Prussia.

13. It has been suggested that *The Contest of the Faculties* is more hostile to absolutism than earlier works. Kant is certainly more openly critical of *unenlightened* absolutism in this work than in previous ones (e.g., *CF*, 7:80). However, the work is in other respects entirely consistent with his earlier political writings, especially regarding the impermissibility of revolution, the necessity of top-down reform by an enlightened ruler, and the desirability of mass education and enlightenment (*CF*, 7:86n, 87–88, 89–91, 92–93).

14. On the term "leading string" in Kant's work, see LaVaque-Manty, chapter 8 of this volume.

15. Hans S. Reiss, ed., *Kant's Political Writings*, trans. H. B. Nisbet (Cambridge: Cambridge University Press, 1991), 274n7. Even nonmaterialistic doctrines can turn man into a machine, however, as Kant indicates in the second *Critique* when he compares Leibnizian freedom to that of a "turnspit [*Bratenwender*]" (*CPrR*, 5:97).

16. Cf. Jean-Jacques Rousseau, *The Social Contract and Other Later Political Writings*, ed. Victor Gourevitch (Cambridge: Cambridge University Press, 1997), 67n, 82–99 [*Of the Social Contract*, Book II, chapter 6; Book III, chapters 1–6].

17. On censorship of religious and political writings under Frederick the Great and his immediate successor, Frederick William II, see Georg Cavallar, "Kant's Judgment on Frederick's Enlightened Absolutism," *History of Political Thought* 14 (Spring 1993): 112–14, 117–18; as well as Frederick Beiser, *Enlightenment, Revolution, and Romanticism: The Genesis of Modern German Political Thought, 1790–1800* (Cambridge: Harvard University Press, 1992), 48–53. Kant's relationship with Frederick the Great's minister of state and head of ecclesiastical affairs, the liberal K. A. F. von Zedlitz, was extremely close, but he ran into problems with von Zedlitz's reactionary successor, J. C. Wöllner. Kant was censured for his religious writings and threatened with "unpleasant measures for [his] continued obstinacy"; he consequently promised to write no further on religious matters, a promise he kept until the death of Frederick William II in 1797. For more details, see Manfred Kuehn, *Kant: A Biography* (Cambridge: Cambridge University Press, 2001), 378–82, 404; and Hunter, chapter 7 of this volume.

18. For more on the concepts of a *lex permissiva* and of "provisional right" (*provisorisch Recht*), see *MM*, 6:223, 247, 256–57, 329; as well as Ellis, *Kant's Politics*.

19. Cavallar, "Kant's Judgment," 115, suggests this may have been Frederick the Great's primary reason for tolerating diverse sects. His grandfather Frederick I's admission of thousands of persecuted but industrious French Huguenots may have provided a model; see C. B. A. Behrens, *Society, Government, and the Enlightenment: The Experiences of Eighteenth-Century France and Prussia* (London: Thames and Hudson, 1985), 123–24. For more on this topic, see Hunter, chapter 7 of this volume.

UNSOCIAL SOCIABILITY: PERPETUAL ANTAGONISM IN KANT'S POLITICAL THOUGHT

Michaele Ferguson

While Immanuel Kant is not widely seen as an important political thinker on a par with Aristotle, Locke, or Rousseau, his work has had a tremendous influence on the past fifty years of scholarship in political theory. His insistence on the imperative of setting laws that could command universal consent inspired John Rawls's attempts to establish the basic principles for a just society by imagining what a rational individual could consent to in abstraction from the particulars of his life situation. His concept of a regulative ideal that should guide our actions even if we can never meet it is the basis for Jürgen Habermas's consensus-oriented political philosophy that aims at identifying procedures and policies that could claim universal validity, even if perhaps this goal is ever beyond our reach. Finally, his prediction of a cosmopolitan future in which federations govern the peaceable relations between states has inspired the nascent literature on cosmopolitan justice that explores how global institutions would have to be designed for all humans to be able to consent to them.

These contemporary appropriations tend to interpret Kant's work as that of a moral philosopher who abstracts away from the complexity of reality in order to identify clear, systematic rules that could guide rational agents in their everyday lives. This familiar way of reading Kant figures him as a rigorous and systematic thinker who seeks to bring the precision of universal moral law to bear on political matters. Those who find this version of Kant appealing try to reconcile apparent inconsistencies between his political writings and his larger body of work either by designating these essays as dilettantish forays into relatively unfamiliar topics, incomplete investigations into matters that were not a central part of his philosophical interests, or (in the case of his earlier works) immature expressions of views later incorporated into his system in more extensive works like the *Critique of Judgment* or *Religion Within the Boundaries of Reason Alone*. Those who find this version of Kant dull and unreceptive to the messiness of human existence are unlikely to think him redeemed by a few uncharacteristic essays on politics and some reflections on the French Revolution. Captivated by conventional interpretations of Kant, opponents and allies alike of Rawls, Habermas, and cosmopolitanism have tended to overlook the critical potential contained in the tensions and contradictions in his political writings.[1]

I suggest in this essay that we can find the resources for an alternative reading of Kant that provides a counterpoint to contemporary neo-Kantianism by taking seriously moments in his political texts where he appears to be inconsistent. If we read these seeming tensions and contradictions in his argument as reflections of the complexity of his position, rather than as symptomatic of the underdevelopment or immaturity of his arguments, a much richer Kant emerges. In this piece, I look specifically at the different accounts he gives of the role of antagonism in moral and political life. The tensions in his view of antagonism come to the fore in his treatment of the concept of "unsocial sociability" in the brief essay "Idea for a Universal History with a Cosmopolitan Purpose."[2]

Commentators on *Idea* usually interpret unsocial sociability in terms of Kant's moral philosophy.[3] They take it to refer to a natural human tendency toward conflictual behaviors fueled by competition, jealousy, and self-interest. These natural unsociable desires are at odds with the categorical imperative that we should make the moral law the maxim of our actions. Since we have free will, humans are caught in the struggle between choosing to do what is good (obeying the moral law for its own sake) and choosing to do what is evil (acting from our selfish desires). For Kant, this is the source of all social conflict, from interpersonal strife all the way up to interstate war: all conflict is the result of the free choices of individuals acting in accord with their natural unsociability. In order to manage this antagonism and achieve perpetual peace, we must counteract the natural tendencies we have to will evil. At first, Kant calls for legal systems and executive powers capable of ensuring our external obedience to the moral law. Gradually, however, he hopes that humans will develop their rationality to the point where their obedience is internal as well. On this reading of Kant, then, we should aspire to overcome our natural unsocial sociability, to make the moral law the maxim of our actions, and to bring into being the kingdom of ends. Interpreters who read antagonism in exclusively moral terms understand it to be a product of our human nature that Kant thinks we can—by means of law and the development of reason—regulate, control, and perhaps overcome. As Allen Wood writes, the "final aim [of Kant's ethical theory] is a human society free from antagonism."[4]

Kant is not only a moral philosopher, however; he is also, importantly, a phenomenologist. That is to say, he is interested in how our experience of the world is shaped by the fact that we humans are particular kinds of beings.[5] In the first *Critique*, for example, he notes that humans organize their perceptions in terms of space and time. This is characteristic of how human beings experience the world, but we cannot therefore infer that reality is structured in terms of space and time, nor that all rational beings would perceive it in this same way. Similarly, in his moral writings Kant frequently notes that the maxims according to which people act are opaque to others: humans are a kind of being who do not broadcast their thoughts to one another, and so we can only guess at what motivates others to act as they do. Each person is a separate subject whose will can never be fully transparent to others, let alone to herself.

I suggest that unsocial sociability for Kant arises in part from this peculiar feature of the human condition—what, borrowing from Hannah Arendt, I call plurality. People come into conflict with one another because their plural wills lead them to pursue different and often incompatible goals. Moreover, the mutual opacity of our thoughts and motivations generates even more opportunities for discord in the form of miscommunication and misunderstanding. We have to make assumptions about what others think, which sets us up to feel confused or even betrayed when they do not act as we would expect. Since we humans cannot but be plural persons with opaque wills, the seeds of mistrust, suspicion, and conflict are forever embedded in human affairs.

Taking this phenomenological account of unsocial sociability together with the moral one, we get a picture of antagonism in Kant's work that is significantly more complex than the moral reading alone would suggest. When we treat "unsocial sociability" as only a moral concept in Kant's work, we think of antagonism as a moral failing, and one that can hopefully be resolved by willing our obedience to the moral law. Insofar as conflict arises from the human condition, however, we cannot eliminate it by designing better institutions, increasing enforcement mechanisms, or developing our rationality. Some antagonism, rather than being a sign of our freedom to will evil, is from this perspective a morally neutral feature of human existence. And rather than being eliminable or manageable, it will continue to reemerge and resist our efforts to contain it. Kant's attempt to regulate conflict away is in tension with his recognition of its persistence; his moral impulses are in tension with his phenomenological ones. What emerges from this way of reading *Idea* is a Kant who can be helpful for thinking critically about the limitations of the Rawlsian turn to procedures as a form of conflict resolution, the Habermasian appeal to consensus and rational will formation, and the cosmopolitan hope for institutions that could guarantee peaceful and just relations around the globe. This Kant—caught himself in the tensions between his moral philosophizing and his phenomenological observations—reveals the persistent tensions and paradoxes of democracy in the context of human plurality.

Antagonism and Purposiveness in Human History

I begin with an account of the role of antagonism in *Idea*. In the First Proposition of that essay, Kant argues that a brief glance at the course of human history is likely to give the impression that it is "an aimless, random process" (*Idea*, 42). Humans are neither creatures of pure instinct, nor entirely governed by reason. Consequently, it is difficult to identify in the activity of the species any consistent patterns or laws at work. Human existence seems instead to be ruled by individual caprice. As Kant writes, "despite the apparent wisdom of individual actions here and there, everything as a whole is made up of folly and childish vanity, and often of childish malice and destructiveness" (41).

The source of this apparent chaos is the free human will. Humans, unlike animals guided only by instinct, are capable of determining their own ends. Yet insofar as humans do not "act in accordance with any integral, prearranged plan like rational cosmopolitans" (*Idea*, 41), we should expect that they will pursue different (and often competing) ends.

This tendency to seek individual ends produces the antagonism that Kant calls *unsocial sociability*, a tendency "rooted in human nature." He explains, "Man has an inclination to *live in society*, since he feels in this state more like a man, that is, he feels able to develop his natural capacities. But he also has a great tendency to *live as an individual,* to isolate himself, since he also encounters in himself the unsocial characteristic of wanting to direct everything in accordance with his own ideas" (*Idea,* 44; emphasis in original). The free exercise of the individual will puts man at odds with society, creating conflict. Indeed, if it were not for the individual will, Kant suggests, "man would live an Arcadian, pastoral existence of perfect concord, self-sufficiency, and mutual love" (45).

Instead, human existence is characterized by chaos, caprice, and conflict, which ultimately make the "course of human events" appear to be "senseless" (*Idea,* 42). The frequency and barbarity of wars in particular call into question any belief that humanity is making moral progress and may even suggest a kind of moral regress. In such a world, what reason do individuals have to strive for improvement? The study of human history, it seems, encourages us to despair for the future and to embrace the nihilistic pursuit of self-interest.

Kant is dissatisfied with such conclusions. In order to make sense of our world, we must presume that humans would not have the capacity to reason if it served no purpose. Consequently, he argues that we need to presuppose that the course of human events is, in fact, driven by a purpose: the full development of reason in the species through the establishment of a cosmopolitan order (*Idea,* 42). Without this idea that the species is progressing toward its fullest development, individual humans would lack sufficient motive to act in accordance with reason: "all practical principles would have to be abandoned, and nature, whose wisdom we must take as axiomatic in judging all other situations, would incur the suspicion of indulging in childish play in the case of man alone" (43). In order to be motivated to act in accordance with reason, we need the sense that such action would be meaningful; the idea of the progress of the species provides human action with this sense of purpose.[6]

Kant suggests that when we examine human history "*on a large scale*" we "will be able to discover a regular progression among freely willed actions" (*Idea,* 41; emphasis in original). Nature acts through human history as a kind of invisible hand, bringing about her purpose for humanity through the unwitting actions of individuals (41).[7] Indeed, it is through our antagonism with one another that we unconsciously bring about nature's end: the rational development of the species under a cosmopolitan moral order. We can further contribute to this progress by intentionally adopting nature's end as our own (50).

Antagonism is the mechanism that nature has provided to drive the improvement of the species. While each of us seeks to pursue our own will, we find our will resisted by other individuals. This resistance, Kant suggests, "encourage[s] man towards new exertions of his powers and thus towards further development of his natural capacities" (*Idea*, 45). In other words, since humans cannot simply get what they want, they are forced by nature into thinking, strategizing, and struggling with other humans to achieve their goals—activities that trigger self-awareness of ourselves as rational beings and the development of our rational capacities. The conflict produced by our plural wills is then transformed into competition by "the desire for honour, power, or property" that "drives [us] to seek status among [our] fellows" (45).[8] And so our unsociable, individual wills produce "social incompatibility, enviously competitive vanity, and insatiable desires for possession or even power" (45). Antagonism thereby drives innovation and progress: "All the culture and art which adorn mankind and the finest social order man creates are the fruit of his unsociability" (46).

Indeed, it is our experience of the conflict produced when every individual pursues freedom without constraint that makes us aware of the need for laws. Antagonism thus motivates us to pursue a society governed by a civil constitution that has "the most precise specification and preservation of the limits of this freedom in order that it can co-exist with the freedom of others" (*Idea*, 45). The conflict between individual wills is thereby managed and made sustainable by the combination of laws and force. Nonetheless, even in such a law-governed society, we would still want to encourage antagonism. One form of conflict Kant sees as crucial for the progress of civil society is that between citizens and their rulers: citizens must be free to exercise their reason in public in order to critically assess society's laws and ensure their legitimacy. It is through this critique that he hopes the continual reform of our political institutions will be possible.[9] Consequently, a civil society must be one that has "the greatest freedom, and therefore a continual antagonism among its members," albeit a civilized antagonism consistent with obedience to the law (45).

Yet it is impossible to sustain a civil society if it remains in conflict with other civil societies. At the international level, the antagonism between individual wills is experienced anew as the antagonism between the wills of individual states. Even the most internally rational civil society is nonetheless subject to "[w]ars, tense and unremitting military preparations, and the resultant distress which every state must eventually feel within itself, even in the midst of peace." The antagonism between states, therefore, drives us to form law-governed federations whose united wills manage the conflict between the differing "individual" wills of each polity (*Idea*, 47). We make international society sustainable through the establishment of "common external agreement and legislation" (48). Our natural unsocial sociability, therefore, rouses us from intellectual laziness and drives us (knowingly or unknowingly) to create the conditions for a cosmopolitan political order.[10]

Notice how in the course of this essay Kant has managed to rehabilitate the concept of antagonism. It seems to us at first that antagonism is the source of the meaninglessness of human existence. On closer inspection, however, we see that it is instead the driving force of human progress. Chaos and conflict in human events, rather than being a reason for despair, are a reason for hope.

Even so, Kant achieves this rehabilitation at the expense of the disruptive force of antagonism in human affairs. The idea of a cosmopolitan future for which we should strive and toward which we must assume nature drives us is an idea of a future in which antagonism is managed and brought under rational regulation. Yet is unsocial sociability fully regulable, as Kant's cosmopolitanism would seem to require?

Unsocial Sociability and the Fact of Human Plurality

To answer this question, we need first to reflect further on what Kant means by "antagonism" or "unsocial sociability." As Wood notes, the phrase "unsocial sociability," far from being a curiosity in one brief and relatively early piece, captures a concept that is central to Kant's work: "its importance for the entirety of Kant's thinking about human nature would be virtually impossible to overestimate."[11] Although the phrase itself is specific to *Idea*, the concept to which it refers appears in one form or another throughout the works gathered together as his so-called political writings, as well as in those that might be characterized as moral anthropology and philosophy. However, it is not entirely clear from one mention to the next what precisely Kant means to include under this concept. Sometimes he is concerned with a tension between the individual and society in general (e.g., *Idea*, 44); at other times, he seems to be referring to a conflict between different individual wills (e.g., *Idea*, 46).[12] Sometimes antagonism involves physical conflict, as in the case of war;[13] sometimes it is represented in terms of inequality and class conflict;[14] and at other times it is simply disagreement or discord,[15] as in the case of public critique of the law.[16] Sometimes the conflict is external—between states or individuals; at other times, it is represented as internal—whether between reason and desire within a single person[17] or between a person's simultaneous attraction to and repulsion from the company of other humans.[18] In the *Metaphysics of Morals,* as I examine later in this essay, this tension is characterized in terms of competing desires for love and respect. The concept of unsocial sociability, even within a single text like *Idea,* involves the elision of many different kinds of antagonism. We could say therefore that the concept is uncharacteristically unclear and undertheorized in Kant's writings.

The moral reading of unsocial sociability finds an underlying unity to all of these different expressions of antagonism in Kant's work: all forms of conflict are an expression of the human propensity for radical evil. All antagonism is reducible to the struggle within the individual between reason and the natural inclination to serve one's self-interest. Competition, war, and inequality are all the consequence of individuals failing to make the moral law the maxim of their actions.

Yet—while I do not dispute that there is a great deal of textual evidence to support this reading—it does not capture the whole of Kant's account of these different forms of antagonism. He is, as I noted at the outset of this essay, a phenomenological thinker as well as a moral philosopher. At stake in all of these forms of antagonism is a concern not just with the moral struggle within each of us, but also with the characteristics of a specifically human existence that structure our experience of what is possible—indeed, that structure that experience of moral struggle itself.

Humans, according to Kant, are a peculiar kind of creature. Unlike bees and beavers, we are not governed solely by instinct, acting together as a collective agent for the benefit of our species (*Idea,* 42). Nor are we united in a rationally chosen common purpose, like Kant's "rational cosmopolitans." The purpose that Kant divines for us is not one of our own choosing; rather, it is nature's purpose, although individuals may come to choose it as their own (42). In other words, we act primarily as distinct individuals and not as coordinated members of the same species.

This peculiarly human quality corresponds roughly to what Arendt has called *plurality*: "the fact that men, not Man, live on the earth and inhabit the world."[19] Humans are plural not simply in terms of number, but also in terms of their desires. Other animals, by contrast, share "immediate, identical needs and wants."[20] However, the plurality of human needs and wants—and, we might say with Kant, the plurality of individual wills—separates us from one another. We cannot know what others want in advance of interacting with them; unlike in the case of bees and beavers, we cannot simply extrapolate from the fact of our shared humanity to an accurate understanding of what individual humans desire. One of the main characteristics of human plurality, then, is our *subjective distance* from one another. Individual thoughts and desires are opaque to others unless they find expression in speech and action, which because of their public nature are then accessible. Even then, we can only infer from her actions what a person's internal state might be; we can never have direct knowledge of it.[21] We are, despite our common humanity, strangers to one another.

This mutual opacity is a characteristic of human beings and not a characteristic of rational beings in general, as Kant himself notes. In *Anthropology from a Pragmatic Point of View*, he imagines a species organized quite differently from our own: "It could well be that on some other planet there might be rational beings who could not think in any other way but aloud; that is, they could not have any thoughts that they did not at the same time *utter*, whether awake or dreaming, in the company of others or alone" (*A*, 7:332). Members of such a species could be mutually transparent (assuming, of course, that language unproblematically expresses their thoughts). However, we humans need not reveal our every thought to one another.[22] The privacy of our thinking, on Kant's view, tempts us to conceal ourselves. "So it already belongs to the original composition of a human creature and to the concept of his species to explore the thoughts of others but to withhold one's own; a neat quality which then does not fail to progress gradually from *dissimulation* to *intentional deception* and finally to *lying*" (*A*, 7:332–38; emphasis in original).[23]

In this passage, Kant slides very quickly from consideration of the "original composition" of humanity—what we might with Arendt call "the human condition"—to consideration of the kind of character that this composition enables. In fact, in his political writings, Kant frequently conflates the givens of the human condition with the tendencies, instincts, and character of the human species—what I will call here "human nature." Yet human nature and the human condition are quite different matters. By nature, Kant suggests that humans have a propensity for conflict, war, lying, deceit, and evil. We have an obligation to strive to correct these natural tendencies by means of moral and civil law. However, no amount of rational regulation can alter the underlying fact of plurality. We cannot eliminate the subjective distance between persons and make their wills mutually transparent. At best, by striving for honesty and accountability, we can hope to mitigate the impact of the opacity of our thoughts on our interactions; but we cannot simply legislate it away. Indeed, as Kant's imaginative example of rational extraterrestrials suggests, in order to rid ourselves of the human condition of plurality, we would have to become entirely different kinds of beings. Insofar as antagonism is a consequence of human nature, then, we can reasonably strive to manage it via moral, civil, and cosmopolitan law. However, insofar as antagonism is a consequence of the human condition of plurality, it is an unalterable feature of human existence.

This conflation of human nature and the human condition may help us to make sense of one of the more perplexing features of Kant's political writings: his tendency to equivocate about the role of antagonism in our cosmopolitan future. On the one hand, Kant calls for a "universal and lasting peace"[24] as "the supreme political good."[25] The cosmopolitan order that brings this peace about is one that "can maintain itself *automatically*" (*Idea*, 48; emphasis in original). On the other hand, Kant's invocation of the famous phrase "perpetual peace" can be read as ironic, since the peace to which it refers is that found only in death. He notes in *Theory and Practice* that "a permanent universal peace by means of a so-called *European balance of power* is a pure illusion."[26] In *Perpetual Peace,* he hints at a possible explanation for this: a federation, he suggests, "may check the current of man's inclination to defy the law and antagonise his fellows, although there will always be a risk of it bursting forth anew" (*PP*, 105). The laws that "regulate the essentially healthy hostility which prevails among the states and is produced by their freedom" (*Idea*, 49), it seems, cannot fully insulate us from the riskiness of antagonism. Indeed, eliminating antagonism would be dangerous, as "a cosmopolitan system of general political security" risks letting "human energies . . . lapse into inactivity" (*Idea*, 49). At times, he calls for "an end to all hostilities" (*PP*, 93); at other times, he insists that we can and should manage "essentially healthy hostility"; and at still other moments, he anticipates that despite our best efforts at regulation and enforcement, even unhealthy hostilities may continue to burst forth anew.[27]

We could read Kant's wavering on this point as symptomatic of his conflicting views on the source of antagonism in human affairs. If antagonism arises solely from human nature, then it should be more or less manageable by law.[28] However, if it arises even in part from the human condition, then we would have to shed our very humanity in order to be rid of it, and so we can expect it to be a permanent feature of politics. Kant is unable to provide a consistent answer about whether cosmopolitanism amounts to the cessation of hostilities or merely their continuation by other means because he has not worked out a consistent account of the origin of antagonisms in human affairs.[29]

Friendship and Antagonism

Perhaps the most troubling consequence of Kant's conflation of nature with condition is that, while he often acknowledges the ineradicability of antagonism in human affairs, his political vision of "a cosmopolitan system of general political security" is an idea that addresses the antagonism arising from human nature, but one that is fundamentally at odds with human plurality. In order to illustrate this point, I make the seemingly unlikely turn to his discussion of friendship in the *Metaphysics of Morals*, one of the many places in his work where the concept of unsocial sociability reappears.

Perfect friendship, according to Kant, "is the union of two persons through equal mutual love and respect" (*Metaphysics*, 261).[30] Two perfect friends would consider themselves to be the two halves of a single self with a single will. Friendship, in its ideal form, is a complete communion, a "fusion into one person" (262); it marks an overcoming of subjective distance. Perfect friends are transparent to one another, essentially indistinct in their sameness, and therefore reliable to such an extent that they should never have cause to doubt each other.

This perfect unity is an impossible ideal to which we can only aspire, for three reasons. First, we can never realize this ideal in practice because it is difficult for us to establish that each friend's love and respect for the other is equivalent. Second, friendship, for Kant, is a delicate balancing act between the sociable love that attracts us to one another and the unsociable respect that repels us (*Metaphysics*, 261). It is difficult for each of us to maintain an exact balance between attraction and repulsion. Third, it is impossible in practice to achieve "the union of two persons." Kant is sharply aware that two persons can never simply be united into one, no matter how much we might wish for this. We always remain different subjects with different wills, each of us ends in ourselves. The ideal of complete communion in friendship is therefore in tension with the fact of human plurality.

For Kant, this tension is manifested when one friend tries to uphold the duty to judge and criticize the other in order to help the latter to improve himself. He writes,

> From a moral point of view it is, of course, a duty for one of the friends to point out the other's faults to him; this is in the other's best interests and is therefore a duty of love. But his other half sees in this a lack of the respect he expected from his friend and thinks that he has either already lost or is in constant danger of losing something of his friend's respect, since he is observed and secretly criticized by him; and even the fact that his friend observes him and finds fault with him will seem in itself offensive. (*Metaphysics*, 262)[31]

We have all likely found ourselves on both sides of this scenario: we have tried gently to point out faults to our friends, and we have received unanticipated, and perhaps unwelcome, criticism from our friends. No matter how honorable the intentions, criticism and the attendant act of judging have the effect of reminding friends of their subjective distance: we are not two halves of a single self, after all. My attempt to be a perfect friend by pointing out your flaws, rather than bringing us closer to communion, reveals that we are and will always be distinct individuals with different perspectives on the world.

For Kant, then, it seems that friendship can persist only through a constant back-and-forth movement. At one moment, we are caught up in the fantasy of communion and feel that the two of us constitute a single self. At the next moment, judgment disrupts that feeling of oneness and reminds us that we are indeed different subjects. To keep going, we must forget that difference, and so we start the cycle over again. Judging and forgetting, judging and forgetting: this is the rhythm of Kantian friendship.[32] Relationships are fragile and must continually be put back together through a kind of willful, collective amnesia; "friendship is something so delicate (*teneritas amicitiae*) that it is never for a moment safe from interruptions" (*Metaphysics*, 262). It involves a constant struggle between attraction and repulsion, sociability and unsociability, forgetting and judgment.

Kant contends that the interruptions in friendship are caused by emotion. He concludes, therefore, that lasting friendships must be grounded in morality, rather than in affect. Morality supplies friends with guidelines to help them maintain an appropriate balance between attraction and repulsion without provoking melodramatic quarrels and reconciliations (*Metaphysics*, 262). In moral friendship, friends recognize that they are two separate persons who are opaque to each other. Nonetheless, moral friends aim to approximate the conditions of perfect friendship: that is, to transcend as much as possible the subjective distance and difference that divides them. People yearn for the intimacy of complete transparency: "[Man] would like to discuss with someone what he thinks about his associates, the government, religion and so forth, but he cannot risk it: partly because the other person, while prudently keeping back his own judgments, might use this to harm him, and partly because, as regards disclosing his faults, the other person may conceal his own, so that he would lose something of the other's respect by presenting himself quite candidly to him" (263). Moral friendship makes this disclosure safe and possible because moral friends share enough ideas and principles in common that they can count on each other to not have anything to gain by revealing each other's secrets. This moral sameness enables "confidence" in the other, a kind of reliability: friends have a good idea of how the other is likely to act, because each can infer from his knowledge of his own thoughts what the other would do. A good moral friend is a person who is smart enough to know when to keep a secret, and who is likely to agree anyhow with his friend's secret opinions, and so can be trusted (263). Moral friendship, then, differs from perfect friendship only in that it is grounded in moral principles rather than emotional attachments. Although Kant does not acknowledge it, the ideal of perfect friendship that denies our plurality by collapsing the space between us continues to govern the aspirations of moral friends, who seek transparent disclosure, the reliability of shared principles, and trustworthiness.

Moral friendship, then, manages the kind of antagonism that arises from human nature (here that associated with emotions), at the same time as it aims to overcome the kind of antagonism that arises from the human condition of plurality: that associated with subjective distance and different individual wills. Kant describes a moral friend as "someone who ... shares his [friend's] general outlook on things" (*Metaphysics*, 263); we can assume, then, that our moral friends will think and will what we would think and will. Yet what reason do we have to think that our moral friends do, in fact, share our general outlook? Since our thoughts are hidden from one another, we cannot know whether our friends share our views; we can only infer that they do from their words and actions. That is, moral friendship—like perfect friendship—relies upon a fiction of sameness, a series of practical assumptions that we make about one another in order to be willing to trust and confide, but assumptions that cannot be grounded in actual knowledge of the other. These working assumptions that we make are always in danger of being disrupted when our friend says or does something we did not anticipate. Our confidences may reveal that we are more different than we had assumed. In order to go on being friends, we may need to acknowledge or forget these differences; and of course, we may find that the trust and confidence we had, once disrupted, cannot be rebuilt. Moral friendship still takes place between two human beings; no matter how closely they hew to the principles of friendship, moral friends are still mutually opaque beings with different wills who by virtue of their difference are capable of reintroducing antagonism to the relationship. Morality may help us to check the destructive influence of emotion in friendship, but it cannot eliminate the impact of plurality on human interaction: moral friends are still capable of miscommunication, misunderstanding, and discovering to their surprise that the other is not who they thought he was.

This concept of moral friendship is Kant's model for political friendship, which he only briefly discusses at the conclusion of this section of *The Metaphysics of Morals* as the "friend of man" (264). While the friend of man takes an "affective . . . interest in the well-being of all men," and so might seem to be engaged in a version of emotional friendship, he is nonetheless guided by a principled commitment to "the *equality* among men" (264). This moral, cosmopolitan friendship also is parasitic upon the idea of perfect friendship. We can see this in *Idea*, where the cosmopolitan federation Kant envisions in the future has "a united power" and "a united will" (47). Whether at the level of civil society or the cosmopolitan federation, his political solution to the challenge of antagonism is to fuse different, conflicting, individual wills into one single, universalizable will. However, just as moral friendship is still in constant danger from the antagonisms arising from plurality, we can expect the cosmopolitan friendship expressed in a united political will to be continually threatened. The belief that our fellow citizens and fellow human beings share our will can only be founded on a practical assumption about what they think and want, and not on knowledge. Consequently, our assumption that our fellows are like us and will what we will, that they are equally committed to the universal moral law as expressed in our shared political institutions, is an assumption that is always vulnerable to disruption when it turns out they do not act as we thought they would. Ironically, the assumption that we have or should have a single, united will risks making us less, rather than more, attentive to the ways in which other human beings are ends in themselves, with their own, individual wills. Rather than ensuring political security, cosmopolitan institutions will continue to be threatened by the antagonisms arising from our mutual opacity.

Constant Danger and Perpetual Peace

We will never be able to fully realize Kant's idea of a cosmopolitan future, therefore, without escaping the human condition. Only a different kind of being would be capable of permanently establishing a united will; plural humans, by virtue of their mutual opacity, generate a constant danger to the presumption of unity. Ironically, we might say that it is our very humanity that prevents us from realizing our full humanity.

In Kant's defense, we might note that he was deeply aware of the tensions between morality and anthropology. Humans are not only rational beings, they are also humans, which limits their capacity to fully realize rational principles in practice. This fact, as other scholars have pointed out, motivated Kant's interest in moral anthropology and applied ethics.[33] We could also point out that the impossibility of realizing the idea of our cosmopolitan purpose does not in any way undermine its role for us as a regulative idea. Ideas like purposiveness in human history are presumptions that it is necessary for us to make in order to make sense of our world.[34] They guide human action; whether human beings can actually realize them is irrelevant to their necessity as ideas. Furthermore, Kant in his political writings frequently notes that his predictions for the future may be incorrect.[35] If we cannot realize what he envisions for the future, that may simply be a reflection of his limited capacity to see the full arc of human history.

My aim here, however, is not to suggest that Kant's cosmopolitanism is an impossible ideal. Instead, I suggest that the pursuit of a cosmopolitan future both requires and is undermined by antagonism. That is, there is a *constitutive tension* at the heart of Kant's political writings: a tension between morality and phenomenology, between the moral law and perpetual antagonism, between the practical assumption that we are in agreement and the persistent possibility that we do not see matters in the same way. It is not just that our unsocial sociability keeps us from fully realizing the cosmopolitan idea in practice; it is also that the cosmopolitan idea needs perpetual antagonism to motivate us to try to realize it in the face of its impossibility.

Antagonism works against the establishment of cosmopolitan order in several ways. In the forms of war, competition, and disagreement, it threatens to undermine the legitimacy and efficacy of institutions that aim to regulate conflict between states and persons. The persistence of antagonism in human affairs, moreover, encourages despair that we humans are not in fact making moral progress, that human affairs are random and capricious, and that the world we live in is essentially meaningless. Despair in turn undermines the motivation to pursue a cosmopolitan legal order: if regulation cannot put a stop to human conflict, why bother trying?

Yet even as antagonism works against the cosmopolitan idea, it is also necessary to it. Our confrontation with the possibility that human affairs are chaotic and meaningless is what prompts us to make the practical assumption that there must be some kind of purposiveness in human history that gives seemingly random events order and meaning. Antagonism, therefore, generates faith in the possibility of a cosmopolitan future and motivates individuals to act so as to further moral and political progress. What is more, we learn from the conflicts between persons and states that we need systems of law and enforcement to peaceably manage human interactions. In this way, antagonism is the source of the impulse to address conflict by means of regulation. Finally, a cosmopolitan future requires antagonism because it is only through encountering obstacles and resistances that humans develop their rational capacities. In a world without conflict, adults risk becoming intellectually and morally lazy and children lack the stimuli they need to exercise their reason. We risk devolving into a society of passive law-abiders with no appreciation of why we might want to obey the law or sustain our political institutions. The pursuit of an ever more extensive and ever more moral political order depends upon at least some of us being able to develop our reason enough to understand why we might want a cosmopolitan future.

On this reading of Kant's political thought, then, the idea of progress toward a cosmopolitan future depends upon humans being perpetually tossed back and forth between our attraction to and repulsion from the idea itself. We need both the hope that humans might someday realize a cosmopolitan future and the experience of the abyss of meaninglessness to reinvigorate that hope when we become discouraged. We need the dream of a world without conflict, and we need conflict to inspire us to have that dream. Rather than overcoming antagonism, therefore, Kantian cosmopolitanism is parasitic upon it.[36]

This Kant is importantly different from the one who inspires neo-Kantian political theory. He is a moral philosopher who attends to the undesirability of the elimination of conflict and the importance of its perpetuation. He is a phenomenologist who notes the limits of our ability to manage or abolish forms of antagonism that arise from the human condition. This is a Kant who can help us to understand the neo-Kantian impulse to regulate antagonisms via universally valid procedures, laws, and institutions. Yet this is also a Kant who can help us to see how this impulse draws strength from its own failure to ever fully eliminate the antagonisms that bring it into being.

NOTES

1. A significant exception is the scholarship that draws inspiration from Hannah Arendt's provocative, if unorthodox, reading of the *Critique of Judgment*, in Hannah Arendt and Ronald Beiner, *Lectures on Kant's Political Philosophy* (Chicago: University of Chicago Press, 1982). This literature focuses primarily on the concept of judgment in politics, however, and does not directly take on the neo-Kantian appropriations mentioned here. See, for example, Linda M. G. Zerilli, *Feminism and the Abyss of Freedom* (Chicago: University of Chicago Press, 2005), chapter 4; and Kennan Ferguson, *The Politics of Judgment: Aesthetics, Identity, and Political Theory* (Lanham, Md.: Lexington Books, 1999).

2. Immanuel Kant, "Idea for a Universal History with a Cosmopolitan Purpose," in Hans S. Reiss, ed., *Kant's Political Writings*, trans. H. B. Nisbet (Cambridge: Cambridge University Press, 1970), 41–53; hereafter *Idea*. In *Religion Within the Limits of Reason Alone* (hereafter *Religion*) and other places, these tensions are not apparent, or at least not as easily noticed. This is what underlies the moral reading of Kant—there is a great deal of textual evidence for it. However, we miss an opportunity here when we read *Idea* in terms of these other accounts or when we treat the tensions in this text as simply a matter of immature or underdeveloped thinking.

3. There is little scholarship specifically on *Idea*, and even less that examines the concept of "unsocial sociability" in particular. The three essays that do provide minor variations on this interpretation are: Allen W. Wood, "Unsociable Sociability: The Anthropological Basis of Kantian Ethics," *Philosophical Topics* 19, no. 1 (1991): 325–52; J. B. Schneewind, "Good Out of Evil: Kant and the Idea of Unsocial Sociability," in *Kant's Idea for a Universal History with a Cosmopolitan Aim: A Critical Guide*, ed. Amélie Oksenberg Rorty and James Schmidt (Cambridge: Cambridge University Press, 2009); and Allen Wood, "Kant's Fourth Proposition: The Unsociable Sociability of Human Nature," in Rorty, *Kant's Idea for a Universal History with a Cosmopolitan Aim*, 112–28. For a version of this reading centered on Kant's moral writings, see Katrin Flikschuh, "Towards a Morality of Outer Freedom: Teleology and Right in the Metaphysics of Morals," (typescript, 2008), 181–82. The support for this kind of reading of unsocial sociability comes primarily from passages in *Religion* that strikingly echo the themes of *Idea*. Immanuel Kant, *Religion Within the Limits of Reason Alone*, trans., Theodore M. Greene and Hoyt H. Hudson (New York: Harper and Row, 1960), 22, 29–30. While I agree that the textual continuities are quite strong, I also feel that the phenomenological observations that are a part of

Idea drop out in the later text. In other words, in *Religion*, Kant's account of the role of antagonism in human progress is exclusively moral. That he himself gives this more restricted account of antagonism in his later works in no way means that we must follow him and let *Religion* govern what we can discover by reading *Idea*.

4. Wood, "Unsociable Sociability," 345.

5. On this topic, see Hunter, chapter 7 of this volume.

6. On the concept of *Idea* as a practical assumption, see Onora O'Neill, "Historical Trends and Human Futures," *Studies in History and Philosophy of Science Part A* 39, no. 4 (2008): 529–34; and Onora O'Neill in chapter 1 of this volume, "Kant and the Social Contract Tradition."

7. For the relation of Kant's idea of the purposiveness of nature in human history to his historical predecessors, contemporaries, and followers, see Eckart Förster, "The Hidden Plan of Nature," in Rorty, *Kant's Idea for a Universal History with a Cosmopolitan Aim*, 187–99; Genevieve Lloyd, "Providence as Progress: Kant's Variations on a Tale of Origins," in Rorty, *Kant's Idea for a Universal History with a Cosmopolitan Aim*, 200–215; and Schneewind, "Good Out of Evil."

8. Wood and Schneewind's moral readings of *Idea* focus only on those aspects of our unsocial sociability that correspond to what Kant in *Religion* calls our "predisposition to humanity": that is, our tendency to "judge ourselves happy or unhappy only by making comparison with others" (*Religion*, 22). This tendency to compare ourselves to others leads to jealousy, rivalry, and a desire for superiority. Consequently they (and Kant in *Religion*) miss that the resistance that plural human wills provide to one another is prior to our tendency toward comparison and competition in the account of antagonism in *Idea*.

9. Immanuel Kant, "An Answer to the Question: 'What Is Enlightenment?,'" in Reiss, *Kant's Political Writings*, 57 (hereafter *Enlightenment*). Paul Guyer provides a detailed account of how Kant thought the process of political reform should take place in "The Crooked Timber of Mankind," in Rorty, *Kant's Idea for a Universal History with a Cosmopolitan Aim*, 129–49.

10. This political order, Kant notes in *Religion* (e.g., 90), is the precursor for the pinnacle of humanity's ultimate hoped-for moral development, the kingdom of ends, in which all persons do not just externally obey the law, but also internally make the moral law the maxim of their actions. For discussion of the difference between a cosmopolitan political order and the kingdom of ends, see Wood, "Unsociable Sociability."

11. Wood, "Kant's Fourth Proposition," 115. Wood prefers the translation "unsociable sociability." I have chosen to use the Nisbet translation "unsocial sociability" here because it is the phrase with which English language readers are likely to be most familiar.

12. See Immanuel Kant, "Perpetual Peace: A Philosophical Sketch," in Reiss, *Kant's Political Writings*, 113 (hereafter *Perpetual Peace*); and *Anthropology from a Pragmatic Point of View*, trans. Robert B. Louden (Cambridge: Cambridge University Press, 2006), 236 (henceforth, *Anthropology*).

13. See, for example, Immanuel Kant, *The Critique of Judgment*, trans. Werner S. Pluhar (Indianapolis: Hackett, 1987), 320, 328 (hereafter *Judgment*); "Conjectures on the Beginning of Human History," in Reiss, *Kant's Political Writings*, 232 (hereafter *Conjectures*); *Perpetual Peace*, 113–14; *Religion*, 29; and *Idea*, 47–49.

14. For example, in *Judgment*, 319–20; and *Conjectures*, 230.

15. For example, in *Perpetual Peace*, 108; and *Idea*, 45.

16. For example, in *Enlightenment*, 57. The criticism of laws and institutions by citizens is a form of antagonism that is a necessary part of the process of political reform for Kant. See Guyer, "Crooked Timber of Mankind," 140–41.

17. For example, in *Judgment*, 318–19; *Religion*, 22; *Idea*, 44; *Anthropology*, 229–30; and *Conjectures*, 223.

18. Immanuel Kant, *The Metaphysics of Morals*, ed. Raymond Geuss, trans. Mary Gregor (Cambridge: Cambridge University Press, 1991), 261 (hereafter *Metaphysics*).

19. Hannah Arendt, *The Human Condition* (Chicago: University of Chicago Press, 1958), 7.

20. Ibid., 176.

21. In his moral philosophy, Kant frequently mentions that we cannot have knowledge of one another's thoughts. For example, consider this passage in *Religion*: "In and through experience we can observe actions contrary to law, and we can observe (at least in ourselves) that they are performed in the consciousness that they are unlawful; but a man's maxims, sometimes even his own, are not thus observable; consequently the judgment that the agent is an evil man cannot be made with certainty if grounded on experience. In order, then, to call a man evil, it would have to be possible a priori to infer from several evil acts done with consciousness of their evil, or from one such act, an underlying evil maxim and further, from this maxim to infer the presence in the agent of an underlying common ground, itself a maxim, of all particular morally-evil maxims" (16).

22. Indeed, Kant notes that self-knowledge is difficult, if not outright impossible (*Metaphysics*, 236, 241). Moreover, humans develop habits that make it difficult for them to judge themselves and others, and they lack an objective viewpoint from which to make such judgments (*Anthropology*, 5, 34).

23. Note how here our natural propensity to dissimulate and lie is made possible by our mutual opacity. The possibility of this form of evil, then, depends upon our being certain kinds of creatures: if our thoughts were immediately broadcast to others, lying would be unthinkable to us, and so a propensity to hide our thoughts from others would be conceptually incoherent.

24. "The Metaphysics of Morals," in Reiss, *Kant's Political Writings*, 174.

25. "The Contest of Faculties," in Reiss, *Kant's Political Writings*, 175.

26. Although perhaps we might achieve it by other means. Immanuel Kant, "On the Common Saying: 'This May Be True in Theory, but It Does Not Apply in Practice,'" in Reiss, *Kant's Political Writings*, 92 (emphasis in original; hereafter *Theory and Practice*).

27. For example, he says that a cosmopolitan society would be "constantly threatened by disunion" and so the idea of such a future can only function for us as a "regulative principle" (*Anthropology*, 236–37).

28. Guyer, for example, reads *Idea* as saying that we can only manage the consequences of our propensity to evil. Insofar as our radical evil is a consequence of our having free will, it cannot be eliminated, but only regulated by increasingly reformed institutions ("Crooked Timber of Mankind," esp. 148–49).

29. Wood makes sense of these tensions by distinguishing between two periods in Kant's history of humankind. The first is the epoch of nature, in which we struggle to bring the antagonism produced by human nature under control by means of political institutions. In the second epoch, that of freedom, we abolish antagonism by developing our rationality under religious institutions ("Unsociable Sociability," 343–44). Kant's seemingly contradictory statements can then be parsed as being relevant only to one epoch or the other. Yet the possibility of controlling, let alone abolishing, antagonism requires a view of human conflict as arising solely from our propensity to radical evil. It also requires viewing all antagonism for Kant as problematic and in need of abolition—a reading that is irreconcilable with Kant's comments that some hostility is "essentially healthy," and that human reason requires a succession of obstacles to overcome in order to develop and not lapse into laziness.

30. Respect for Kant is respect for personhood; that is, respect that the other is an end in himself.

31. I have altered Mary Gregor's translation to better reflect Kant's text. For the original German, see Immanuel Kant, *Werkausgabe*, vol. 8, *Die Metaphysik der Sitten*, ed. Wilhelm Weischedel (Frankfurt am Main: Suhrkamp, 1991), 610.

32. Kant condescendingly describes such behavior among "uncultivated people": "Such people cannot part with each other, and yet they cannot be at one with each other since they need quarrels in order to savor the sweetness of being united in reconciliation" (*Metaphysics*, 262).

33. On the relationship of Kant's ethics to his anthropology, see Wood, "Unsociable Sociability"; Robert B. Louden, *Kant's Impure Ethics: From Rational Beings to Human Beings* (New

York: Oxford University Press, 2000); Patrick R. Frierson, *Freedom and Anthropology in Kant's Moral Philosophy* (Cambridge: Cambridge University Press, 2003); Holly L. Wilson, "Kant's Integration of Morality and Anthropology," *Kant-Studien* 88 (1997): 87–104; Sharon Anderson-Gold, "Kant's Ethical Anthropology and the Critical Foundations of the Philosophy of History," *History of Philosophy Quarterly* 11, no. 4 (1994): 405–19; and Roger Sullivan, "The Influence of Kant's Anthropology on His Moral Theory," *Review of Metaphysics* 49 (1995): 77–94.

34. See note 6.

35. See, for example, *Theory and Practice*, 91.

36. This dynamic of a cosmopolitan idea parasitic upon that which it purports to reject echoes Jacques Derrida's treatment of the concept of the "regulative Idea" in *Rogues: Two Essays on Reason,* trans. Pascale-Anne Brault and Michael Naas (Stanford: Stanford University Press, 2005), 83–86.

KANT'S POLITICAL THOUGHT IN THE PRUSSIAN ENLIGHTENMENT

Ian Hunter

Introduction

This chapter provides an historical account of Immanuel Kant's political and religious writings by situating them in the context of the Prussian Enlightenment. "Enlightenment" or *Aufklärung* was the term adopted by protagonists during the eighteenth century to name a series of cross-cutting public debates over the reform of Prussia's religious and political constitution and its social and economic order.[1] These debates were centered in Berlin and the small university towns of Halle and Königsberg. They drew their protagonists from the north-German *Bildungsbürgertum*—the stratum of Protestant university-educated theologians, pastors, bureaucrats, jurists, and professors—who communicated via journalism, sermonizing, and academic disputations, and through interlinking memberships of university faculties, Protestant congregations, Masonic lodges, and private clubs and debating societies. This social and literary network formed the public that Kant addressed in his political and religious writings. Given its composition, however, membership of this public was not entirely distinct from or opposed to membership of the state or church, with much depending in this regard on the persona adopted by officials and clergy when engaging in the debates. Neither did the shared educational qualification of the *Bildungsbürgertum* mean that its members were united by a homogenous rational or moral culture—no more than is the tertiary-educated middle class in today's Western societies. What linked the members of this public was the Protestant intellectual culture transmitted in north-German universities and churches. This is also what divided them, as this culture itself remained fractured by opposed intellectual formations, ethical styles, and political commitments, as we shall see.

Kant's political and religious writings were shaped by the Protestant rationalist philosophy (metaphysics) of the north-German universities, preeminently that of Leibniz and Wolff, albeit significantly transformed and distinguished by Kant's own elaboration of a critical, transcendental idealist variant. This is not to say that Kant's views on particular political and religious questions were determined by his philosophical doctrines. Rather, the way in which Kant understood the domains of politics and religion as such was shaped by the kind of philosophical demeanor that Kant cultivated. Kant thought about Prussia's political and religious constitution in the persona of a Protestant rationalist metaphysician. His rationalist natural law conception of politics is thus marked by the metaphysical separation of an ideal domain—understood in terms of harmonious relations established between self-governing rational beings—from an empirical or historical domain. Concomitantly, the domain of empirical or historical politics is understood in terms of the obstacles posed to the realization of ideal rational self-legislation by man's animal nature or sensuous passions and interests. This style of thinking contrasted sharply with Pufendorf's natural law and with German public law as expounded by Johann Jacob Moser. Pufendorf derived political and juridical norms from a Hobbesian anthropology that placed them at the disposal of the civil sovereign;[2] while Moser derived them from the complex web of imperial and territorial enactments that formed the public law constitution of the German empire.[3] Similarly, while religious rationalism (Neology) was significant among Lutheran theologians and clergy—because of their shared exposure to Wolffian metaphysics—Kant's philosophical theology may still be regarded as the theology of a rationalist philosopher. This is not least because for Kant the historical or revealed doctrines of Lutheran Christianity—the soteriological narrative of the Fall, Christ's vicarious atonement, and mankind's regeneration and redemption—are all treated as symbols of mankind's self-purifying capacity to govern itself through the pure practical reason of Kant's own moral philosophy.[4]

Our task, then, is to outline the manner in which Kant's political and religious writings were shaped by the particular academic-philosophical milieu in which he was formed and the distinctive philosophical persona that he cultivated. This contextual analysis holds the key to distinguishing his way of engaging with the debates of the Prussian Enlightenment from that of such groups as the public-law jurists, Lutheran theologians, reform absolutists, and others who staked their own claim to the mantle of *Aufklärung*. To achieve this historical contextualization, it is necessary to observe two interlinked protocols. First, we must be careful not to allow Kant's construction of the ideal (a priori) and empirical domains to organize the relation between philosophy and historiography, for this would turn history into the space in which an ideal philosophy is empirically manifested. Our task, though, requires that we treat the separation of the ideal ("theory") and the empirical ("practice") as itself a characteristic of a particular style of philosophical activity—one taught in the rationalist faculties of the north-German universities—for which we must offer an historical account. Second, for the same reason we must not treat the history of political and religious thought in late eighteenth-century Prussia as if it were characterized by the gradual surfacing of ideal juridical and moral norms in empirical domains of (autocratic) politics and (orthodox) religion destined for rational transformation, or else irrationally resistant to such. In fact this style of philosophical historiography was itself an ideological expression of philosophical rationalism for which we must also offer an historical account, by tracing the interests that anchored it in the political and religious contests of the Prussian *Aufklärung*.

If, then, we approach Kant's philosophy as the basis of his political and religious thought, this does not mean treating it as the source of ideal concepts and norms through which he was able to illuminate and reshape the merely empirical domains of politics and religion, providing the theory for a practice of enlightenment. Rather, it means treating his philosophy as the instrument by means of which he cultivated a distinctively rationalist-philosophical outlook and persona, which in turn shaped a distinctively rationalist-philosophical way of thinking about Prussia's political and religious constitution. To the extent that it was grounded in the cultivation of a distinctive sense of self and social mission, Kant's philosophical engagement in the Prussian political and religious controversies of the late eighteenth century was not fundamentally different from the ideological engagements of the public-law jurists, reform absolutists, Orthodox Lutherans, and others who competed with the Kantians in the Prussian public sphere.[5] We can begin, then, by briefly characterizing the Kantian style of philosophical culture and the distinctive persona of the philosopher to which it gives rise, before outlining Kant's philosophical politics and philosophical theology.

The Morals of Metaphysics

Kant's political and religious writings are based in his moral rather than his theoretical philosophy, even if his moral philosophy itself relies on two key planks of the *Critique of Pure Reason*.[6] These planks are the elaboration of a formal and critical (as opposed to a material and dogmatic) conception of the metaphysical subject, and the related critical demonstration of moral freedom—the capacity of an intellectual being to be self-acting independent of empirical causation and sensuous inclination—in the third antinomy of the Transcendental Dialectic. In the *Groundwork of the Metaphysics of Morals* Kant famously construes the principle of morality not as something arising from man's empirical nature and historical way of life but as formal and a priori—"the ground of obligation must not be sought in the nature of the human being or in the circumstances of the world in which he is placed, but solely a priori in concepts of pure reason"—as this is the only way of ensuring that morality will apply universally and unconditionally (*GW*, 4:389).[7] The formal character of Kant's moral philosophy might thus seem to present an insuperable obstacle to the task of historical contextualization that we have set ourselves. After all, if the principle of Kantian morality is indeed discovered independently of experience, through moral reason's reflexive recovery of its own a priori concepts, then it can hardly be the product of a particular historical style of philosophizing characteristic of philosophy faculties in Protestant northern Germany.

In fact reflection on the formal character of Kantian philosophy leads not to a terminus but to a switch point between philosophical and historical lines of inquiry. Philosophical inquiry into Kant's moral philosophy begins by accepting the formal construction of the principle of morality. It then works within the problem-space of how such a principle—arrived at through formal reflection independent of all anthropological assumptions and sociohistorical purposes—might still ground obligations effective on sensuously distracted human beings acting in concrete historical circumstances.[8] Historical inquiry, however, begins by treating the formal construction of the moral principle as the concrete historical activity of Kantian philosophers. It then regards the image of sensuously distracted human beings acting under the command of pure practical reason as indicative of the particular (metaphysical) moral anthropology that informs this philosophical activity. Needless to say, it is not our intention here to offer a full-scale justification for adopting the historical approach, only to provide some prima facie reasons for its permissibility.[9]

In the first place it can be observed that Kant's formal universal construction of moral philosophy has not been generally accepted within the domain of philosophy itself. Philosophers working in the Hegelian tradition thus regard Kant's formal principle as too concrete, in the sense of being tied to unacknowledged metaphysical assumptions associated with the theological notion of the self-determining intellect. They also regard it as too abstract, in that these assumptions remove morality from the process of institutional innovation and transformation that lies at the heart of Hegelian historicism.[10] This is not to indicate a preference for Hegelian over Kantian philosophy, only to show that despite its self-understanding—as universal moral reason's reflexive recovery of its a priori principle—Kant's formalism is simply one philosophical construction of moral reason among several on offer.

Second, the programmatic and material dimension of Kant's formal method can itself be gleaned from the fact that he ascribes concrete moral consequences to the use of the method itself. For Kant, to refuse an ethics based on empirical views of human character, and to adopt instead a moral principle grounded in the concept of pure rational being, is more than just a methodological protocol for arriving at a true moral philosophy. In fact he regards this methodology as an ethical imperative required to secure the moral purity of those undertaking moral philosophy:

> Now the moral law in its purity and genuineness . . . is to be sought nowhere else than in a pure philosophy; hence, this, (metaphysics) must come first, and without it there can be no moral philosophy at all. That which mixes up these pure principles with empirical ones does not even deserve the name of philosophy . . . much less does it deserve the name of a moral philosophy, since by this very confusion it actually damages the purity of morals themselves and acts against its own end. (GW, 4:389–90)

Kant thus identifies the formal purity of his construction (its capacity to derive the principle of moral philosophy from concepts independent of empirical morality) with its moral purity (its capacity to preserve the morals of philosophers against the corrupting effects of empirical reasoning). This is warrant enough for approaching Kant's formal method historically, as the programmatic means for cultivating a particular kind of moral persona for the philosopher. In an important regard Kant's metaphysics of ethics is an ethics for metaphysicians.

This way of approaching Kant's moral philosophy allows us to adjust our understanding to its proper scale, setting, and significance. This philosophy was a cultural program of moral cultivation that was shaped by its competition with similar programs amid the academic rivalry and journal combat of the Prussian Enlightenment. Kant had been prompted to write his first morals treatise, the *Groundwork* of 1785, by the publication of Christian Garve's Cicero translation and commentary, the *Philosophische Anmerkungen and Abhandlung zu Ciceros Büchern von den Pflichten* (Philosophical remarks and essays on Cicero's Books on the Duties) that had appeared in 1783.[11] Garve had been responsible for the first negative review of the *Critique of Pure Reason*. Published in the *Göttingische Anzeigen von gelehrten Sachen* in January 1782—and heavily reworked by the editor Georg Feder—Garve's review annoyed Kant by minimizing the distinctively transcendental features of the first *Critique* and assimilating it to Humean skepticism and Berkleyean idealism.[12] Garve's Cicero edition thus gave Kant the opportunity to avenge himself on his critic, even if he did so indirectly by elaborating a moral philosophy that repudiated Garve's Ciceronian conception of the duties, root and branch.

As Manfred Kuehn has observed, Ciceronian duties are derived from the roles or offices that organize civil life in the public sphere of the *res publica*—the political commonwealth; individuals are obligated by honor to cultivate the moral persona required to occupy a particular office.[13] In deriving duty from the inner imperative of a self-legislating rational being, and in treating society as the reciprocal communication of this legislation among a universal community of such beings, Kant was not just attacking Garve's Ciceronian ethics of office. In fact he was repudiating the whole Ciceronian conception of a society of civil offices whose historical anchorage was the Prussian ordering of public offices to which Garve's moral philosophy was adapted.[14] This is a pointer to the cultural and political significance of Kant's ostensibly formalistic claim that "the ground of obligation must not be sought in the nature of the human being or in the circumstances of the world in which he is placed, but solely a priori in concepts of pure reason" (*GW*, 4:389).

To get some sense of the complex cultural-political terrain on which such debates took place—largely terra incognita in studies of Kant's moral philosophy—we can situate the Garve-Kant conflict in relation to somewhat similar events that took place in the first decades of the century. In 1713 the famous public-law jurist and public intellectual Christian Thomasius published his *Cautelen zur Erlernung der Rechtsgelehrtheit* (Precautions for the study of jurisprudence).[15] A distillation of his private seminar for advanced law students at the University of Halle, Thomasius's *Cautelen* offers cautionary advice on how such students should negotiate the entire field of academic sciences taught in the universities of Brandenburg-Prussia: public law, theology, medicine, metaphysics, rhetoric, history, natural law, and more; although it is only his advice on how law students should study moral philosopher that concerns us on this occasion. Negatively, this advice was designed to warn his students off the metaphysical moral philosophy and natural law taught in the philosophy faculties that supported Lutheran scholasticism (*Cautelen*, 108–36). Thomasius had two main concerns in this regard: to attack the notion that the sensuous inclinations of the will can be controlled by speculative reason; and to repudiate the related idea that individuals might derive the norms of natural law through the speculative holiness of their own reason, through which they discern divine law (275–97). Positively, Thomasius sought to imbue his students with an Epicurean natural law (political psychology) according to which sensuous inclinations and passions are constitutive of the will. This means that morality consists in the inner restraint or calming of the passions—a practice of tempering violent passions by cultivating countervailing moderate ones—as opposed to subordinating the passions to reason (325–63).

On this basis, Thomasius could separate morality from law—which pertains only to the sovereign's coercive maintenance of external peace—but also from a distinct ethical domain that he called decorum (364–404). Decorum concerns rules designed to fit individuals for life in society in areas of conduct lying beyond legal control and moral principles. Thomasius's construction of decorum compares significantly with the Kant-Garve conflict, as its fundamental premise is that social intercourse requires us to interact with individuals whose religious and moral principles may be fundamentally unlike our own. This means that we must not attempt to impose our own "true" or "pure" morality on our social *confrères*—an indecorous purism that Thomasius associates with Quakers, monks, and scholastics—and should instead cultivate forms of conduct capable of rendering us agreeable to others whose morals we do not share. Such forms of conduct derive from the manners of those who are regarded as the finest representatives of the estate to which we belong, and they include the appropriate modes of relating oneself to the inhabitants of estates higher or lower than one's own. It is through the imitative acquisition of these manners—the modes of dress, speech, and demeanor suited to the occupancy of particular estate or official positions—that we learn the forms of decent conduct that make society possible between religiously and politically fractured groups, within the liminal parameters set by law and morality. Thomasius impresses on his law students that they have a special obligation to cultivate the discipline of decorum, as it is only in the law faculty that this discipline can flourish, for this is the faculty that is charged with preserving social intercourse and civil order regardless of conflicts of religious and moral principle.

Thomasius's moral philosophy can thus be understood as an ethics for law students destined for juridical and political office in a confessionally divided society. To what extent, then, may Kant's moral philosophy be regarded as an ethic for philosophy students being oriented to a different social mission and destination? We have already observed that Kant's formal conception of moral philosophy imports substantive metaphysical-moral ideas associated with the cultivation of a particular intellectual persona. The persona of the moral metaphysician is one who overcomes the moral corruption attendant on empirical moral philosophies of the Garve and Thomasius type by purifying his intellect through pure concepts of morality. The central metaphysical conception around which Kant's moral ideas cohere—the notion of a pure (in both senses) rational being (*Vernunftwesen*) capable of conforming its will to self-legislated moral laws—was definitive of the metaphysical scholasticism attacked by Thomasius. Kant had inherited this figure of thought from Protestant scholasticism via Wolff's rational psychology.[16]

It is striking that that the very conception of "metaphysical holiness" against which Thomasius warns his law students—the notion of a self-legislating rational will that he regards as a threat to his students' moral modesty and a risk to their occupancy of civil office—is precisely the conception that Kant holds out to his philosophy students. No longer presented as a substance as in earlier rational psychology, rational being nonetheless remains a powerful competitor in the battle of moral self-conceptions. Kant thus tells his students (and readers) that they should regard themselves in a "twofold way," with the first side resting "on [man's] consciousness of himself as an object affected through the senses" and the second "on consciousness of himself as an intelligence, that is, as independent of sensuous impressions in his use of reason (hence as belonging to an intelligible world)" (*GW*, 4:457). Rather than arising from moral reason's formal recovery of its pure concepts, it is Kant's concrete struggle for dominance in the field of competing moral programs—particularly the conflict between his metaphysics of morals and Garve's ethics of office—that shapes his conception of the moral subject as a self-legislating intelligence mired in sensuous inclinations that it must overcome:

> So it comes about that mankind claims for himself a will which allows nothing to be imputed to it that belongs merely to his desires and inclinations; and, on the other hand, that he regards as possible, in fact as necessary through it, actions that can be done only by disregarding all desires and sensuous incitements. The causality of such actions lies in him as intelligence and in the laws of effects and actions that follow the principles of an intelligible world. Of this he knows nothing more than that in it reason alone—in fact pure reason independent of sensibility—gives the law. Additionally, that since it is there, as intelligence only, that he is his proper self (while as man he is only the appearance of himself), those laws apply to him immediately and categorically, so that what inclinations and impulses (hence the whole nature of the sensible world) incite him to, cannot infringe the laws of his will as intelligence. (*GW*, 4:457–58)

Kant's construction of moral obligation—in terms of the imperative force of a self-legislating intelligence impacting on a sensuously distracted being—is thus indicative of a learned way of relating to the self. This was available to students in the Protestant rationalist tradition as a form of moral self-culture for a particular philosophical persona, and was in competition with such rival forms as Thomasius's and Garve's in the journal wars of the Prussian Enlightenment. It was on the basis of this conception of the moral subject and moral obligation that Kant elaborated his philosophical theology and natural law politics. This is the (historiographical) sense in which Kant's religion and politics may be regarded as ideologically anchored in the cultural politics of Protestant philosophical rationalism.

Kant's political and religious discourses are tied to his moral philosophy by an array of concepts clustered around the two key figures of "autonomy" and the "kingdom of ends." In the *Groundwork*, the conceptions of autonomy and the kingdom of ends are elaborated on the basis of a figure of thought deeply rooted in the history of Christian university metaphysics, namely, the notion of the "end in itself." First developed as part of the metaphysical characterization of God, the notion of a being "whose existence is in itself an end" ("increate being") contrasts with other beings ("creatures") whose existence is determined by ends imposed by another (*GW*, 4:428–29). On this originally Christian-Aristotelian doctrine, value or the good is determined by the end or purpose that determines the (teleological) existence of things. As a pure autotelic intellect that intuits the end for which it exists—"I am that I am"—God thus possesses "absolute value" via the intrinsic purpose of self-creation. Conversely, his "creatures" possess only relative value in relation to the ends prescribed for them.[17]

In transposing this figure of the self-legislating intelligence to man, Kant produces an analogue for the relation between the divine mind and its creatures: namely, in the relation between man's self-legislating pure intelligence—as an end in itself possessing absolute value—and his embodied self whose relative value derives from desires or ends arising from sensuous inclinations.[18] This is the source of Kant's conception of the person as a rational being to be respected as an end in itself, and of humanity as a dignity or value to be respected absolutely. These conceptions have been widely celebrated as bulwarks preserving humanity against its instrumental misuse for alien ends. In this regard, though, it should be observed that for Kant humanity is not man but something quite different, namely, "rational being in man." This is what makes it possible for Kant to combine absolute respect for humanity with condescending toleration of (empirical) man, as can be seen in his moral prohibition of suicide as a means of ending suffering and (in this sense) obtaining happiness: "It [humanity] demands the duty of morality, and it is only man who demands happiness, which must be unconditionally subordinated to morality. . . . Personhood, or humanity in my person . . . is therefore thought of as a subject that is destined to give moral laws to man, and to determine him, as occupant of the body, to whose jurisdiction the control of all man's powers is subordinated" (*Lectures on Ethics*, 27:627).

The concepts of autonomy and the kingdom of ends that illuminate Kant's religious and political philosophy are thus accompanied by a penumbra of metaphysical ideas in whose half-light we can make out the persona of the rationalist metaphysician, formed through the thinking of these ideas. Kant thus characterizes autonomy in terms of the capacity of rational beings to be subject only to laws of their own making: "Hence the will is not merely subject to the law but subject to it in such a way that it must be viewed as also giving the law to itself" (*GW*, 4:431). We should recall, though, that this notion of self-legislation is grounded not in historically existing men, but in the conception of an autotelic intelligence that conforms its existence to laws of its own intuition.

In a similar fashion, Kant lays the basis for his conception of polity and society via the concept of the "kingdom of ends in themselves." He characterizes this as a "systematic union of different rational beings through common laws." This union takes place through suspension of the subjective ends and inclinations that individuate empirical persons, leading to a "whole both of rational beings as ends in themselves and also of the personal ends that each may set himself" (*GW*, 4:433). Here we should recall, though, what it is that qualifies rational beings as ends in themselves, namely, their status as pure intelligences whose self-legislative willing is governed by the end of their own intellectual existence. This means that the reciprocal unity of their legislative wills in a harmonious kingdom is predetermined by the fact that as pure intelligences they must all will the same thing: namely, their own existence as pure intelligences. This fundamental feature of Kant's moral philosophy was first observed by Heinz Heimsoeth:

> A pluralistically constructed "realm of spirits," of immortal individuals (of the kind in Berkeley's world or in Swedenborg's), is the tacit background of [Kant's] rational faith. . . . Every interpretation of the categorical imperative (which commands me always to behave in such a way that the maxim of my will could serve as the principle of *universal* law) in an individualistic sense changes its meaning and essentially misinterprets Kant's intent. For Kant, too, everything comes down to a community of rational beings, which is made possible by the fact that all of them will essentially the same thing and that in the spiritual-rational core of their being they are totally alike. Only "empirical" self is individual in the sense of something unique; the special character of individuals is merely a fact; it is not itself something of importance and value.[19]

Perhaps we have done enough to show that we cannot understand Kant's religious and political ideas by assimilating them to modern concepts whose meanings are presumed to be transparent: concepts, for example, of the secular autonomy of reason, or of republican government understood as the people's self-legislative "general will." If we are to understand Kant's construction of these concepts then we must begin by tracking them to the metaphysical philosophy from which they emerged and to the persona of the metaphysician formed by this philosophical activity.

Kant's Political Metaphysics

Somewhat paradoxically, the historical understanding of Kant's political thought has suffered from its modernizing adaptation to meet the needs of two highly successful twentieth-century normative philosophies, those of John Rawls and Jürgen Habermas. Kant's figure of a kingdom of pure self-legislating intelligences or "noumenal selves" continues to inform these philosophies. It lies behind Rawls's construction of selfless legislators occupying the "original position" behind a "veil of ignorance"; and it drives Habermas's model of the rational participants in a democratically deliberative public sphere.[20] Understandably, though, these modernizing adaptations strip the kingdom of ends of key metaphysical elements, particularly Kant's construction of self-legislation in terms of the autotelic willing of a community of pure intelligences.[21] This would not be a problem were it not for the fact that the adaptations are then used to interpret the historical Kant. When this occurs, however, then crucial features of the politics of Protestant metaphysical rationalism drop from sight, as does its distinctive place in the war of position that characterized the Prussian Enlightenment.[22]

The basic elements of Kant's political thought were elaborated in his *Rechtslehre,* or *Doctrine of Right,* in 1797, initially bearing the title *Metaphysische Anfangsgründe der Rechtslehre* (Metaphysical elements of the doctrine of right). Despite Kant's claim that his philosophy is not based in a conception of human nature, his political thought may be appropriately viewed as a particular species of natural law.[23] As we have just seen, it is indeed based on a moral anthropology (or angelology)—of man as a pure self-determining intelligence—and it shares the general aim of natural law in deriving juridical and political norms through natural (as opposed to revealed) reflection on what is required for the governance of man as a being with a certain kind of nature. The leading idea of Kant's *Rechtslehre* is that natural law norms—the "principle of right"—may be arrived at through reflection on what is needed for rational beings to achieve rightful ownership of different parts of the globe. This gives rise to a politics based on the protection of reciprocally determined natural rights.

Kant's *Rechtslehre* is thus based on the metaphysical anthropology of man the self-determining pure intelligence that he elaborated in his metaphysics of morals. In fact Kant's political and legal doctrine is formed on the basis of the extraordinary conception that right or justice originates when this pure intelligence, existing outside space and time, seeks to exercise its freedom "externally" by occupying the global surface of the earth (*MM*, 6:247–55).[24] It is on this ground that Kant formulates his principle of right or justice—as the harmonization of the external freedom of each with the external freedom of all in accordance with a universal law—and thence his conception of the juridical community (*MM*, 6:229–31). Kant thus constructs juridical community as the devolved form of the moral community. This emerges when rational beings form a common will on the basis of the "universal reciprocal coercion" required to harmonize individual external claims to the surface of the earth, as opposed to universal reciprocal intellection that characterizes their angelesque community in the moral "kingdom of ends in themselves" (6:231–33).

Formulated in this historically oriented manner, the metaphysical doctrines underlying Kant's construction of justice and politics appear recondite and even esoteric to us moderns, not least because of the depth at which they have been buried in such exoteric receptions as those of Habermas and Rawls. It is thus worth supplying a full quotation that encapsulates them, this one taken from Kant's working notes to the *Rechtslehre*—the *Vorarbeiten zur Rechtslehre*—where the connection between the metaphysical anthropology and his conception of justice is starkly apparent:

> When right [justice] is thought of between men as pure intelligences, in no relation to things or to each other in space and time, then it is easy to determine according to general rules. One need consider nothing but freedom and the exercise of choice [*Willkür*] in relation to each other, either immediately or by means of things. Yet one can say in general that all external right—regarded as possession of the choices of others (because one has control of their willing)—is grounded in the idea of a community of wills [*Gemeinschaft der Willkühr*]. And when for the sake of concretely realising this right man is viewed as a being of the senses [*Sinnenwesen*], then the idea of a community of wills requires, firstly, the sensible [*sinnliche*] condi-

tions for determining right in relation to things, under which alone a communal will is possible; second, such [conditions] through which [a communal will] becomes real; third, the condition for the use of persons as things through which a unified will becomes necessary. (23:299–300)

The central elements of Kant's juridical and political philosophy flow directly from this metaphysical picture of the sensory conditions required to actualize the common willing of a community of pure intelligences. It is on this basis that Kant grounds his construction of right or justice by posing the philosophical problem of "noumenal possession" (*possessio noumenon*): how can a pure intelligence existing outside space and time occupy the physical surface of the earth? According to Kant's metaphysical anthropology, cosmology, and cosmography this problem is inescapable and fundamental. As noumenal or spiritual beings men are metaphysically compelled to make use of the earth in order to redeem it from the morally vacuous status of *res nullius*—an ownerless thing—and in order to obtain embodiment for themselves in the world of space and time.[25] Right for Kant is thus fundamentally understood in terms of the empirical actualization of the idea of the communal willing of a community of pure intelligences through which they harmonize their occupancies of the surface of the earth.

The spherical character or global character of the earth's surface turns out to be crucial for this construction, as it is the continuous and finite nature of the sphere that establishes contiguity among the rational beings seeking to occupy it. This is what allows their exercises of "external freedom" to conflict—were the earth an infinite plane then there would be neither conflict nor law, says Kant—and gives rise to right or justice as the principle that resolves this conflict through communal will harmonization (*MM*, 6:248–56). Noumenal or rightful possession of the earth—that is, the capacity of pure intelligences existing outside space and time to occupy the surface of the earth without infringing one another's choices—is thus reciprocally related to the formation of a communal will. This is understood in terms of the harmonization of the choices of each with the choices of all through "universal reciprocal coercion" in accordance with a universal law (6:232–33). It permits the universe of rational beings to achieve a justly distributed possession of the surface of the earth without having to physically attach themselves to it and thereby lose their noumenal freedom.

For Kant, the achievement of unified external willing via universal reciprocal coercion is thus the devolved juridical analogue of the intellectually unified willing of pure intelligences in the moral kingdom of ends. This in turn holds the key to Kant's way of conceiving politics. Right begets politics because even though the exercise of choice in the "state of nature" determines the possibility of (natural) right, this right remains "provisional" until there is a means of enforcing the common will's universal reciprocal coercion, which entails entrance into the civil condition or state (*MM*, 6:256; 409). Kant thus conceives of the state as the public juridical embodiment of the universal reciprocal coercion that is required to permit a totality of pure intelligences to achieve rightful possession of the earth. This "state in idea"—viewed as the instrument of the harmonized will of a community of rational beings—is thus treated as the moral norm or archetype for all actually existing states:

> A state (*civitas*) is a union of a multitude of human beings under laws of right. Insofar as these are a priori necessary as laws, that is, insofar as they follow of themselves from concepts of external right as such (are not statutory), its form is the form of a state as such, that is, of the state in idea, as it ought to be in accordance with pure principles of right. This idea serves as a norm (*norma*) for every actual union into a commonwealth (hence serves as a norm for its internal constitution). (*MM*, 6:313)

Kant therefore conceives political authority and the state as the sensory condition for actualizing the otherwise noumenal community of rational wills through which a rightful possession of the earth is achieved. This is the light in which to view his specification of the three juridical attributes of the citizens of the "ideal republic":

> The members of such a society (*societas civilis*) that is, a state, unified for law-giving, are called citizens (*cives*). And their juridical attributes—inseparable from their essence (as such)—are [first], rightful freedom, to obey no other law than one to which [the citizen] has given his consent; [second], civil equality, or recognising among the people no superior over him except one whom he has just as much of a moral capacity to bind juridically as the other has to bind him; third, the attribute of civil independence, [meaning] that he owes his exis-

tence and preservation, not to the choice of another among the people, but rather to his own rights and powers as a member of the commonwealth, such that in juridical matters his civil personality may not be represented by another. (*MM*, 6:314)

In viewing it as a community of free, equal, and self-governing citizens, each obeying only those laws that all would will in common, Kant conceives the state or republic as the sensory actualization of a metaphysical potentiality: that is, as the phenomenal machinery that gives effect to the communal willing of a universe of noumenal intelligences seeking to occupy the globe.

We are now in a position to characterize Kant's juridical and political thought as "metaphysical" in a descriptive rather than pejorative sense. Kant's principle of right and conception of the state are metaphysical in the sense of being based on one of the central thought figures of the discipline of German university metaphysics: the idea of man as a rational being or pure intelligence distracted by the sensuous inclinations associated with his material embodiment.[26] In the *Rechtslehre,* Kant treats this idea as something that it is permissible to think (without claiming to know), as a practical principle for making sense of the possibility of noumenal or metaphysical possession. As a result of our discussion, though, it should be said that entertaining the notion of noumenal possession is the result of learning (being taught) to think the idea of sensuously embodied rational being: that is, to think using the instruments of rationalist metaphysics in the persona of a metaphysician. This is what permits philosophers to envisage right or justice in terms of the harmonized willing of a totality of world-seeking rational beings, and to view the state as the actualization of this mutually coercive willing.

If we recall our earlier redescription of the formal or a priori character of Kant's practical philosophy—as itself a moral objective associated with cultivating the persona of the metaphysician—then we can bring a properly historical perspective to bear on Kant's conception of the ideal form of the state. In teaching that his conception of the state—as the harmonized and irresistible collective willing of rational citizen-sovereigns—represents the ideal norm for all historically existing states, Kant should be seen as expounding the characteristic view of the state held by a certain kind of historically existing intellectual: the Protestant German university metaphysician. The historian cannot thus afford to treat late eighteenth-century Prussia as the (imperfectly) realized form of the Kantian ideal state, for his task is to treat the Kantian ideal state as something whose thinking first became possible for a certain kind of intellectual in late eighteenth-century Prussia. The fact though that Kant and his followers do treat Prussia as such an imperfect realization of an ideal state is an important clue as to the character of Kantian political thought. It indicates that this thought assumes the form of a normative political hermeneutics. This is a hermeneutics that uses metaphysics to project an ideal form of the state as a means of revealing the "true" nature of an historical state rendered imperfect by the projection itself.

The particularity of this metaphysical-hermeneutic way of advancing juridical and political norms within the cultural politics of the Prussian Enlightenment can be seen by briefly developing our comparison of Kant's natural law with the Pufendorfian form. Rather than positing rational beings seeking harmonious willing in order to guarantee natural rights, Pufendorf constructed natural law norms in a quite different way and for quite other purposes. He posited man as a passion-driven historical being whose need for mutual security can only be satisfied through the imposition of norms of sociability by a political "superior."[27] Pufendorf was a one of the *gelehrte Räte*, or academic advisers, to the Protestant princely territorial states of Sweden and Brandenburg, and his objective was to reconstruct natural law in terms of norms of sociability required to render historical man peaceable, as opposed to norms of rationality advanced to render ideal man actual.[28] Pufendorf's natural law was designed to place norms of sociability at the disposal of a secular territorial sovereign or state, removing them from the hands of clerical and academic estates whose claims to judge morals and politics on the basis of universal rationality and righteousness were regarded as a threat to such states. This strategy had a particular resonance in Brandenburg-Prussia, where the centralizing dynastic government was seeking to subordinate and pacify religiously fractious clergy and estates.[29]

This does not mean that Pufendorf's natural law political thought was nonnormative or merely historical in the sense of failing to capture the formal grounds of moral judgment or the ideal form of the state.[30] In fact this view of Pufendorf belongs to those whose commitment to formal judgment and the ideal state is indicative of a rival cultural and political program. This is the program formulated via a metaphysical political hermeneutics designed to project the imperfection of the historical state from the standpoint of those—university metaphysicians—claiming custodianship of its pure idea. No less normative and programmatic than Kant's, the natural law political thought of Pufendorf was formulated in a different academic and literary genre. It was not a political hermeneutics for a university metaphysicians, but a political theory-program for the *politici* and juristically trained officials of the secularized Protestant territorial states of northern Germany.[31] This is what permitted Pufendorf's natural law to be adapted to a characteristic array of concrete political and juridical uses: as a semi-official political philosophy for high court officials; as a means of integrating imperial public law (the Westphalian treaties in particular) into the political objectives of the princely territorial state; as a political psychology for the juristically trained officials of this kind of state (most notably in Thomasius's teaching at Halle); and as an ideological weapon used against Christian natural law, which sought to subordinate political objectives to "higher" legal norms and rights based in divine reason.[32]

Most of the features of Kant's political thought fall into place when it is seen as a political metaphysics and political hermeneutics for the stratum of Protestant rationalist philosophers. We have seen that Kant's conception of the state is projected as the solution to a specific metaphysical problem: how can a universe of rational beings or pure intelligences achieve rightful possession of corporeal objects? This leads to a conception of the state as the ideal form of the required reciprocal coercive harmonization of wills into an irresistible general will. The unification of wills and powers in Kant's version of sovereignty thus takes place not in the register of concrete sovereign state building—how to form a unified and unchallengeable agency of political decision and action—but in the register of moral and political legitimation. Neither, though, does Kantian legitimacy depend on the model of a contractual agreement among the people to delegate powers to a sovereign, as Kant's agreement of wills is necessitated by the metaphysical problem of noumenal possession.[33] For Kant, sovereignty and the state should be seen as the expression of the reciprocal harmonization of wills that allows rational beings to possess the surface of the globe, that is, of metaphysical right or justice: "The well-being of a state must not be understood as the welfare of its citizens and their happiness" but as "that condition in which its constitution conforms most fully to principles of right" (*MM*, 6:318).

Kant thus does not formulate sovereignty as the principle of a set of political arrangements required to achieve a territory's domestic peace and external security: a unified agency for making and enforcing law, a standing army, a taxation system, and so on. He constructs it, rather, as a principle of political legitimacy based on the representative exercise of the people's collective will. As a principle of legitimacy, Kantian popular sovereignty does not require that the consensual unification of the people's will has ever actually taken place, as it is the pure projection of a metaphysical moral requirement: "It [the unification of wills] is instead only an idea of reason, which, however, has its undoubted practical reality, namely to bind every legislator to give his laws in such a way that they could have arisen from the united will of a whole people and to regard each subject, insofar as he wants to be a citizen, as if he has joined in voting for such a will. For this is the touchstone of any public law's conformity with right." (*TP*, 8:297).

As the repository of this principle of legitimacy, Kant's central political concept—republicanism—is thus a normative concept within his political metaphysics. It refers to the way a government can legislate *as if* its laws had arisen from the will of the people, which is how Kant conceptualizes political freedom and equality (*PP*, 8:352–53; *MM*, 6:314). Deploying a Trinitarian language, Kant argues that the condition for this legitimate form of government is the separation between the legislative and executive (and judicial) "persons" of the general will. This allows the (executive) ruler to act as the "servant" of the "public will," thereby distinguishing him from the "despot" who enforces laws of his own making and hence imposes his "private will"; although it is not immediately clear why laws enacted in accordance with this division of political persons should be regarded as if they had arisen from the people's united will.

This can be clarified if we recall that Kant regards the formation of a rightful general will as constitutive of the a priori idea of the state, hence as independent of all historically existing political arrangements. Republican political arrangements—the separation of the legislative, executive, and judicial persons of the state—are thus regarded not as constitutive of the general will, but as a schematism for the empirical representation of its idea. This is why Kant characterizes republicanism via the Trinitarian analogy—"the general united will consists of three persons (*trias politica*)" (*MM*, 6:313)—treating the people's united will as the ineffable political godhead whose governance of the visible political universe is only manifested by the republican division of governmental persons. Despite the fact that he occasionally discusses the divided powers as establishing reciprocal checks and balances for the empirical exercise of sovereignty, Kant's fundamental conception of them is as the unified coordinate means of manifesting the supreme unified will. Kant's central political principle—the unified will of the people as the test of political legitimacy—is thus not itself determined by republican political arrangements. This can be seen from the fact that when Kant applies this test—for example, to show the illegitimacy of laws arbitrarily privileging a noble social estate—he does so not by asking whether republican governments might actually pass such laws (clearly they have), but by asking instead whether such a law could be universalized in a community of rational beings.[34]

This is a pointer to the fact that Kant's conception of the general will is driven by a metaphysical principle—the a priori harmonization of wills required to allow a universe of rational beings to occupy the globe—that no conceivable set of historical political arrangements could exemplify, except, that is, as the object of a normative political hermeneutics based on this principle. It is for this reason that Kant can interpret Frederick the Great as the legitimate embodiment of the principle of republican government—because the will of the people is not the historical people's actual will but an ideal harmonization capable of being represented by a single ruler—while simultaneously arguing that actual government must gradually approximate the ideal form of the democratic republic (*PP*, 8:352–53). It is also why he can treat the state as irresistible and irreproachable—as the manifest form of the people's own right-creating will that makes political resistance a crime—and yet regard it as intrinsically imperfect; as no empirical historical state can fully embody the pure idea of the state as the unified will of a community of rational beings (*MM*, 6:318–23).

In fact, Kant's pure idea of the state is not linked to historical governments as a norm for their concrete political reform. Rather, this linkage is envisaged in terms of the progressive approximation of the empirical people to the unified willing of the ideal community of rational beings, through a protracted process of historical refinement. It is this projected process—and not the division of governmental powers—that allows Kant to treat a monarchical government as republican, insofar as the monarch governs in a way that fosters the maturation of the people's powers of reason:

> Consequently, it is a duty to enter into such a system of government [in which citizens obey laws of their own making], but in the interim it is the duty of monarchs, even though they rule as autocrats, to govern in a republican (not democratic) way, that is, to treat people according to principles which are commensurate with the spirit of laws of freedom (as a people with developed reason would prescribe them

for itself), although they would not literally be asked for their consent. (CF, 7:91)

Kant's predominant conception of the historically existing Prussian state is thus of an *Erziehungsstaat*, a pedagogical or tutelary state. Here the state is envisaged as legislating in the name of the self-legislative will of a community of pure rational beings as a means of bringing this community into historical existence. This is what Kant means by *Volksaufklärung*, or the enlightenment of the people. It is this pedagogical conception of the state—transforming the people in accordance with the metaphysician's conception of a community of rational beings—that linked the political ideas of rationalist philosophy faculties to those of the socially adjacent Masonic lodges and illumination societies.[35] With their internal hierarchy organized around a Leibnizian philosophical ascent from sensuous to intelligible being, the lodges provided the rationalist philosophers with a social space for a certain kind of political activity. This took the form of an enclave politics dedicated to the total rational transformation of the people, hence a politics significantly removed from the work of those for whom *Volksaufklärung* meant the improvement of peasant agricultural practices; even if the same individuals sometimes advocated both programs as they shifted intellectual personae between metaphysician and public law political adviser.[36]

In this regard Kant's conception of concrete politics bears a striking resemblance to that of other Protestant metaphysicians and lodge members—especially Fichte's—but also to Herder's.[37] In conceiving the *Bildung* of a moral nation through culture and language, however, Herder's conception of the pedagogical state was attuned to the interests of the Lutheran clerical estate, and was self-consciously opposed to the Kantian cultivation of a community of pure reasoners.[38] According to Kant, since the enlightenment of the people concerns only their natural (not positive) rights as derived from universal reason, then "the natural heralds and expositors of these among the people are not officially appointed by the state but are free teachers of law, that is philosophers who, precisely because this freedom is allowed them, are objectionable to the state, which always desires to rule alone; and they are decried, under the name of enlighteners [*Aufklärer*] as persons dangerous to the state" (CF, 7:89). If we recall, though, that the positing of a gap between the ideal state and the historical commonwealth is itself an instrument for the cultivation of the persona of the rationalist metaphysician, then the project to close this gap by means of the pedagogical state is indicative of the theory-program of the Protestant rationalist philosophers. That at least is the hypothesis that will govern our discussion of Kant's intervention in the debate over the enlightenment or rationalization of religion.

Rational Religion and the Prussian Religious Constitution

In his 1793 essay "On the Common Saying: 'That May be Correct in Theory, but It Is of No Use in Practice,'" Kant offered to exemplify the utility of his principle of political legitimacy—"what a people cannot decree for itself, a legislator cannot decree for a people"—by asking the following question: "Can a law prescribing that a certain religious constitution, once arranged, is to continue permanently, be regarded as issuing from the real will of the legislator (his intention)?" This question can be readily answered, Kant argues, by asking two further questions: "May a people itself make it a law that certain articles of faith and forms of external religion, once adopted, are to remain forever? And so: May a people hinder itself, in its posterity, from making further progress in religious insight or from at some time correcting old errors?" According to Kant, these questions show that "an original contract of the people that made this a law would itself be null and void because it conflicts with the vocation and end of humanity." As a result of the fact that in this contract the actual legislative will of the people is not in accordance with its fully developed rational will—the "vocation and end of humanity"—such a religious constitution "is not to be regarded as the real will of the monarch." The people (or their rational philosophical representatives) thus have a natural right to protest this constitution, albeit noncoercively (*TP*, 8:305).

In the context of the intense journal combat over the intellectual character and political consequences of being enlightened, Kant's "On the Common Saying" was intended to settle a number of scores.[39] Against Christian Garve's criticism that his formal morality lacked motivating power and practical consequences—made in Garve's essay collection of 1792—Kant wished to show that, as he had developed it in his doctrine of right, his moral philosophy provided practical grounds for determining the legitimacy of state laws. This was also aimed at negating the Hobbesian view that only the state can determine political rights and obligations—in accordance with the ends of social peace and happiness—while simultaneously rebutting the view (put recently by August Wilhelm Rehberg) that metaphysics was the politically destabilizing source of French Jacobinism. Of particular importance for grasping the context of Kant's essay, though, is the case chosen to exemplify his principle of political legitimacy—the indefinite maintenance of a particular religious constitution—as this was a thinly veiled reference to Kant's own immediate engagement with the Prussian religious constitution and indeed the Prussian state.[40]

In June 1792 the second of the essays that would form part of Kant's *Religion Within the Bounds of Bare Reason* was refused approval by the Prussian government's Immediate Examination Commission, to which he had chosen to send it prior to publication in the *Berlinische Monatsschrift*. Established by Friedrich Wilhelm II in 1791 to assist with the enforcement of the 1788 Edict on Religion, the commission formed part of a set of measures designed to contain Protestant religious rationalism. These measures were overseen by the king's minister for religious affairs, Johann Christoph Wöllner. In arguing that the theology and sacraments of biblical (Lutheran) Christianity should be seen as the merely external form of a true inner religion—in fact a moral religion based on his metaphysical conception of man's self-purifying and self-legislating rational will—Kant's essay treated revealed historical religion as a vestige destined to wither away. This would occur, Kant prophesied, as the progressive refinement of human reason rendered unnecessary the material rewards and sanctions of the historical biblical revelation and ecclesial faith, displacing them with a "kingdom of virtue" understood as a community of morally self-governing rational beings.[41] In other words, in the rejected essay of 1792 Kant used his own moral philosophy to determine what humanity's vocation and destiny would be: perfection of the pure "rational being in man" and the formation of a global community of such beings.

The argument put in "On the Common Saying" in the following year—that the legislative maintenance of a particular religious constitution (even if consented to) is illegitimate because it conflicts with the "vocation and end of humanity"—was thus a defense of Kant's own censored religious philosophy. In this way, Kant proclaimed himself one of the "natural heralds and expositors" of the people's natural religious rights. In doing so, however, he was advancing his own religious philosophy as the authentic expression of the people's "real" legislative will—that is, the will that they would form were their reason to be fully developed—with his moral philosophy determining what reason looks like when it is fully developed.

Apparently Wöllner was not entirely convinced by Kant's revelation of the people's "real" will in religious affairs. In October 1794, soon after the publication of Kant's *Religion,* the philosopher received a royal order declaring that in this work and associated writings he had "abused his philosophy for the purpose of distorting and disparaging several principal and fundamental doctrines of Holy Scripture and of Christianity," and that considering his "duty as a teacher of the young" and the king's well-known religious policy, this conduct was irresponsible and must cease forthwith (*CF*, 7:6).

A good deal of the twentieth-century commentary on Kant's brush with the Prussian authorities relied on Wilhelm Dilthey's view of it: namely, as an attempt by the state to stand in the way of humanity's path to *Aufklärung,* manifest here in Kant's recovery of a "pure religion of reason" from within the historical husk of positive religion.[42] Dilthey's neo-Kantian view, though, is quite anachronistic. It portrays the historical events in which Kant was a philosopher-protagonist from the protagonistic viewpoint of Kant's own philosophy: as an attempt to block humanity's rational emancipation by blocking humanity's philosopher of rational emancipation. In fact Dilthey treats Kant's philosophy of the manifestation of reason in history as if it were reason's own historical self-manifestation, once again displaying the covert identification of philosophy (as a local institutional cultivation of the intellect) with reason (envisaged as the universal self-clarificatory power of the human mind). He is thus quite unable to offer an account either of the local factional position assumed by Kant's religious philosophy in the cultural-political conflict over Protestant religious rationalism, or of the historical circumstances and significance of this conflict in the context of the Prussian religious constitution. So too the twentieth-century commentary that has followed Dilthey's template study in this regard, in which Wöllner and the edict are treated as symptoms of a gathering anti-Enlightenment storm.[43]

The Prussian religious constitution—whose illegitimacy Kant purported to demonstrate with such single-minded clarity in the 1790s—had its beginning in 1614. That was the year in which, immediately following his conversion of the Hohenzollern dynasty to the Calvinist religion, Elector Johann Sigismund issued an edict intended to prohibit the Lutheran clergy of Brandenburg and Prussia from calumniating the territories' Calvinist minority as heretics.[44] More broadly, the edict was intended to bridge the theological gulf between the two Protestant confessions. This was only the first of a long series of public law enactments and treaties—further princely decrees and confessional formulas, compacts between the Calvinist rulers of Brandenburg-Prussia and their Lutheran estates, the imperial public law treaties of Westphalia—that would eventually include the Religious Edict of 1788. Rather than a singular act of legislative will, this series recorded the contingent unfolding of two factors central to Prussian religious and political history. The first of these was the protracted campaign by the Calvinist ruling house to integrate its Lutheran nobles and cities (the "estates") into a princely territorial state. A central strategy in this campaign was the attempt to reform the liturgy and theology of the Lutheran Church, integrating Lutheranism and Calvinism under the Augsburg Confession, as a means of overcoming a key source of estate cultural identity and political resistance.[45] The second great source of the Prussian religious constitution was provided by the two great imperial public law religious peace treaties to which Brandenburg was a signatory, the Peace of Augsburg (1555) and the Peace of Westphalia (1648). The former established the right of Protestant princes to reform their territorial churches in accordance with their own religious convictions, while the latter granted imperial legal recognition to the empire's three main religions: Lutheranism, Catholicism, and Calvinism.[46]

During the seventeenth century, the religious conflict between Brandenburg's Calvinist rulers and their Lutheran estates inched toward a stalemate. The Hohenzollern electors gradually abandoned their attempt to achieve a Calvinist reformation of the Lutheran Church and opted instead for a biconfessional system in which the state would not officially endorse a particular religion.[47] In the middle of the century this pragmatic tendency toward political secularization and limited religious toleration coalesced with the formal legal declaration of toleration in the Treaty of Osnabrück (Westphalia). The Treaty was remarkable in formalizing the legal parity between the confessions that had been evolving under imperial public law, and also for the fact that, in the negotiations that produced it, the question of religious truth had been dropped from the agenda in favor of achieving the purely secular end of social peace.[48] As a result of these developments, and under the stewardship of the "Great Elector," Friedrich Wilhelm (1640–1688), by the end of the seventeenth-century Brandenburg-Prussia's religious constitution had assumed the form of a multiconfessional system of public churches, which is what religious toleration meant as a concrete historical reality.[49] This multilayered arrangement of public law was managed by a state that refused to endorse a particular religion—"political secularization"—and formulated its policy in terms of maintaining the religious peace between its rival confessional communities, even if the dynasty remained committed to Calvinism as the court religion.[50]

Such was the religious constitution—remarkably stable during the eighteenth century and unchanged at its end—whose illegitimacy Kant purported to demonstrate because it was not based on the pursuit of (rational) religious truth and thus could not have been "decreed by the people for itself." Kant was of course right on this point of fact: none of the rival congregations would or could have freely willed a constitution that relativized their truth claims and subjected them to indifferentist state management. As Moser observed with regard to great public law treaties of religious peace that framed the religious constitution of the empire—the treaties of Augsburg (1555) and Westphalia (1648)—their role was not to act as vehicles for the pursuit of religious truth, but to suspend this pursuit as a means of achieving piece between the rival confessions: "[The law of] Religious Peace does not concern the essence of religion. In other words, through such, neither the Catholic religion is required to recognize the Protestant as true or erroneous, nor the Protestant the Catholic; but this issue is to be wholly set aside by both parties. . . . The whole purpose of the Religious Peace is thus that both sides would cease treating each other with hostility and persecuting each other for the sake of religion."[51] In being framed by these fundamental public law enactments, the Brandenburg-Prussian system of regulated multiconfessionalism could never have been grounded in the consent of rational beings seeking religious truth—thereby achieving Kantian legitimacy—as it was designed to remove religious truth as a ground of religious rights, grounding the latter instead in the state's maintenance of social peace. Public law was incapable of being grounded in Kant's principle of right.

By the last third of the seventeenth century, two distinct (but historically related) forms of theological rationalism had emerged as destabilizing forces in the cultural politics underpinning the Prussian religious constitution. First, from the beginning of the century, by elaborating the scholastic account of how God as immaterial intellectual being could occupy corporeal things, Lutheran university metaphysics had provided a philosophical defense of the Eucharistic and Christological doctrines enshrined in the anti-Calvinist formula of Lutheran faith, the Formula of Concord.[52] In carrying out this program, the Protestant metaphysicians presented a major obstacle to the political-juristic campaign to minimize such incendiary doctrines in the interests of religious harmony and civil peace. Second, by offering their own account of how a divine intellect or substance manifested itself in the corporeal cosmos, secular metaphysicians purported to provide a true rationalist explication for theological doctrines, the most significant examples being Leibniz's "monadology" and Spinoza's metaphysical materialism.[53] This secular metaphysics thus also threatened to undermine the constitution's relegation of ultimate truths in favor of social peace, especially when it was used to justify natural political rights against the state. Through its uncompromising commitment to a single underlying rational religious truth, secular metaphysics threatened the constitutional management of the existing array of public religions, as this was premised on the separation of civil rights from religious truth. Secular university metaphysics gave rise instead to utopian programs offering to dissolve and reunite the confessions on a new rational metaphysical basis (Leibniz), or to dissolve them altogether and replace them with a philosophy that harmonized faith and reason (Spinoza).[54]

It is no accident, then, that defenses of Brandenburg-Prussia's state-managed multiconfessionalism—for its achievement of relative religious peace after a protracted period of religious civil war—assumed a strongly antimetaphysical character, oriented to history, public law, and politics.[55] In these defenses minimally doctrinal "fideist" forms of Protestantism were paired with (Hobbesian) political and juridical doctrines designed to separate church and state by providing them with mutually exclusive ends: the church as custodian of a religious truth incapable of civil enforcement, and the state as coercive enforcer of peace regardless of religious truth.[56] In his combative defense of this position, Christian Thomasius drew heavily on his father Jacob's history of philosophy, according to which metaphysics had arisen from the miscegenation of Greek philosophy and Christian faith.[57] The indelible mark of this illicit hybridization could be seen in all of those metaphysical doctrines—secular and theological—where God is pictured as a divine mind whose intellection of the forms of things brings meaning to the material cosmos. Not only did such doctrines mix God pantheistically with the world, but they also convinced men that they could regenerate themselves by exercising the intellect that joined them to the divine mind, thereby giving rise to "enthusiast" programs to reshape the religious and political constitution in accordance with the free exercise of this intellect.[58] Thomasius used this historical critique to wage a disputation war against both Lutheran university metaphysics and the new secular metaphysics of the Leibnizians and Spinozists. We have already noted that he was particularly opposed to metaphysical conceptions of natural law according to which individuals could discern public religious and political norms through their own purified reason. Thomasius regarded this as a double infringement: of the individual's private faith and the state's determination of public right.[59]

However alien it might be to the political sensibilities of those now living in religiously pacified societies under politically secularized states, the occasional action taken against outbreaks of religious rationalism in Brandenburg-Prussia during the seventeenth and eighteenth centuries was neither anti-Enlightenement nor indicative of the state's attempt to block the progress of reason and freedom.[60] It represented rather the routine defense of the public law constitution of managed multiconfessionalism that, as the source of the most liberal regime of religious toleration in Europe, staked its own claim to be enlightened. As new research by Michael Sauter has shown, Wöllner—chief architect of the edict and long portrayed as the poster boy for anti-Enlightenment reaction—was himself an active participant in the *Volksaufklärung*: not that envisioned in terms of a self-governing community of rational beings, but that dedicated to improving the legal entitlements and economic existence of the agricultural peasantry.[61] For its part, the Pufendorfian "civil philosophy" and Moserian *Staatsrecht* (public law) that supported the Prussian religious constitution were no less deeply embedded in the academic culture of Protestant northern Germany than the religious rationalism of the metaphysicians. This is the appropriate historical context in which to situate the Religious Edict of 1788 and the attempted censoring of Kant's rationalist theology in the 1790s, which was one of several similar actions taken against rationalist clergy and theologians at this time.

Kant's Religion and the Prussian Religious Edict

In reaffirming the state's protection of "all three main confessions of the Christian religion, namely the Reformed, Lutheran, and Roman Catholic" (article 1), the Religious Edict was maintaining the public law basis of Prussian religious toleration, which it then formally extended to include "the sects previously publicly tolerated in our states": the Jewish nation, the Herrnhutter, Mennonites, and Bohemian Brethren (article 2).[62] Despite the widespread portrayal of it as an attempt to enforce a particular confessional truth—recalling Kant's reference to the illegitimacy of a law prescribing "certain articles of faith and forms of external religion"—the edict required only that clergy teach the doctrines of the religions into which they had been ordained, which was of course a condition for maintaining the system of public confessions. This is clear not only from the fact that the edict relativizes truth across all of the confessions—and is thus neutral between competing articles of faith—but also from the fact that it accepts that clergy, like other subjects, may believe what they like in private, so long as this does not interfere with the performance of their public office (article 2). No less inimical to the stability of the system of public religions are the practices of proselytism and conversion undertaken secretly by the confessions, the Catholics in particular (article 4), but also publicly by rationalist Protestant clergymen, who deviate so greatly from the Augsburg Confession that their preaching may regarded as an attempt to convert their flocks to a new (philosophical) religion (articles 7 and 8). From the viewpoint of the edict and its public law architects, it is thus the religious rationalists who should be regarded as sectarians. So convinced are they of the truth of metaphysics that they refuse to accept the relativistic maintenance of a plurality of such truths and set about converting people to reason: "One is not ashamed to again resuscitate the miserable and long-refuted errors of the Socinians, Deists, Naturalists, and other sects, and to spread these in a brazen and shameless way among the people under the utterly misused name of *Aufklärung*" (article 7).

Kant's religious philosophy occupied a place in a crowed spectrum of positions that stretched from various forms of pietistic and sacramental Lutheranism—often combined with public law defenses of state oversight—through to the radical naturalism of a figure like Carl Friedrich Bahrdt. Bahrdt argued that the world was based on natural rational laws, and that man was quite capable of governing himself through reason without the divine intervention of Christ who was in any case only a man.[63] The Protestant teaching that religion should focus on inner morality rather than external ritual and sacraments was widespread across this continuum, not least because the meaning of morality was construed in quite different ways. Within this spectrum, Protestant religious rationalism (the "theological enlightenment") was defined by the problem of reconciling a metaphysical conception of morality—the idea that as the bearer of a self-governing pure intellect man could effect his own moral regeneration—with the core

Christological teaching of the Protestant churches: namely, that owing to his fallen nature man's moral regeneration and salvation is dependent on Christ's vicarious atonement for human sin.[64] Formed by the impact of Leibniz-Wolffian metaphysics on Protestant religious culture, this problem-space was one that Kant shared with many other north-German philosophers and "Neologians," including Johann Friedrich Stapfer, Johann Joachim Spalding, Karl Friedrich Stäudlin, Samuel Reimarus, Gottfried Lessing, and Johannes Salomo Semler, to name only some of the more significant.[65] Late eighteenth-century religious rationalism thus represented a resurgence of a conflict at the heart of Prussia's religious constitution that had emerged with the appearance of secular metaphysics in the second half of the seventeenth century.[66] It was thus no accident that one of the defining controversies of the late eighteenth-century debate over what it meant to be enlightened should have broken out over F. H. Jacobi's sensational allegation that Lessing had been a Spinozist, or philosophical atheist.[67]

We have already argued that Kant's moral philosophy represents a particular improvisation on the secular "morals of metaphysics"—centered on the figure of a sensuously distracted morally self-legislating pure intelligence—which we have treated as the means of cultivating a particular kind of intellectual persona. Kant's *Religion Within the Bounds of Bare Reason* may be regarded as an exercise in transposing this philosophical figure into the register of Protestant Christianity, for which purpose he deployed two key strategies to reconcile it with the Christology and soteriology of the Protestant churches. First, he elaborated a complex metaphysical hermeneutics that permitted the biblical account of man's fall and redemption to be interpreted as a drama played out entirely within the confines of philosophical subjectivity or the persona of the philosopher. On the central issue of the Fall and human sinfulness, Kant advanced both the (pagan) philosophical conception of sin—as the product of the sensuous nature to which man's rational being was mortgaged—and the Christian conception that regards sin as the product of man's disobedience before God's law. Kant presents these alternatives as an aporia that he then proceeds to resolve by arguing that man indeed chooses to sin, but does so by choosing the sensuous nature that makes his sinning inevitable (*RE*, 6:22–32). Setting aside the logical coherence of this resolution—Kant himself declares it to be a "mystery" beyond human understanding—it presents a clear example of Kant's hermeneutic method of transposing the biblical account of man's relation to God into a metaphysical account of man's relation to his own moral subjectivity. Kant sets up a similar aporia and resolution with regard to the relation between man's responsibility for his own moral regeneration and Christ's vicarious atonement for human sinfulness.[68] On the one hand, morality is understood in terms of man's capacity for autonomous rational willing. On the other, though, man's nature has been so corrupted by sin that only an access of external goodness via Christ's grace can redeem him. This aporia is again resolved within the philosophical persona—where it takes the form of a secular "spiritual exercise"—via the notion that man's rational purification of his own sensuous nature can be regarded as a kind of moral rebirth, brought about "as if" by an access of a Christlike rational purity (*RE*, 6:62–78). In other words, Kant interprets the historical Redeemer as if he were a symbol of the timeless "rational being in man," thereby viewing man as self-redeeming on the basis of his own reason.

Kant's second strategy for reconciling metaphysical morality with Christian doctrine was via the deployment of an accommodationist philosophical history—an account of the "vocation and destiny of humanity"—having much in common with similar histories provided by Reimarus, Semler, and Spalding.[69] If the Bible treats Christ as the real historical incarnation of God, rather than as a symbol of our inner rational being—"*homo noumenon*"—that is because it was written for the infancy of mankind; that is, for the time when the sensuous side of man's double nature was dominant, and crude historical narratives were required to render the noumenal side visible. Now, though, in late eighteenth-century Protestant Germany, it was possible to provide a rational interpretation of the Scriptures, whose content turns out to be Kant's own metaphysical simulacrum of the Christian mysteries. History itself has thus effected a progressive winnowing of the sensuous biblical husks from religion's inner rational core, leading to the revelation of Kant's "pure moral religion" to an historically enlightened humanity (*RE*, 6:107–22). In other words, in a remarkable *coup de thèatre*, Kant situates his own metaphysical hermeneutics not just as one source of morally improving biblical interpretations, but as the finally true interpretation: in fact as the vehicle through which the world of self-determining noumenal beings discloses itself in empirical history through a "pure rational religion." Kant thus understands his hermeneutic purification of historical biblical Christianity as heralding the translation of the noumenal community into history and into the public domain, giving the true meaning of the biblical promise regarding the building of God's kingdom on earth:

All this is not to be expected from an external revolution . . .—Rather, it is in the principle of pure rational religion, of such religion as a constantly occurring (though not empirical) divine revelation, that the basis for that transition to this new order of things must lie. . . . There is, however, ground for saying "that the kingdom of God is come unto us," even if only the principle of the gradual transition from church faith to universal rational religion and thus to a (divine) ethical state on earth has taken root universally and somewhere also publically, although the actual establishment of this state lies an infinite distance away from us. (*RE*, 6:122)

Both of Kant's strategies—the metaphysical hermeneutics and the accommodationist philosophical history—are driven by the figure of self-purifying rational being which, we have argued, forms part of the spiritual discipline for cultivating a particular moral persona: that of the academic secular metaphysician. If Kant's *Religion* offered a rational philosophy of religion then it did so by way of providing a rational religion for philosophers. In the *Religion* Kant was staking the ideological claim of Prussia's university metaphysicians to mediate the conflict between secular metaphysics and Protestant Christology and soteriology, proclaiming in fact that his own metaphysics of self-purifying rational being exemplifies the form in which an historically purified Christianity would give birth to a "pure moral religion." By combining this metaphysical hermeneutics of Protestant Christianity with his political metaphysics of the ideal republic, Kant was able to effect an uncompromising double delegitimation of Prussia's religious constitution: as both an obstacle to the eschatological unfolding of a pure religion of reason, and as illegitimate in relation to the "real" political will of the people. This is will the people would acquire at the end of the process of historical-rational purification but that in the meantime could be discerned and declared by the "free teachers of law, that is the philosophers" (*CF*, 7:89).

The distinctiveness of Kant's ideological position is clear when compared with that of the public law jurists and officials charged with the ongoing management of the Prussian religious constitution itself. In his *Vörtrage über Recht und Staat* (Lectures on law and state) given to the Prussian crown prince in 1791–1792, for example, the public law jurist Carl Gottlieb Svarez repeated the Pufendorfian and Moserian construction of the state's powers of religious supervision. Svarez instructed the future king Friedrich Wilhelm III that the state has the right and responsibility to regulate the system of public churches, but that this regulation is restricted to managing the impact of the churches on public peace and must on no account presume to a view on religious truth or "dogmatic principles."[70] These were also the terms in which public jurists defended the Religious Edict of 1788.[71]

Kant's position, though, was also distinctive in relation to other groups with whom he shared the space of Protestant religious rationalism, particularly the moderate rationalist theologians. In his response to the Religious Edict, Johann Semler could thus argue that the measure should be supported because it represented the maintenance of the system of public religions from which all of the churches benefited.[72] In a sophisticated division of offices, Semler observed that the edict concerned the duties of a citizen that involved accepting the existence of an array of public churches regardless of the truth of any of them. As far as the duties of clerical office are concerned, however, the clergy should teach as true the basic doctrines that define a particular church, keeping their rational religious reservations as a matter for their private persona. Semler acknowledged that new principles of reason would indeed lead to changes in the historical teachings of the church. Such changes, though, must take place not on the basis of an individual's philosophical insight into ultimate rational truths, but through modifications to its historical teachings undertaken by the church itself as a corporate body.

We have observed that the Prussian religious constitution was based not in the natural rights of a harmonized general will but in a complex series of public law measures for the pacifying management of an array of public religions. In their different ways, the public law jurists and the moderate rationalist theologians operated within this constitution, whose tolerationist regime was itself widely regarded as "enlightened" at the time.[73] They did so not on the basis of an autonomous philosophical subjectivity—*homo noumenon*—but in accordance with a pluralized set of offices and duties created by the constitution itself. Contextualized against this historical reality, Kant's political and religious thought may thus be regarded as advancing the factional cultural politics of the Protestant metaphysical rationalists. This was committed to a single metaphysical persona regarded as the only true moral self, and was hostile to any set of political arrangements that could not be viewed as the expression of an ideally harmonized community of rational wills. In this regard, Kant's thought assumed the form of a prophetic religious and political hermeneutics. This showed how the historical religious constitution appeared when viewed from the perspective of a future community of self-legislating rational beings whose present personification is the university metaphysician himself.

NOTES

1. Michael J. Sauter, *Visions of the Enlightenment: The Edict on Religion of 1788 and the Politics of the Public Sphere in Eighteenth-Century Prussia* (Leiden: Brill, 2009), 23–48; and James Schmidt, "The Question of Enlightenment: Kant, Mendelssohn, and the *Mittwochgesellschaft*," *Journal of the History of Ideas* 50, no. 2 (1989): 269–91.
2. Fiammetta Palladini, "Pufendorf, Disciple of Hobbes. The Nature of Man and the State of Nature: The Doctrine of *Socialitas*," *History of European Ideas* 34 (2008): 26–60; and Ian Hunter, *Rival Enlightenments: Civil and Metaphysical Philosophy in Early Modern Germany* (Cambridge: Cambridge University Press, 2001), 148–96.
3. Michael Stolleis, *Geschichte des öffentlichen Rechts in Deutschland. Erster Band: Reichspublizistik und Policeywissenschaft 1600–1800* (Munich: C. H. Beck, 1988), 258–67; and Mack Walker, *Johann Jakob Moser and the Holy Roman Empire of the German Nation* (Chapel Hill: University of North Carolina Press, 1981).
4. Walter Sparn, "Kant's Doctrine of Atonement as a Theory of Subjectivity," in *Kant's Philosophy of Religion Reconsidered*, P. J. Rossi and M. Wreen (Indianapolis: Indiana University Press, 1991), 103–12.
5. The polemical dimension of the following account thus flows not from any anti-Kantian animus in the author, but directly from the methodological decision to suspend the metaphysics supporting Kant's distinction between theory and practice; that is, to treat this metaphysics as neither true nor false, but rather as an historical fact in an historiographic account capable of empirical truth and falsity.
6. For the contrary view—that Kant's legal and political philosophy is not dependent on his metaphysics of morals—see chapter 3 in this volume by Thomas Pogge.
7. I have occasionally modified Mary Gregor's translation.
8. For powerful examples of work carried out within these intellectual parameters, see Christine M. Korsgaard, *Creating the Kingdom of Ends* (Cambridge: Cambridge University Press, 1996); and Allen W. Wood, *Kant's Ethical Thought* (Cambridge: Cambridge University Press, 1999).
9. For more, see Ian Hunter, "The Morals of Metaphysics: Kant's *Groundwork* as Intellectual *Paideia*," *Critical Inquiry* 28, no. 4 (2002): 908–29; and Hunter, *Rival Enlightenments*, 274–93.
10. For a recent and illuminating example of this approach to Kantian formalism, see George di Giovanni, *Freedom and Religion in Kant and His Immediate Successors: The Vocation of Humankind, 1774–1800* (Cambridge: Cambridge University Press, 2005).
11. Christian Garve, *Philosophische Anmerkungen and Abhandlung zu Ciceros Büchern von den Pflichten* (Breslau, 1783).
12. Anonymous [Garve/Feder], "Critique of Pure Reason by Immanuel Kant. 1781. 856 pages in Octavo," *Zugabe zu den Göttingischen Anzeigen von gelehrten Sachen*, January 19, 1782, 40–48. Reprinted in *Kant's Early Critics: The Empiricist Critique of the Theoretical Philosophy*, ed. and trans. Brigitte Sassen (Cambridge: Cambridge University Press, 2000), 53–59.

13. Manfred Kuehn, "Kant's Critical Philosophy and Its Reception—The First Five Years (1781–1786)," in *The Cambridge Companion to Kant and Modern Philosophy*, ed. Paul Guyer (Cambridge: Cambridge University Press, 2006), 644–48.

14. On the ethics of office and its role in ordering moral life in a society of offices, see above all Conal Condren, *Argument and Authority in Early Modern England: The Presupposition of Oaths and Offices* (Cambridge: Cambridge University Press, 2006).

15. Christian Thomasius, *Cautelen zur Erlernung der Rechtsgelehrtheit* (Halle, 1713; repr. Hildesheim: Olms, 2006). This was the German translation of the Latin original, *Cautelae Circa Praecognitia Jurisprudentiae* (Halle, 1710). Subsequent citations to *Cautelen* are given parenthetically in the text.

16. The still unsurpassed account of the relation between Kant's moral philosophy and Wolff's rational psychology is provided in Josef Schmucker, *Die Ursprünge der Ethik Kants in seinen vorkritischen Schriften und Reflektionen* (Meisenheim am Glan: Anton Hain, 1961). See also two important papers by Heinz Heimsoeth: "Persönlichkeitsbewußtsein und Ding an sich in der Kantischen Philosophie," in Heinz Heimsoeth, *Studien zur Philosophie Immanuel Kants*, vol. 1, *Metaphysische Ursprünge und ontologische Grundlagen* (Cologne: Cologne University Press, 1956), 227–57; and "Zur Frage nach Grund und Herkunft der Moral," in *Konkrete Vernunft: Festschrift für Erich Rothacker*, ed. G. Funke (Bonn: H. Bouvier, 1958), 207–18.

17. One of the most influential formulations of this set of doctrines in Protestant scholasticism can be found in Christoph Scheibler, *Opus Metaphysicum: Duobus Libris Universum Hujus Scientiae Systema Comprehendens* (Giessen, 1617).

18. Considering the late twentieth-century disinterest in this key historical source for Kant's metaphysics of morals, it is important to observe that some of his contemporaries regarded it as central. Garve thus offers an historical argument that Kant's duplex construction of the intelligible and sensible worlds was historically grounded in scholastic theological constructions of the gulf between divine and human intelligence. See Christian Garve, *Übersicht der vornehmsten Principien der Sittenlehre, von dem Zeitalter des Aristotles an bis auf unsere Zeiten*, vol. 8 of *Gesammelte Werke*, ed. K. Wöfel, Series II (Hildesheim: Georg Olms, 1986 [1798]), 354–60.

19. Heinz Heimsoeth, *The Six Great Themes of Western Metaphysics and the End of the Middle Ages*, trans. R. J. Betanzos (Detroit: Wayne State University Press, 1994), 215–16.

20. See in particular Rawls's comment that "the description of the original position interprets the point of view of noumenal selves, of what it means to be a free and equal rational being," in *A Theory of Justice* (Cambridge: Harvard University Press, 1971), 255–56.

21. See, for example, Thomas Pogge's modernizing reading of Kant's *Rechtslehre* in chapter 3 of this volume.

22. For a partial exception in the recent literature, see Katrin Flikschuh, *Kant and Modern Political Philosophy* (Cambridge: Cambridge University Press, 2000). Flikschuh, though, does not recover the historical character of Kant's metaphysics of rational being, treating it instead as a formal presupposition for a transcendent metaphysics.

23. For the contrary view, see Arthur Ripstein's chapter in this volume.

24. *The Metaphysics of Morals*, in *Immanuel Kant: Practical Philosophy*, trans. and ed. Mary J. Gregor (Cambridge: Cambridge University Press, 1996), 402–9. I will cite from this edition even though it contains an unauthorized editorial reconstruction of the text dealing with noumenal possession. For a summary of the changes introduced, see Mary J. Gregory, "Translator's Note on the Text of *The Metaphysics of Morals*," 355–57. Readers seeking an English translation of Kant's construction of noumenal possession in the form that he authorized should consult Gregor's earlier stand-alone translation, *Immanuel Kant: The Metaphysics of Morals*, intro, trans., and notes Mary J. Gregor (Cambridge: Cambridge University Press, 1991), 68–90.

25. *MM*, 6:246–47. Note that this section—"§2, The Juridical Postulate of Practical Reason"—has been relocated in Gregor's new Cambridge translation (1996). To view it in its proper place, readers should consult the *Akademie* edition (6:246–47) or Gregor's 1991 translation at 68–69.

26. See Hunter, *Rival Enlightenments*, 52–58, 102–15, 279–316.

27. Samuel Pufendorf, *The Law of Nature and of Nations in Eight Books*, trans. C. H. Oldfather and W. A. Oldfather, vol. 2 (Oxford: Clarendon Press, 1934), book 1, chapter 6, 87–112.

28. Ian Hunter, "The Love of a Sage or the Command of a Superior: The Natural Law Doctrines of Leibniz and Pufendorf," in *Early Modern Natural Law Theories: Strategies and Contexts in the Early Enlightenment*, ed. T. J. Hochstrasser and P. Schröder (Dordrecht: Kluwer, 2003), 169–94. See also Laursen, chapter 9 of this volume.

29. Michael J. Seidler, "Pufendorf and the Politics of Recognition," in *Natural Law and Civil Sovereignty: Moral Right and State Authority in Early Modern Political Thought*, ed. I. Hunter and D. Saunders (Basingstoke: Palgrave, 2002), 235–51.

30. For an example of this view, see Christine M. Korsgaard, *The Sources of Normativity* (Cambridge: Cambridge University Press, 1996), 25–32. For the prototype, see Gottfried Wilhelm Leibniz, "On the Principles of Pufendorf," in *Leibniz: Political Writings*, ed. P. Riley (Cambridge: Cambridge University Press, 1972), 64–76.

31. For helpful terms of comparison in this regard, see Horst Dreitzel, "Naturrecht als politische Philosophie," in *Die Philosophie des 17. Jahrhunderts*, vol. 4, *Das heilige Römische Reich deutscher Nation, Nord- und Ostmitteleuropa*, ed. H. Holzhey and W. Schmidt-Biggemann (Basel: Schwabe, 2001), 836–48.

32. Horst Dreitzel, "Samuel Pufendorf," in Holzhey, *Die Philosophie des 17. Jahrhunderts*, 4:757–812.

33. Cf., Flikschuh, *Kant and Modern Political Philosophy*, 157; and Onora O'Neill's argument in chapter 1 of this volume that Kantian political authority is not grounded in consent or contract but in the principle of right understood as a rational imperative.

34. *MM*, 6:329. See Robert Pippin's parallel comment, "Mine and Thine: The Kantian State," in Guyer, *Cambridge Companion to Kant*, 441, note 4.

35. On this linkage, see Martin Mulsow, "Vernünftige Metempsychosis: Ueber Monadenlehre, Esoterik und geheime Aufklärungsgesellschaften im 18. Jahrhundert," in *Aufklärung und Esoterik*, ed. M. Neugebauer-Wölk (Hamburg: Felix Meiner, 1999), 211–73; and Gerhard W. Fuchs, *Karl Leonhard Reinhold—Illuminat und Philosoph: Eine Studie über den Zussamenhang seines Engagements als Freirmaurer und Illuminat mit seinem Leben und philosophischen Wirken* (Frankfurt am Main: Peter Lang, 1994).

36. See Schmidt, "The Question of Enlightenment"; and Sauter, *Visions of the Enlightenment*, 105–40.

37. Fichte argued for the state's role in educative transformation of its "immature" citizens, by coercion if necessary, in Johann Gottlieb Fichte, *Addresses to the German Nation*, ed. G. A. Kelly, trans. R. F. Jones and G. H. Turnbull (New York: Harper Torchbooks, 1968 [1808]). See in particular the eleventh address.

38. On this difference, see Horst Dreitzel, "Herders politische Konzepte," in *Johann Gottfried Herder, 1744–1803*, ed. G. Sauder (Hamburg: Felix Meiner, 1987), 267–98.

39. Useful selections from the debate are provided in Norbert Hinske, ed., *Was ist Aufklärung?: Beiträge aus der Berlinischen Monatsschrift*, 2nd ed. (Darmstadt: Wissenschaftliche Buchgesellschaft, 1977); and James Schmidt, ed., *What Is Enlightenment?: Eighteenth-Century Answers and Twentieth-Century Questions* (Berkeley and Los Angeles: University of California Press, 1996). In order to capture the diverse spectrum of religious and political positions in play, these sources should be supplemented by Dirk Kemper's microfilm collection of works published in response to the 1788 Edict on Religion: Dirk Kemper, ed., *Mißbrauchte Aufklärung?: Schriften zum preußischen Religionsedikt vom 9. Juli 1788* (Hildesheim: Georg Olms, 1996).

40. For more on the strategic aspects of Kant's writings, see Laursen, chapter 9 of this volume.

41. Immanuel Kant, *Religion Within the Bounds of Bare Reason*, trans. Werner S. Pluhar (Indianapolis: Hackett, 2009), 127–37; *Akademie* edition, 6:115–24.

42. Wilhelm Dilthey, "Der Streit Kants mit der Zensur über das Recht freier Religionsforschung," *Archiv für Geschichte der Philosophie* 3 (1890): 418–50.

43. For examples, see Paul Schwartz, *Der erste Kulturkampf in Preussen um Kirche und Schule (1788–1798)* (Berlin: Weidmann, 1925); Klaus Epstein, *The Genesis of German Conservatism* (Princeton: Princeton University Press, 1966); Frederick C. Beiser, *Enlightenment, Revolution, and Romanticism: The Genesis of Modern German Political Thought, 1790–1800* (Cambridge: Harvard University Press, 1992); Thomas P. Saine, *The Problem of Being Modern: Or, the German Pursuit of Enlightenment from Leibniz to the French Revolution* (Detroit: Wayne State University Press, 1997); and Allen W. Wood, "General Introduction," in *Immanuel Kant: Religion and Rational Theology*, trans. and ed. Allen W. Wood and George di Giovanni (Cambridge: Cambridge University Press, 1996), xi–xxiv.

44. Wolfgang Gericke, *Glaubenszeugnisse und Konfessionspolitik der Brandenburgischen Herrscher bis zur Preussischen Union 1540 bis 1815* (Bielefeld: Luther, 1977), 22–29, 132–36.

45. See the illuminating account in Bodo Nischan, *Prince, People, and Confession: The Second Reformation in Brandenburg* (Philadelphia: University of Pennsylvania Press, 1994).

46. For an overview, see Martin Heckel, "Zur Entwicklung des deutschen Staatskirchenrechts von der Reformation bis zur Schwelle der Weimarer Verfassung," in *Martin Heckel Gesammelte Schriften: Staat, Kirche, Recht, Geschichte*, ed. K. Schlaich (Tübingen: J. C. B. Mohr, 1989), 366–401.

47. Paul Schwartz, "Die Verhandlungen der Stände 1665 und 1668 über die Religionsedikte," *Jarhrbuch für brandenburgische Kirchengeschichte* 30 (1935): 88–115.

48. On this, see above all Martin Heckel, "Die religionsrechtliche Parität," in Schlaich, *Martin Heckel*, 227–323; and Martin Heckel, "Religionsbann und landesherrliches Kirchenregiment," in *Die lutherische Konfessionalisierung in Deutschland*, ed. H.-C. Rublack (Gütersloh: Gerd Mohn, 1992), 130–62.

49. Hartmut Rudolph, "Öffentliche Religion und Toleranz: Zur Parallelität preußischer Religionspolitik und josephinischer Reform im Lichte der Aufklärung," in *Im Zeichen der Toleranz: Aufsätze zur Toleranzgesetzgebung des 18. Jahrhunderts in den Reichen Joseph II., ihren Voraussetzungen und ihren Folgen*, ed. P. F. Barton (Vienna: Institute for Protestant Church History, 1981), 221–49.

50. Gerd Heinrich, "Religionstoleranz in Brandenburg-Preußen: Idee und Wirklichkeit," in *Preussen, Versuch einer Bilanz*, vol. 2, *Beiträge zu einer politischen Kultur*, ed. M. Schlenke (Reinbeck: Rowohlt, 1981), 61–88.

51. Johann Jacob Moser, *Neues teutsches Staatsrecht*, vol. 1, *Von Teutschland und dessen Staats-Verfassung überhaupt* (Stuttgart: Mezler, 1766), 264.

52. For an overview, see Walter Sparn, "Die Schulphilosophie in den lutherischen Territorien," in Holzhey, *Die Philosophie des 17. Jahrhunderts*, 4:475–97.

53. Hunter, *Rival Enlightenments*, 115–26.

54. On these metaphysical programs and their cultural and political impact, see Walter Sparn, "Formalis Atheus?: Die Krise der protestantischen Orthodoxie, gespiegelt in ihrer Auseinandersetzung mit Spinoza," in *Spinoza in der Frühzeit seiner Religiösen Wirkung*, ed. K. Gründer and W. Schmidt-Biggemann (Heidelberg: Lambert Schneider, 1984), 27–64; and Walter Sparn, "Das Bekenntnis des Philosophen: Gottfried Wilhelm Leibniz als Philosoph und Theologe," *Neue Zeitschrift für Systematische Theologie* 28 (1986): 139–78. For Leibniz's reunion project, see Gerda Utermöhlen, "Die irenische Politik der Welfenhöfe und Leibniz' Schlichtungsversuch der Kontroverse um den papstliche Primat," in *Religion und Religiosität im Zeitalter des Barock*, ed. D. Breuer (Wiesbaden: Harrossowitz, 1995), 191–200.

55. Notker Hammerstein, *Jus und Historie: Ein Beitrag zur Geschichte des historischen Denkens an deutschen Universitäten im späten 17. und im 18. Jahrhundert* (Göttingen: Vandenhoeck & Ruprecht, 1972).

56. The locus classicus is Samuel Pufendorf, *De Habitu Religionis Christianae ad Vitam Civilem* (Lund, 1687). English version: *Of the Nature and Qualification of Religion in Reference to Civil Society*, ed. S. Zurbuchen (Indianapolis: Liberty Fund, 2002). For an illuminating account of Leibniz's attack on Pufendorf's relegation of the metaphysical project for a reunification of the churches in favor of a state-managed *Religionspolitik*, see Detlef Döring, "Samuel

von Pufendorfs Stellung zur Reunion der Konfessionen in der Kritik von G. W. Leibniz," *Leibniz: Tradition and Aktualität* (Hanover: International Leibniz Congress, 1988), 197–204.

57. Christian Thomasius, *Introductio ad Philosophiam Aulicam* (Leipzig, 1688). On Thomasius's use of his father's antimetaphysical history, see Ralph Häfner, "Jacob Thomasius und die Geschichte der Häresien," in *Christian Thomasius (1655–1728): Neue Forschungen im Kontext der Frühaufklärung*, ed. F. Vollhardt (Tübingen: Max Niemeyer, 1997), 141–64; and Sicco Lehmann-Brauns, *Weisheit in der Weltgeschichte: Philosophiegeschichte zwischen Barok und Aufklärung* (Tübingen: Niemeyer, 2004), 308–15.

58. Lehmann-Brauns, *Weisheit in der Weltgeschichte*, 70–99.

59. Christian Thomasius, "The Right of Protestant Princes Regarding Indifferent Matters or *Adiaphora*," in *Christian Thomasius: Essays on Church, State, and Politics*, ed. and trans. I. Hunter, T. Ahnert, and F. Grunert (Indianapolis: Liberty Fund, 2007), 49–127.

60. For an indication of some of the other occasions on which the authorities had acted against religious rationalism, see Ian Hunter, "Kant's *Religion* and Prussian Religious Policy," *Modern Intellectual History* 2, no. 1 (2005), 10–11.

61. See Sauter, *Visions of the Enlightenment*, 1–47; and Sauter, "Visions of the Enlightenment: Johann Christoph Woellner and Prussia's Edict on Religion of 1788," in *Monarchisms in the Age of Enlightenment: Liberty, Patriotism, and the Public Good*, ed. H. Blom, J. C. Laursen, and L. Simonutti (Toronto: Toronto University Press, 2003), 217–39.

62. The text of the edict is reproduced in Kemper, *Mißbrauchte Aufklärung*, 226–34.

63. Carl Friedrich Bahrdt, *Briefe eines Staatesministers über Aufklärung* (Strasbourg, 1789).

64. See the helpful discussion by Walter Sparn, "Vernünftiges Christentum. Uber die geschichtliche Aufgabe der theologischen Aufklärung im 18. Jahrhundert in Deutschland," in *Wissenschaften im Zeitalter der Aufklärung*, ed. R. Vierhaus (Göttingen: Vandenhoeck & Ruprecht, 1985), 18–57. See also Karl Aner, *Die Theologie der Lessingzeit* (Halle: Niemeyer, 1929).

65. On the striking degree to which Kant shared the views of these figures, see Josef Bohatec, *Die Religionsphilosophie Kants in der "Religion innerhalb der Grenzen der bloßen Vernunft": Mit besonderer Berücksichtigung ihrer theologisch-dogmatischen Quellen* (Hamburg: Hoffmann & Campe, 1938). See also Frieder Lötzsch, *Vernunft und Religion im Denken Kants: Lutherisches Erbe bei Immanuel Kant* (Köln: Böhlau, 1976).

66. See Sparn, "Formalis Atheus?"

67. Gérard Vallée, ed., *The Spinoza Conversations Between Lessing and Jacobi: Texts with Excerpts from the Ensuing Controversy* (Lanham: University Press of America, 1988).

68. See the illuminating discussion of this in Walter Sparn, "Kant's Doctrine of Atonement as a Theory of Subjectivity," in *Kant's Philosophy of Religion Reconsidered*, ed. P. J. Rossi and M. Wreen (Indianapolis: Indiana University Press, 1991), 103–12.

69. For a helpful discussion of this context, see di Giovanni, *Freedom and Religion in Kant*, 1–30.

70. Carl Gottlieb Svarez, *Vorträge über Recht und Staat*, ed. H. Conrad and G. Kleinheyer (Köln: Westdeutscher, 1960), 505–6.

71. See, for example, Jakob Friedrich Rönnberg, *D. Jacob Friedrich Roennberg Hofrath und Professor zu Rostock etc. über Symbolische Bücher im Bezug aufs Staatsrecht* (Rostock, 1790).

72. Johann Salomo Semler, *Verteidigung des Königl.[iches] Ediktes vom 9. Jul. 1788 wider die freimüthigen Betrachtungen eines Ungenannten* (Halle, 1788). For a discussion of the context of Semler's intervention in the debate, see Sauter, *Visions of the Enlightenment*, 49–103.

73. Rudolph "Öffentliche Religion und Toleranz."

KANT ON EDUCATION

Mika LaVaque-Manty

Kant's late *Pädagogik* (1803) is one of his many too often overlooked works. Its contribution to Kant's moral and political philosophy is significant: it addresses one of the fundamental problems of the eighteenth-century Enlightenment—how to foster people's civic independence—and so enriches our understanding of Kant's theory of autonomy. Kant had a lifelong interest in education. As his recent biographer Manfred Kuehn has suggested, this interest stemmed in part from Kant's own schoolboy experience at the hands—the metaphor is deliberate—of stern Pietists.[1] Kant lectured on education throughout his university career; *Pädagogik* is actually based on his university lectures. He even raised funds to support a school in Dessau founded by radical educational reformers, the so-called *Philanthropinen* movement.

This chapter puts *Pädagogik* and Kant's educational theory in general in the context of his theory of autonomy and explores in particular the political preoccupations, on the one hand, and political implications, on the other, of that theory. I chart the social and political landscape around the education of children in the German *Aufklärung*, focusing especially on the *Philanthropinen* and the movement's charismatic founder, Johann Bernhard Basedow.[2] The question all participants in the education debates were addressing was about the scope and nature of children's education. Most enlighteners believed in extending the reach of education to broader classes of people than had been customary; the idea was that education would foster greater civic independence and, simply, greater "enlightenment" for more people.

The enlighteners also correctly believed that the means of that education mattered, and reformers like the *Philanthropinen* advocated some radically new methods. Kant largely adopted Basedow's methods and elaborated on them in his own theory: central were an emphasis on free play on children's own terms and pace, on the one hand, and an opposition to rote memorization and physical punishment, on the other.

Thinking about these ideas against the backdrop of Kant's theory of autonomy will enrich our understanding of that theory. For example, I argue that Kant's idea of autonomy is far more dynamic than it sometimes seems: autonomy can be context dependent, and it can come in degrees and kinds. This, in turn, can help us understand Kant's sometimes problematic discussions of citizenship in a new light.

Discipline and Instruct

Like Kant's other very late works, *Pädagogik* remains incomplete. Incomplete, that is, at least by Kant's own exacting architectonic standards. It was based on the lectures Kant gave on education over several decades.[3] The organization of the book is occasionally unclear: different recorders of the lectures offer slightly different outlines, and some recordings have more gaps than others. Also, the book is repetitive in ways that Kant, however interested in hammering his point, probably would not have intended had he had more time and energy to work on the publication. But it is still eminently readable, as Kant's lecture-based books and essays often are, and the structure accessible even to nonexperts. Indeed, had Kant had more time to structure the book to fit it in his overall system, it may well have been more difficult: where we now have occasionally tiresome repetition, we might have had opaque and extremely complex structure. For something as practical as a book on education, simplicity seems eminently preferable.

None of this means Kant's educational theory doesn't have a clear structure. The key distinction in it maps onto a key distinction in Kant's philosophy overall: that between the two "worlds" of mechanisms, cause, and nature, on the one hand, and freedom, on the other. Humans find themselves in these two worlds simultaneously: They are both subjects to the natural world of cause and effect and are themselves part of it. They are also themselves causes in a world of rational freedom.[4] In other words they are, in Kant's memorable words, ambiguous hybrids of cattle and angels. As animals, humans need discipline; as rational beings, they need instruction and cultivation (*P*, 9:441, 449).[5] The former will keep us from acting on bad impulses; the latter will allow us to be free, that is, to act as autonomous agents.

The problem with the perspectives of these two worlds is that they are simultaneous, but in some tension. Therefore, one "of the greatest problems of education is how to combine subjection to legitimate constraint (*den gesetzlichen Zwang*) with one's facility to exercise one's freedom. For constraint is necessary! How do I cultivate freedom when there is constraint? I must accustom my pupil to put up with a constraint on his freedom and to direct him to use his freedom well" (*P*, 9:453). Right from the beginning, Kant sees education in a broader social context. "Two human inventions can be considered the most difficult, namely, the art of government and the art of education; and we still disagree over what they even mean," Kant says (9:446). Whatever they mean, they are related. Education is one key means to addressing the difficulties in the art of government: it is a way of generating citizens and improving humankind. Education directly addresses what I have elsewhere called enlightenment's "autonomy problem": how to foster people's civic independence when they aren't currently independent.[6] Too much fostering, and independence won't come about (that is the perennial problem of paternalism); too little, and people will remain metaphorical children all their lives. This is one reason that makes the problem of education "the most difficult question" humanity confronts (9:446).

Given this view, it seems odd that where later commentators have thought that what Kant has to say about the art of government is worth paying attention to—at least to some extent, and increasingly, as this volume attests—his views on education have received far less notice.[7] As a sign of how little philosophical interest it has generated, there was no high-end scholarly English translation until 2007.[8] Annette Churton's now dated 1899 translation is charming and eminently accessible (in part because Kant's German in his lectures was quite accessible), but it is not adequate for scholarly exegetical purposes.[9] I argue that *Pädagogik* remains an excellent introduction to early modern thinking about the education of children. On both practical and philosophical grounds, its virtues arguably surpass Locke's or Rousseau's more famous ideas about education.

On its face, the idea that there must be constraints suggests Kant wouldn't have a problem with a thoroughgoing paternalism. But this is really just a statement of the abstract principle Kant and most other liberals endorse: freedom, as opposed to license, is intelligible only against some constraints. This will become clear in the paragraph that follows the one I quoted above. The foremost principle of all education is that "one must grant the child from its earliest childhood freedom in all things (except where it might harm itself, as for example when it tries to grab a knife), as long as this happens so it doesn't impinge on others' freedom—for example, when the child screams or is too boisterously cheerful, it begins to annoy others" (*P*, 9:454).[10] The qualification may in reality mean many restrictions, but it is still important that the primary principle is freedom—and from the child's earliest childhood on, to boot. This is analogous to Kant's thinking in political matters: the state must guarantee and protect citizens' external freedom even before the citizens are fully autonomous—are fully capable of exercising their internal freedom—because external freedom is a precondition for the development of full moral autonomy. Most readers are probably familiar with Kant's argument in "What Is Enlightenment?" and may remember that Kant's concept of freedom may indeed strike us as limited ("Argue as much as you want, but obey!"—*WE*, 8:41). The same is, in some ways, true in terms of education. At the level of principle, though, Kant's antipaternalism is important.

Context for the *Pädagogik*: The *Philanthropinen* Movement

Still, to say that education is important is to state a triviality; to say that education must cultivate human freedom is to beg the key question: how? For us, it is worth considering whether Kant's views on education are worth paying attention to in the way his views on politics are. There are good reasons to think so. First, Kant himself noted that although education is a universal and transhistorically difficult human problem, there was something in the air right then: "For only now are people beginning to judge correctly and understand clearly what a good education involves" (*P*, 9:444). One might dismiss this as typical self-congratulatory Enlightenment Whiggishness, but Kant is right in many ways. Children are being noticed in new ways in the eighteenth century; in fact, according to some controversial views, children are being noticed for the first time *as* children.[11] Whether modernity invented childhood does not matter for us: it is enough to note that children are noticed in new ways.

When children matter, education matters. At the time, it was common for the children of the nobility and even the wealthy bourgeoisie to receive education at home by tutors—Kant had served as one early in his career—but there were schools as well. And there was a call for more and new kinds of schools. In general, the institutional arrangements of education were as much in question as the specific pedagogical approaches educators would employ.

Among the most influential and radical educational reformers were the so-called *Philanthropinen*.[12] They were influential in general: an anonymous book review in the *Neue allgemeine deutsche Bibliothek* in 1796 began by calling the Dessau *Philanthropinum* "one of the most beneficial phenomena of our century."[13] (Pretty high praise in the eventful eighteenth century.) They were particularly important for Kant, too, as I will detail later. Because of this influence, we need to have a sense of Basedow's ideas.

The *Philanthropinen* movement emerged in the 1770s, when its founder Johann Bernhard Basedow opened his school in Dessau. The school, the *Philanthropinum*, was based on the educational ideas Basedow had outlined in a 1768 pamphlet, *Vorstellung an Menschenfreunde* (A presentation to friends of humanity).[14] Basedow's ideas, in turn, had been heavily influenced by the educational theories of Locke and Rousseau, although Basedow wasn't just parroting them (even if he sometimes quotes both at great length). Rather, there are many ways in which Basedow modified the earlier ideas of Locke and Rousseau and even went against them.

There were three central and very radical ideas in Basedow's thinking. First, he saw education as a collective good that was in the state's interest, and argued that therefore the state, not the church, should be in charge of it.[15] Second, he argued for a *common* education, almost (though not fully) independent of social class (*MB*, 17). Finally, he and the *Philanthropinen* in general were in favor of pedagogy we might call child centered: learning was to resemble play and it was to be on the children's terms (*MB*, 42–47; *EW*, 259–260). All of his ideas are very much in keeping with and inspired by Enlightenment ideals, and it is worth saying a bit more about each, although I will focus on the final one.

Basedow was not opposed to religious education, but because the goal of all education was the happiness of the state and its citizens, its oversight had to be the state's responsibility (*VM*, 12–19, 33–35; *MB*, 21–27, 185–208). It was fine and in fact desirable that state religion be taught in schools, and schools had no obligation to offer religious education that was critical of state religion. However, even state religion had to be taught tolerantly, and the children from religiously dissident families could not be kept from attending schools simply on the grounds of their religion (*VM*, 35–38). Moreover, religious education should not begin until a child was capable of understanding it—after the child had already learned many other things (*MB*, 135–147). At the same time, the development of patriotic feelings was an important goal of education (*MB*, 42). But even the cultivation of patriotic feelings was not just for mindless obedience; its purpose was to ensure that all even minimally educated people would have appropriate civic virtues (*VM*, passim).

It is this idea of the reciprocity between the collective happiness of the state, on the one hand, and the citizens that constituted the state, on the other, that undergirds Basedow's second central idea: an education that is far more independent of social class than any previous and many later educational theories had it. Although Basedow thought that the children of the "great masses" and the children of the bourgeois and the gentry might actually go to different schools, their education would be the same. "Because people of every estate are still people, and children, children, the beginning of instruction [in the schools for the better-off people] can be nothing other than what it is in the large schools" for the masses, Basedow said (*VM*, 61). The idea was that at an early age, it was impossible to tell whether someone was going to become more highly educated, and so everyone needed to be offered the same basic skills for practical life (*MB*, 17). In regions with sufficient resources, basic elementary education could be followed by *bürgerliche Schule*—"citizen school"—at what we could call middle-school level (*VM*, passim.). Even though this began to differentiate educational opportunities, it didn't do it on the basis of any given individual's resources, but on the basis of geography. And, again, even in these schools the assumption was that it wasn't predetermined whether a child would become more highly educated. The emphasis was also on education for practical life, not for further schooling (*VM*, §§23, 39; *MB*, 42). Only at age fifteen would there be enough evidence, in Basedow's view, of whether a child should be even more highly educated. Perhaps ironically, at that age financial resources came directly back into the picture: only absolute geniuses from poor families should be offered a free high school and university education at state cost; all others had to show sufficient economic resources to be able to support themselves. Presumably Basedow wasn't after too radical a change in people's economic mobility. Furthermore, the number of people allowed to pursue higher education, that is, schooling past their fifteenth year, would be strictly set by the state (*VM*, §19).

These were Basedow's ideas for the infrastructural organization of education. Bringing about such changes alone or even by a small movement, even if the ideas had been less radical, would naturally be slow and difficult process, and the early *Philanthropinen* never saw these ideas realized on a large scale. However, the "microeducational" ideas, namely, the actual pedagogy, could be put in practice much more easily. Basedow argued for the immediate establishment of experimental schools, and that is the kind of purpose the *Philanthropinum* tried to fulfill. Although experimenting was important because it was impossible to know fully in advance what kinds of methods would work best at different levels, he did have important principles in mind.

These ideas were the most radical part of Basedow's program. I have already mentioned Basedow's idea of the first two stages of education as a preparation for practical *living*, not for school. For Basedow, however, the emphasis on the practical wasn't in the first instance because it was all the common classes would need in the future. After all, these stages of education were for everybody. Rather, the idea was that the practical was something everyone would need, regardless of one's station in life and future plans. That wasn't just an empirical observation, but in fact had its own causal efficacy: it *would* bring about a more egalitarian, republican state.

A set of key principles would bring about the practical goals. The central notion was that learning, especially early learning in the common elementary school (*Volksschule*), was to be on the child's terms. In general, all education should happen with means appropriate to the child's developmental stage. This meant that early teaching should resemble play as much as possible. A full half of a child's day in the *Volksschule* should be some kind of physical (*körperlich*) play or "work" (*VM*, 59). The subjects of the *Volksschule* were the same for all: reading, writing, arithmetic, *Realien* (history and what we would now call elementary social and natural sciences), practical knowledge of nature and of the law. Rote memorization was absolutely banned; instead, children should learn through "real" remembering via playful exercises and practices (*MB*, 95–100). Physical education was important, both through simple gymnastic exercises as well as physical games (*MB*, 62–65). Basedow opposed physical punishment.

Physical Autonomy

The best evidence of Kant's enthusiasm for the *Philanthropinen* are two early (1776) essays he wrote in support of Basedow's Dessau school. In these essays, he rejects "slow reformism" in favor of a "speedy revolution" when it comes to changing education. The essays are fundraising pamphlets; at the end, Kant lists when and where he will be available to sell subscriptions to the school. His enthusiasm outlasted Basedow's ouster from the school and a slightly conservative turn by other educational reformers.[16] In *Pädagogik*, he frequently refers to the school. The references are not uncritical cheerleading, but it does seem obvious that Kant believes Basedow's ideas were more promising than many other educational proposals at the time. One of the reasons he appreciates the *Philanthropinum* is that it is experimental (*P*, 9:451, 467). Educational reform, he believes, is necessarily experimental because it is difficult to know in advance what the right means of bringing children up are.

But there are some general principles, and the goal of *Pädagogik* is to outline them. Kant doesn't just repeat Basedowian principles. He modifies them and, most interesting for us, puts them in the framework of his critical philosophy. In terms of overall areas, the goals of education are the following: The purpose of discipline, as I suggested above, is to restrain our animal nature. The purpose of acculturation is to ascertain that we have sufficient information and abilities to pursue our ends, whatever they might be. These include discretion (the ability to conduct oneself in society) and some degree of refinement (which, surprisingly perhaps, allows us to use others for our ends). The fundamental goal of *practical* education is to train our morality so that we will choose only good ends.

These theoretical goals are important and recognizably Kantian, but we get an interesting purchase on them if we begin by thinking of the book more pragmatically: the first conception of autonomy that arises will be in an important sense physical. The immediate purpose of the book is, after all, pragmatic. Recall that it is largely based on lectures he gave at the University of Königsberg on education. Many of Kant's students were likely to work, as Kant had, as private tutors. And although their charges were likely to be children whom they taught school subjects, Kant believed it was worth their while to know about childrearing from the infancy on. They might, as he points out, often be the only educated people in a household and so were important conduits of the proper childrearing methods (*P*, 9:456). The book's section on physical education therefore begins with newborns and goes through the various developmental stages in remarkably sophisticated degree (at least if we remember that Kant never married or, as far as we know, had children).

Some more context. Here, from an English translation of Johann Amos Comenius's influential illustrated 1658 encyclopedia *Orbis Sensualium Pictus* (The visible world), is the early modern story of early childhood in a nutshell:

> The Infant is wrapped in Swadling-clothes, is laid in a Cradle, is suckled by the Mother with her breasts, and fed with Pap.
> Afterwards it learneth to go by a Standing stool, playeth with Rattles, and beginneth to speak.
> As it beginneth to grow older, it is accustomed to Piety and Labour, and is chastised if it be not dutiful.[17]

No excerpt this brief and general can tell the whole story of childrearing or even of the ideology of childrearing, but what is interesting is exactly that this short a description does include, as a matter of course, the standing stool as the device with which the child learns to walk. Comenius's Latin term for the standing stool is *Serperastro*; the German translation is *Gängelwagen*, and, according to the Brothers' Grimm dictionary, is one of the first printed occurrences of the term. The more common English translation is "walking cart."

Closely related to the walking cart are leading strings (*Leitbande* or *Gängelbande* in German). Both the cart and the strings were childrearing devices commonly used in Europe from the middle ages well into modernity. They were tools to help children learn to walk while their parents tried to balance children's need for self-direction with concern for safety. One doesn't have to be a parent to understand what a crucial watershed a child's learning to walk is. It is particularly crucial in terms of its scale: the entire physical object, that is, the child's body, is now under control of her self-direction, in a way that allows her to move to new places and new heights. Her self-direction isn't perfect, of course, nor is it very reflective. Because of that, learning to walk comes with numerous risks: the child may hurt herself in new ways and, in particular, the risks to her head from falling from new heights make things more dangerous. So the understandable dual pull on parents: walking has to be *her* activity, and so ultimately unaided, but at the same time she by definition does not yet have all the skills necessary to avoid the risks involved.

Gängelwagen is a child-sized version of what we know as a walker, commonly used these days by adults with disabilities and by the elderly. Leading strings are either a kind of harness or simply reins or a leash. Walking carts and leading strings can even serve slightly different purposes: leading strings remain useful long after a child has learned to walk as a way of controlling him. But the overall purpose is the same: they are tools that try to balance safety, control, and assistance for someone who can't be trusted to move about by himself.

Elsewhere, I have written about Kant's tendency to use the terms *Gängelwagen* and *Leitbande* as metaphors for things he doesn't like: political paternalism, nonautonomous thinking, dogmatic beliefs.[18] They are helpful metaphors for things Kant wants to criticize in part because he dislikes the real thing just as much, as the *Pädagogik* shows. Kant spends several pages discussing the common methods of teaching children to walk and thoroughly condemns both walkers and leading strings. The latter in particular he singles out for an attack; they are not only useless, but they are also "in particular very harmful" (P, 9:461). They can, in Kant's view, cause permanent damage to the child's upper body by distorting and deforming the still soft bones in the ribcage. In general, such "aids" (*Hülfsmittel*) teach children bad habits: children don't learn to walk as steadily on their own feet if they get used to being helped. "It is best," Kant says, "to let the children crawl on the ground until they eventually start walking on their own" (9:461). He also thinks people have exaggerated worries about how hard children fall. And, he suggests, letting them fall a few times teaches them to move lightly and to turn their bodies in ways that are not damaging to them when they do fall (9:461). Furthermore, Kant wants to disabuse people of the particularly problematic belief that children should never be allowed to fall forward because they will hurt their faces. Quite the contrary, letting them fall forward, he thinks, teaches them to use the most important "natural tool" they have: their hands (9:462).

All this leads to an overall theoretical-practical point: the more "artificial tools" one uses in teaching children, the more dependent they will remain on "instruments." "In general, it would be better if one used fewer instruments right from the start and just let the children learn more things by themselves. That way, they would learn things more thoroughly" (P, 9:462).

Children's free exercise of their bodies on their own terms and at their own pace makes them stronger, teaches them independence, and gives them ownership of their actions and behavior. "Foremost is that the child always help itself" (9:466).

So artificial aids are bad, self-direction—even when it means clumsiness and stumbling—is good. This is consistent with the familiar understanding of Kant as an advocate of autonomy, although it is important to note that the sort of self-direction Kant is interested in in the case of concrete walking carts and leading strings is physical. There is a connection between the importance of a child's physical self-direction and Kant's theory of autonomy as "using one's own understanding," which the metaphorical leading strings might hamper. It is little remarked that Kant thinks physical self-cultivation—"gymnastics in the strict sense" (*MM*, 6:445)—is a moral duty, as I elaborate below. So the importance of the physical isn't limited to how children learn to walk; it extends to how children grow up and how adults develop themselves.

Exercising Autonomy

The reviewer who praised the *Philanthropinen* in the *Neue allgemeine deutsche Bibliothek* in 1796 thought one of the benefits of the *Philanthropinum* had been the introduction of physical education. The book under review was one specifically inspired by that aspect of the Basedowian philosophy: Johann Christoph Friedrich GutsMuths's *Gymnastik für die Jugend* (Gymnastics for Youth). GutsMuths had intended his book for children and youth who weren't able to attend progressive experimental schools or who were simply tutored at home. GutsMuths's book is a combination of philosophical justifications for exercises, detailed descriptions of those exercises, and discussions of their history and context. It reflected an increasingly popular appreciation of physical education, and GutsMuths made a career of such books. He also wrote *Games for the Practice and Strengthening of the Body and Mind, Intended for Youth, Their Educators, and All Friends of Innocent Youthful Joy* and *A Small Self-study Guide of the Art of Swimming*. *Gymnastik* was quickly translated into other European languages and was particularly influential in Britain.

In general, whether they considered Basedow's egalitarianism too radical or not, one thing most of the reformers agreed on was the importance of physical education. There were some differences, but on the whole what is striking is their accord. People generally also thought that the physical was strongly connected to the rational and the moral. In 1790, Peter Villaume wrote in the *Deutsche Monatsschrift*: "Of all the periods of a human life, none is as important as youth. At this time, the previously weak and undeveloped body receives its perfection and strength. Before this, one could say with a kind of hindsight that the child had only vegetated; now it begins to live. Reason awakens, feelings begin to rule, he rises to the dignity of a moral being."[19] Against this light, it is less surprising that even Kant, the supposed paragon of the cerebral, argued for physical exercise as a moral duty: "Finally, cultivating the *powers of his body* (gymnastics in the strict sense) is looking after the *basic stuff* (the matter) in a human being, without which he could not realize his ends. Hence the continuing and purposive invigoration of the animal in him is an end of a human being that is a duty to himself" (*MM*, 6:445). Part of the rationale for this injunction is simply the idea that the physical body is where moral personhood necessarily resides in the case of humans (as opposed to, say, angels), and so it needs to be maintained. Villaume's view is explicit; but even Kant is implicit about the there being a strong connection between human agency and the physical body.

Villaume's and Kant's points are about physical exercise well into adulthood, but exercise should of course begin quite early. In fact, think back to the leading strings and walking carts: it begins literally with the child's first steps. Even budding and inchoate awareness of what my body can and cannot do plays a role in my developing a sense of myself as an autonomous person. Errors and failures are important for learning to understand the limits of that exercise, "for one cannot straightaway do all that that one *wants* to do, without having first tried out and exercised one's powers," Kant argues in *The Doctrine of Virtue* (*MM*, 6:477). This is true of all aspects of our human agency, but again in the first instance, when we think of children, it is particularly true of one's physical abilities. So it makes sense, if we return to the Basedowian *Volksschule*, that half of a child's day is spent on physical play and exercise: those are the ways in which the child can be self-directed on her own terms. Young children aren't yet fully rational agents, but there is a way in which they can be self-directed on their own terms: there are *some* things in which they themselves can be the sources of their actions, and in which it is only harmful to have their minds be under the direction of others. So here we have the beginnings of a theory of agency:

Leading strings for the child, like rote memorization or physical punishment for the *Volksschüler*, are an externally imposed *illegitimate constraint*. However well intentioned, they are, in this kind of Enlightenment theory, a kind of tyranny.[20] We can put things in another way: when Kant says that "[n]othing is more harmful than a nagging, slavish discipline used to break the [child's] will (*Eigenwille*)" (*P*, 9:465), the idea is that a child does indeed have her will and that attempts to break it include physical discipline.

None of this is to say that Kant wants to permit everything; the constraints remain, and some of them might appall us (e.g., a hard bed is good for discipline, excessive caressing of the child is bad [*P*, 9:464–65]). But the general idea requires respect for the freedom of the child's will almost from the beginning. And the will—as a budding *rational* will—is indeed always there. Even a child less than a year old always cries "with some reflection (*Reflexion*), however vague," Kant says (9:461).[21] All this suggests that autonomy does come in an important sense in degrees and is inextricably connected to our physical embodiment.

Still, the culmination of human autonomy is in moral autonomy, which aims at setting good ends *in general*. Kant is often taken to be a hedonist about nonmoral ends, but as Barbara Herman has suggested, this may get things backward: the very idea of autonomy presupposes a social orientation toward other persons as ends.[22] At the same time, this can't come about through a conceptual stipulation, lest the theory of autonomy lose its purchase on what people are even minimally like. Seeing the theory of moral education as both continuous with and a culmination of the lesser kinds of training answers the empirical worry.

Moral Education

Let us turn again to the reformer who inspires Kant, not to reduce his theory to its social and political context, but to illustrate it. In radical contrast to the prevailing practices and attitudes of the day, and in keeping with his child-centered orientation, Basedow thought religious education could only begin in middle school when the child had developed a sufficient understanding to make any real sense of the instruction. Otherwise, Basedow suggested, the child's proper understanding and thus *real* faith would be threatened or impeded (*MB*, 122). He outlined these ideas in eight lengthy pieces of advice to parents and educators (*MB*, 135–47); we can get a good sense of their logic from a letter Kant wrote to Christian Heinrich Wolke, the director of the *Philanthropinum*, in support of a friend's son's application to the school. The view Kant outlines is ostensibly his friend's, Robert Motherby's, but what he says captures the school's (and Basedow's) own pedagogical idea:

> In matters of religion, the spirit of the Philanthropin agrees perfectly with the boy's father. He wishes that even the natural awareness of God (as the boy's growth in age and understanding may gradually make him arrive at it) should not be aimed at devotional exercises directly but only after he has realized that these are valuable merely as a means of animating an effective conscience and a fear of God, so that one does one's duties as though they were divinely commanded. (*Correspondence*, 10:192)[23]

Although religious education should be postponed, it didn't mean that children's moral or religious development was unimportant. It was simply that proper moral development would be hindered by a too early religious education, especially if it took the form of religious memorization, "mere words," as Basedow called it (*VM*, 57). For Kant, the problem in such an approach to religious and moral education is that morality and faith would interfere with one another in problematic ways. First, rote memorization of religious formulas, especially before a child can understand them, only brings about a "contrived concept of piety" (*P*, 9:495). Even worse, when religion and morality are combined in formulaic teaching, children fail to understand why something is morally wrong. Children should be taught to despise vice "not only on the ground that God has forbidden it, but because vice itself is despicable" (9:450). Here, again, the point is recognizable to those familiar with Kant's moral theory: despite the importance of religious faith, it disrespects morality to argue that it binds us only because God has so ordered.

Instead, moral education should be based on experience and proceed through relaxed play as well as through instructive moral conversations (*MB*, 102–107). The latter is particularly important for Kant, who argues for a "catechism of right" (*Katechismus des Rechts*) in order to develop children's sense of right and wrong (*Rechtschaffenheit*) (*P*, 9:490). Such a catechism would pose tricky moral questions for children to think about. The questions Kant proposes as an example are familiar to anyone who knows their moral philosophy. Is it acceptable to omit paying a debt if one uses the money to help someone in immediate need? Is it acceptable to lie to prevent a bad outcome? Kant's answers are equally predictable (no and no). Despite this, and despite the way the approach and its answers are scripted, they do make the process of moral education importantly interactive, as opposed to purely mechanical: they respect the child's reasoning capacities by an involvement with those capacities.[24]

Conclusion

Education, when it is properly conducted with sensitivity to the child's level of development (P, 9:455), will produce citizens who have the capacities to conduct themselves well in society and, most important, set morally permissible ends for themselves. These citizens are, as we know from Kant's views here and elsewhere (in *Rechtslehre* and *Theory and Practice*, for example), primarily men. One of the goals of education is to avoid, at all costs, effeminacy (*Weichlichkeit*), Kant says (9:463), and we know as a general rule that Kant believes that education should end when a person is physically and morally capable of becoming a father (9:453). Interestingly, though, these assumptions and pronouncements about gender are less central to Kant's theory of education than Kant himself may have thought. That is not only because the German term *das Kind* is in the grammatical neuter; so is the German word for "girl" (*das Mädchen*). Part of Kant's idea is that prepubescent children can be understood, in some ways, as genderless, even if we know that not to be true in practice, then or now. This is clearly what Kant has in mind in his lectures on education. But grammatical gender and social facts have only a contingent, even tenuous connection.

NOTES

1. Manfred Kuehn, *Kant: A Biography* (Cambridge: Cambridge University Press, 2001), chapter 1.
2. Given the lack of standardized orthography in eighteenth-century German, we find the word *Philanthropin* and its cognates spelled with and without the *h* in contemporary literature. I have spelled it with the *h* throughout, but anyone interested in searching electronic databases should use both spellings.
3. The most important of them are now included in volume 25 of the *Akademie* edition.
4. For a different view of the consequences of Kant's distinction, see Hunter, chapter 7 of this volume.

5. Translations are my own unless otherwise noted.
6. Mika LaVaque-Manty, "Kant's Children," *Social Theory and Practice* 32, no. 3 (2006): 365–88, and *The Playing Fields of Eton: Equality and Excellence in Modern Meritocracy* (Ann Arbor: University of Michigan Press, 2009).
7. Few recent examples are Barbara Herman, "Training to Autonomy: Kant and the Question of Moral Education," in *Philosophers on Education: Historical Perspectives,* ed. Amélie Oksenberg Rorty (London: Routledge, 1998), 254–71; Barbara Herman, *Moral Literacy* (Cambridge: Harvard University Press, 2007); G. Felicitas Munzel, "*Menschenfreundschaft*: Friendship and Pedagogy in Kant," *Eighteenth-Century Studies* 32, no. 2 (1998): 247–59; Paul Saurette, *The Kantian Imperative: Humiliation, Common Sense, Politics* (Toronto: University of Toronto Press, 2005); and Tamar Schapiro, "What Is a Child?," *Ethics* 109, no. 4 (1999): 715–38.
8. Immanuel Kant, *Anthropology, History, and Education,* ed. Günter Zöller and Robert B. Louden (Cambridge: Cambridge University Press, 2007).
9. Immanuel Kant, *Education,* trans. Annette Churton, intro. Caroline Rhys Davids (London: Kegan Paul, Trench, Trübner, 1899; repr. Ann Arbor: University of Michigan Press, 1960).
10. I use the impersonal and objectifying word "it" to refer to the term "the child" in order to capture Kant's gender-neutral language. The German *das Kind* is in the grammatical neuter.
11. Philippe Ariès, *Centuries of Childhood: A Social History of Family Life* (London: J. Cape, 1962).
12. It might be worth noting here that the term *Philanthropinen* does not have the connotation we most commonly associate with it these days, namely, the financial support of worthy public causes. It did involve varying degree of paternalism—though far less in Basedow's case than in, say, the slightly later Swiss variants. The key idea, however, is a general concern for humanity, and if a convenient term were available, the best translation would evoke a kind of hybrid between humanists and humanitarians.
13. Anonymous, "Review of Gutsmuth's *Gymnastik für die Jugend,*" *Neue allgemeine deutsche Bibliothek* 21, no. 2 (1796): 459–61.
14. Johann Bernhard Basedow, *Vorstellung an Menschenfreunde,* ed. Theodor Fritzsch (Leipzig: Reclam, 1906), 17. Hereafter cited parenthetically in the text as *VM*. *Methodenbuch* and *Elementarwerke,* both of which are in Basedow, *Ausgewählte Schriften* (Langenfalza: Hermann Beyer & Söhne, 1880), will be cited parenthetically as *MB* and *EW*.
15. "Aufsätze, das Philanthropin betreffend" [Essays concerning the Philanthropin], 2:449.
16. Basedow's ouster was by all accounts as much on the grounds of bad management skills and drinking problems as it was politics, but his followers in the school and in the educational movement in general dialed back his egalitarianism in a massive compendium, *Allgemeine Revision des gesammten Schul- und Erziehungswesens,* which Basedow's successor Johann Heinrich Campe edited and published in 1785–1792.
17. Johann Amos Comenius, *Joh. Amos Commenii Orbis Sensualium Pictus. Hoc Est, Omnium Fundamentalium in Mundo Rerum, & in Vitâ Actionum, Pictura & Nomenclatura. Joh. Amos Commenius's Visible World. Or, a Picture and Nomenclature of All the Chief Things That Are in the World; and of Mens Employments Therein,* ed. Charles Hoole (London: J. Kirton, 1659), 244.
18. LaVaque-Manty, "Kant's Children."
19. Peter Villaume, "Über die Gewalt der Leidenschaften in den Jünglingsjahren," *Deutsche Monatsschrift* 2 (1790): 153–75.
20. Schapiro, "What Is a Child?," makes a similar argument about Kant's view of children; see in particular 735–36.
21. Different versions of the lecture notes of Kant's students have different ages here. Some have three, others have eight months.
22. Herman, *Moral Literacy,* chapters 5–6.
23. *Immanuel Kant, Correspondence,* ed. and trans. Arnulf Zweig (Cambridge: Cambridge University Press, 1999).

24. The most famous vehicle for moral conversations of this kind was Campe's reworking of the Robinson Crusoe story in *Robinson der jüngere,* which was translated into a dozen European languages within a few years of its publication in 1781. In the book, the story of the famous castaway is interspersed with model conversations about right and wrong, about good and bad choices the characters make. Its conversations are so scripted Kant might have found them unhelpful; at least he never mentions them, despite his friendly correspondence with Campe over the years.

KANT, FREEDOM OF THE PRESS, AND BOOK PIRACY

John Christian Laursen

Immanuel Kant is known for calling for intellectual freedom and freedom of the press in his famous essay of 1784, "What Is Enlightenment?" In *Theory and Practice* he called the press "the sole palladium of the people's right" (*TP*, 8:304) and in the best interest of princes (8:302), and in his lectures on anthropology he called it "a great [*grosses*] means of testing the correctness of own our judgments" (*A*, 7:129). In many of his later works he promotes a politics of publicity.[1]

Why, then, is there no clearly established right to freedom of the press in his great *Metaphysics of Morals* of 1797? Part of the answer can be found in a further puzzle about the book. When John Ladd translated part of it in 1965 for the Library of Liberal Arts, he left out a short section entitled "What Is a Book?"[2] Few interpreters from the philosophers' camp have known what to make of such a peculiar question.[3] Why did Kant discuss such an odd question in a metaphysics of morals?

Kant's section "What Is a Book?" is actually about book piracy, or the unauthorized reprinting of books. It turns out that this was a major economic, legal, and philosophical issue in late eighteenth-century Germany. Luckily for us, a contemporary author and publisher, Ernst Martin Gräff, put together in 1794 a running commentary on over sixty books, pamphlets, and journal articles of the time on the issue of book piracy, and we will draw on this resource in order to bring out some of the special features of Kant's argument.[4] A review of some of the forgotten elements of this debate throws light on the politics of authorship of the day, and on the place of freedom of the press in Kant's philosophy of law.

Kant's section "What Is a Book?" was not his first exploration of the matter. In 1784, philosophy professor Martin Ehlers of Kiel intervened in an ongoing debate about book piracy with a book entitled *On the Injustice of Book Piracy According to Natural Penal Law*.[5] The next year, Kant published an essay in the *Berlinische Monatsschrift* with the title "On the Injustice of Book Piracy."[6] Appearing a dozen years later, "What Is a Book?" was a recapitulation of points he had made in the earlier article.

What could make such an apparently insignificant question so important? It may seem strange indeed to make a big issue of book piracy. But from the point of view of the material conditions of intellectual life, book piracy may have been more of a threat to eighteenth-century writers than state censorship. As long as one managed to stay out of prison, censorship of books could actually increase an author's or publisher's income by making books famous. As we know from many sources, including a passage in Goethe's autobiography, a good book bonfire could increase reader demand.[7] But book piracy threatened authors and publishers by depriving them of income. Unauthorized reprints of books kept authors' honoraria low and publishers' risks high.[8]

When Ehlers and Kant set to work on the issue of book piracy, they already had a literature at hand. Ehlers reports in his introduction that he had read an address in English "attached to Grandison" thirty years before (xiii); he must have meant Samuel Richardson's *Address to the Public* of 1754, protesting the piracy of Richardson's novel, *The History of Sir Charles Grandison*.[9] For the German-speaking world, the jurist J. S. Pütter had published *Book Piracy According to the True Basic Principles of Law* in 1774.[10] More recently, there had been essays in the *Deutsches Merkur* and the *Deutsches Museum* in 1783. Ehlers explained that he had been working on the issue before those pieces came out (xviff.), but he still felt obliged to dedicate the last fifty-eight pages of his book to a close refutation of the *Museum* article.

Ehlers was concerned to *refute* the *Museum* piece because it *defended* book piracy. In fact, the prevailing view in the period seems to have been to justify the practice.[11] Respectable publishers all over Europe engaged in the trade.[12] As Christian Sigmund Krause, author of the piece, put it, "A published book is a secret divulged."[13] It makes no more sense to forbid reprinting books than to forbid students from using the ideas they have been taught by their teachers. The whole point of publishing is taken to be the dissemination of ideas, and that is precisely what reprinting does. We shall return to Ehlers's answers to these arguments.

As professor of philosophy at the University of Kiel, Ehlers's natural idiom was the language of natural law, refounded for Protestant Germany in the works of Grotius and Pufendorf, and developed by Thomasius, Wolff, and many other figures. Ehlers sought to resolve all questions concerning authors' rights in terms of natural penal law. Natural penal law covers only a small part of a person's duties: out of one hundred duties, ninety-five are matters of civil law or morals, and only five belong to natural penal law (14). It sets only minimal standards: "a righteous man before the penal law can still be an evil man before God" (18). But they are firm standards that the civil authorities should enforce.

In Ehlers's hands, natural penal law was very much a property-centered paradigm. "All rights that a man has according to nature are founded on a chief concept, namely, the existence of property" (6). The security of property "is indisputably the first basic principle of human happiness" (7). With the exception of true cases of life-or-death need, everyone must leave to others the full possession of their rightful property (16–17). "The inviolability of the right of property is clearly the ground of every civil union and every society" (108). Marxists would probably call this an artisanal conception of natural law.

There are three sources of property, Ehlers writes. It belongs to you if you have received it directly from God or nature; if you have won it from nature; or if you have obtained it by contract (19). Indisputably, he says, the power to think is given to you directly by God or nature and you are entitled to the products of that power, which are your thoughts (20). That other people have facilitated your thinking does not give them a shared right to your thoughts (21). The only time anyone has a right to your thoughts is in the same cases of dire need that justify the invasion of other sorts of property (23–24). Otherwise, other people can obtain your thoughts only through contract with you (24).

If a person obtains your thoughts through contract, the person is bound by the conditions of that contract, Ehlers insists. A contract can allow for the recipient of your thoughts to pass those thoughts along, or it can forbid it (36). Even in the case of oral communication, contractual limits on the right to repeat things can be understood from the nature of the ideas that have been communicated (30–31). If what you say may cause harm upon being repeated, it is understood that you do not want it repeated (41). But there are practical limits to your rights. The chief reason why you cannot charge for everything you say in speech and for further dissemination of it by others is that it is practically impossible to prove when and what you have added to someone's knowledge by speaking with them (44–45). But in the case of writings, there is no question of forgetting what was said; there is ample time for returning to your text to see if it has been passed on by others (47).

Whatever can be said for protecting handwritten materials from unauthorized use can be said with more force for printed materials, Ehlers writes (57). It should be taken for granted that authors want to be compensated for the use of their property in their ideas. If they do not want compensation, they can print the work at their own cost and distribute it for free (61); they can sell the publishing rights to a publisher and give the proceeds to deserving people; or they can give the publishing rights to deserving people (62). But none of this can be made a duty by natural penal law. Luther's idea that writers write for the greater glory of God or the good of mankind does not mean that they have no property rights. After all, no matter how well meaning they may be, authors and their families may need money to live, too (63). In fact, Ehlers asserts, it is a sort of tyranny when worthy scholars, who do so much for the world, cannot make a respectable living because of book piracy (115).

This matter of the economic effects of book piracy drives a wedge between the interests of publishers and of writers. Since publishers cannot afford to pay writers much because their competitors can bring the same book out without paying anything, a writer often makes only one-thirtieth of what a publisher makes from a book (130). Booksellers live like government ministers, while authors starve (130).[14] The quality of books also suffers: booksellers seek quick sales, rather than good books (126). As part of his strategy to redress the imbalance, Ehlers insists that the issue of book piracy is always a matter of the rights of the writer against the pirates, and only a matter of the right of the publisher insofar as the writer has transferred rights to the publisher (172). (Kant will reverse this, as we shall see.) Gräff later asserted that Ehlers's book "belongs to the best writings on this subject," but regretted that he gave all of the rights to the author and none to the legitimate publisher.[15] As a publisher, he approved of all efforts to strengthen the rights of publishers.

As Ehlers explains it, it is not necessary for a book to contain an explicit prohibition of book piracy because it is generally known that writers do not authorize it (65).¹⁶ If anyone has any doubts about the author's intentions to prohibit reprinting, he can simply ask the author. Thus, the purchase of a book with the intention to reprint it openly violates the conditions with which books are sold (67). Knowing buyers of reprinted books are like knowing receivers of stolen goods (72–73). Although he is arguing from the point of view of natural penal law, Ehlers points out that according to civil law, intellectual property is like any other property (87).

Ehlers's book was a call for the matter of book piracy to become an object of *Staatspolicey,* or state policy (125). "Privileges" issued by individual princes to individual printers had been available since shortly after the beginning of printing, but they did not protect authors, nor did they protect very much in a Germany divided up among dozens of princedoms, bishoprics, etc. In 1794, Prussia became one of the first larger states to prohibit book piracy when it enacted the Prussian Code.¹⁷ Although he lived and worked in Danish-ruled north Germany, Ehlers dedicated his book to Emperor Joseph, in the hopes that he would push for imperial legislation that would cover all of Germany. Gräff quoted another 1783 proposal for such legislation, including its conclusion: "When [will this be enacted]? Not yet in the year 2440?"¹⁸

In the tradition of natural law and enlightened absolutism,¹⁹ Ehlers is willing to trust a great deal to princes. Censorship by the best scholars of all faculties is acceptable to him, although he also mentions favorably the system of no censorship, but with authors' and publishers' responsibility for libel, slander, and so forth (132–33).²⁰

For our purposes, perhaps the most interesting part of Ehlers's argument is his insistence that books do not consist solely of paper and printed letters, but more important, of the authors' thoughts (96–97). Words alone do not make a book; they must be organized into thoughts (155). It is not the reproduction of the letters that constitutes piracy, but the reproduction of thoughts (172). Ehlers is a philosophical voluntarist, asserting that intellectual freedom is important because "desires, drives, and actions depend, as long as one is free, on the ideas that a man has" (131). This sort of argument sets the stage for Immanuel Kant's view of book piracy.

The first paragraph of Kant's 1785 essay "On the Injustice of Book Piracy" reads like a direct criticism of Ehlers's book.²¹ Those who "regard the publication of a book as a use of property in a copy . . . and then want, nevertheless, to restrict the use of this right by the reservation of certain rights . . . so that unauthorized publication of it would not be permitted . . .

can never succeed in this" (8:79). There are two reasons: one is that "the author's property in his thought . . . is left to him regardless of the unauthorized publication" (8:79). The other is that it is unrealistic to expect buyers to give express consent to restrictions on reprinting, and Ehlers's presumption of the consent of the buyer to such restrictions is stretching presumptions too far (8:79).

Kant's alternative makes the issue a matter of agency law. Book piracy, for Kant, is the transaction of business in the name of another without his consent. Only the authorized publisher has the right to sell books in the writer's name. "This is undoubtedly present in the elementary concepts of natural right," Kant writes (8:80).

In defense of his reasoning, Kant points out that "everything comes down to the concept of a book . . . as a work of an author" (8:80). If a book is a commodity that the author can trade to the public with or without reservation of rights, then apparently the case is hopeless, because booksellers do not in fact require buyers to assume financial responsibility if their copies are used for reprinting. However, if the book is conceived of as a use of the author's powers, as "speech," the author cannot in fact alienate those powers entirely, but only give another (the publisher) the right to "speak" on his behalf by selling his books (8:80–81). Thus, the authorized bookseller is not just selling a thing, but also acting as an agent for the transmission of the author's thoughts. The unauthorized book pirate is usurping this agency. One of the peculiarities of Kant's argument is that this means that it is not the author, but the authorized publisher, who is damaged by book piracy (8:82).

As long as the chief right in the publication of books is a right of agency, Kant argues, it cannot be obtained by the mere fact of buying a thing, that is, a copy of the book. Quite opposite to Ehlers's reasoning, according to which when you buy a thing (the book), you obtain it with an implied reservation of the right to reprint, in Kant's version, you obtain nothing but a thing, and the right to reprint it would require an additional agency agreement. This follows from what Arthur Ripstein in chapter 2 of this volume describes as Kant's view of property as "a relation between persons with respect to things." It is undergirded by Kant's "explanation of how everyone can be bound by some other person's unilateral act," which in this case is the author's conferral of the right to reproduce his work on the publisher (51).

There are other distinctions between Ehlers's and Kant's arguments. Ehlers argued that abridgments or translations should be subject to the same protections against piracy as original texts; Kant asserted that abridgments and translations are not the same speech, so they are not protected (8:86–87). Ehlers argued that certain types of lacework and other artistry should be considered the property of the one who thought them up; Kant asserted that paintings, sculpture, and other works of art could be freely copied because they are *opera* or works, whereas speech is *operae* or actions (8:86). Apparently, Kant is assuming some sort of distinction between image and word; surely today many would contest Kant's claim that sculpture and painting are not speech.

Kant's essay also represented a different political strategy from Ehlers's. Where Ehlers hoped for an imperial rescript, Kant packaged his argument as a matter of the principles of natural and Roman agency law that, with suitable elaboration, could be taken to court right away (8:87). This was in keeping with his standard practice of reinterpreting established principles and institutions to allow for what he thought reason required. He may have had less confidence in the reforming instincts of the absolute rulers, and more confidence in the ability of philosophers like himself to persuade judges and other authorities that the right was already in existence. This strategy is comparable to the reform strategy in the United States today that bypasses Congress and tries to persuade the Supreme Court to recognize an implicit reform or right already present in the Constitution.

Kant's distinction between the thing and the speech it contains is surely a reflection of his larger critical philosophy, with its distinction between phenomena and noumena. We can never be sure if the phenomena of property or republics actually instantiate the rights that they are supposed to, but we can be sure of the noumena or rights they are supposed to instantiate. So what he says about book piracy seems fully consistent with what Elisabeth Ellis says about his reliance on provisional right as opposed to conclusive right in much of his work: it is an effort to move us closer to a state of right while admitting that we might not even recognize it if we had it.[22] In this essay, as elsewhere in his legal philosophy, Kant blended natural law with his own philosophy in ways that certainly transformed the tradition. Ehlers and other previous natural lawyers would not have recognized many of his distinctions.

Gräff commented on Kant's essay in the *Berlinische Monatsschrift* that it was "uncommonly enlightening." What he seemed to like best about it was that it insisted that even the author of a work did not have the right to give to a book pirate the rights already given to another publisher.[23] He added that "Mr. K. has been misunderstood in almost all of his opinions and principles; since these claims have been understood and expressed by some very differently from the way they should be understood and expressed, according to my opinion and conviction."[24] That is perhaps not surprising. Kant's political strategy was usually to make fine and abstract philosophical distinctions. He had no confidence in manifestos or confrontational demands for major political change. Not only did he want to avoid trouble with the authorities such as the rebuke he received in 1794 for publishing *Religion Within the Limits of Reason Alone*, but he also generally thought it best to persuade rather than berate, insinuate rather than demand, and bring out the implications of what everyone could accept rather than harangue people. He preferred modes of writing that massaged people into changing their minds.

Others made more radical demands. The 130-page preface to Johann Lorenz Schmidt's 1741 German translation of Matthew Tindal's *Christianity as Old as Creation* [orig. 1730] was a ringing endorsement of the right to express themselves of Tindal, Anthony Collins, and other deists.[25] The same author also translated Spinoza and Boullainvilliers, considered scandalous at the time for their materialism and atheism. Two years after Kant's first essay on book piracy, in 1787, Carl Friedrich Bahrdt brought out an essay on freedom of the press in which he made radical claims that the right to share one's thoughts in print was a human right (*Menschenrecht, Recht des Menschen*). He went so far as to call for "Woe to the prince who hinders this!"; "Oh you tyrants of humanity. . . . It is true, your minds are armored with metal and your backs are covered with Russian leather, but I will smash the bronze and tear the skin: so that you will feel my blows and at least scream[!]"[26] Kant would never use such rhetoric. He preferred to work from the inside on people's (including rulers' and officials') minds, subtly changing their minds in order to change their behavior. This required dressing his proposals in the most abstract, uncontroversial, and innocuous language, so that by the time the reader had finished reading he would find himself having to agree with Kant's outcome.

At this point we know why Kant included a version of his discussion of books and book piracy in his *Metaphysics of Morals* of 1797. A book is still a writing that presents the author's discourse or speech (*Rede*) (*MM*, 6:289). The pirate still commits "the crime of stealing the profits from the publisher" (6:289). Book piracy is still "forbidden as a matter of right (or law, *von rechtswegen verboten*)" (6:290). Our remaining question is this: what does the foregoing analysis tell us about rights to freedom of the press in Kant's philosophy of law?

As already mentioned, there is no doubt that Kant was broadly in favor of intellectual freedom, public debate, and freedom of the press. He was by no means alone in thinking that freedom of the press was a central element of liberty or freedom. Ever since John Milton's *Areopagitica* of 1644, thinkers such as John Toland (who reprinted Milton), Matthew Tindal (who wrote his own essays in favor of freedom of the press), and Anthony Collins in England; Spinoza, Justus van Effen, and Elie Luzac in the Netherlands; and Schmidt, August Ludwig von Schlözer, Johannes Kern, Christoph Martin Wieland, Wilhelm Wekhrlin, and Bahrdt in Germany had vindicated freedom of the press in print.[27] Why, then, is there no explicit mention in Kant's philosophy of law of a general, high-profile right to freedom of the press? It will be suggested here that the answer can be found in Kant's rhetorical-political strategy. That is, he did not have to spell out a possibly tendentious right to press freedom as long as it would be obvious that it was included in the most abstract general rights, and he could reinforce that view with apparently minor specific details such as his brief discussion of "What Is a Book?" Anyone who read his philosophy of law would come away with the impression that it definitely provided for freedom of the press, without him actually having to spell it out.

Kant's "universal principle of right" is that "any action is right if it can coexist with everyone's freedom in accordance with a universal law, or if on its maxim the freedom of choice of each can coexist with everyone's freedom in accordance with a universal law" (*MM*, 6:230). At this very general level, we have no guidance from Kant on how to apply it to questions about freedom of the press. In principle, with possible exceptions including book piracy, there does not seem to be any reason why one person's use of the press could not coexist with the next person's.

Kant explicates the universal principle by showing that it is connected with an authorization to use coercion. If anyone hinders someone else's freedom, an authorization to use coercion to prevent that hindrance is created (*MM*, 6:231). For example, coercion to make a debtor pay his debts can coexist with freedom for everyone, including the debtor, Kant asserts (6:232). Without coercion to enforce repayment, no one could rely on contract; coercion actually creates freedom of contract.

How could an authorization to use coercion apply to freedom of the press? Where limits on freedom of the press are created by governments, coercion to prevent it would imply a right to coerce the government, which is completely ruled out by Kant's theory of obligation and sovereignty. On the other hand, coercion against book pirates violates no such theory, and this is why Kant can use his section on "What is a Book?" to demonstrate such a right.

How can Kant discourage princes from limiting press rights? Only by persuading them that press rights are indeed natural rights, justified by reason. And the better part of his writings can be read as a sort of Trojan horse, designed to plant ideas inside the city walls, which can later break out and tear down those walls. The very abstract discussion in the *Metaphysics of Morals* hides this sort of strategy. It is yet another example of his practical use of provisional theory for immediate progress in an imperfect world.[28]

There is one innate right, Kant writes: "freedom (independence from being constrained by another's choice), insofar as it can coexist with the freedom of every other in accordance with a universal law, is the only original right belonging to every man by virtue of his humanity" (*MM*, 6:237). One of the few remarks he makes about this right is relevant for our purposes: one is authorized "to do to others anything that does not in itself diminish what is theirs . . . [which includes] such things as merely communicating his thoughts to them" (6:238). Sometimes censorship has been justified on the ground that errors and lies should not be free, but Kant specifically states that this innate freedom authorizes communication "whether what he says is true and sincere or untrue and insincere" (6:238).

The rest of private right consists of "external rights," which can be enforced by governments against private citizens. The agency right against book pirates surely falls in this category. "What is a Book?" is part of Kant's chapter on external right. Crucially, public right exists only to enforce private right, and this should shield the authors' rights against the princes (*MM*, 6:255–56). Indeed, nothing in his substantial discussions of public law explicitly gives princes the right or duty to engage in censorship.

Abstract discussions of legal principles that may include, and in any event do not rule out, freedom of the press, coupled with specific rejection of book piracy, may seem a thin wedge with which to open the case for press rights in Kant's philosophy of law. My point is that that is all it takes: the details are implied from the big picture. On the point that Kant does not justify rights of coercion against princes if they violate press rights through censorship, it must be remembered that he does not justify rights of coercion against princes if they violate any rights whatsoever, so that is no reason to conclude that he did not believe in any sort of press rights. Rather, our review of a small part of the German debate over book piracy—the contrast of Kant's view with that of Martin Ehlers—has served to contextualize a small section of Kant's *Metaphysics of Morals,* and show how it was in fact a philosophical response to an important social issue in late eighteenth-century Germany. It was an engagé contribution to the vindication of the rights of authors. Now that similar issues have arisen concerning Internet and music piracy,[29] Kant's ideas may repay renewed attention.

NOTES

1. See Allen Wood, *Kant's Ethical Thought* (Cambridge: Cambridge University Press, 1999), 306–9; Francis Cheneval, *Philosophie in weltbürgerliche Bedeutung* (Basel: Schwabe, 2005); Elisabeth Ellis, *Kant's Politics: Provisional Theory for an Uncertain World* (New Haven: Yale University Press, 2005), 155–80; Ciaran Cronin, "Kant's Politics of Enlightenment," *Journal of the History of Philosophy* 41, no. 1 (2003): 53–57; Katerina Deligiorgio, "Universalisability, Publicity, and Communication: Kant's Conception of Reason," *European Journal of Philosophy* 10, no. 2 (2002): 143–59; and J. C. Laursen, *The Politics of Skepticism in the Ancients, Montaigne, Hume, and Kant* (Leiden: Brill, 1992), chapter 9.

2. Immanuel Kant, *The Metaphysical Elements of Justice,* trans. John Ladd (Indianapolis: Bobbs-Merrill, 1965). "What Is a Book?" is found at 437–38 of Mary Gregor's translation in the 1996 Cambridge edition.

3. See short discussions in Karl Vörlander, "Einleitung," Immanuel Kant, *Kleinere Schriften zur Geschichtsphilosophie, Ethik und Politik* (Hamburg: Felix Meiner, 1913), 18–50; Klaus Blesenkemper, *"Publice Age": Studien zum Öffentlichkeitsbegriff bei Kant* (Frankfurt: Haag & Herchen, 1987), 211–12; and Adrian Johns, *Piracy: The Intellectual Property Wars from Gutenberg to Gates* (Chicago: University of Chicago Press, 2009), 54–55.

4. Ernst Martin Gräff, *Versuch einer einleuchtenden Darstellung des Eigenthums und der Eigenthumsrechte des Schriftstellers und Verlegers* (Leipzig, 1794). Reprinted in Reinhard Wittmann, ed., *Quellen zur Geschichte des Buchwesens,* vol. 1, *Nachdruck und geistiges Eigentum* (Munich: Kraus, 1981), 191–588.

5. Martin Ehlers, *Ueber die Unzulässigkeit des Büchernachdrucks nach dem natürlichen Zwangsrecht* (Dessau: Buchhandlung der Gelehrten, 1784), xxxvi, 195. Hereafter, page numbers to this edition will be cited parenthetically in the text.

6. Immanuel Kant, "Von der Unrechtmässigkeit des Büchernachdrucks," *Berlinische Monatsschrift* 5 (1785): 403–17. English translation: "On the Wrongfulness of Unauthorized Publication of Books" in Kant, *Practical Philosophy,* trans. and ed. Mary Gregor (Cambridge: Cambridge University Press, 1996), 23–35. Akademie edition, 8:79–87. See also Stephen Palmquist, ed., *Four Neglected Essays by Immanuel Kant* (Hong Kong: Philopsychy Press, 1994), 38–45.

7. J. W. von Goethe, *The Autobiography of Johann Wolfgang von Goethe* [translation of *Aus meinem Leben: Dichtung und Wahrheit*], trans. John Oxenford (London: Bohn, 1848–1849; repr., intro. Karl J. Weintraub, Chicago: University of Chicago Press, 1974), 1:156.

8. See Pamela Selwyn, *Everyday Life in the German Book Trade: Friedrich Nicolai as Bookseller and Publisher in the Age of Enlightenment, 1750–1810* (University Park: Pennsylvania State University Press, 2000), 219–37; Reinhart Siegert, "Nachdruck und 'Reichsbuchhandlung,'"

in *Buchkulturen: Beiträge zur Geschichte der Literaturvermittlung*, ed. Monika Estermann, Ernst Fischer, and Ute Schneider (Wiesbaden: Harrassowitz, 2005), 265–82; Ludwig Fertig, "'Krieg mit dem Zensor' und 'Druck-Diebe': Zur Behinderung des Berufsschriftstellers Jean Paul durch Zensur und Nachdruck," *Jahrbuch der Jean-Paul-Gesellschaft* 22 (1987): 114–26; Reinhard Wittmann, "Der gerechtfertigte Nachdrucker?: Nachdruck und literarisches Leben im achtzehnten Jahrhundert," in Reinhard Wittmann, *Buchmarkt und Lektüre im 18. und 19. Jahrhundert* (Tübingen: Niemeyer, 1982), 69–92; and Wolfgang von Ungarn-Sternberg, *Ch. M. Wieland und das Verlagswesen seiner Zeit* (Frankfurt: Buchhändler-Vereinigung, 1974).

9. See Mark Rose, *Authors and Owners: The Invention of [English] Copyright* (Cambridge: Harvard University Press, 1993), 116–17. See also Stephen Parks, ed., *English Publishing, the Struggle for Copyright, and the Freedom of the Press: Thirteen Tracts, 1666–1774* (New York: Garland, 1975).

10. J. S. Pütter, *Der Buchernachdruck nach ächten Grundsätzen des Rechts* (Göttingen, 1774; repr., Munich: Kraus, 1981).

11. See John A. McCarthy, "Literatur als Eigentum: Urheberrechtliche Aspekte der Buchhandelsrevolution," *MLN* 104, no. 3 (1989): 531–47.

12. See, e.g., Robert Darnton, "The Science of Piracy: A Crucial Ingredient in Eighteenth-Century Publishing," *SVEC [Studies on Voltaire and the Eighteenth Century]* 12, no. 3 (2003): 3–29.

13. Translation borrowed from Martha Woodmansee, "The Genius and the Copyright," *Eighteenth-Century Studies* 17 (1984): 444.

14. On the economic situation of authors, see Hans Jürgen Haferkorn, "Der freie Schriftsteller: Eine literatursoziologische Studie . . . zwischen 1750 und 1800," *Archiv für Geschichte des Buchwesens* 5 (1962–1964): 523–712.

15. Gräff, *Versuch*, 213, 286.

16. Gräff reprints a condition prohibiting reprinting suggested by another author in 1791 to be printed in all books, but comments that it would be too easy for the book to fall into the hands of someone who would not be bound by that legal obligation (*Versuch*, 366–67).

17. See Reinhart Koselleck, *Preussen zwischen Reform und Revolution* (Stuttgart: Klett, 1967). Gräff reprints the relevant sections in *Versuch*, 185–98.

18. Gräff, *Versuch*, 362.

19. See H. M. Scott, ed., *Enlightened Absolutism: Reform and Reformers in Later Eighteenth-Century Europe* (Ann Arbor: University of Michigan Press, 1990); H. Blom, J. C. Laursen, and L. Simonutti, eds., *Monarchisms in the Age of Enlightenment: Liberty, Patriotism, and the Common Good* (Toronto: University of Toronto Press, 2007).

20. He repeated this point in a later essay on freedom of the press in general: "Entwurf einer dem gemeinen Besten zuträglichen Pressfreyheit," in Martin Ehlers, *Staatswissenschaftliche Aufsätze* (Kiel: Konigl. Schulbuchhandlung, 1791), 177–87.

21. This was not noticed by Vörlander in his introduction to the Felix Meiner edition of the *Kleinere Schriften*, nor Mary Gregor in her introduction to Kant's essay on book piracy in *Practical Philosophy*, 25, 628. She was aware of an earlier book by Ehlers, *Über die Lehre von der menschlichen Freiheit* (1782), which she believes Kant had in mind when he referred to Ehlers in a review of Schulz (1783), in *Practical Philosophy*, 628.

22. Elisabeth Ellis, *Provisional Politics: Kantian Arguments in Policy Context* (New Haven: Yale University Press, 2008).

23. Gräff, *Versuch*, 328.

24. Ibid., 331. Gräff does not give any examples of these misunderstandings. He does point out that Fichte's later essay on book piracy (1793) shows no signs of him having read Kant's essay (327).

25. [Matthew Tindal], *Beweis, dass das Christentum so alt als die Welt sey*, trans. J. L. Schmidt (Frankfurt and Leipzig [Hamburg], 1741).

26. J. C. Laursen and J. van der Zande, eds., *Early French and German Defenses of Freedom of the Press: Elie Luzac's Essay on Freedom of Expression (1749) and Carl Friedrich Bahrdt's on Freedom of the Press and Its Limits (1787) in English Translation* (Leiden: Brill, 2003), 122, 126–27.

27. See the introductory surveys in Laursen, *Early French and German Defenses of Freedom of the Press*, 1–34, 89–106.

28. See Ellis, *Kant's Politics*, passim; and Ellis, *Provisional Politics*, passim.

29. See, for example, Lawrence Lessig, *Free Culture: The Nature and Future of Creativity* (New York: Penguin, 2004); and Jessica Litman, *Digital Copyright* (Amherst: Prometheus, 2001).

SELECTED BIBLIOGRAPHY

Allison, Henry E. *Idealism and Freedom: Essays on Kant's Theoretical and Practical Philosophy.* Cambridge: Cambridge University Press, 1996.
———. *Kant's Theory of Freedom.* Cambridge: Cambridge University Press, 1990.
———. *Kant's Transcendental Idealism: An Interpretation and Defense.* Rev. and enlarged ed. New Haven: Yale University Press, 2004.
Ameriks, Karl. *Interpreting Kant's Critiques.* Oxford: Clarendon Press, 2003.
———. *Kant and the Fate of Autonomy: Problems in the Appropriation of the Critical Philosophy.* Cambridge: Cambridge University Press, 2000.
Ameriks, Karl, and Otfried Höffe, eds. *Kant's Moral and Legal Philosophy.* Translated by Nicholas Walker. Cambridge: Cambridge University Press, 2009.
Anderson-Gold, Sharon. "Kant's Ethical Anthropology and the Critical Foundations of the Philosophy of History." *History of Philosophy Quarterly* 11, no. 4 (1994): 405–19.
———. *Unnecessary Evil: History and Moral Progress in the Philosophy of Immanuel Kant.* Albany: State University of New York Press, 2001.
———. "War and Resistance: Kant's Doctrine of Human Rights." *Journal of Social Philosophy* 19, no. 1 (1988): 37–50.
Archibugi, Daniele. "Immanuel Kant, Cosmopolitan Law, and Peace." *European Journal of International Relations* 1, no. 4 (1995): 429–56.
Arendt, Hannah, and Ronald Beiner. *Lectures on Kant's Political Philosophy.* Chicago: University of Chicago Press, 1982.
Armstrong, A. C. "Kant's Philosophy of Peace and War." *The Journal of Philosophy* 28, no. 8 (1931): 197–204.
Arntzen, Sven. "Kant on Duty to Oneself and Resistance to Political Authority." *Journal of the History of Philosophy* 34, no. 3 (1996): 409–24.
———. "Kant's Denial of Absolute Sovereignty." *Pacific Philosophical Quarterly* 76, no. 1 (1995): 1–16.
Atkinson, R. F. "Kant's Moral and Political Rigorism." *Dodone* 19, no. 3 (1990): 9–30.
Axinn, Sidney. "Kant, Authority, and the French Revolution." *Journal of the History of Ideas* 32, no. 3 (1971): 423–32.
———. "Kant on World Government." In *Proceedings of the Sixth International Kant Congress,* edited by G. Funke and T. M. Seebohm. Washington, D.C.: Center for Advanced Research in Phenomenology and the University Press of America, 1989.
Baiasu, Sorin. "Kantian Metaphysics and the Normative Force of Practical Principles." *Journal of International Political Theory* 3 (2007): 37–56.
Baiasu, Sorin, Sami Pihlström, and Howard Williams, eds. *Politics and Metaphysics in Kant.* Cardiff: University of Wales Press, 2011.
Batscha, Zwi, ed. *Materialen zu Kants Rechtsphilosophie.* Frankfurt am Main: Suhrkamp, 1976.
Baumann, Peter. "Zwei Seiten der Kantischen Begründung von Eigentum und Staat." *Kant-Studien* 85, no. 2 (1994): 147–59.
Baynes, Kenneth. "Kant on Property Rights and the Social Contract." *The Monist* 72, no. 3 (1989): 433–53.
———. *The Normative Grounds of Social Criticism: Kant, Rawls, and Habermas.* Albany: State University of New York Press, 1992.

Beck, Gunnar. "Autonomy, History, and Political Freedom in Kant's Political Philosophy." *History of European Ideas* 25, no. 5 (1999): 217–41.
———. *Fichte and Kant on Freedom, Rights, and Law.* Lanham, Md.: Lexington Books, 2008.
———. "Immanuel Kant's Theory of Rights." *Ratio Juris* 19, no. 4 (2006): 371–401.
Beck, Lewis White. "Kant and the Right of Revolution." *Journal of the History of Ideas* 32, no. 3 (1971): 411–22.
———. "Kant's Two Conceptions of Will." *Annales de Philosophie Politique* 4, (1962): 119–37.
Beiner, Ronald, and William J. Booth, eds. *Kant and Political Philosophy: The Contemporary Legacy.* New Haven: Yale University Press, 1996.
Beiner, Ronald, and Jennifer Nedelsky. *Judgment, Imagination, and Politics: Themes from Kant and Arendt.* Lanham, Md.: Rowman and Littlefield, 2001.
Beiser, Frederick C. *Enlightenment, Revolution, and Romanticism: The Genesis of Modern German Political Thought, 1790–1800.* Cambridge: Harvard University Press, 1992.
———. *The Fate of Reason: German Philosophy from Kant to Fichte.* Cambridge: Harvard University Press, 1987.
Bernasconi, Robert. "'Will the Real Kant Please Stand Up?': The Challenge of Enlightenment Racism to the Study of the History of Philosophy." *Radical Philosophy* 117 (2003): 13–22.
Bielefeldt, Heiner. "Autonomy and Republicanism: Immanuel Kant's Philosophy of Freedom." *Political Theory* 25, no. 4 (1997): 524–58.
———. "Towards a Cosmopolitan Framework of Freedom: The Contribution of Kantian Universalism to Cross-Cultural Debates on Human Rights." *Annual Review of Law and Ethics* 5 (1997): 349–62.
Bohman, James, and Matthias Lutz-Bachmann. *Perpetual Peace: Essays on Kant's Cosmopolitan Ideal.* Cambridge: MIT Press, 1997.
Booth, William James. *Interpreting the World: Kant's Philosophy of History and Politics.* Toronto: University of Toronto Press, 1986.
Bottici, Chiara. "The Domestic Analogy and the Kantian Project of Perpetual Peace." *Journal of Political Philosophy* 11, no. 4 (2003): 392–410.
Brandt, Reinhard. *Eigentumstheorien von Grotius bis Kant.* Stuttgart: Frommann-Holzboog, 1974.
———. "Das Erlaubnisgesetz." In *Rechtsphilosophie der Aufklärung*, edited by R. Brandt, 233–85. Berlin: Walter de Gruyter, 1982.
———. "Gerechtigkeit bei Kant." *Jahrbuch für Recht und Ethik* 1 (1993): 25–44.
———. "Die politische Institution bei Kant." In Göhler, *Politische Institutionen*, 335–57.
———. "Das Problem der Erlaubnisgesetze im Spätwerk Kants." In *Immanuel Kant: zum ewigen Frieden*, edited by Otfried Höffe, 47–60. Berlin: Akademie, 2011.
Breitenbach, Angela. "Kant Goes Fishing: Kant and the Right to Property in Environmental Resources." *Studies in History and Philosophy of Biomedical and Biological Sciences* 36 (2005): 488–512.
Brocker, Manfred. *Kants Besitzlehre: Zur Problematik einer transzendentalphilosophischen Eigentumslehre.* Würzburg: Königshausen & Neumann, 1987.
Buhr, Manfred, and Steffan Dietzsch. *Immanuel Kant: Zum ewigen Frieden: Ein philosophischer Entwurf: Texte zur Rezeption, 1796–1800.* Leipzig: Reclam, 1984.
Burg, Peter. *Kant und die Französische Revolution.* Berlin: Duncker & Humblot, 1974.
Byrd, B. Sharon. "Kant's Theory of Punishment: Deterrence in Its Threat, Retribution in Its Execution." *Law and Philosophy* 8, no. 2 (1989): 151–200.
———. "Two Models of Justice." *Annual Review of Law and Ethics* 1 (1993): 45–68.
Byrd, B. Sharon, and Joachim Hruschka. "From the State of Nature to the Juridical State of States." *Law and Philosophy* 27, no. 6 (2008): 599–641.

———, eds. *Kant and Law*. Aldershot, UK: Ashgate, 2006.
———. *Kant's Doctrine of Right: A Commentary*. Cambridge: Cambridge University Press, 2010.
Capps, Patrick. "The Kantian Project in Modern International Legal Theory." *European Journal of International Law* 12, no. 5 (2001): 1003–25.
Carr, C. L. "Kant's Theory of Political Authority." *History of Political Thought* 10 (1989): 719–31.
Carroll, David. "Rephrasing the Political with Kant and Lyotard: From Aesthetic to Political Judgments." *Diacritics* 14, no. 3 (1984): 74–88.
Carson, Thomas L. "Perpetual Peace: What Kant Should Have Said." *Social Theory and Practice* 14, no. 2 (1988): 173–214.
Caruth, Cathy. *Empirical Truths and Critical Fictions: Locke, Wordsworth, Kant, Freud*. Baltimore: Johns Hopkins University Press, 1991.
Carvounas, David. *Diverging Time: The Politics of Modernity in Kant, Hegel, and Marx*. Lanham, Md.: Lexington Books, 2002.
Cassirer, Ernst. *Kant's Life and Thought*. Translated by James Haden. New Haven: Yale University Press, 1981.
Castillo, Monique. *Kant et l'avenir de la culture: Avec une traduction de Réflexions de Kant sur l'anthropologie, la morale, et le droit*. Paris: Presses universitaires de France, 1990.
Cavallar, Georg. *Kant and the Theory and Practice of International Right*. Cardiff: University of Wales Press, 1999.
———. "Kantian Perspectives on Democratic Peace: Alternatives to Doyle." *Review of International Studies* 27, no. 2 (2001): 229–48.
———. "Kant's Judgment on Frederick's Enlightened Absolutism." *History of Political Thought* 14 (Spring 1993): 103–32.
———. "Kant's Society of Nations: Free Federation or World Republic?" *Journal of the History of Philosophy* 32, no. 2 (1994): 461–82.
———. *Pax Kantiana: Systematisch-historische Untersuchung des Entwurfs "Zum ewigen Frieden" (1795) von Immanuel Kant*. Vienna: Böhlau, 1992.
———. *The Rights of Strangers: Theories of International Hospitality, the Global Community, and Political Justice Since Vitoria*. Aldershot, UK: Ashgate, 2002.
Cederman, Lars-Erik. "Back to Kant: Reinterpreting the Democratic Peace as a Macrohistorical Learning Process." *The American Political Science Review* 95, no. 1 (2001): 15–31.
———. "Modeling the Democratic Peace as a Kantian Selection Process." *Journal of Conflict Resolution* 45, no. 4 (2001): 470–502.
Chadwick, Ruth F. The Market for Bodily Parts: Kant and Duties to Oneself. *Journal of Applied Philosophy* 6, no. 2 (1989): 129–40.
Cohen, Alix. *Kant and the Human Sciences: Biology, Anthropology, and History*. Basinstoke: Palgrave Macmillan, 2009.
Coole, Diana H. *Negativity and Politics: Dionysus and Dialectics from Kant to Poststructuralism*. New York: Routledge, 2000.
Corlett, J. A. "Foundations of a Kantian Theory of Punishment." *The Southern Journal of Philosophy* 31, no. 3 (1993): 263–83.
Cronin, Ciaran. "Kant's Politics of Enlightenment." *Journal of the History of Philosophy* 41, no. 1 (2003): 51–80.
Cummiskey, David. *Kantian Consequentialism*. New York: Oxford University Press, 1996.
Danilovic, Vesna, and Joe Clare. "The Kantian Liberal Peace (Revisited)." *American Journal of Political Science* 51, no. 2 (2007): 397–414.
Davidovich, Adina. *Religion as a Province of Meaning: The Kantian Foundations of Modern Theology*. Minneapolis: Augsburg Fortress, 1993.

Davis, Kevin R. "Kantian 'Publicity' and Political Justice." *History of Philosophy Quarterly* 8, no. 4 (1991): 409–21.

———. "Kant's Different 'Publics' and the Justice of Publicity." *Kant-Studien* 83, no. 2 (1992): 170–84.

De Federicis, Nico. *Gli imperativi del diritto pubblico: Rousseau, Kant, e i diritti dell'uomo.* Pisa: PLUS-Pisa University Press, 2005.

Deggau, Hans-Georg. *Die Aporien der Rechtslehre Kants.* Stuttgart: Frommann-Holzboog, 1983.

De Laurentiis, Allegra. "Kant's Shameful Proposition: A Hegel-Inspired Criticism of Kant's Theory of Domestic Right." *International Philosophical Quarterly* 40, no. 3 (2000): 297–312.

Deleuze, Gilles. *Kant's Critical Philosophy: The Doctrine of the Faculties.* Translated by Hugh Tomlinson and Barbara Habberjam. Minneapolis: University of Minnesota Press, 1985.

Deligiorgi, Katerina. *Kant and the Culture of the Enlightenment.* Albany: State University of New York Press, 2005.

———."Universalisability, Publicity, and Communication: Kant's Conception of Reason." *European Journal of Philosophy* 10, no. 2 (2002): 143–59.

Denis, Lara, ed. *Kant's Metaphysics of Morals: A Critical Guide.* Cambridge: Cambridge University Press, 2010.

Dietze, Anita, and Walter Dietze, eds. *Ewiger Friede?: Dokumente einer deutschen Diskussion um 1800.* Leipzig: Kiepenheuer, 1989.

Di Giovanni, George. *Freedom and Religion in Kant and His Immediate Successors: The Vocation of Humankind, 1774–1800.* Cambridge: Cambridge University Press, 2005.

Dilthey, Wilhelm. "Der Streit Kants mit der Zensur über das Recht freier Religionsforschung." *Archiv für Geschichte der Philosophie* 3 (1890): 418–50.

Djaballah, Marc. *Kant, Foucault, and the Forms of Experience.* New York: Routledge, 2008.

Dodson, Kevin E. "Autonomy and Authority in Kant's *Rechtslehre*." *Political Theory* 25, no. 1 (1997): 93–111.

Doyle, Michael W. "Kant, Liberal Legacies, and Foreign Affairs." *Philosophy and Public Affairs* 12, no. 3 (1983): 205–35.

———. "Liberalism and World Politics." *The American Political Science Review* 80, no. 4 (1986): 1151–69.

Easley, Eric S. *The War over Perpetual Peace: An Exploration into the History of a Foundational International Relations Text.* New York: Palgrave Macmillan, 2004.

Ebbinghaus, Julius. *Gesammelte Schriften.* 4 vols. Bonn: Bouvier, 1986–.

Ellis, Elisabeth. "Citizenship and Property Rights: A New Look at Social Contract Theory." *Journal of Politics* 68, no. 3 (2006): 544–55.

———. *Kant's Politics: Provisional Theory for an Uncertain World.* New Haven: Yale University Press, 2005.

———. *Provisional Politics: Kantian Arguments in Policy Context.* New Haven: Yale University Press, 2008.

Elshtain, Jean Bethke. "Kant, Politics, and Persons: The Implications of His Moral Philosophy." *Polity* 14, no. 2 (1981): 205–21.

Enderlein, Wolfgang. "Die Begründung der Strafe bei Kant." *Kant-Studien* 76 (1985): 303–27.

Erp, H. H. H. van. "Das Problem der politischen Repräsentation bei Kant, Hegel, und Marx." *Philosophisches Jahrbuch* 101, no. 1 (1994): 165–77.

Etzioni, Amitai. "Toward a Kantian Socioeconomics." *Review of Social Economy* 45, no. 1 (1987): 37–47.

Eze, Emmanuel Chukwudi, ed. *Race and the Enlightenment: A Reader.* Oxford: Blackwell, 1997.

Fackenheim, Emil L. "Kant's Concept of History." *Kant-Studien* 48 (1957): 381–98.
Fackenheim, Emil L., and John W. Burbidge. *The God Within: Kant, Schelling, and Historicity.* Toronto: University of Toronto Press, 1996.
Fenves, Peter D. *A Peculiar Fate: Metaphysics and World-History in Kant.* Ithaca: Cornell University Press, 1991.
Ferry, Jean-Marc. *Europe, la voie kantienne: Essai sur l'identité postnationale.* Paris: Cerf, 2005.
———. *La question de l'histoire: Nature, liberté, esprit: Les paradigmes métaphysiques de l'histoire chez Kant, Fichte, Hegel entre 1784 et 1806.* Bruxelles: Editions de l'Université de Bruxelles, 2002.
Fimiani, Mariapaola. *Foucault y Kant: Crítica, clínica, ética.* Caracas: Monte Ávila Editores Latinoamericana, 2006.
Fleischacker, Samuel. "Kant's Theory of Punishment." *Kant-Studien* 79 (1988): 434–49.
———. *A Third Concept of Liberty: Judgment and Freedom in Kant and Adam Smith.* Princeton: Princeton University Press, 1999.
Flikschuh, Katrin. *Kant and Modern Political Philosophy.* Cambridge: Cambridge University Press, 2000.
———. "Kantian Desires: Freedom of Choice and Action in the *Rechtslehre*." In Timmons, *Kant's Metaphysics of Morals*, 185–208.
———. "Kant's Sovereignty Dilemma: A Contemporary Analysis." *Journal of Political Philosophy* 18, no. 4 (2010): 469–93.
———. "Reason, Right, and Revolution: Kant and Locke." *Philosophy and Public Affairs* 36, no. 4 (2008): 375–404.
Förster, Eckart. "The Hidden Plan of Nature." In Rorty, *Kant's Idea for a Universal History with a Cosmopolitan Aim*, 187–99.
Foucault, Michel. "What Is Critique?" In *The Politics of Truth*, edited by Sylvère Lotringer, 41–81. New York: Semiotext(e), 1997.
———. "What Is Enlightenment?" In *The Foucault Reader*, edited by Paul Rabinow, 32–50. New York: Pantheon Books, 1984.
Franceschet, Antonio. *Kant and Liberal Internationalism: Sovereignty, Justice, and Global Reform.* New York: Palgrave Macmillan, 2002.
Freeman, Samuel Richard, ed. *Collected Papers: John Rawls.* Cambridge: Harvard University Press, 1999.
Frierson, Patrick R. *Freedom and Anthropology in Kant's Moral Philosophy.* Cambridge: Cambridge University Press, 2003.
Fulda, Hans Friedrich. "Kants Postulat des öffentlichen Rechts." *Jahrbuch für Recht und Ethik* 5 (1997): 267–90.
Gailus, Andreas. *Passions of the Sign: Revolution and Language in Kant, Goethe, and Kleist.* Baltimore: Johns Hopkins University Press, 2006.
Galston, William A. *Kant and the Problem of History.* Chicago: University of Chicago Press, 1975.
———. "What Is Living and What Is Dead in Kant's Practical Philosophy?" In Beiner, *Kant and Political Philosophy*, 207–23.
Gartzke, Erik. "Kant We All Just Get Along?: Opportunity, Willingness, and the Origins of the Democratic Peace." *American Journal of Political Science* 42, no. 1 (1998): 1–27.
Gaubatz, Kurt Taylor. "Kant, Democracy, and History." *Journal of Democracy* 7, no. 4 (1996): 136–50.
Gerhardt, Volker. *Immanuel Kants Entwurf "Zum ewigen Frieden": Eine Theorie der Politik.* Darmstadt: Wissenschaftliche Buchgesellschaft, 1995.
Gerrand, Nicole. "Misuse of Kant in the Debate About a Market for Human Body Parts." *Journal of Applied Philosophy* 16, no. 1 (1999): 59–67.
Gillroy, John Martin. "Making Public Choices: Kant's Justice from Autonomy as an Alternative to Rawls' Justice as Fairness." *Kant-Studien* 91, no. 1 (2000): 44–72.

Göhler, Gerhard et al., eds. *Politische Institutionen im gesellschaftlichen Umbruch: Ideengeschichtliche Beiträge zur Theorie politischer Institutionen*. Opladen: Westdeutscher, 1990.

Gregor, Mary. "Kant on 'Natural Rights.'" In Beiner, *Kant and Political Philosophy*, 50–75.

———. "Kant's Approach to Constitutionalism." In *Constitutionalism: The Philosophical Dimension*, edited by Alan S. Rosenbaum, 69–87. New York: Greenwood Press, 1988.

———. "Kant's Theory of Property." *Review of Metaphysics* 41 (1988): 757–87.

Grenberg, Jeanine. *Kant and the Ethics of Humility: A Story of Dependence, Corruption, and Virtue*. Cambridge: Cambridge University Press, 2005.

Guyer, Paul, ed. *The Cambridge Companion to Kant*. Cambridge: Cambridge University Press, 1992.

———. *Kant and the Claims of Taste*. 2nd ed. Cambridge: Cambridge University Press, 1997.

———. *Kant and the Experience of Freedom: Essays on Aesthetics and Morality*. Cambridge: Cambridge University Press, 1996.

———. "Kantian Foundations for Liberalism." *Annual Review of Law and Ethics* 5 (1997).

———. *Kant on Freedom, Law, and Happiness*. Cambridge: Cambridge University Press, 2000.

———. "Kant's Deduction of the Principles of Right." In Timmons, *Kant's Metaphysics of Morals*, 23–64.

———. *Kant's System of Nature and Freedom: Selected Essays*. Oxford: Oxford University Press, 2005.

Habermas, Jürgen. "Kant's Idea of Perpetual Peace, with the Benefit of Two-Hundred Years' Hindsight." In Bohman, *Perpetual Peace*, 113–54.

———. *The Structural Transformation of the Public Sphere: An Inquiry into a Category of Bourgeois Society*. Translated by Thomas Burger with the assistance of Frederick Lawrence. Cambridge: MIT Press, 1989.

Hansson, Sven Ove. "Kant and the Revolutionary Slogan 'Liberté, Egalité, Fraternité.'" *Archiv für Geschichte der Philosophie* 76, no. 3 (1994): 333–39.

Hedrick, Todd. "Race, Difference, and Anthropology in Kant's Cosmopolitanism." *Journal of the History of Philosophy* 46, no. 2 (2008): 245–68.

Henrich, Dieter. *Aesthetic Judgment and the Moral Image of the World: Studies in Kant*. Stanford: Stanford University Press, 1992.

———. *The Unity of Reason: Essays on Kant's Philosophy*. Edited by Richard Velkley. Cambridge: Harvard University Press, 1994.

Herb, Karlfriedrich, and Bernd Ludwig. "Naturzustand, Eigentum, und Staat: Immanuel Kants Relativierung des 'Ideal des Hobbes.'" *Kant-Studien* 84 (1993): 283–316.

Herman, Barbara. "A Cosmopolitan Kingdom of Ends." In Reath, *Reclaiming the History of Ethics*, 187–213.

———. *Moral Literacy*. Cambridge: Harvard University Press, 2007.

———. *The Practice of Moral Judgment*. Cambridge: Harvard University Press, 1993.

———. "Training to Autonomy: Kant and the Question of Moral Education." In *Philosophers on Education: Historical Perspectives*, edited by Amélie Oksenberg Rorty, 254–71. New York: Routledge, 1998.

Hill, Thomas E. "Hypothetical Consent in Kantian Constructivism." *Social Philosophy and Policy* 18, no. 2 (2001): 300–329.

———. "A Kantian Perspective on Political Violence." *The Journal of Ethics* 1, no. 2 (1997): 105–40.

———. "Kant on Wrongdoing, Desert, and Punishment." *Law and Philosophy* 18, no. 4 (1999): 407–41.

———. *Respect, Pluralism, and Justice: Kantian Perspectives*. Oxford: Oxford University Press, 2000.

Hinske, Norbert. *Was ist Aufklärung?: Beiträge aus der Berlinischen Monatsschrift*. 2nd ed. Darmstadt: Wissenschaftliche Buchgesellschaft, 1977.
Hodgson, Louis-Philippe. "Kant on Property Rights and the State." *Kantian Review* 15 (2010): 57–87.
———. "Kant on the Right to Freedom: A Defense." *Ethics* 120 (2010): 791–819.
Höffe, Otfried. *Categorical Principles of Law: A Counterpoint to Modernity*. University Park: Pennsylvania State University Press, 2002.
———. *Kant's Cosmopolitan Theory of Law and Peace*. Cambridge: Cambridge University Press, 2006.
———. "Kants universaler Kosmopolitismus." *Deutsche Zeitschrift für Philosophie* 55, no. 2 (2007): 179–91.
Holtman, Sarah Williams. "Kant, Ideal Theory, and the Justice of Exclusionary Zoning." *Ethics* 110, no. 1 (1999): 32–58.
———. "Toward Social Reform: Kant's Penal Theory Reinterpreted." *Utilitas* 9, no. 1 (1997): 3–21.
Hruschka, Joachim. "The Permissive Law of Practical Reason in Kant's 'Metaphysics of Morals.'" *Law and Philosophy* 23, no. 1 (2004): 45–72.
———. "Rechtsstaat, Freiheitsrecht, und das Recht auf Achtung von seinen Nebenmenschen." *Annual Review of Law and Ethics* 1 (1993): 193–206.
Huhn, Tom. *Imitation and Society: The Persistence of Mimesis in the Aesthetics of Burke, Hogarth, and Kant*. University Park: Pennsylvania State University Press, 2004.
Hunter, Ian. "Kant's *Religion* and Prussian Religious Policy." *Modern Intellectual History* 2, no. 1 (2005): 1–27.
———. "The Love of a Sage or the Command of a Superior: The Natural Law Doctrines of Leibniz and Pufendorf." In *Early Modern Natural Law Theories: Strategies and Contexts in the Early Enlightenments*, edited by T. J. Hochstrasser and P. Schröder, 169–93. Dordrecht: Kluwer, 2003.
———. "The Morals of Metaphysics: Kant's *Groundwork* as Intellectual *Paideia*." *Critical Inquiry* 28, no. 4 (2002): 908–29.
———. *Rival Enlightenments: Civil and Metaphysical Philosophy in Early Modern Germany*. Cambridge: Cambridge University Press, 2001.
Huntley, Wade L. "Kant's Third Image: Systemic Sources of the Liberal Peace." *International Studies Quarterly* 40, no. 1 (1996): 45–76.
———. "An Unlikely Match?: Kant and Feminism in IR Theory." *Millennium-Journal of International Studies* 26, no. 2 (1997): 279–320.
Hurrell, Andrew. "Kant and the Kantian Paradigm in International Relations." *Review of International Studies* 16, no. 3 (1990): 183–205.
Hutchings, Kimberly. *Kant, Critique, and Politics*. New York: Routledge, 1996.
Jacobs, Brian, and Patrick Kain, eds. *Essays on Kant's Anthropology*. Cambridge: Cambridge University Press, 2003.
Jaffro, Laurent. *Le sens moral: Une histoire de la philosophie morale de Locke à Kant*. Paris: Presses universitaires de France, 2000.
Jahn, Beate. "Kant, Mill, and Illiberal Legacies in International Affairs." *International Organization* 59, no. 1 (2005): 177–207.
Japaridze, Tamar. *The Kantian Subject: Sensus Communis, Mimesis, Work of Mourning*. Albany: State University of New York Press, 2000.
Kaufman, Alexander. "Reason, Self-legislation, and Legitimacy: Conceptions of Freedom in the Political Thought of Rousseau and Kant." *The Review of Politics* 59, no. 1 (1997): 25–52.
———. *Welfare in the Kantian State*. New York: Oxford University Press, 1999.
Kersting, Wolfgang. "Kant ist nicht Bushs Hofphilosoph." *Die Welt*, February 11, 2004.
———. "Kant's Concept of the State." In Williams, *Essays on Kant's Political Philosophy*, 143–65.

———. *Kant über Recht*. Paderborn: Mentis, 2004.
———. "Politics, Freedom, and Order: Kant's Political Philosophy." In Guyer, *Cambridge Companion to Kant*, 342–66.
———. *Wohlgeordnete Freiheit*. Berlin: Walter de Gruyter, 1984.
Kim, John Namjun. "Kant's Secret Article: Irony, Performativity, and History in *Zum ewigen Frieden*." *The Germanic Review* 82, no. 3 (2007): 203–26.
Kleingeld, Pauline. "Approaching Perpetual Peace: Kant's Defence of a League of States and His Ideal of a World Federation." *European Journal of Philosophy* 12, no. 3 (2004): 304–25.
———. "Kant, History, and the Idea of Moral Development." *History of Philosophy Quarterly* 16 (1999): 59–80.
———. "Kant on Historiography and the Use of Regulative Ideas." *Studies in History and Philosophy of Science* 39 (2008): 523–28.
———. "Kant's Cosmopolitan Patriotism." *Kant-Studien* 94 (2003): 299–316.
———. "Kant's Second Thoughts on Race." *The Philosophical Quarterly* 57, no. 229 (2007): 573–92.
———, ed. *Toward Perpetual Peace and Other Writings on Politics, Peace, and History*. New Haven: Yale University Press, 2006.
Kneller, Jane, and Sidney Axinn. *Autonomy and Community: Readings in Contemporary Kantian Social Philosophy*. Albany: State University of New York Press, 1998.
Knippenberg, Joseph M. "Moving Beyond Fear: Rousseau and Kant on Cosmopolitan Education." *The Journal of Politics* 51, no. 4 (1989): 809–27.
Kofman, Sarah. *Le respect des femmes: (Kant et Rousseau)*. Paris: Galilée, 1982.
Korsgaard, Christine M. *The Constitution of Agency: Essays on Practical Reason and Moral Psychology*. Oxford: Oxford University Press, 2008.
———. *Creating the Kingdom of Ends*. Cambridge: Cambridge University Press, 1996.
———. "The Right to Lie: Kant on Dealing with Evil." *Philosophy and Public Affairs* 15, no. 4 (1986): 325–49.
———. *The Sources of Normativity*. Cambridge: Cambridge University Press, 1996.
———. "Taking the Law into Our Own Hands: Kant on the Right to Revolution." In Reath, *Reclaiming the History of Ethics*, 297–328.
Kosch, Michelle. *Freedom and Reason in Kant, Schelling, and Kierkegaard*. Oxford: Oxford University Press, 2006.
Krieger, Leonard. "Kant and the Crisis of Natural Law." *Journal of the History of Ideas* 26, no. 2 (1965): 191–210.
Kuehn, Manfred. *Kant: A Biography*. New York: Cambridge University Press, 2001.
Kühl, Kristian. *Eigentumsordnung als Freiheitsordnung: Zur Aktualität der Kantischen Rechts-und Eigentumslehre*. Freiburg: Alber, 1984.
Landa, Dimitri. "On the Possibility of Kantian Retributivism." *Utilitas* 21, no. 3 (2009): 276–96.
Laursen, John Christian. *The Politics of Skepticism: in the Ancients, Montaigne, Hume, and Kant*. Leiden: Brill, 1992.
———. "The Subversive Kant: The Vocabulary of 'Public' and 'Publicity.'" *Political Theory* 14, no. 4 (1986): 584–603.
Laursen, John Christian, Luisa Simonutti, and Hans Blom. *Monarchisms in the Age of Enlightenment: Liberty, Patriotism, and the Common Good*. Toronto: University of Toronto Press, 2007.
Laursen, John Christian, Johan van der Zande, Elie Luzac, and Karl Friedrich Bahrdt. *Early French and German Defenses of Freedom of the Press: Elie Luzac's Essay on Freedom of Expression (1749) and Carl Friedrich Bahrdt's On Freedom of the Press and Its Limits (1787) in English Translation*. Leiden: Brill, 2003.
LaVaque-Manty, Mika. *Arguments and Fists: Political Agency and Justification in Liberal Theory*. New York: Routledge, 2002.

———. "Kant's Children." *Social Theory and Practice* 32, no. 3 (2006): 365–88.
———. *The Playing Fields of Eton: Equality and Excellence in Modern Meritocracy.* Ann Arbor: University of Michigan Press, 2009.
LeBar, Mark. "Kant on Welfare." *Canadian Journal of Philosophy* 29, no. 2 (1999): 225–49.
Lillich, Richard B. "Kant and the Current Debate over Humanitarian Intervention." *Journal of Transnational Law and Policy* 6 (1996): 397–404.
Loriaux, Sylvie. "Kant on International Distributive Justice." *Journal of Global Ethics* 3, no. 3 (2007): 281–301.
Losurdo, Domenico. *Immanuel Kant: Freiheit, Recht, und Revolution.* Köln: Pahl-Rugenstein, 1987.
Louden, Robert B. *Kant's Impure Ethics: From Rational Beings to Human Beings.* New York: Oxford University Press, 2000.
Löwith, Karl. *Meaning in History: The Theological Implications of the Philosophy of History.* Chicago: University of Chicago Press, 1949.
Lucht, Marc. "Toward Lasting Peace: Kant on Law, Public Reason, and Culture." *American Journal of Economics and Sociology* 68, no. 1 (2009): 303–26.
Ludwig, Bernd. "'The Right of a State' in Immanuel Kant's *Doctrine of Right.*" *Journal of the History of Philosophy* 27, no. 3 (1990): 403–15.
Ludwig, Bernd, and Werner Stark. *Kants Rechtslehre.* Hamburg: Meiner, 1988.
Lutz-Bachmann, Matthias, and James Bohman. *Frieden durch Recht: Kants Friedensidee und das Problem einer neuen Weltordnung.* Berlin: Suhrkamp, 1996.
Lyotard, Jean-François. *Enthusiasm: The Kantian Critique of History.* Translated by Georges Van Den Abbeele. Stanford: Stanford University Press, 2009.
———. *Lessons on the Analytic of the Sublime: Kant's Critique of Judgment.* Translated by Elizabeth Rottenberg. Stanford: Stanford University Press, 1994.
Marwah, Inder S. "A Matter of Character: Moral Psychology and Political Exclusion in Kant and Mill." PhD diss. University of Toronto, 2011.
Maus, Ingeborg. "Zur Theorie der Institutionalisierung bei Kant." In Göhler, *Politische Institutionen,* 358–86.
May, Todd G. "Kant the Liberal, Kant the Anarchist: Rawls and Lyotard on Kantian Justice." *The Southern Journal of Philosophy* 28, no. 4 (1990): 525–38.
Merkel, Reinhard, and Roland Wittmann. *"Zum ewigen Frieden": Grundlagen, Aktualität, und Aussichten einer Idee von Immanuel Kant.* Berlin: Suhrkamp, 1996.
Mertens, Thomas Johannes Marie. "Cosmopolitanism and Citizenship: Kant Against Habermas." *European Journal of Philosophy* 4, no. 3 (1996): 328–47.
———. "War and International Order in Kant's Legal Thought." *Ratio Juris* (1995): 296–314.
Meyer, Michael J. "Kant's Concept of Dignity and Modern Political Thought." *History of European Ideas* 8, no. 3 (1987): 319–32.
Mieszkowski, Jan. *Labors of Imagination: Aesthetics and Political Economy from Kant to Althusser.* New York: Fordham University Press, 2006.
Mori, Massimo. *La pace e la ragione: Kant e le relazioni internazionali: Diritto, politica, storia.* Bologna: Il mulino, 2008.
Mulholland, Leslie Arthur. *Kant's System of Rights.* New York: Columbia University Press, 1990.
Munzel, G. Felicitas. *Kant's Conception of Moral Character: The "Critical" Link of Morality, Anthropology, and Reflective Judgment.* Chicago: University of Chicago Press, 1999.
———. "*Menschenfreundschaft*: Friendship and Pedagogy in Kant." *Eighteenth-Century Studies* 32, no. 2 (1998): 247–59.
Munzer, Stephen R. "Kant and Property Rights in Body Parts." *Canadian Journal of Law and Jurisprudence* 6, no. 2 (1993): 319–41.
Muthu, Sankar. *Enlightenment Against Empire.* Princeton: Princeton University Press, 2003.

———. "Justice and Foreigners: Kant's Cosmopolitan Right." *Constellations* 7, no. 1 (2000): 23–45.
Neal, Patrick. "In the Shadow of the General Will: Rawls, Kant, and Rousseau on the Problem of Political Right." *The Review of Politics* 49, no. 3 (1987): 389–409.
Nichols, Mary P. "Kant's Teaching of Historical Progress and Its Cosmopolitan Goal." *Polity* 19, no. 2 (1986): 194–212.
Nicholson, Peter. "Kant on the Duty Never to Resist the Sovereign." *Ethics* 86, no. 3 (1976): 214–30.
Nussbaum, Martha. "Kant and Cosmopolitanism." In Bohman, *Perpetual Peace*, 25–57.
O'Neill, Onora. *Autonomy and Trust in Bioethics*. Cambridge: Cambridge University Press, 2002.
———. *Bounds of Justice*. Cambridge: Cambridge University Press, 2000.
———. *Constructions of Reason: Explorations of Kant's Practical Philosophy*. Cambridge: Cambridge University Press, 1989.
———. "Constructivism in Rawls and Kant." In *The Cambridge Companion to Rawls*, edited by Samuel Freeman, 347–67. Cambridge: Cambridge University Press, 2003.
———. "Kant: Rationality as Practical Reason." In *The Oxford Handbook of Rationality*, edited by Alfred R. Mele and Piers Rawling, 93–109. Oxford: Oxford University Press, 2004.
———. "Reason and Politics in the Kantian Enterprise." In Williams, *Essays on Kant's Political Philosophy*, 50–80.
———. *Towards Justice and Virtue: A Constructive Account of Practical Reasoning*. Cambridge: Cambridge University Press, 1996.
———. "Vindicating Reason." In Guyer, *Cambridge Companion to Kant*, 280–308.
Owona, Kisito. *Kant et l'Afrique: La problématique de l'universel*. Paris: Harmattan, 2007.
Parish, Randall, and Mark Peceny. "Kantian Liberalism and the Collective Defense of Democracy in Latin America." *Journal of Peace Research* 39, no. 2 (2002): 229–50.
Payne, Charlton, and Lucas Thorpe, eds. *Kant and the Concept of Community*. Rochester: University of Rochester Press/North American Kant Society, 2011.
Penner, James. "The State Duty to Support the Poor in Kant's Doctrine of Right." *The British Journal of Politics and International Relations* 12, no. 1 (2010): 88–110.
Philonenko, Alexis. *La théorie kantienne de l'histoire*. Paris: J. Vrin, 1986.
———. *Théorie et praxis dans la pensée morale et politique de Kant et de Fichte en 1793*. Paris: J. Vrin, 1968.
Pippin, Robert B. "Mine and Thine?: The Kantian State." In *The Cambridge Companion to Kant and Modern Philosophy*, edited by Paul Guyer, 416–46. Cambridge: Cambridge University Press, 2006.
Pogge, Thomas W. "Cosmopolitanism and Sovereignty." *Ethics* 103, no. 1 (1992): 48–75.
———. "An Egalitarian Law of Peoples." *Philosophy and Public Affairs* 23, no. 3 (1994): 195–224.
———. "Is Kant's *Rechtslehre* Comprehensive?" *The Southern Journal of Philosophy* 36, no. 1, Spindel Supplement: Kant's *Metaphysics of Morals* (1998): 161–87.
———. "Kant's Theory of Justice." *Kant-Studien* 79 (1988): 407–33.
Prauss, Gerold. *Kant über Freiheit als Autonomie*. Frankfurt am Main: Vittorio Klostermann, 1983.
———. *Moral und Recht im Staat nach Kant und Hegel*. Freiburg: Alber, 2008.
Rawls, John. "Justice as Fairness: Political Not Metaphysical." *Philosophy and Public Affairs* 14, no. 3 (1985): 223–51.
———. "Kantian Constructivism in Moral Theory." *The Journal of Philosophy* 77, no. 9 (1980): 515–72.
Rawls, John, and Barbara Herman. *Lectures on the History of Moral Philosophy*. Cambridge: Harvard University Press, 2000.

Raz, Joseph. "Facing Diversity: The Case of Epistemic Abstinence." *Philosophy and Public Affairs* 19, no. 1 (1990): 3–46.
———. *The Morality of Freedom*. New York: Oxford University Press, 1986.
Reath, Andrews, Barbara Herman, and Christine M. Korsgaard, eds. *Reclaiming the History of Ethics: Essays for John Rawls*. Cambridge: Cambridge University Press, 1997.
Reich, Klaus. *The Completeness of Kant's Table of Judgments*. Translated by Jane Kneller and Michael Losonsky. Foreword by Lewis White Beck. Stanford: Stanford University Press, 1992.
———. *Rousseau und Kant*. Tübingen: Mohr Siebeck, 1936.
Reiss, Hans. "Kant's Politics and the Enlightenment: Reflections on Some Recent Studies." *Political Theory* 27, no. 2 (1999): 236–73.
Riley, Patrick. "Federalism in Kant's Political Philosophy." *Publius* 9, no. 4 (1979): 43–64.
———. *Kant's Political Philosophy*. Totowa, N.J.: Rowman and Littlefield, 1983.
———. "On Kant as the Most Adequate of the Social Contract Theorists." *Political Theory* 1, no. 4 (1973): 450–71.
———. *Will and Political Legitimacy: A Critical Exposition of Social Contract Theory in Hobbes, Locke, Rousseau, Kant, and Hegel*. Cambridge: Harvard University Press, 1982.
Ripstein, Arthur. "Authority and Coercion." *Philosophy and Public Affairs* 32, no. 1 (2004): 2–35.
———. "Beyond the Harm Principle." *Philosophy and Public Affairs* 34, no. 3 (2006): 215–45.
———. *Force and Freedom: Kant's Legal and Political Philosophy*. Cambridge: Harvard University Press, 2009.
Rorty, Amélie Oksenberg, and James Schmidt, eds. *Kant's Idea for a Universal History with a Cosmopolitan Aim: A Critical Guide*. Cambridge: Cambridge University Press, 2009.
Rosen, Allen D. *Kant's Theory of Justice*. Ithaca: Cornell University Press, 1993.
Rottenberg, Elizabeth. *Inheriting the Future: Legacies of Kant, Freud, and Flaubert*. Stanford: Stanford University Press, 2005.
Sandel, Michael J. *Liberalism and the Limits of Justice*. Cambridge: Cambridge University Press, 1982.
Saner, Hans. *Kant's Political Thought: Its Origins and Development*. Chicago: University of Chicago Press, 1973.
Saurette, Paul. *The Kantian Imperative: Humiliation, Common Sense, Politics*. Toronto: University of Toronto Press, 2005.
Schaller, Walter E. "From the *Groundwork* to the *Metaphysics of Morals*: What Happened to Morality in Kant's Theory of Justice? *History of Philosophy Quarterly* 12 (1995): 333–45.
Schmidt, James. "The Question of Enlightenment: Kant, Mendelssohn, and the *Mittwochsgesellschaft*." *Journal of the History of Ideas* 50, no. 2 (1989): 269–91.
———, ed. *What Is Enlightenment?: Eighteenth-Century Answers and Twentieth-Century Questions*. Berkeley and Los Angeles: University of California Press, 1996.
Schmucker, Josef. *Die Ursprünge der Ethik Kants in seinen vorkritischen Schriften und Reflektionen*. Meisenheim am Glan: Anton Hain, 1961.
Schneewind, J. B. "Good Out of Evil: Kant and the Idea of Unsocial Sociability." In Rorty, *Kant's Idea for a Universal History with a Cosmopolitan Aim*, 94–111.
———. *The Invention of Autonomy: A History of Modern Moral Philosophy*. Cambridge: Cambridge University Press, 1998.
Schott, Robin May. *Cognition and Eros: A Critique of the Kantian Paradigm*. Boston: Beacon Press, 1988.
Scruton, Roger. "Contract, Consent, and Exploitation: Kantian Themes." In Williams, *Essays on Kant's Political Philosophy*, 213–27.

Seidler, Victor J. *Kant, Respect, and Injustice: The Limits of Liberal Moral Theory*. London: Routledge and Kegan Paul, 1986.

Seung, T. K. *Kant's Platonic Revolution in Moral and Political Philosophy*. Baltimore: Johns Hopkins University Press, 1994.

Shaw, Brian J. "Rawls, Kant's *Doctrine of Right*, and Global Distributive Justice." *Journal of Politics* 67, no. 1 (2005): 220–49.

Shell, Susan Meld. *The Embodiment of Reason: Kant on Spirit, Generation, and Community*. Chicago: University of Chicago Press, 1996.

———. *Kant and the Limits of Autonomy*. Cambridge: Harvard University Press, 2009.

———. "Kant on Just War and 'Unjust Enemies': Reflections on a 'Pleonasm.'" *Kantian Review* 10 (2005): 82–111.

———. "Kant on Punishment." *Kantian Review* 1 (1997): 115–35.

———. "Kant's Theory of Property." *Political Theory* 6, no. 1 (1978): 75–90.

———. *The Rights of Reason: A Study of Kant's Philosophy and Politics*. Toronto: University of Toronto Press, 1980.

Simmons, A. John. *Justification and Legitimacy: Essays on Rights and Obligations*. Cambridge: Cambridge University Press, 2001.

———. "The Principle of Fair Play." *Philosophy and Public Affairs* 8, no. 4 (1979): 307–37.

Smith, S. R. "Equality, Identity, and the Disability Rights Movement: From Policy to Practice and from Kant to Nietzsche in More Than One Uneasy Move." *Critical Social Policy* 25, no. 4 (2005): 554–76.

Sørensen, Georg. "Kant and Processes of Democratization: Consequences for Neorealist Thought." *Journal of Peace Research* 29, no. 4 (1992): 397–414.

Stammen, Theo, and Tobias Bevc. *Kant als Politischer Schriftsteller*. Würzburg: Ergon, 1999.

Stekeler-Weithofer, Pirmin. "Willkür und Wille bei Kant." *Kant-Studien* 81 (1990): 304–20.

Stern, David S. "Autonomy and Political Obligation in Kant." *The Southern Journal of Philosophy* 29, no. 1 (1991): 127–47.

Sullivan, Roger J. "The Influence of Kant's Anthropology on His Moral Theory." *Review of Metaphysics* 49 (1995): 77–94.

Surprenant, C. W. "Cultivating Virtue: Moral Progress and the Kantian State." *Kantian Review* 12, no. 1 (2006): 90–112.

Szymkowiak, Aaron. "Kant's Permissive Law: Critical Rights, Sceptical Politics." *British Journal for the History of Philosophy* 17, no. 3 (2009): 567–600.

Taylor, Robert S. "Democratic Transitions and the Progress of Absolutism in Kant's Political Thought." *Journal of Politics* 68, no. 3 (2006): 556–70.

———. "A Kantian Defense of Self-Ownership." *Journal of Political Philosophy* 12, no. 1 (2004): 65–78.

———. "Kantian Personal Autonomy." *Political Theory* 33, no. 5 (2005): 602–28.

———. "Kant's Political Religion: The Transparency of Perpetual Peace and the Highest Good." *The Review of Politics* 72, no. 1 (2010): 1–24.

———. *Reconstructing Rawls: The Kantian Foundations of Justice as Fairness*. University Park: Pennsylvania State University Press, 2011.

Tierney, Brian. "Kant on Property: The Problem of Permissive Law." *Journal of the History of Ideas* 62, no. 2 (2001): 301–12.

———. "Permissive Natural Law and Property: Gratian to Kant." *Journal of the History of Ideas* 62, no. 3 (2001): 381–99.

Timmons, Mark, ed. *Kant's Metaphysics of Morals: Interpretative Essays*. Oxford: Oxford University Press, 2002.

Tonella, Giovanni. *L'idea repubblicana in Kant: Tra riforma e negazione del diritto di resistanza*. Padova: Il poligrafo, 2009.

Tosel, André. *Kant révolutionnaire: Droit et politique*. Paris: Presses universitaires de France, 1988.

Tuck, Richard. *The Rights of War and Peace: Political Thought and the International Order from Grotius to Kant.* Oxford: Oxford University Press, 1999.
Tully, James. "The Kantian Idea of Europe: Critical and Cosmopolitan Perspectives." In *The Idea of Europe: From Antiquity to the European Union,* edited by Anthony Pagden, 331–58. Cambridge: Cambridge University Press, 2002.
Tunick, Mark. "Is Kant a Retributivist?" *History of Political Thought* 17, no. 1 (1996): 60–78.
Uleman, Jennifer K. "On Kant, Infanticide, and Finding Oneself in a State of Nature." *Zeitschrift für Philosophische Forschung* 54, no. 2 (2000): 173–95.
Unruh, Peter. *Die Herrschaft der Vernunft: Zur Staatsphilosophie Immanuel Kants.* Baden-Baden: Nomos, 1993.
Varden, Helga. "Kant's Non-Voluntarist Conception of Political Obligations: Why Justice Is Impossible in the State of Nature." *Kantian Review* 13, no. 2 (2008): 1–45.
Velkley, Richard L. *Freedom and the End of Reason: On the Moral Foundation of Kant's Critical Philosophy.* Chicago: University of Chicago Press, 1989.
Waldron, Jeremy. *The Dignity of Legislation.* Cambridge: Cambridge University Press, 1999.
———. "Kant's Legal Positivism." *Harvard Law Review* 109, no. 7 (1996): 1535–66.
———. *The Right to Private Property.* New York: Oxford University Press, 1990.
———. "What Is Cosmopolitan?" *Journal of Political Philosophy* 8, no. 2 (2000): 227–43.
Waligore, Timothy. "Cosmopolitan Right, Indigenous Peoples, and the Risks of Cultural Interaction." *Public Reason* 1, no. 1 (2009): 27–56.
Walker, Thomas C. "Two Faces of Liberalism: Kant, Paine, and the Question of Intervention." *International Studies Quarterly* 52, no. 3 (2008): 449–68.
Waltz, Kenneth Neal. "Kant, Liberalism, and War." *The American Political Science Review* 56, no. 2 (1962): 331–40.
Weinrib, Ernest J. "Poverty and Property in Kant's System of Rights." *Notre Dame Law Review* 78, no. 3 (2003): 795–828.
Weinstock, Daniel M. "Natural Law and Public Reason in Kant's Political Philosophy." *Canadian Journal of Philosophy* 26, no. 3 (1996): 389–411.
Westphal, Kenneth R. "Do Kant's Principles Justify Property or Usufruct?" *Annual Review of Law and Ethics* 5 (1997): 141–94.
———. "How 'Full' Is Kant's Categorical Imperative?" *Annual Review of Law and Ethics* 3 (1995): 465–509.
———. "Kant on the State, Law, and Obedience to Authority in the Alleged 'Anti-Revolutionary' Writings." *Journal of Philosophical Research* 17 (1992): 383–426.
———. "Republicanism, Despotism, and Obedience to the State: The Inadequacy of Kant's Division of Powers." *Annual Review of Law and Ethics* 1 (1993): 263–81.
Williams, David Lay. "Ideas and Actuality in the Social Contract: Kant and Rousseau." *History of Political Thought* 28, no. 3 (2007): 469–95.
Williams, Howard. "Back from the USSR: Kant, Kaliningrad, and World Peace." *International Relations* 20, no. 1 (2006): 27–48.
———, ed. *Essays on Kant's Political Philosophy.* Chicago: University of Chicago Press, 1992.
———. *Kant's Critique of Hobbes.* Cardiff: University of Wales Press, 2003.
———. *Kant's Political Philosophy.* New York: St. Martin's Press, 1983.
Williams, Howard, and Daniela Kroslak. "Die Idee eines liberal-demokratischen Friedens." *Zeitschrift für Philosophische Forschung* 53, no. 3 (1999): 428–39.
Williams, Michael C. "The Discipline of the Democratic Peace." *European Journal of International Relations* 7, no. 4 (2001): 525–53.
———. "Reason and Realpolitik: Kant's 'Critique of International Politics.'" *Canadian Journal of Political Science* 25, no. 1 (1992): 99–120.

Wilson, Holly L. "Kant's Integration of Morality and Anthropology." *Kant-Studien* 88 (1997): 87–104.
Wit, Ernst-Jan C. "Kant and the Limits of Civil Obedience." *Kant-Studien* 90, no. 3 (1999): 285–305.
Wood, Allen W. "The Final Form of Kant's Practical Philosophy." *The Southern Journal of Philosophy* 36, suppl. 1 (1998): 1–20.
———. *Kantian Ethics*. Cambridge: Cambridge University Press, 2008.
———. "Kant's Compatibilism." In *Self and Nature in Kant's Philosophy*, edited by Allen W. Wood, 73–101. Ithaca: Cornell University Press, 1984.
———. *Kant's Ethical Thought*. Cambridge: Cambridge University Press, 1999.
———. "Kant's Fourth Proposition: The Unsociable Sociability of Human Nature." In Rorty, *Kant's Idea for a Universal History with a Cosmopolitan Aim*, 112–28.
———. "Kant's Historical Materialism." In Kneller, *Autonomy and Community*, 15–38.
———. "Kant's Project for Perpetual Peace." *Cultural Politics* 14 (1998): 59–76.
———. *Kant's Rational Theology*. Ithaca: Cornell University Press, 1978.
Yack, Bernard. "The Problem with Kantian Liberalism." In Beiner, *Kant and Political Philosophy*, 224–44.
Zammito, John H. *The Genesis of Kant's Critique of Judgment*. Chicago: University of Chicago Press, 1992.
———. *Kant, Herder, and the Birth of Anthropology*. Chicago: University of Chicago Press, 2002.
———. "A Text of Two Titles: Kant's 'A Renewed Attempt to Answer the Question: "Is the Human Race Continually Improving?"'" *Studies in History and Philosophy of Science Part A* 39, no. 4 (2008): 535–45.

INDEX

absolutism, 135–49, 229
acquisition. *See* property
agency, 110–34, 157, 230–31
antagonism, 151–66
Arendt, Hannah, 152, 157–58
aristocracy, 9
Aristotle, 3–4, 150
atheism, 199, 232
Aufklärung. *See* enlightenment
Augsburg Confession, 194, 198
authorization, 62–67, 110–14, 130n22, 229–30, 233
autonomy, 8, 20–21, 178–80, 208–11, 220
 physical, 8, 215–20

Bahrdt, Carl Friedrich, 198, 232–33
balance of power, 132n38, 159
barbarism, 12, 18, 67–68, 73n57
Basedow, Johann Bernhard, 20, 208–9, 212–15, 218–21
Berkeley, George, 175, 180
Berlin, Isaiah, 75, 99n34
Berlinische Monatsschrift, 3, 135, 192, 226, 231
book piracy, 12, 21, 225–37
Boullainvilliers, Henri de, 232
Brandenburg-Prussia. *See* Prussia

Calvinism, 193–95
categorical imperative, 16, 35–36, 46, 69n11, 81, 95n8, 96n13
Catholicism, 194–95, 197–98
censorship, 2, 144, 192, 197, 226, 229, 234.
 See also freedom of the press
Christology, 199, 201
Cicero, 175
citizenship, 137–40, 184–85, 222
 active and passive, 40–41n17, 144–45
civil condition, 14, 56, 60, 65, 67, 73n50, 104–8, 117–18, 184. *See also* right
clergy, 170–71, 193
coercion, 47–51, 84–85, 104, 115–18, 182–85, 233–34
Collins, Anthony, 232–33

consent, 11, 16–17, 25–40, 47–49, 58–63, 113, 130n19, 230
 hypothetical, 27–30
 possible, 32
constitution, 59, 65, 71–72n36, 124, 143–46, 184, 187
 mixed, 9
 republican (see rightful)
 religious, 170–72, 191–97, 199, 201–3
 rightful, 31–34, 37–39, 88–89, 92, 109
cosmopolitanism, 156–60, 163–66

Dante, 13
deists, 198, 232
democracy, 10, 39, 144, 153, 189
 deliberative, 1, 7, 181
democratic peace hypothesis, 1, 7, 10, 13
dependence, 6, 46–47, 139, 145
despotism, 12, 18, 67–68, 127, 134n51, 140, 144, 148
devils, nation of, 88–89, 94
Dilthey, Wilhelm, 193

Ebbinghaus, Julius. *See* independence thesis
education, 8, 20, 139, 208–24
 moral, 220–22
Effen, Justus van, 233
Ehlers, Martin, 21, 226–32, 235
Emperor Joseph, 229
enlightenment, 8, 19–20, 135–49, 170–207, 190–91, 198, 208, 212
equality, 92–95, 97–98n23
Erziehungsstaat. *See* state, tutelary
ethics, 7, 79, 89, 93, 164, 174–78
 dependence of the doctrine of right on, 74–95, 96–97n16, 128n4, 184
 interpretations of Kant's, 2–3, 150–52

Fichte, Johann Gottlieb, 132n36, 190
Formula of Concord, 195
Frederick II (the Great), 10, 143, 189
Frederick William, 194
Frederick William II, 192
Frederick William III, 202

freedom, 6, 8–11, 18, 48–53, 65, 77–78, 85–88, 91–94, 98n30, 103–4, 129n6, 211
  intellectual, 21, 138–41
  of the press, 21, 138, 147, 225–35
  states' right to, 110–15, 117–22
  universal law of, 77–78 (see also right)
friendship, 19, 160–63

Garve, Christian, 175–78, 191
Geismann, Georg, 90
Gilmore, Grant, 43
God, 69n10, 179, 188, 195–96, 199–201, 221, 227–28
Gräff, Ernst Martin, 225, 228–29, 231
Grotius, Hugo, 42, 63, 227

Habermas, Jürgen, 4, 7, 150–51, 153, 181–82
Hegel, Georg Wilhelm Friedrich, 4, 42, 174
Herder, Johann Gottfried, 190
Herman, Barbara, 2, 220
Hobbes, Thomas, 3, 41n19, 42–44, 59, 61, 66, 88, 103, 115, 121, 131n26, 171, 191, 196
human condition, 16, 37–38, 60, 152, 158
human history, 154, 168n29, 201
human nature, 16, 43, 152–60, 168n29, 181
Hume, David, 43–44, 59, 175

independence, 40–41n17, 46–48, 109, 118–22, 126, 218
independence thesis, 89–90, 92, 99n39, 100n42

Jacobi, F. H., 199
Jacobinism, 192
justice, 7–8, 10, 36–39, 42–68, 75, 99n37, 182–83, 185, 187, 226, 229
  circumstances of, 43–45, 59
  conditions of, 45–51, 78–80
  universal principle of (see right, universal principle of)
Kant, Immanuel, works
  "An Answer to the Question: What Is Enlightenment?," 8, 18–19, 21, 65, 135–48, 211, 225
  Anthropology from a Pragmatic Point of View, 18, 67, 158, 168n22, 168n27, 225
  Conjectural Beginning of Human History, 69n3
  Conflict of the Faculties, 3, 9, 139, 149n13, 189–90, 193, 201
  Critique of the Power of Judgment, 3, 4, 6, 8, 70n22, 81, 151, 156–57, 166n1

Critique of Pure Reason, 3, 10, 12, 34–36, 63, 69n7, 70n28, 71n30, 73n50, 138, 173, 175
Critique of Practical Reason, 3, 15, 69n10, 95–96n9, 149n15
Doctrine of Right (Part I of Metaphysics of Morals), 3, 18, 21, 26, 36–37, 71n30, 71–72n36, 73n50, 131–32n32, 144–45, 181–82, 185, 191, 222
Doctrine of Virtue (Part II of Metaphysics of Morals), 45, 59, 77, 93, 219
Groundwork of the Metaphysics of Morals, 2–4, 8, 36, 47, 69n7, 73n50, 81, 96n13, 137, 173–75, 178–80
"Idea for a Universal History with a Cosmopolitan Aim," 45, 139, 146, 151, 153–57, 159
Metaphysics of Morals, 2–3, 5, 8, 11, 13–15, 21, 26, 36, 45–47, 49, 51–55, 57–60, 63–68, 70n22, 77, 79–82, 84, 89–90, 93, 102–4, 106, 144–45, 147–48, 157, 160, 163, 182–85, 187–89, 218–19, 225, 232–35
"On the Common Saying: 'That May Be Correct in Theory, but It Is of No Use in Practice,'" 11, 26, 31–32, 34, 37, 119, 132n38, 143, 145, 148, 159, 188, 191, 222, 225
Pädagogik, 208–11, 215, 217, 220–22
Religion Within the Boundaries of Mere Reason, 142, 151, 167n8, 167n10, 168n21, 192–93, 199–201, 232
Towards Perpetual Peace, 10, 13–15, 26, 33, 88–89, 93, 109, 127, 141, 143–44, 146, 151, 159, 164
"Vigilantius's Lecture Notes," 73n5, 130n18, 179
"What Does It Mean to Orient Oneself in Thinking?," 138
Kern, Johannes, 233
kingdom of ends, 152, 178–81
Korsgaard, Christine, 2
Krause, Christian Sigmund, 226

la Mettrie, Julien Offray de, 142
law, 40–41n17, 60, 67, 107–8. See also right, justice
  metaphysical circumstances of, 52–60
  moral, 174, 179
  natural, 42–44, 171, 181, 186–87, 226–31
  permissive, 26, 71n29, 146
  philosophy of, 226, 233–34
  public, 51–64, 201–2
  Roman, 46, 57, 60, 231

rule of, 66, 79
universal, 9-10, 26, 36, 41n25, 46, 53, 58, 77–79, 81–84, 89, 96n13, 96–97n16, 103–4, 180–83, 233–34
Leibniz, Gottfried Wilhelm, 171, 190, 196–97
Lessing, Gottfried, 199
liberalism, 74–76, 80, 95
Locke, John, 3–5, 21, 26, 42–44, 51, 53, 59–61, 66, 72n44, 106, 129n12, 150, 210, 212 Louis XVI, 144, 147
Luther, Martin, 228
Lutherans, 171–72, 176. See also Protestants
Luzac, Effie, 233

Machiavelli, Niccolò, 3, 143
marriage, 71n29, 135
Marx, Karl, 3, 227
Mendelssohn, Moses, 135–36
metaphysics, 171, 174–91, 195–203
Mill, John Stuart, 3, 74–75
Milton, John, 233
minority, condition of, 136–38
Möhsen, J. K. W., 135–36
Montesquieu, 10
moral anthropology, 164, 173, 181
moral subject, 88, 178, 200. See also persons
Moser, Johann Jacob, 171, 195, 197, 201
multiconfessionalism, 195–97

Nazi regime, 18, 68. See also barbarism
neo-Kantianism, 7, 151, 166, 181, 193

obligation, 50, 61–62, 68, 69n7, 71n29, 73n50, 93–94, 129nn14–15, 132n37, 175, 177–78
  to enter a rightful condition, 9–10, 14, 31, 37, 59–60, 63–68, 84, 91, 96n14, 102, 109, 129n15
O'Neill, Onora, 2, 99n36

paternalism, 8, 20, 210–11, 217
persons, 77, 88, 96n11
phenomenology, 19, 152–53, 157, 164, 166, 166–67n3
Philanthropinen movement, 208–18
Plato, 3, 171–72n36
plurality, 63, 77–78, 152–53, 156–60
possibility, 32, 35–39, 64–65, 71n30, 187. See also right, provisional
priests, 136–37, 140, 142. See also clergy
property, 48–58, 61, 104–6, 132n36, 227–31. See also right, property
  in land, 56, 100n46, 129n14, 183

Protestants, 170–171, 185–87, 190–203
Prussia, 143–44, 170–207, 229
  religious constitution of, 170–72, 191–97, 199, 201–3
  as tutelary state, 20, 143, 185–86, 190, 201–2
Prussian Code, 229
public sphere, 7, 172, 175
publicity, 12, 93–94
Pufendorf, Samuel, 42, 171, 186–87, 197, 201, 227
Pütter, J. S., 226

rationalism, 19–20, 171–72
Rawls, John, 4, 7, 18, 21, 26, 30, 43, 62, 74–100, 150–51, 153, 181–82
reason, idea of, 11, 31–34, 71n76, 164
  judicial postulate of practical, 93
  public, 137–38, 140
rebellion, 41n19, 100n47. See also revolution
Rechtslehre. See also Immanuel Kant, works: *Doctrine of Right*
  meaning of, 80
  as a game, 84–91
reciprocity, 48–49, 52, 58–60, 70n24, 106–8, 116–18, 120, 213
reform, 144–47, 149n13
  of education, 20, 208–9, 212, 215 (see also *Philanthropinen* movement)
  of the Prussian constitution, 170, 231
Rehberg, August Wilhelm, 192
Reich, Klaus, 90
Reimarus, Samuel, 199–200
religion, 171–72, 191–202, 212–13, 221
Religious Edict of 1788, 194, 197–98, 202
representation, 63–64, 110, 144–45, 188–89
republics, 33, 38, 67–68, 88–89, 140, 143–45, 147–48, 184–85, 188
revolution, 12, 66, 137, 201. See also rebellion
  French Revolution, 12, 151
Richardson, Samuel, 226
right. See also justice
  conclusive right, 14, 18, 55, 57, 63, 104–5, 107–9, 116–19, 123–25, 231
  cosmopolitan right, 108
  definition of right, 76–81, 96n12, 96n16
  private right, 50–52, 55–56, 61–63, 70n22, 73n50, 234
  property right, 49–60, 70n22, 116, 132n36, 228 (see also property)
  provisional right, 5, 14–15, 52–57, 63, 104–9, 116–19, 123–25, 130–31n24, 184, 231
  public right, 48, 57, 63, 65, 71n33, 234

right *(continued)*
  right of humanity, 72n42, 232
  right of nations, 70n23, 108, 133n41
  universal principle of, 26, 34–38, 45–46, 81–86, 233
Rousseau, Jean-Jacques, 3–4, 21, 26, 37, 42, 63, 103, 150, 210, 212

Sandel, Michael, 43
Schlözer, August Ludwig von, 233
Schmidt, Johann Lorenz, 232–33
self-government, 141–45, 148
self-legislation, 175, 177–81, 190
Semler, Johannes Salomo, 199–200, 202
separation of powers, 10, 144
slavery, 6, 46, 113
sociability, 186. *See also* unsocial sociability
social class, 9, 32, 95, 212–13
social contract, 10–11, 16, 25–39, 42–43, 61–65
  as an idea of reason, 11, 16, 31–35, 37–39, 65, 67–68, 188
  as a norm, 11, 65, 184–85
soteriology, 199, 201
sovereignty, 115, 144, 147–48, 185–88
Spalding, Johann Joachim, 199–200
Spinoza, Benedict, 196–97, 199, 232–33
Stapfer, Johann Friedrich, 199
  in the international system, 101, 108–10, 115–22, 131–32n32, 133n40, 155–56
state, 60–66, 68, 102–4, 110, 112–19, 121, 124–25, 136, 139, 143–44, 159, 170, 184–91, 193–97, 201–2, 211–14
  as agent of the people, 63–64, 113
  distinctive powers of, 56–57, 59, 131n25
  federal, 13, 18, 122–28, 163
  origin of, 66, 107
  tutelary, 20, 190 (see also Prussia)
  versus voluntary association, 110–14, 126, 128n2, 130n22, 133n50
  world, 13, 18, 101–34
state of nature, 10–11, 37, 44, 52, 55–59, 61–64, 67–68, 70n24, 73n55, 84, 101, 104–8, 184

Stäudlin, Karl Friedrich, 199
Svarez, Carl Gottlieb, 201–2

Thomasius, Christian, 176–78, 187, 196–97, 227
Tindal, Matthew, 232–33
Toland, John, 233
transcendental idealism, 75–76, 92, 95n9, 171
Treaty of Westphalia, 187, 194–95
two-stage justification, 28, 91

Ulpian, 47, 57
unsocial sociability, 19, 37, 44–45, 150–68

volenti non fit iniuria, 27, 60
Volksaufklärung, 190, 197
voluntary association, 61–62, 65, 112, 114, 126–28, 229

war, 13, 70n23, 109, 155–60
  debt-financed, 14, 147
  power to declare, 144
Wednesday Society (*Mittwochgesellschaft*), 135
Wekhrlin, Wilhelm, 233
Wieland, Christoph Martin, 233
will, 9–10, 153, 182–85
  and choice, 69n13, 77–78
  general will, 52, 58, 68, 187–88
  individual will, 58–59, 154–56
  partial will, 9
  particular will, 58–59
  private will, 10, 31, 60, 188
  public will, 31, 188
  unilateral will, 10, 53–55, 58
  united will, 9–11, 32, 51, 55–59, 68, 163–64, 188
Wolff, Christian, 171, 177, 199, 227
Wöllner, Johann Cristoph, 20, 149n17, 192–93, 197
women, 5–6, 34, 94–95

Zöllner, Johann Friedrich, 135–36

www.ingramcontent.com/pod-product-compliance
Lightning Source LLC
Chambersburg PA
CBHW021358290426
44108CB00010B/297